Pythagoras

His Life and Teachings

D1593189

Pythagoras

His Life and Teachings

A COMPENDIUM OF CLASSICAL SOURCES

Thomas Stanley

(From the 1687 edition of *The History of Philosophy*)

Preface by
MANLY P. HALL

Introduction by
HENRY L. DRAKE

Edited by
JAMES WASSERMAN

With a Study of Greek and Latin Sources by
J. DANIEL GUNTHER

IBIS PRESS
Lake Worth, FL

Published in 2010 by Ibis Press
An imprint of Nicolas-Hays, Inc.
P. O. Box 540206
Lake Worth, FL 33454-0206
www.ibispress.net

Distributed to the trade by
Red Wheel/Weiser, LLC
65 Parker St. • Ste. 7
Newburyport, MA 01950
www.redwheelweiser.com

First Edition 2010

Library of Congress Cataloging-in-Publication Data

Stanley, Thomas, 1625–1678.
  Pythagoras : his life and teachings : a compendium of classical sources / by
Thomas Stanley ; preface by Manly P. Hall ; introduction by Henry L. Drake ;
edited by James Wasserman ; with a study of Greek and Latin sources by
J. Daniel Gunther. — 1st ed.
    p. cm.
  Includes bibliographical references.
  ISBN 978-0-89254-160-7 (alk. paper)
  1. Pythagoras and Pythagorean school. I. Wasserman, James, 1948– II. Title.
B243.S67 2010
182'.2–dc22   2010000399

ISBN 978-0-89254-160-7

Cover painting by Longhi, Pietro (1702–1785)
Photo Credit : Cameraphoto Arte, Venice / Art Resource, NY

Book design and production by Studio 31
www.studio31.com

Manufactured in the USA

CONTENTS

PART ONE: THE LIFE OF PYTHAGORAS

PART TWO: DISCIPLINES AND DOCTRINES OF THE PYTHAGOREANS

PART THREE: THE DOCTRINE OF PYTHAGORAS

Section I. Mathematical Sciences

Section II: Philosophy

Section III. Symbols

PART FOUR: PYTHAGOREAN COMMENTATORS

FOREWORD

JAMES WASSERMAN AND J. DANIEL GUNTHER

The book you are holding is the work of Thomas Stanley (1625–1678), as published in 1687. It consists of the long section he devoted to Pythagoras in his masterful and massive tome *The History of Philosophy*. The timeless brilliance of Stanley's work is that it presented a survey of the classical writers of antiquity that remains as contemporary today as it was over three hundred years ago.

A biographical sketch of the author is given by Manly Palmer Hall in the Preface, along with a profound overview of Pythagorean philosophy by Dr. Henry L. Drake in the Introduction. Manly P. Hall (1901–1990) founded the Philosophical Research Society in 1934. He was a prolific author and lecturer, and remains a primary exponent of the Mystery Traditions in Western culture, especially because of his inspiring and comprehensive magnum opus, *The Secret Teachings of All Ages*. Dr. Drake (1906–1978), a close and loyal friend of Mr. Hall, served as vice-president of the Society for nearly three decades, in addition to editing a collection of Plato's complete works. In 1970, the Philosophical Research Society produced a facsimile edition of Stanley's work on Pythagoras in a limited printing of 2000 copies. The Society has kindly allowed us to include Mr. Hall's Preface and Dr. Drake's Introduction to that facsimile. Our thanks to Paul Austad and the members of the Copyright Committee for their generosity.

We have reset the text from the 1687 edition of *The History of Philosophy* to make it more accessible to the modern reader. We have generally regularized spelling, replaced obsolete words that may not be found in a modern dictionary, and used contemporary conventions of punctuation. At the same time, we have endeavored to leave as much of Stanley's expression intact as possible. The reader will do well to allow the archaic tone of the language to become both familiar and pleasant; its pacing seems to call forth a contemplative state of mind. The editing has been done "silently" because of the extent of the work involved. Here is a representative sample of the original book that you may compare with the typeset text on

C H A P. IV.

Silence.

(a) **M**Oreover, *he enjoyned thofe that came to   (a) Jamb.
him Silence for five years, making tryal*
how firmly they would behave themfelves in the moft
difficult of all continencies ; for fuch is the govern-
ment of the tongue, as is manifeft from thofe who
have divulged myfteries.

This πεντατῆς σιωπῆ, a quinquennial filence,
was called ἐχεμυθία, (and fometimes, but lefs
frequently, ἐχερημοσύνη) (b) ἀπὸ τῆ ἔχειν ἐν ἑαυτῷ   (b) Hefych.
ᶖ λόγον, from keeping our fpeech within our
felves.

The reafon of this filence was, (c) *That the*   (c) Simplic. in
foul might be converted into her felf from external Epictet.
things, and from the irrational paffions in her, and
from the body even unto her own life, which is to
live for ever. Or, as (d) *Clemens Alexandrinus*   (d) Strom. 5.
expreffeth it, *That his difciples, being diverted from*
fenfible things, might feek God with a pure mind.
Hence (e) *Lucian* to the demand, how *Pythagoras*   (e) In vit. act.
could reduce men to the remembrance of the
things which they had formerly known, (for he
held Science to be only Reminifcence) makes him
anfwer, *Firft, by long quiet and filence, fpeaking no-*
thing for five whole years.
X x x   **Yet**

page 122. Thanks to Yvonne Weiser of Ibis Press for helping to define and clarify this task, thereby making it possible.

We have also attempted to correct and contextualize the extensive Greek language references throughout the text. Thomas Stanley wrote at a time when it was expected that the average reader had been schooled in Latin and Greek, with a well-rounded knowledge of the classics. Not surprisingly therefore, he made numerous references in Greek; often just a single word for clarification; at other times, phrases and sentences with only brief abbreviations noting the source. To complicate matters, the Greek typeface of Stanley's day was quite different from that employed today, as may be seen from the sample page provided. It was a florid script that incorporated a number of "abbreviations" representing various letter combinations that could potentially increment the standard Greek alphabet set by a great many additional characters. These characters are no longer used today, and to a student accustomed only to modern Greek typefaces, even though such texts are visually striking, they are virtually unreadable.

The initial task was to regularize the Greek references to the convention of a modern Greek typeface in order to make them accessible. Each quotation was then verified with the source document in Greek. Even so, it quickly became apparent that Stanley's copious references would present an enormous challenge to the reader without some sense of context. His knowledge was encyclopedic, encompassing not only the masters of Greek philosophy, mathematics, music, poetry, geography and history, but the Patristic literature as well. Therefore, many of these references are discussed in the annotated appendix with additional material incorporated to clarify the meaning or context of the original quote. A complete bibliography has been included, detailing all the reference works utilized.

We have included a small Glossary with a number of terms, especially those from musical theory which may be unfamiliar to the non-technical reader. In such cases, the first occurrence of the word is presented in bold type to indicate that it may be found in the Glossary. Certain other words are included as well for the reader's convenience. Comments in editorial brackets are ours, while those in parenthesis are by Stanley. We have tried to retain as much of Stanley's original organization of the text as practical. Because of the large number of chapters and various divisions of his original, we have decided to number the extensive endnotes sequentially for clarity. While we have spared no effort in trying to understand and clarify as much of the text as possible, some of Stanley's original work was not clear to either of us.

For the reader in search of the next step in the study of Pythagoras, we recommend two books from Phanes Press: *The Pythagorean Sourcebook and Library*, compiled and translated by Kenneth Sylvan Guthrie, edited and introduced by David Fideler. It includes many of the texts to which Stanley refers. *The Manual of Harmonics of Nicomachus the Pythagorean*, translation and commentary by Flora R. Levin, will help to clarify the complex musical material Stanley presents.

This project would not have been possible without the diligent efforts of Wileda Wasserman, who meticulously and painstakingly typed the manuscript from which all further production advanced. Nicole Laliberte cheerfully persisted through untold hours of out-loud proofreading sessions to insure the most accurate reconstruc-tion of Stanley's text. Thanks to Julia and Daniel Pineda for their help in proofreading the finished manuscript, to Mike Estell for his assistance with Greek and Latin sources, and to Dennis Deem for communicating the principles of geometric drawing so many years ago. Special thanks to David L. Vagi, author of *Coinage and History of the Roman Empire*, for sourcing photos and writing cap-tions for the ancient Greek coins that grace these pages, and for his help with the map (whose place names, for the most part, reflect Stanley's spelling). Thanks also to Classical Numismatic Group, Inc. and Numismatica Ars Classica for permission to reproduce their images of the coins.

Walking in the company of such giants as Pythagoras, Thomas Stanley, Manly Hall, and Henry Drake has been a great honor for both of us.

PREFACE

MANLY P. HALL

It is now generally acknowledged that Thomas Stanley was the first English historian of philosophy. He had an orderly but versatile mind and gained distinction during his own lifetime, as a poet and a translator of poetical works. His father Sir Thomas Stanley was the author of some prose and poetical fragments, but never attained the recognition that came to his illustrious son.

The Thomas Stanley, with whom we are directly concerned, was born in Hertfordshire, England in 1625. His early education was under the personal direction of William Fairfax, son of the translator of Tasso, the 16th century Italian poet. While still young, Stanley became a good classical scholar, with fluency in French, Italian and Spanish languages.

When Stanley went to Pembroke Hall, Cambridge, Fairfax accompanied him. Stanley graduated from Cambridge with the degree of Master of Arts in 1641, and took up residence in the Middle Temple, where he combined the practice of law with his studies of philosophy and the classics, and the composition of poetry. During the Civil War he apparently considered it discreet to travel on the continent, where he devoted himself principally to his literary projects. Stanley died in London on April 12, 1678.

If it seems extraordinary that Thomas Stanley could have studied in both Cambridge and Oxford and graduated at the age of sixteen, it should be noted that he entered Cambridge in his fourteenth year, apparently having received most of his fundamental education by private tutoring. Actually, he issued the first volume of *The History of Philosophy* in 1655, when he was only thirty years old. The engraved frontispiece [reproduced here on page 17] shows Stanley as a young and handsome man, with long hair hanging on his shoulders. His son of the same name was also educated at Pembroke Hall and at the age of fourteen made a translation of Aelian's *Various Histories*, which passed through three editions.

The *History of Philosophy* was issued in sections between 1655 and 1662. It was reprinted complete in one large folio volume in

1687, and this is referred to as the second edition. There was a third edition in 1700, and a fourth (which included a life of the author) in 1743. Parts of the work were translated into Latin and French. The present text was taken from the edition of 1687. At the beginning of the section devoted to Pythagoras is an engraved portrait of the philosopher. [See frontispiece.]

Stanley's account of the Italic Sect is compiled from most records preserved by ancient authors and draws heavily upon the historical writings of Diogenes Laertius, who flourished in the 3rd century A.D. Stanley's account of the Pythagorian system is quite extensive, covering nearly one hundred double column pages, in folio. It is divided into convenient headings under which related material is organized in proper sequence. Very little of basic importance can be added to Stanley's compilation, and writings on Pythagoras are few and for the most part difficult to secure.

In order to make Stanley's text available at a time when there is considerable demand for authentic information on the Pythagorian philosophy, it seems desirable that Stanley's contribution should be republished. The earlier editions, though not listed as great rarities, are extremely difficult to find, and demand has long exceeded the supply.

There are other books which are useful to the study of the Pythagorean philosophy. One of these is the *Theoretic Arithmetic,* compiled by Thomas Taylor. On the title page of this volume, Taylor describes his book as "Containing the substance of all that has been written on this subject by Theo of Smyrna, Nicomachus, Iamblichus, and Boetius." Only one hundred copies of this book were issued in London in 1816. It is so rare that I reprinted the volume in 1934, and this reprint is also long out of print. Taylor also translated the *Life of Pythagoras* by Iamblichus. This first appeared in London in 1818 and there have been several reprints.

It seems to me that Stanley's study of the Italic Sect will interest several types of readers. It has been said that Orpheus, Pythagoras and Plato excelled all the other Greeks in their contributions to the enlightenment of mankind. Orpheus was the divine theologian, Pythagoras the great scientist, and Plato the inspired philosopher. The Orphic Mysteries have descended to us only in the form of

hymns and fragments of mystical rituals. Very little has survived of the authentic writings of Pythagoras, and his words have been preserved mostly as quotations in the writings of other ancient scholars. Most of the dialogues of Plato have descended to this present time, but it remained for the Neo-Platonists to restore the esoteric parts of his teachings.

On August 20, 1955, special observances were held on the Island of Samos to honor the 2,500th. Anniversary of the founding of the first school of Philosophy by Pythagoras. A special set of four postage stamps was issued, two of which contained reproductions of a Samian coin depicting Pythagoras. Another stamp showed a map of

Samos, and there was a third design featuring the celebrated 47th Proposition of Euclid, now generally referred to as the Pythagorean Theorem.

In the Ceramicus in Athens, Greece, there stands a monument popularly believed to be the Tomb of Pythagoras. A white limestone shaft is supported by a platform of four receding squares. The monument has been the subject of considerable speculation by those concerned with Pythagorean symbolism.

While it is obvious that many doctrines have been attributed to Pythagoras upon very slender evidence, it is also true that he was an original thinker, whose concepts strongly influenced the course of all Western learning. We believe that the republishing of Stanley's researches may assist in defining the actual boundaries of Pythagorean religious, philosophical and scientific speculations. Of special interest, are the philosophical disciplines which he taught, and which have continued to have exponents even to the present time. His theories on symbolic numbers have inspired countless books on numerology and divination by such devices as the wheel of Pythagoras, described by the English Rosicrucian writer Robert Fludd in his *De Numero et Numeratione*. There is also a Greek Cabala, by which numbers are substituted for the letters of the Greek alphabet. These numbers are then involved in an esoteric system similar to Jewish Cabalism. Godfrey Higgins goes into considerable detail on this subject in his massive work *Anacalypsis*.

In these days of unrest, the political thinking of Pythagoras and his contributions to practical philosophy are most timely. There has long been an interest in those theories of the Pythagoreans which are primarily concerned with problems of health. Here also many little known beliefs, traceable to the Pythagorean School, are set forth. There is also a brief discussion of the descent of the Pythagorean School and later scholars, who are known to have been in legitimate descent from the Master.

So far as is known, there is no surviving likeness of Pythagoras. A small Samian coin is considered a possible portrait, but this is found in such poor condition that it gives no idea of the great philosopher's appearance. He is nearly always represented as bearded and of noble appearance, and is sometimes accompanied by a bear. The portrait in my book *The Secret Teachings of All Ages, is* a composite of traditional likenesses.

Dr. Oliver, who issued several important volumes on Masonic Symbolism, notes in his posthumously published work *The Pythagorean Triangle*, that Justin Martyr (100–165?), an early Church Father, approached a Pythagorean teacher and sought to enter his school. He was rejected, however, because he lacked proper qualifications in geometry, astronomy and music.

The Life of Pythagoras by M. Dacier, translated into English in 1707, and including a translation of the "Golden Verses," translated from the Greek by M. Rowe, Esq., is worthy of careful study. It includes the elaborate commentaries of Hierocles, who seems to have been an Alexandrian Neoplatonist. On the title page of Dacier's book is the same Samian coin reproduced on the Greek stamp of 1955.

Bronze coins naming Pythagoras, and showing him placing a wand against a celestial globe, were issued on the island of Samos during the 2nd and 3rd centuries A.D.

From M. Dacier, *The Life of Pythagoras*

The distinguished Masonic scholar, General Albert Pike, thus summarizes the deeper learning that arose in the Golden Age of the Hellenic States: "Among the Greeks, the scholars of the Egyptians, all the higher ideas and severer doctrines on the Divinity, his Sovereign Nature and Infinite Might, the Eternal Wisdom and Providence that conducts and directs all things to their proper end, the Infinite Mind and Supreme Intelligence that created all things, and is raised far above external nature—all these loftier ideas and nobler doctrines were expounded more or less perfectly by Pythagoras, Anaxagoras, and Socrates, and developed in the most beautiful and luminous manner by Plato, and the philosophers that succeeded him." (See *Morals and Dogma*).

We sincerely trust that the republication of Thomas Stanley's history of the Pythagorean sect will be of practical use to the many students of Greek learning and the societies dedicated to the study of the Pythagorean writing. In his biographical article, S. Austin Allibone summarizes the value of the *History of Philosophy* by Stanley in these carefully chosen words: "To those who would make a vast parade of learning at little expense, it is of great utility."

INTRODUCTION

DR. HENRY L. DRAKE

After many centuries, Pythagoras' name still flares across the conscious horizon of learned men. He was a polydynamic figure whose encyclopedic understanding influenced the ancient world in a strange and powerful way. Born in Samos about 580 B.C., the impact of his life and work is felt, even today, in the areas of science, mathematics, music, religion, mysticism, and philosophy. The world has not heard the last of Pythagoras, but there is a record as to how we first heard of him. His father Mnesarchus, engraver of rings, with his wife Parthenis, visited the oracle of Delphi and were told that she would bear a son who would excel in grace and wisdom.

This early sage was accepted by some as a Hero, meaning that he was, indeed, a virtuous man who possessed divine powers. He was regarded as one who had come to earth for the specific purpose of enlightening mankind. He sought to produce an advanced type of human being—the insightful, creative man of character, inquiring mind, depth of feeling, thoughtful disposition, practical understanding, and above all, spiritual sensitivity.

According to Pythagoras each individual has within his basic nature certain qualities which, when cultivated under proper instruction, make it possible for him to mature into the likeness of a divine being. Manly P. Hall states, "Pythagoras believed that ultimately man would reach a state where he would cast off his gross nature and function in a body of spiritualized ether . . . From this he would ascend into the realm of the immortals, where by divine birthright he belonged."

Pythagoras chose to reveal his deeper meanings only by the spoken word. If he left any writings they have been lost. What we know of him derives mainly from his disciples, the Pythagoreans. His chief biographers, among them Porphyry, Iamblichus, and Diogenes Laertius, wrote of Pythagoras several hundred years after his demise. Plato and Aristotle left us meaningful insights about the Pythagoreans. Plato's significant dialogues the Phaedo and Timeaus are deeply influenced by Pythagorean ideas and ideals. Plato, speaking of Pythagoras, says that he taught his disciples, "A way of Life." They so revered him that, after his death, none ever took credit for any Pythagorean theory or discovery, but referred them to The Master, or That Man, as they called Pythagoras, thus evidencing their esteem for his greatness.

Vagueness surrounds the life and work of Pythagoras as well as his affirmed charismatic nature. It is appropriate to ponder what significant difference, if any, this makes. He, as with other great teachers, taught a meaning common to all mankind. The fact of Christ's existence, or the exact words of Buddha, is secondary to the significant truth inherent in the message they portrayed. Pythagoras' message is as vital now as it was then as a way for man to follow in pursuing and developing his own being and well-being. The message is that what one man has done each man can do. This Pythagoras taught, stressing that each must attain integration of his soul for himself, since there is no vicarious attainment. Legitimate integration comes only from a depth of commitment to and an insightful understanding and application of fundamental, Divine principles which, being scientific, are the same for all mankind.

During Pythagoras' youth, he was recognized for temperance, serenity, gentleness, prudence, and for his abilities generally. Even at this age, he was respected and honored. His discourse attracted many, including significant persons, so that some said this man must be the son of a deity, perhaps Apollo. Coming to knowledge, and understanding its functioning within himself, he attended to those endeavors which aided him in comprehending reality. His abilities to relate with others, and "Living like some good genius," caused worthy reports regarding him to spread. Men of insight such as Thales, Bias, and many others, took note of him, and he came to be called, the "fair-haired Samian."

As Pythagoras matured, he was regarded as comely, and his presence was one of power and awesomeness. Recognizing his own power, he was ever mindful of his manner of speaking, for a reproach from him, would to some, be like death. In habits he was modest, partaking little of food and drink, and often, only of honey. He cared not only for the body, but for the emotion, and mind as well. He was not subject to excess and, "No man ever saw him rejoice or mourn." He composed his soul with the Lyre, and strove to maintain harmony within his being. He would walk with small groups of companions in groves or temples which were pleasant and remote from the confusion of daily living. When the tyrant Polycrates came to power, Pythagoras realized that under such a government he could not pursue learning or disseminate his findings. It was then that he left his country to found his Academy in Crotona.

At an advanced age, Pythagoras married Theano, a disciple and a good woman. After his death, she assisted with the government of the school. Of this marriage, seven children are mentioned, three sons and four daughters. One daughter, Damo, is said to have been left the writings of her father for safekeeping with the admonition, to which she was faithful, that she, at no cost, should communicate them to anyone outside of the family. Some maintain that Pythagoras left nothing in writing; others even name works ascribed to him, for instance, The Sacred Discourse, and The Magical Virtues of Herbs. Among the many men influenced by The Master are: Plato, Aristotle, Marcus Aurelius, Julian, St. Augustine, St. Thomas Aquinus, and Francis Bacon.

Pythagoras' instruction came from his contact and studies with the wise of many countries, and from the unfoldment of his own inner being. He first voyaged to Therecydes. It was from the mentor Anaximander that he learned of nature's secrets. He was a disciple of Pherecydes and a student of Hermodanias. Before he established himself at Crotona, in Southern Italy, it is possible that he visited Phoenica, Palestine, Chaldea, Persia, Arabia, and India. His wish for truth also determined him to venture a voyage to Egypt, where, with the aid of King Amasis, he became acquainted with the priests of Heliopolis and Memphis. These priests, not prone to share their wisdom with strangers, and wishing to test Pythagoras, confronted him with the most difficult disciplines. Nevertheless, he gained their confidence and was finally accepted into the Mysteries of Isis, at Thebes.

In Babylon the Magi received Pythagoras kindly and initiated him into their arcanum, including music, the mathematical sciences, and sublime methods of worshiping the gods. He learned of the motions of the stars and their effects upon the nativities of men. The Magi also shared their remedies for many diseases, and taught

him the principles ruling the Universe. It was here too that he came
to know the Zoroastrians.

While in India, Pythagoras visited the Brahmans. These worthy
priests communicated deep insights to Pythagoras regarding aspects
of the mind, nature of the soul, means of solving the vicissitudes of
life, and methods by which man becomes a positive agent in his own
evolutionary process. He was allowed to share in profound doctrines
taught at Elephanta and Ellora.

Pythagoras was also instructed by the Rabbis regarding the
inner traditions of Moses. He went to Crete and Sparta to learn the
renowned laws of Minos and Lycurgus. In Phoenicia the significance
of the Adonic mysteries were conferred upon him. He learned all
there was to know from the Greek philosophers, and was probably
an initiate of the Eleusinian mysteries. The probability of these travels is strengthened in that such journeys were possible, travel was the
best manner of acquiring knowledge, and Pythagoras' teachings were
influenced by oriental philosophy and mysticism.

When Pythagoras returned to Samos, he lived in a cave outside
of the city, that he might devote himself to developing his philosophy and way of life. He was now regarded by his countrymen with
even greater admiration than before, for he seemed to them even
wiser and more majestic. He was asked to instruct them in the deeper
meaning of what he had learned, especially regarding the symbolic
way to knowledge.

It appears that Pythagoras was, indeed, one of those dedicated to
clarifying for man the real purpose of existence. Penetrating mind
and conviction of feeling may ponder well the validity of the opinion
that esoteric meanings existed in early times and, having been passed
on from master to disciple, have been perpetuated even to us, and,
living on, operate constructively in various ways and at many levels.

Admission to Pythagoras' Academy was by choice and by trial.
The choice was selective and the trials difficult, for this was not a
school where instruction was sold. The Pythagoreans did not ". . .
open their souls like the gates of an inn, to everyone that came to
them." There is another sense in which the instruction was not open.
Pythagoras' lectures were delivered from behind a screen, and were
veiled in language to be fully understood only by the most advanced

disciples. In this manner the esoteric instruction was perpetuated and kept pure, as was the case with mystery schools.

Before admission to the Academy, Pythagoras would know the petitioner: his relations with parents, friends, and associates, the appropriateness of his laughter, silence, and manner of discourse, his handling of anger, passion, and ambition, his capacity for joy and grief, and what caused these sentiments. All elements of the personality were seriously appraised.

Included in the prerequisites was the severe probation of five years silence, which assured poise under difficult circumstances. To those who were to know philosophy, science, and the mysteries, a reason for silence was given: "That the soul might be converted into herself from external things, and from the irrational passions in her, and from the body, even into her own life, which is to live forever." Again, he who is silent hears what is said. Profundity is to stop talking and to learn to meditate. "We ought either to be silent, or to speak things that are better than silence." A stone thrown at random is more worthy than speaking an idle word. In communication use few words, and say much.

Pythagoras would observe the countenance and bearing of the petitioner and, from this, determine many things he desired to know. If the person was found desirable—a lover of knowledge, capable of learning, retaining, and following what he would be taught—he was admitted. Otherwise, he was summarily dismissed.

The mind alone sees and knows. Hence, it must be freed of the fetters which have hampered it since infancy. In no other way can it comprehend what is true, or perceive if the senses are functioning properly. Thus, once disciples were accepted, Pythagoras assisted them with many exercises for the purification of mind and soul, especially the strengthening of will.

Pythagoras advised his disciples that it is best to commence one's day in silent meditation, and thus compose one's own soul. He felt that meditation placed one in the presence of powerful constructive and directive forces. This practice he himself pursued, often retiring into the desert for the purpose, though he placed no merit upon solitude as such.

There were also disciplines such as abstinence regarding food and sleep, temperance, and not being attached to honors. Important too, was their strict rule of secrecy concerning speaking of their more profound doctrines with outsiders, nor did they accept, without caution, the opinion of others. The hearts and minds of the uninitiated are not prepared for basic instruction and, "The goods of wisdom ought not to be communicated to those whose soul is not purified." The Master admonished his disciples not to conceal faults with words, but amend them with constructive action, and to appreciate one who legitimately reproves us, for this leads to improvement through self-discovery. He maintained that it is better to lie on the ground with settled and calm nature, than to lie upon a golden bed and be troubled. No man is free who cannot command himself. Only the most dedicated disciple could pass Pythagoras' means of testing. Yet, the procedures for qualification and purification were indispensable for those who desired to know That Man.

It was at Crotona, a seaport of much wealth and commercial activity, that Pythagoras, about the year 529 B.C., established his Academy. It was a secret scientific-religious brotherhood. The school prospered with centers of the society developing in other parts of the known world. The number of disciples and auditors numbered several hundred. The more serious students were divided into the classes of Probationers or Exoterics, and Mathematicians or Esoterics. To attain advancement in this academy, it was required that science, especially mathematics and astronomy, be mastered as subjects best fitted for the enlightenment of man. The disciples needed also to deepen their religious insights, master their feelings, and purify their souls, thus mitigating the necessity for rebirth.

Wisdom results when the intellect is so integrated as to partake in intuitive cognition of vital causes. Pythagoras taught that with developed capacities one may comprehend and become a part of creative principles by relating to them with one's inner being. He accepted the reality of a constant interchange of energies and consciousness between the universe and man. Man and his greater environment are related as microcosm and macrocosm, and at no point in time or space is there a break in continuity, no dichotomy. Again, true wisdom is hidden from the profane and must be discovered by looking, not outward, but inward. Therein is to be revealed all that man will ever know.

The Master was accredited the ability to communicate to each disciple what was most proper for him to know at a particular time. Not being alike, it is fitting that they not partake alike. The distinction between Exoteric and Esoteric disciples was significant, for the latter were entitled to an inner instruction in which the others were not privileged to partake. This distinction had to do with the difference between the lesser and greater initiations, between lesser preparatory concerns, and complete consecration.

By degrees, the serious disciple experienced a transition from the mundane to the contemplation of incorporeal elements in nature. Gradually, the eye of the mind turned inward toward the realization of eternal principles which do not change and which, when partaken of, make man wise. Pythagoras believed mathematics capable of abstracting the soul from sensibles, preparing it for intellectual and emotional ascension, and making it possible to intuit things inherent in Divine mind. The Master, "Seeing that they could not in words express incorporeal forms and first principles, had recourse to demonstration by Numbers," realizing that God himself is the number of numbers. Without mastering mathematics, the disciple could never become a Pythagorean. Men usually know what they want, but seldom what they need. Pythagoras assisted his disciples with the needs required by nature to comprehend the meaning and purpose of life.

The Pythagorean community was an unusual experiment in human relations. It comprised a close membership adhering to strictly prescribed rules, which they regarded as reversed ordinances. The brothers were thus united in a common purpose. A friend, they held to be another self. With the understanding, derived from Pythagoras, they established true friendships, with the depth of his meaning becoming practical reality. They were aware that friendship symbolizes the good that exist between God and man, soul and body, and man and woman, binding all relations together. The brothers recognized too that discord, wherever appearing, is the cause of dissension and disintegration.

In this society personal possessions meant nothing. The brothers saw no point in accumulating personal wealth, seeing that overabundance is as pointless as severe need. Upon entering the society, everything that a brother owned became the common property of all, for the best interest of each. Should one leave the society, he took with him the estate he brought. The brothers would then erect a tomb for him, as if he were dead. Thus they outgrew egoistic interest, which could never promote the principles for which they stood.

Pythagoras advised his disciples not to rise from their beds after sun up. Rather, they must be about their duties and, as the sun rose, see therein the image of God. He instructed them never to do anything they had not first premeditated. He had no approval for the student who made an appointment and then broke it, and disregarded one who broke a vow. In relating, the student was to speak clearly, constructively, and directly. Moderation in all things was demanded, for an excess, even of virtue, can be a vice.

Notwithstanding Pythagoras' severe disciplining, his disciples accepted his directives without question, for they respected That Man. They looked upon him, not as an ordinary human being, but as one, who possessing godly aspects, was in a class between man and the gods. No mere human, they felt, could accomplish such things as he had achieved. They recognized that when he spoke, the aim was to cure, for he regarded teaching as the highest form of preventive and curative therapy.

In directing the Academy, Pythagoras established additional procedures for the strengthening of soul and body. Included was the practice of piety, morality, temperance, obedience, government, fidelity, and respect for law. Instruction also entailed the structure and meaning of the world soul, the universe, and the law of cause and effect which makes one see that he will reap what he deserves. Religious insights, along with natural mysticism, were stressed, for Pythagoras saw that one must align with God and the gods as principles, or spiritual development would be stultified. Man is never to assume that he has been overlooked by God and the gods, who are his agents, for man is always under their supervision.

The curriculum also included harmony, music, the dance, gymnastics, and proper diet. Having discovered harmony, Pythagoras applied it to order body and soul. By music the manner and passions may be modified to produce health. Through the appreciation of music, angers, griefs, fears, and various desires were exorcised and directed toward virtue. There were melodies for evening relaxation, and others that roused the energies. Pythagoras had music within himself, and applying the ears of his soul to the inner harmony of the world, used it to heal. On one occasion a murder was prevented by the introduction of quieting music. The dance was practiced as conducive to agility of body and health of soul. In healing, poultices and potions from herbs were frequently used. Physical and psychological therapy, by means of color and verse, as those of the *Odyssey* and *Illiad,* were well known to the Pythagoreans. Pythagoras' efforts were spent in the process of unfolding, developing, and deepening the natural potentials of those he accepted for instruction. He saw his disciples and himself as conscious parts of a universal, vital, moving process, and advised all to cooperate with this process, since it involves an inevitable necessity.

The Master taught that, "A man must be made good, then a god." In the order of ascent, the attainment is first made by achieving in daily life, from hence, under instruction, one comes gradually to comprehend, and then to resemble the Divine. He concluded that, most important of all, a man must inform his soul concerning what is good and what is ill, for one is good only when he knows and practices the good. Everyone is destined eventually to know universals, not with the physical eye, but by intellectual and intuitive insight. Then, as The Golden Verses say, man stripped of flesh is freed to higher ether: "A deathless God divine, mortal no more."

The Master maintained that philosophy has to do with real things. He means real essences, incorporeal and eternal realities. All other things are what they are by participating in these realities. Such is the nature of material things, which are corruptible. Science, he points out, has to do with corporeals and not with essentials, and the knowledge of particulars must always follow the science of essentials, or universals. In consciousness, he who understands universals will also understand particulars, but not the reverse.

Pythagoras was practical with his philosophy, for he held it to be in vain if incapable of curing man's passions. As medicine cures the body, there is no benefit in philosophy unless it expels the diseases of the soul. What then are the anchors, the helpers, of the soul? He answers: Wisdom, Magnanimity, and Fortitude, for the virtues are solid, the rest are trifles.

Progress at the Academy actually amounted to a series of initiations. The most significant phase of instruction concerned the fundamental concept that number is the essence of things—that everything is essentially number. Authorities disagree as to how this concept is to be understood. Aristotle's opinion is that the two ways of viewing numbers namely as primal essences, or as the symbols of existence, do not exclude one another. The principle explanation maintains that numbers are the Form, the very essence and meaning of things, and do not exist apart from things. Number *per se* was presented as the quality of things, as the substance and law which holds the universe together. So powerful was this concept that it was further stated that number rules over gods and men and are therefore, the condition and definition of knowledge.

All numbers are divisible into either Odd, or Even, which are the universal constituents of numbers and of things. A third class was accepted, namely, the Odd-Even. The Odd was identified with the Limited, while the Even was associated with the Unlimited. All things partake of the Limited and the Unlimited, the Limited to be equated with the perfect, and the Unlimited with the imperfect. In addition to these opposites, there were the One and Many, Right and Left, Masculine and Feminine, Rest and Motion, Straight and Crooked, Light and Darkness, Good and Evil, Square and Oblong. Certain meanings were also assigned to each of these categories. The Pythagoreans felt it to be observable that each thing contains within itself these opposite characteristics.

Regarding first principles, Pythagoras taught that from the opposition of Unity and Duality, other opposites may be deduced, such as: Spiritual and Corporeal, Form and Substance, and Deity and Matter, which is itself derived from Deity as the original Unity. Unity is the condition of all beginning, and from it arose infinite Duality. Unity and Duality produced numbers and, from these, points, and other mathematical and geometrical forms. Unity is the efficient or moving cause of things. Duality is fundamental matter out of which, when impressed by Unity, creation is produced. The Neo-Pythagoreans regarded Unity as the One and correlated it with Deity, a formless Form lying beyond all opposites as the cause of causes. Duality is to be identified with diversity, as the fragmentor of Being.

The opposites are held together by Harmony, present in each thing, as the unifier of the many which brings discord into accord. Pythagoras assigned special importance to this principle, seeing that it was a necessary condition of each discrepant unit of being: for instance, it is inherent in musical structure, and in the constitution of individuals.

To understand Pythagoras we cannot minimize his preoccupation with numbers and their application to specific concepts and objects. His theory applies specific numbers to everything, both animate and inanimate—for example, to man, plant, and earth. He also applied numbers to concepts: two is equated with opinion, four with justice, five with marriage, seven with timeliness.

The decad was regarded as the inclusive, culminating, sacred number. The Pythagoreans, therefore, divided the universe into ten spheres: first was the circle of the Divine Fire, then the seven spheres of the planets, the earth, and Antichthon, which they proposed as a counter earth. This we never see, since its motion always keeps it at 180° from the earth, kept from view by the sun. They conceived of the heavenly bodies, not so much as physical bodies, but as energy centers, serving as agencies through which Divine intelligence expresses.

The Tetractys, representing universal forces and processes, forms a pyramid by the use of 10 dots. It was the most revered symbol of the Pythagoreans. To construct the figure, four dots are used to form the base, three are placed above these, and then two upon them, and finally one. The one is unity, the two, diversity, the three, equilibrium, while the four is the smallest number of lines that can enclose a square.

Pythagoras draws attention to the properties of the ten basic numbers:

1. The Monad, accepted before all others, because having no diversity, it is always the same;
2. The Duad, the audacious, because the first to separate from the One;
3. The Triad, because it grows out of the Duad, or great mother and the Monad, or divine father;

4. The Tetrad, because it provides the foundation of structure;
5. The Pentad, or equilibrium, because it divides ten into equal halves;
6. The Hexad, because it comprises the form of forms, and concerns the perfection of parts;
7. The Heptad, because it is the number of life and law;
8. The Ogdoad, because it symbolizes counsel, prudence, and love;
9. The Ennead, because it contains the first square of an odd number (3 x 3), and entails boundary or limitation;
10. The Decad, because it is the most inclusive, number, involving all arithmetic and harmonic possibilities.

From the first ten numbers all others were created, since these involve the nature of all numbers.

Pythagorean metaphysics teaches that creation was the result of a central fire formed in the center of the universe. This fire is the One, or Monad and therefore, is good. It is the moving principle of all, including the gods and heavenly bodies. Pythagoras was convinced that the central fire always was; hence, it was not appropriate to speculate upon a beginning of this first cause. As the objects of time and space were regarded mathematically, so the central fire was regarded dynamically. It is the spirit or soul of individuals, as well as of the universe, and is fused throughout the entirety of Being.

The stars are highly evolved phases of the universe, having everything that the earth has, except more perfect. Pythagoras discovered Venus to be both a morning and evening star. He knew the motion of the heavenly bodies, and was aware of the unchangeable regularity of their orbits. In this he saw something divine. From the revolution of heavenly bodies he arrived at his theory of a universal year.

The heavenly bodies give off a sound which the Pythagoreans called the harmony of the spheres. The tones produced by these bodies is in relation to their size, distance, density, and movement. As the planetary system produces a harmony, so too does the universe in its entirety, and as living creatures breathe, so do the planets and the universe.

In the Pythagorean schema the universe entails three levels of being, which correlate with three levels of consciousness. There is the Supreme World, the Superior World, and the Inferior World. The Supreme is the highest, a subtle spiritual essence. The Superior World is that of essential principles such as Numbers and Ideas, and is the abode of the immortals. The Lower World is inhabited by those creatures which partake of material substance. The Supreme world contains within itself the nature and capacity of the lesser two.

Human souls, requiring experience which will eliminate ignorance, take on bodies. The soul, however, must discover how to extract itself from matter, or better, to incorporate the principle of matter into itself. As long as it experiences on the earth plane, it requires a body through which to function. Separated from the body, the soul in the other world experiences the exact sort of life it has set up for itself by causes established during its earthly existence. The later Pythagoreans regarded man's soul as a part of the world soul and, for this reason, considered it divine and imperishable. Another reason for this is that soul has its number and harmony, both of which are imperishable.

The Pythagoreans also believed in Daemons. At times these forms appear to men and assist in directing the processes of their lives. They may, in fact, as may man himself, be regarded as agencies or facilitators of a purposeful plan extent in the world process. The Daemons in consciousness stand midway between man and the gods. Man is under divine direction, and cannot accomplish his transformation to the Hero state without the help of the Daemons, gods, and God. To achieve this greatest good, man must follow the order and spirit of Nature, rather than the dictates of irrationality, and emotional abandonment. Therefore, it is one's duty to purify the soul, and not to depart earthly responsibilities of one's own accord.

Of Pythagoras' Golden Verses, his cryptic way of presenting important truths, seventy-one are recorded, exemplified by those quoted: Verses XIII–XVI read, "Observe justice in all your actions and words; neither use yourself, in any manner, to act without reason. But always make this reflection, that it is ordained by destiny for all men to die; and that the goods of fortune are uncertain; and that, as they may be acquired, they may likewise be lost."

Verses XVII–XX read, "Support with patience your lot, be it

what it will, and never repine at it; but endeavor what you can to remedy it. And consider that fate does not send the greatest portion of these misfortunes to good men."

Verses XL–XLIV read, "Never suffer sleep, to close your eyelids, after going to bed—till you have examined by reason, all your actions of the day. Wherein have I done amiss? What have I done? What have I omitted that I ought to have done? If in this examination, you find that you have done amiss, reprimand yourself severely for it, and if you have done any good, rejoice."

Verses LIX–LX read, "Likewise know, that men draw upon themselves their own misfortunes voluntarily, and of their own free choice, wretches as they are! They neither see, nor understand, that their good is near them. There are very few of them who know how to deliver themselves out of their misfortunes. Such is the fate that blinds mankind, and takes away their senses. Like huge cylinders, they roll to and fro, always oppressed with ills without number. For fatal contention is innate in them and pursuing them everywhere, tosses them up and down, nor do they perceive it. Instead of provoking and stirring it up, they ought to be yielding to avoid it."

At times, Pythagoras taught by means of aphorisms, some of which follow: "Decline from public ways, walk in unfrequented paths," meaning that wisdom must be sought in solitude; "Assist a man in raising a burden, but do not assist him in laying it down," meaning that the diligent merit assistance, but the indolent deserve no help; "Having departed from your house, turn not back, for the furies will be your attendants," meaning that once the disciple sets foot upon the path of truth, he must not turn back to former ignorant ways, which will only cause confusion and suffering.

According to our informants, Pythagoras was known for his prophecies and miracles. His very presence was surrounded by a charismatic splendor. One report states that Pythagoras, while walking from Sybaris to Crotona, came upon fishermen and told them the exact number of fish they would have in their nets. The fishermen said that, if this be true, they would do whatever he commanded. When the fish were counted there were exactly the number foretold. Pythagoras requested that the fish be returned to the sea, whereupon he paid them for their catch, and proceeded to Crotona.

Pythagoras had unusual influence upon rational and irrational creatures alike. One time, stroking a bear, which had done harm to the people, he gave her maize and fruits and directed her not to attack living creatures. As reported, the bear went to the woods and caused no further damage to any living thing. At times, Pythagoras would relate what another had in mind before the other had spoken it. He foretold earthquakes. On one occasion he predicted correctly that a certain ship, though under pleasant breeze at the time, would be wrecked. He was known for counteracting pestilence, and caused violent winds to cease. He is also said to have had the ability to visit the other world and bring back reports to friends of their deceased acquaintances. Pythagoras too spoke of his former lives. Once he appeared, at the same time, before two of his disciples who were at different places, and had conversation with them both. He practiced the art of divination by numbers, and is reported to have developed a round object containing numbers and letters by means of which he could analyze character, and predict future events.

Among the achievements to be accredited Pythagoras are:

1. An improved status of mathematics to a level above mere practicality by introducing the method of axioms, postulates, definitions, and proofs;
2. The discovery and proof of the angle-sum of a triangle;
3. Demonstration that the square erected on the hypotenuse of a right triangle is equivalent in area to squares erected on its other two sides;
4. The concept that the earth is a globe, and astronomical thoughts which led Copernicus to affirm that from the Pythagoreans he arrived at his heliocentric hypothesis;
5. Founded the harmonic science as a result of his laws yielding the fourth, fifth, and octave of a note;
6. The first to use the terms philosophy, and mathematics;
7. Combined geometry and arithmetic, as much later the relation between algebra and geometry was established;
8. Developed the principle that numbers are the essences of all things;

9. Brought to clearer focus the meaning of transmigration and the immortality of the soul;
10. Discovered a Way for man by establishing his relation to universals;
11. Made prophecy and mystical experience commensurate with practical living;
12. Formulated essential parts of Euclid's Elements of Geometry. Based on such thoughts and discoveries, Pythagoras' Academy came to be recognized as the most significant scientific school of the ancient world.

Pythagoras died at the age of 80. His demise came as he counseled with friends at the home of one Milo. The home was set afire out of envy by Clyo, a wealthy, prominent, but tyrannical man who, having applied for discipleship, was found unworthy, and so refused. Others say that the Crotonians, for political reasons, perpetrated the massacre in which some forty of the brothers lost their lives.

The cause may, indeed, have been political, for it cannot be denied that Pythagoras and his disciples were zealous in matters of statescraft. They presented directives and laws of good government to many cities so that their magistrates eliminated dissension from their midst. The Pythagoreans had also acquired a powerful influence upon the magistrates and administrations of these cities by establishing a political conference, which amounted to promoting aristocratic government. During this time democratic trends had gained the ascendancy. The result was, the Pythagoreans were persecuted.

It is possible that Pythagoras, aided by his associates, escaped to Metapontum, and there died sometime later. He may have gone to the temple of the Muses, and after forty days, passed on as a result of not having drunk or eaten during this time. Thus ended the career of a noble and wise man, one of the greatest scientists and most prophetic of mystics the world has produced and known.

Part One

The Life of Pythagoras

Celts

ETRURIA
TYRRHENIA

ITALY

CORSICA

Rome

Adriatic Sea

SARDINIA

Tyrrhenian Sea

Metapontum   Tarentum
Heraclea
Syrus   Bay of
Sybaris   Tarentum

Crotona

MAGNA GRAECIA   Caulonia

SICILY   Messena   Locri
        Rhegium
Himera   Tauromenium
Centorpa   Catana   Ionian
Agrigentum   Sea
        Gela   Syracuse

Carthage

MALTA

Numidia

Mediterranean Sea

Tripolitana

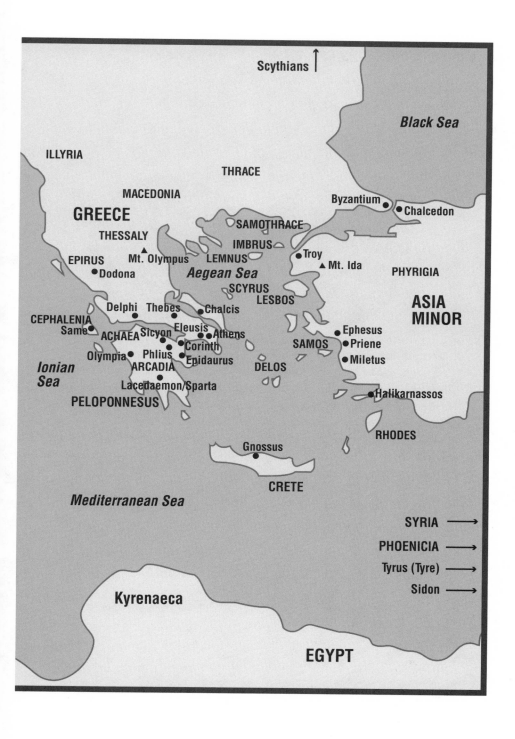

Scythians ↑

Black Sea

ILLYRIA

THRACE

MACEDONIA

Byzantium ● ●Chalcedon

GREECE

THESSALY

SAMOTHRACE

IMBRUS

EPIRUS ▲ Mt. Olympus LEMNUS Troy

●Dodona Aegean Sea ▲ Mt. Ida PHYRIGIA

SCYRUS

LESBOS ASIA MINOR

Delphi ●Thebes ●Chalcis

CEPHALENIA ●Eleusis ●Ephesus

Same● ACHAEA ●Sicyon ●Athens ●Priene

Olympia ●Phlius ●Corinth SAMOS ●Miletus

ARCADIA ●Epidaurus

Ionian Sea DELOS

Lacedaemon/Sparta

PELOPONNESUS Halikarnassos

RHODES

Gnossus

CRETE

Mediterranean Sea

SYRIA →

PHOENICIA →

Tyrus (Tyre) →

Sidon →

Kyrenaeca

EGYPT

Among the earliest coins from Southern Italy, this silver stater of c.540–530 B.C. *was issued at Metaptontum, a city some ancient authorities claim to be the home town of Pythagoras' father. The coin has an unusual configuration in which the barley ear of the reverse form-fits within the raised design of the obverse. This required precision in the cutting of the dies and in the striking of the coin. This unusual minting process may be attributable to Pythagoras, though it is far from certain.*

Photo courtesy of Numismatica Ars Classica

CHAPTER I

The Country, Parents, and Time of Pythagoras

The Italic Sect was distinct from the Ionic, in respect of the author, place, discipline, and doctrine. It was denominated from that part of Italy which, from the frequency of Greek colonies, was called Magna Graecia. Yet was not the author, Pythagoras, an Italian,[1] for though some think his father was of Metapontum;[2] some, a Tyrrhene of Etruria in Italy; yet Diogenes and others report him a Tyrrhene of the race of those who inhabited Lemnus, Imbrus, and Scyrus.[3] And that coming upon traffic to Samos, he settled there and was made free. With these concurs Aristoxenus (to whom Clement of Alexandria joins Aristarchus and Theopompus[4]), who says in his life of Pythagoras, that he was born in one of those islands which the Athenians won and expelled thence the Tyrrhenians. Whence Suidas says that Pythagoras was a Samian, but by birth a Tyrrhenian, brought over young by his father from Tyrrhenia to Samos.[5] And indeed, his country seems inscrutable to Lycus;[6] and to Josephus no less difficult to find out than that of Homer.[7]

Nor is it strange that the country of his father should be questioned, since it is not agreed concerning his name and quality.[8] Justin calls him Demaratus (and Johannes Sarisburiensis, from Justine, Maratus[9]), others, Mamercus. But the greatest part of writers agree, that he was called Mnesarchus.[10] His profession, according to Hermippus and others, a graver of rings; according to others, a merchant.[11]

Some there are who affirm he was a Phliasian. Pausanias reports that he was son of Euphron, grandson of Hippasus, who upon the taking of Phlius by the Dorians, fled to Samos. Others, that he was the son of Hippasus. Hippasus was son of Euthyphron of Cleonymus, who was banished out of Phlius; and that Mamercus (or rather Mnesarchus) lived in Samos, whence Pythagoras was said to be a Samian.[12] Cleanthes relates he was a Syrian, of the city Tyrus in Syria (or rather in Phoenicia), whence making a voyage to Samos for traffic, at such time as the Samiams were much oppressed with famine, he furnished them with corn; in requital whereof, they made him free of their country. Hippobotus says that Pythagoras was a Samian.[13]

Indeed, the most general and approved opinion is that Mnesarchus was a Samian, descended from Ancaeus, who first brought a colony into Samos. And that Pythagoras, his son, was born at Sidon in Phoenicia; but by education, as well as extraction, a Samian also. This is ratified by the authority of Iamblichus, who begins his life with the following fabulous narration.

It is reported that Ancaeus, who lived at Same in Cephalenia, was descended from Jupiter[14] (others say from Neptune and Astypalaea), an opinion occasioned by his virtues or some particular greatness of soul.[15] In prudence and magnanimity he excelled all other Cephalenians. This Ancaeus was commanded by the Pythian Oracle to gather together a colony out of Cephalenia, Arcadia, and Thessaly, augmenting it from Athens, Epidaurus, and Chalcis. And that having got them together under his command, he should people an island, named from the richness of the soil Melamphyllos (blackleaf), and call the city which they built Samos, from Same in Cephalenia.[16] The Oracle was thus:

> Instead of Same, Samos thou (an isle)
> Shalt plant Aneaeus, which men Phyllas style.

That this colony was drawn from those several places appears not only from their religious rites and sacrifices (which are derived from the countries out of which those people came), but also from the affinities and mutual conventions made by the Samians. Mnesarchus and Pythais, the parents of Pythagoras, are said to be descended from the family of the same Ancaeus who planted this colony there. (Of Pythais it is confirmed by Apollonius.[17]) Which nobleness of their extraction, being much celebrated amongst their countrymen, a Samian poet declared him to be the son of Apollo in these words:[18]

> Pythais of all Samians the most fair,
> Jove-loved Pythagoras to Phoebus bare.

Which report was raised thus. This Mnesarchus the Samian, being upon occasion of traffic at Delphi with his wife, who was at that time newly with child and not known to be so; he enquired of the Oracle concerning his voyage to Syria. The Prophetess told him that his journey should be, according to his mind, very advantageous. That his wife was already with child, and should bring forth a son that should exceed all men that ever were in Beauty and Wisdom, and through the whole course of his life bring much benefit to mankind. Mnesarchus considering that the Oracle would not have spoken of his son, seeing that he demanded nothing concerning him, if there were not something extraordinary to be expected from him, immediately hereupon changed the name of his wife, which was Parthenis, to Pythais, from the Prophetess.

And as soon as she was delivered at Sidon in Phoenicia, they called the child Pythagoras. For Epimenides, Eudoxus, Xenocrates (and others mentioned by Apollonius[19]) are to be rejected who affirm Apollo at that time lay with Pythais,[20] and got her with child (she not being so before) and thereupon foretold it by the Prophetess. This is not to be admitted. But that the soul of Pythagoras, being of the regimen of Apollo (whether as a follower, or some other way more near to him), was sent to men none can doubt—since it may be evinced by these circumstances of his birth, and the universal wisdom of his mind. This much (says Iamblichus) concerning his generation. Whence we see the Greeks did so much admire his wit that they thought it could be nothing less than divine, and thereupon fabled Apollo to be his father.

Pythagoras was the youngest of three sons: the eldest Cleanthes calls Eunostus;[21] Laertius and Suidas called him Eunomus; the second was called Tyrrhenus. He had likewise an uncle Zoilus, mentioned by Laertius.

The reasons for establishing the times concerning Pythagoras's life will hereafter be set forth upon the occasion of his going into Italy. In the meantime, I shall desire it may be admitted, that he was born about the third year of the fifty-third **Olympiad** [ca. 562 b.c., see Glossary—Ed.]. That being eighteen years old, he heard Thales and others. Then he went to Phoenicia, thence into Egypt, where he stayed twenty-two years; afterwards at Babylon twelve years; then returned to Samos, being fifty-six years old; and from thence went into Italy. The particulars whereof shall in their several places be more fully discoursed.

The island of Samos, off the Ionian coast, was a prolific issuer of coinage. This silver tetradrachm was struck in about 450 B.C. It shows the badge of the city, a facing lion scalp, and on its reverse the forepart of ox and an olive branch. The ΣΑ above the ox indicates it is a coin of the Samians.
Photo courtesy of Classical Numismatic Group, Inc.

His First Education and Masters

Mnesarchus (says Iamblichus) returning from Syria to Samos with much wealth and abundance of merchandise, built a Temple which he dedicated to Apollo the Pythian, and brought up his son in several excellent disciplines. He committed him sometimes to Creophilus, sometimes to Pherecydes of Syria, and to almost all the Prefects of the Temple, as being blessed with the fairest and most divine son that ever man had.[22]

Some there are who affirm that Pythagoras was a wrestler;[23] and that when Pherecydes first discoursed among the Greeks concerning the immortality of the soul, Pythagoras the Samian, moved at the novelty of the discourse, changed from being a wrestler to a philosopher.[24] But these relations seem to have been occasioned by confounding Pythagoras the philosopher with a wrestler of that name, his contemporary, of whom more hereafter.

Cleanthes[25] and Suidas[26] relate that Pythagoras first heard Pherecydes the Syrian at Samos; and in the second place Hermodomas, τῷ Κρεοφυλίῳ, "the Creophylian," at the same Samos, then very old.[27] Hermodamas was his name, but he was surnamed Creophylus, wherefore perhaps instead of τῷ Κρεοφυλίῳ, should be read, τῷ Κρεοφύλῳ.[28] Or else he was termed a Creophylian, as well as surnamed Creophylus,[29] because he was reported to be descended from Creophylus, a Samian, who in times past entertained Homer as his guest, and was, as some say, his master and his rival in poetry.[30] But when Apuleius says Hermodamas (or Leodamas, as he calls him) was disciple to that Creophilus, he makes an error no less in chronology than when he says Pythagoras was disciple of Plato, unless the whole text be corrupted.[31]

Pythagoras, his father dying, grew up in prudence and temperance, being while he was yet very young generally much respected and honored even by the most aged.[32] His presence and discourse attracted all persons. To everyone on whom he looked, he appeared worthy of admiration, insomuch that many averred he was the son of a deity. He, being thus confirmed by the great opinions that were

had of him, by the education of his infancy, and by his natural excellence, made himself daily more worthy of these advantages. He
adorned himself with devotions, with sciences, with excellent conversation, with constancy of mind, with grave deportment, and with
a sweet inimitable serenity; never transported with anger, laughter,
emulation, contention, or any other disorder; living like some good
genius come to converse in Samos. Hereupon, though young, a great
report was spread of him to Thales at Miletus, to Bias at Priene—
two of the sages—and to all the cities thereabout. Many in all those
parts commending the young man made him famous, calling him by
a proverb:

The Samian Comer or, The fair-hair'd Samian.

About this time began the tyranny of Polycrates. Pythagoras,
now eighteen years old, foreseeing the event, and how obstructive
it would prove to his designs and to the pursuit of learning, which
he intended above all things, being young and desirous of knowledge, he left his country to go to travel.[33] He stole away privately
by night, taking with him Hermodamas (surnamed Creophylus, and
descended, as was reported, from that Creophylus who was host to
Homer). They made a voyage to Pherecydes at Lisbus (to whom,
Laertius says, he was recommended by his Uncle Zoilus); and to
Anaximander, the natural philosopher; and to Thales at Miletus.
    With each of these he conversed severally in such manner that
they all loved him, admired his parts, and communicated their
learning to him. Under Anaximander, the Milesian, he is said to
have studied the knowledge of natural things.[34] Thales entertained
him kindly; and wondering at his excellence above other youths
which much surpassed the report he had received, assisted him as far
as he was able in sciences. Withal, accusing his own age and infirmity, he advised Pythagoras to make a voyage to Egypt there to get
acquaintance with the priests of Memphis and Diospolis.[35] He said
that of them he had learned those things for which he was by many
esteemed wise, though he were not of such forwardness, neither by
nature or education, as he saw Pythagoras to be. Whence he pre-

saged that if he conversed with those priests, he should become the most divine and wisest of men.

This Pherecydes fell sick at Delos. That he outlived not the fifty-seventh Olympiad [ca. 548–544 B.C.] is manifest from a letter which he wrote the day before his death to Thales, who died the first year of the Olympiad following.[36] And though the greater part of authors write that at the same time when the Cylonians in Crotona conspired against the Pythagoreans (which was not long before Pythagoras died), Pythagoras was gone from Italy to Delos to visit and bury Pherecydes—yet Dicaearchus and other more accurate authors (says Porphyry) aver that Pythagoras was present when that conspiracy broke forth; and that Pherecydes died before Pythagoras departed from Samos.[37] The former relation has imposed, among others, upon the learned Salmasius, who to reconcile this with other circumstances concerning Pherecydes, is constrained to imagine another person of the same name.[38] It was therefore before Pythagoras left Samos that Pherecydes, being desperately seized by a **Phthiriasis**, he went to visit him and attended him in his sickness until he died. And then performed the rites of funeral as to his master.[39] For Laertius and Porphyry add that after the death and burial of Pherecydes, Pythagoras returned to Samos out of a desire to enjoy the society of Hermodamus.

Phavorinus, in the seventh book of his various History,[40] and Porphyry,[41] relate that after he had lived awhile with Hermodamas, he first taught wrestlers—and of them Eurimenes—to diet with flesh (whereas other wrestlers used to eat dried figs, cheese-curds, and whey) whereby Eurimenes became victor at the Olympic Games. But Laertius and Iamblichus observe that this is falsely ascribed to Pythagoras the Samian (for he allowed not the eating of flesh), but was indeed the invention of Pythagoras, son of Eratocles, of whom more hereafter.[42]

How He Traveled to Phoenicia

He learned of Thales above all things to husband his time. And forbearing wine and flesh, and having before refrained from eating much, he accustomed himself to such meats as were light and easy of digestion. By such means he procured a habit of watchfulness, clearness of mind, and an exact constant health of body.[43]

He made a voyage to Sidon, as well out of a natural desire to the place itself, esteeming it his country, as conceiving that he might more easily pass from thence into Egypt. Here he conferred with the prophets, successors of Mecus the physiologist, and with others, and with the Phoenician priests, and was initiated into all the mysteries of Byblus, and Tyre, and several of the principal[44] sacred institutions in diverse other parts of Syria. He underwent these things not out of superstition, as may be imagined, but out of love to knowledge, and a fear lest anything worthy to be known, which was preserved amongst them in the miracles or mysteries of the gods, might escape him. Withal not being ignorant that the rites of those places were deduced from the Egyptian ceremonies, by means whereof he hoped to participate of the more sublime and divine mysteries in Egypt, which he pursued with admiration as his master Thales had advised him.

How He Traveled to Egypt

Some Egyptian mariners passing accidentally along that coast which lies under Carmel (a Phoenician mountain where he spent much of his time in private retirement at the Temple), willingly received him into their ship.[45] But observing during the voyage how temperately he lived, keeping his usual diet, they began to have a greater esteem for him. And perceiving some things in the excellence of his demeanor, more than human, they reflected within themselves how that he appeared to them as soon as they landed, coming down from the top of the mountain Carmel (which they knew to be more sacred than other hills, and not trode upon by the vulgar), easily and directly, neither stones nor precipices obstructing his passage. And how that coming to the side of the ship,[46] he asked, whether they were bound for Egypt; and they, answering that they were, he went into the vessel, and silently sitting down in a place where he might least disturb the mariners in case they should be in any stress.

He continued in the same posture two nights and three days—without meat, drink, or sleep (except when none perceived he slumbered a little, sitting in the same unmovable posture, and this constantly to the end). They noted how that the voyage proceeded direct, beyond their expectation, as if assisted by the presence of some god. Laying all these things together, they concluded and persuaded themselves that some Divine Genius did indeed come along with them from Syria to Egypt. The rest of the voyage they performed prosperously, observing a greater respect then formerly in their words and actions, as well to one another as towards him, until they at last arrived upon the coast of Egypt by a most fortunate passage without any storm.

As soon as they landed they reverently took him up, and seating him on the cleanest part of the sand, reared an extemporary altar before him, on which they laid part of all the sorts of provisions which they had as the first fruits of their lading, and drew up their vessel in the same place where they first put to sea. Pythagoras, though weakened with long fasting, was not sick, either at his land-ing or by their handling of him. Nor did he, when they were gone, abstain long from the fruits which they had laid before him, but took them and preserved his constitution therewith undisturbed, till he came to the next hours.[47] From thence he went to search after all the Temples with diligent and exact inquisition.

Antiphon, in his book concerning such as were eminent for virtue,[48] extolled his perseverance when he was in Egypt. He said Pythagoras, designing to become acquainted with the institution of the Egyptian priests, and diligently endeavoring to participate thereof, desired Polycrates the tyrant to write to Amasis king of Egypt—with whom he had friendship (as appears also by Herodotus[49]) and hospitality (formerly)—that he might be admitted to the aforesaid doctrine. Coming to Amasis, the Pharoah gave him letters to the priests.

He went first to those of Heliopolis; they sent him to the priest of Memphis as the more ancient, which was indeed but a pretence of the Heliopolitans. (For the Egyptians imparted not their mysteries to everyone, nor committed the knowledge of divine things to profane persons, but to those only who were to inherit the kingdom; and of priests, to those who were adjudged to excel the rest in education, learning, and descent.[50]) From Memphis, upon the same pretence, he was sent to Thebes. They, not daring for fear of the king to pretend excuses, but thinking that by reason of the greatness and difficulty thereof he would desist from the design, enjoined him very hard precepts, wholly different from the institution of the Grecians. These he readily performed to their so great admiration that they gave him power to sacrifice to the gods, and to acquaint himself with all their studies—which was never known to have been granted to any foreigner besides. Clement of Alexandria relates particularly that he was disciple to Sonchedes, an Egyptian arch-prophet.[51]

Diogenes says that while he lived with these priests, he was instructed in the learning and language (as Antiphon also affirms) of the Egyptians,[52] and in their three kinds of writing: Epistolic, Hieroglyphic, and Symbolic—whereof one imitates the common way of speaking, the rest allegorical by Enigmas.[53] They who are taught by the Egyptians learn first the method of all the Egyptian letters, which is called Epistilographic; the second, Hieratic, used by those who wrote of sacred things; the last and most perfect Hieroglyphic, whereof one is **Curiologic**, the other Symbolic.

Of the Symbolic, one is properly spoken by Imitation; another is written as it were Tropically; another on the contrary does allegorize by allusion and parable. For instance, in the hieroglyphic way, to express the Sun they made a circle; the Moon, a crescent. Tropically they do properly traduce and transfer and express by exchanging some things, and variously transfiguring others. Thus when they deliver the praises of kings in theological fables, they wrote with embossed symbolic characters. Of the third kind, by allusion and parable, let this be an example: All other stars, by reason of their oblique course, they likened to the bodies of serpents; but the Sun to that of a beetle, because having formed a ball of cow-dung, and lying upon its back, it rolls it about (from claw to claw). They say, moreover, that this creature lives six months underground, and the other half of the year upon the earth; and that it emits seed into the globe (of the earth) and so generates, there being no female of that species. Hitherto Clemens.[54]

Thus being acquainted with the learning of that nation, and enquiring into the commentaries of the priests of former times, he knew the observations of innumerable ages, as Valerius Maximus says.[55] And living admired and beloved of all the priests and prophets with whom he conversed, he informed himself by their means accurately concerning everything; not omitting any person eminent at that time for learning, or any kind of religious rites; nor leaving any place unseen by going into which he conceived that he might find something extraordinary.[56] For he went into the adyta of the Egyptians[57] (and, as Clemens says, permitted himself to that end to be circumcised[58]) and learned things not to be communicated concerning the gods and mystic philosophy. He traveled to all the priests, and was instructed by every one in that wherein they were particularly learned. In Egypt he lived twenty-two years in their private sacred places, studying Astronomy and Geometry, and was initiated (not cursorily or casually) into all the religious mysteries of the gods.

Laertius says he made three cups of silver and presented them to each (Society) of the Egyptian priests; which, as we said, were three: of Heliopolis, Memphis, and Thebes.

CHAPTER 5

How He Went to Babylon

Amasis, dying in the third year of the sixty-third Olympiad[59] [ca. 522 b.c.] (which was the 223rd of Nabonasser), his son Psamminitus succeeded him, who is by Cresias named Amistaeus. And he seems to be the same whom Pliny calls Semniserteus[60] (though others interpret it of Amasis[61]), in whose reign, says he, Pythagoras was in Egypt. At this time, Cambyses invaded and conquered Egypt,[62] by whom Pythagoras was taken prisoner and sent to Babylon. There he lived with the most excellent among the Chaldeans,[63] the Persian Magi (for so Cicero,[64] Apuleius,[65] and Eusebius[66] term them), in respect that Babylon was then under that monarchy. This is the meaning also of Valerius Maximus,[67] and Lactantius,[68] who affirm, that he went from Egypt to the Persians (not to Persia, as some conceive[69]), and resigned himself to the most exact prudence of the Magi to be formed.

The Magi received him kindly, and instructed him in the most profound and sublime mysteries of the worship of the gods.[70] By their means also he arrived at the height of Arithmetic, Music, and other Mathematical Sciences. From them, says Valerius Maximus, he with a docile mind, received the motions of the stars: their power, property, and effects, their states and periods;[71] the various effects of both in the nativities of men, as likewise the remedies of diseases, which are purchased at vast rates by sea and land.[72]

Of the Chaldeans with whom he lived in Babylon, Diogenes particularly mentions Zabratus, by whom he was cleansed from the pollutions of his life past, and instructed from what things virtuous persons aught to be free, and learnt the discourse concerning Nature (Physic), and what are the principles of the Universe.[73] This Zabratus was probably the same with that Zoroastres, one of the Persian Magi, whom Apuleius says he chiefly had for teacher, terming him, *Omnis divini Arcanum antistate* ["Chief Priest of every Divine Mystery"].[74] He was also probably the same as Nazaratus, the Assyrian, whom Alexander, in his book of Pythagorean Symbols, affirms to have been master to Pythagoras.[75] Also the same person whom

Suidas calls Zares;[76] Cyril, Zaran; Plutarch, Zaratas. Whence some conceive that they all mean Zoroastres, the Magus, who was also called Zarades, as evidently appears from Theodoret and Agathias.[77] Indeed, he could not hear Zoroastres himself, as being some ages later; yet it appears from the relation of Apuleius, that many conceived Pythagoras to have been a follower of Zoroastres. Perhaps him whose doctrine Pythagoras embraced (for Clemens says he explained Zoroastres the Persian Magus[78]), posterity believed to have been his master. This Nazaratus the Assyrian was also by some supposed to be the Prophet Ezekiel, which opinion Clemens disputes. Nevertheless (as Mr. Selden observes), the most accurate chronology teaches that Ezekiel and Pythagoras flourished together, between the fiftieth and fifty-third Olympiad [ca. 576 to 565 B.C.]; and therefore the account of time hinders not, but that this Nazaratus might be Ezekiel.

Diogenes (in his treatise of *Incredible Things Beyond Thule*[79]) adds that Pythagoras went also to the Hebrews, which Lactantius expressly denies.[80] Eusebius says he is reported to have heard the Persian Magi, and the diviners of the Egyptians, at the time some of the Jews were gone to Babylon, others to Egypt.[81] That he conversed with the Jews at Babylon (says the Bishop of Armagh[82]) may be argued, for that he transferred many of their doctrines into his philosophy, as Hermippus declares in his first book of things concerning Pythagoras, cited by Josephus.[83] And in his first book of Lawgivers, cited by Origen.[84] This is likewise confirmed by Aristobulus the Jew, a Peripatetical philosopher, in his first book to Philometor. He moreover was induced to believe that the Books of Moses were translated into Greek before the Persian Empire;[85] whereas it is much more probable that Pythagoras received that part of his learning from the conversation which he had with the Hebrews.

Alexander adds that Pythagoras heard the Galatae and the Brahmans.[86] From Chaldea, says Apuleius, he went to the Brahmans. These are wise persons of the nation of India, for which reason he went to their Gymnosophists. The Brahmans conferred many things to his philosophy: what are the documents of minds; what the exercises of bodies; how many are the parts of the soul; how many the vicissitudes of life; what torments or rewards, according to their merits, are allotted to men after death.

Diogenes adds that he went also to Arabia and lived with the king there.[87] But it is not easy to find the name of the court of the king of that wandering nation.

As concerning his learning, it is generally said that he learned the most excellent parts of his philosophy of the Barbarians.[88] Diogenes affirms he gained the greatest part of his wisdom from these nations. The sciences which are called Mathematical, he learnt of the Egyptians, and the Chaldeans, and the Phoenicians; for the Egyptians, were of old studious of geometry; the Phoenicians, of numbers and proportions; the Chaldeans, of astronomical theorems, divine rites, and worship of the gods; and other institutions concerning the course of life, he learned and received of the Magi.[89] These are more generally known, as being committed to writing; but the rest of his institution are less known.

Hermippus says he embraced the opinions of the Thracians;[90] which some interpret of Pittaeus, whose father Hyrrhadius was of that country.[91] But with more reason may it be understood of Orpheus, from whom Iamblichus acknowledged that Pythagoras derived much of the theological part of his science.

CHAPTER 6

How He Returned to Samos

Having lived at Babylon twelve years,[92] he returned to Samos about the fifty-sixth year of his age (that he was redeemed by one Gyllus, Prince of Crotona, Apuleius cites but for a less creditable relation). Being known by some of the most ancient persons, he was looked upon with greater admiration than before, for he seemed to them more wise, more beautiful, and more divinely majestic. His country summoned him to some public employment that he might benefit the generality, and communicate his knowledge. Which he, not refusing, endeavored to instruct them in the symbolical way of learning, altogether resembling that of the Egyptians in which he himself had been taught. But the Samians not affecting this way, did not apply themselves to him.

Pythagoras, though he saw that no man came to him or sincerely affected his learning, endeavored nevertheless all possible ways to continue amongst them, not despising or undervaluing Samos because it was his country. And while he was very desirous that his countrymen should taste, though against their wills, the sweetness of his Mathematics, he observed in a gymnasium, a young man that played at tennis dexterously and nimbly, but otherwise poor and indigent. Imagining that this youth would be wholly guided by him, if without labor he should supply him with necessaries, when they had done washing, he called him to him. He told him that he would continually furnish him with all things sufficient for his maintenance, if he would learn briefly, and without labor, and constantly (that he might not be over-burdened), some Mathematics—which he himself, when he was young, had learned of the Barbarians, which had now left him by reason of old age and forgetfulness.

The youth promising, and being allured by the hopes of maintenance, he endeavored to initiate him in Arithmetic and Geometry, drawing the demonstration of each in a table. And teaching him, he gave the young man for every scheme (or diagram) three **oboli** as a reward and compensation. And this he continued to do a long time

55

out of a love of glory, and industriously brought him into the theory by an exact method.

But when the young man, having made a good progress, was sensible of the excellence, both of the pleasure and the consequences in Mathematics, the wise man perceiving it, and that he would not now quit his learning, what inconvenience soever he might suffer, pretended, that he had no more **trioboli** to give him. "Tis no matter," said the youth, "I am able to learn and receive your Arithmetics without it." Pythagoras replied, "But I have not sufficient to find food for myself, wherefore I must now give over to acquire necessaries for everyday, and daily food; nor is it fit now to be taken up with tables and fruitless studies." Whereupon the young man, loathe to be hindered from continuing his learning, replied, "I will supply you, and in some manner requite you; for I will give you for every scheme three oboli."

And from thenceforward became so much in love with Mathematics, that he alone of all the Samians was commended with Pythagoras, being likewise of the same name, son of Eratocles. His Aleiptiek Commentaries are extant, and his directions to the wrestlers of the time, to eat flesh instead of dried figs—which by some are falsely ascribed to Pythagoras the son of Mnesarchus (as was formerly intimated), but by Pliny,[93] to one of that name who professed exercises of the body, which agrees with the relation of Iamblichus.

TRAVELS TO DELOS, DELPHI, CRETE, AND SPARTA

Not long after, according to the relation of Iamblichus, Pythagoras went to Delos, where he was much admired by the inhabitants.[94] For he prayed only at the Altar of Apollo Genitor[95] (which stands behind the horn altar), called unbloody, because at it were offered only wheat, barley, and cakes,[96] but no victim—as Aristotle says in his Treatise concerning the Delian Commonwealth—and applied himself to none but the attendants thereof.

From Delos, Iamblichus says he went to all places of Oracle.[97] At Delphi he wrote an elegy upon the Tomb of Apollo whereby he declared that Apollo was son of Silenus, but slain by Pytho, and buried in the place called Trisops, which was so named for that the three daughters of Triopas mourned there for Apollo.[98] At Delphi also (Aristoxenus says) he learned many moral documents of Themistoclea.[99]

He went also to Crete and Sparta to acquaint himself with the Laws of Minos and Lycurgus, which at that time were much renowned, as Justine[100] and Iamblichus[101] affirm.

Neither was Crete less famous for religious ceremonies. It was esteemed the place where Jupiter was born and brought up by the Corybantes—or Dactyli priests of Cybele—in a cave of the Mountain Ida, which they so named after that of Phrygia whence they came. They had also a tradition that Jupiter was buried there, and showed his tomb. Here Pythagoras addressed himself to the priests of Morgus, one of the Idaen Dactyli, who purified him with the Ceraunian Stone (so called in that it is conceived to be a piece of Jupiter's thunderbolt, and therefore perhaps used by his priests[102]). In the morning he lay stretched forth upon his face by the seaside; at night by a river, crowned with a wreath made of the wool of a black lamb.

He also applied himself to the Cretan Epimenides, that eminent soothsayer, as Apuleius calls him.[103] He went down with him into the Idean Cave, wrapped in black wool, and stayed there three times nine days according to the custom.[104] He saw the throne which is made yearly there for Jupiter, and wrote an epigram upon his tomb, beginning thus:

Here Zan deceased lies, whom Jove they call.

Thus was he initiated into all religious rites, Grecian as well as Barbarian.[105]

This silver stater was issued for Olympic Games held in the early 4th century B.C.—*perhaps for the 98th Olympiad of 388* B.C. *It honors honors Zeus, the supreme deity of the Greek pantheon and patron of the Games by showing a round shield emblazoned with his eagle tearing at a ram, and on the reverse his thunderbolt.*
Photo courtesy of Numismatica Ars Classica

CHAPTER 8

How He Went to Olympia and Phlius

After he had made enquiry into the laws and customs of Crete and Lacedaemon, he went down to the Olympic Games.[106] Having given a proof of his multiplicious knowledge to the admiration of all Greece, being demanded what his appellation was, he answered that he was not *Sophos*, wise (for excellent men had already possessed that name), but *Philosophos*, a lover of wisdom.

But some relate this as done at Sicyon in discourse with Leon, tyrant of that place; others at Phlius, distant from Sicyon a hundred furlongs.[107] Of the latter are Heraclides in his book of the breathless woman;[108] and Sosicrates in his successions.[109] The testimony of Heraclides is thus delivered by Cicero.[110]

He went, as is reported, to Phlius and discoursed upon some things learnedly and copiously with Leo prince of the Phliasians. Leo, admiring his wit and eloquence, demanded in what art he did most confide. Pythagoras answered, that he knew no art, but was a philosopher. Leo wondering at the novelty of the name, asked who were philosophers, and what difference there is between them and others? Pythagoras answered that human life seemed to resemble that public convention which is celebrated with the pomp and games of all Greece. For as some by bodily exercises aim at the glory and nobility of a crown; other are led away by gain in buying or selling. But there is a certain kind of person, and those of the better quality, who seek neither applause nor gain, but come to behold and curiously observe what is done, and how. So we, coming out of another life and nature into this life, as out of some city into the full throng of a public meeting—some serve glory, other riches. Only some few there are, who despising all things else, studiously enquire into the nature of things. These he called Enquirers after wisdom, that is, *Philosophers*.

Thus, whereas learning before was called "Sophia," Wisdom, and the prosessors thereof, *Sophoi*, wisemen (as Thales and the rest of whom we treated in the first book), Pythagoras, by a more modest appellation, named it "Philosophy," or Love of Wisdom. He called its prosessors "Philosophers," conceiving the attribute of wise not to belong to men but to God only—that which is properly termed Wisdom, being far above human capacity.[111] For though the frame of the whole heaven, and the stars which are carried about in it, if we consider their order, is fair; yet is it such but by participation of the primary intelligible, who is a nature of numbers and proportions, diffusing itself through the universe, according to which, all these things are ordered together and adorned decently. Wisdom therefore is a true knowledge, conversant about those fair things which are first, and divine, and unmingled, and always the same; by participation whereof, we may call other things fair. But philosophy is an imitation of that science, which likewise is an excellent knowledge, and did assist towards the reformation of mankind.

How He Lived at Samos

Having been a diligent auditor and disciple of all these, he returned home and earnestly addicted himself to enquiry after such things as he had omitted.[112] First, as soon as he returned to Ionia (says Antiphon, cited by Porphyry, repeated and enlarged by Iamblicus), he built in his country within the city a school which even yet is called the Semicircle of Pythagoras.[113] Here the Samians, when they would consult about public affairs, would assemble, choosing to enquire after things honest, just, and advantageous in that place which he, who took care of them all, had erected. Without the city he made a cave proper for his study of philosophy, in which he lived for the most part day and night, and discoursed with his friends, and made enquiry into the most useful part of Mathematics, taking the same course as Minos son of Jupiter. And so far did he surpass all whom he taught, that they, for the smallest theorem, were reputed great persons.

Pythagoras now perfected the science of the celestial bodies and covered it with all demonstrations Arithmetical and Geometrical. Nor this only, but he became much more admired for the things he performed afterwards. For philosophy had now received a great increase, and all Greece began to admire him; and the best and most studious persons, for his sake, reported to Samos desiring to participate of his institutions.

His Voyage to Italy

But Pythagoras, being engaged by his countrymen in all embassies, and constrained to be interested in their public negotiations, perceived that if he should comply with the laws of his country and continue there, it would he hard for him to study Philosophy. For which reason all former philosophers ended their lives in foreign countries.[114] Weighing all these consideration, and to avoid civil employments—or as others say, declining the negligence of learning which at that time possessed the Samians—he departed into Italy, preferring that place before his country, which contained most persons fervently desirous of learning.

But before we speak of his actions in Italy, it will be requisite as well to settle the time of his coming and the state of that country as it was at that time. It was a received opinion amongst the more ancient but less learned Romans that Pythagoras was contemporary with King Numa. The occasion of that tradition might perhaps arise from those books which were found in the sepulcher of Numa, 805 years after his death. Antius Valerius, cited by Livy,[115] and Cassius Hemina, by Pliny,[116] relate these were supposed to contain Pythagorean philosophy. But that opinion is long since refuted by the more learned Romans and Grecians: Cicero, Titus Livius, Dionysius Halicarnassaeus, Plutarch, and others.

They who have looked more strictly into the time of Pythagoras seem to follow two different accounts. Iamblichus says that he lived in Egypt twenty-two years; that he was carried from thence by Cambyses; that he lived in Babylon twelve years; that from thence he returned to Samos being fifty-six years old; that from Samos he went into Italy in the sixty-second Olympiad [ca. 528 B.C.]—Eryxidas, a Chalcidean, being victor at the Olympic Games. From whence it follows that he went into Egypt about the third year of the fifty-third Olympiad [ca. 562 B.C.]; and that he was born in the second year of the forty-eighth Olympiad [ca. 583 B.C.]; and that it was the fifty-second Olympiad [ca. 568–565 B.C.], when he, in the eighteeenth year of his age, heard Thales, Pherecydes and Anaximander.

This account seems to be followed by Laertius, Porphyry, Themistius, Suidas (from Laertius), and others, who affirm he went from Samos into Italy at the time Polycrates was tyrant of Samos, conceiving it unfit for a philosopher to live under such a government. For by Diodorus,[117] Pythagoras is acknowledged in the sixty-first Olympiad [ca. 532 B.C.], Thericles being Archon; by Clement of Alexandria, about the sixty-second Olympiad [ca. 528 B.C.], under Polycrates;[118] and in the second year of the sixty-fourth Olympiad [ca. 519 B.C.], Polycrates was betrayed and put to death by Oroetas. This account Antilochus also seems to follow, who reckons from the time of Pythagoras to the death of Epicurus, 312 years. Epicuras died in the second year of the 127th Olympiad [ca. 267 B.C.]; the 312th year upwards is the first of the forty-ninth Olympiad [ca. 580 B.C.]. Neither is Livy much different from this computation, who makes him to come into Italy, Servio Tullio regnante, who died about a year or two before. And this account might be the occasion of making him live to ninety years, as Laertius says many do; and to 104 years, as the nameless author of his life in Photius, the year of his death being according to Eusebius the fourth of the seventieth Olympiad [ca. 493 B.C.].

But this account may, with good reason, be questioned. For if it be granted (as by Iamblichus himself, and other good authorities it is affirmed) that Pythagoras was in Egypt when Cambyses subdued it, and that he was carried away captive by him into Babylon, the time of his going into Italy must of necessity be much later. For Cambyses invaded Egypt in the fifth year of his reign, which is the third year of the sixty-third Olympiad [ca. 522 B.C.], and the 223rd year of Nobonassar, of which there is no question in chronology. This is so because the seventh year of Cambyses is known to be the 225th year of Nabonassar. Ptolemy in his *Almegest* relates an astronomical observation of a Lunar eclipse at Babylon on the seventeenth day of the month Phamenoth, according to the Egyptians, which is with us the sixteenth of July, one hour before midnight.[119]

From whence now it follows that he if lived twenty-two years in Egypt, that then he went thither in the third year of the fifty-eighth Olympiad [ca. 542 B.C.]; and that if he stayed in Babylon twelve years; he went into Italy about the end of the sixty-sixth Olympiad [ca. 509 B.C.]; and that if he were then fifty-six years old, he was not born before the first year of the fifty-third Olympiad [ca. 564 B.C.]. And according to this account, they who make him live but seventy or eighty years, do not much differ in the time of his death from them, who according to the other account, make him live so much longer. For they who give him most years do not make him to die later, but to be born sooner.

This account they seem to follow who affirm he went from Samos to Italy.[120] For he could not brook Syloson, the brother of Polycrates, on whom (being a private person after his brother's death) Darius Hystaspis afterward bestowed the tyranny of Samos in requital of a garment which Syloson had given him before he came to the empire. And thus perhaps is Strabo to be understood. He says Pythagoras, as they reported, in the time of Polycrates, seeing the tyranny begun, forsook the city and went from thence to Egypt and Babylon out of love to learning. And returning home, and seeing that the tyranny continued still, he went into Italy where he ended his days.[121] By this "continuation of the tyranny," seems to be meant the reign of Syloson—who ruled so cruelly that many persons forsook the city, insomuch that it became a proverb:

> A Region vast
> By Syloson laid waste.

With both these accounts agree what Cicero[122] and Aulus Gellius[123] affirm concerning his coming into Italy—that it was in the reign of Tarquinius Superbus. But to neither can that of Pliny be accommodated. Pliny says that Pythagoras observed the nature of the star Venus about the forty-second Olympiad [ca. 608 B.C.], which was of the city of Rome the 142nd year.[124] There must therefore be either an error in both the numbers; or, which I rather believe, in Pliny himself, occasioned, perhaps by mistaking Tarquinius Priseus (under whom they both fall) for Tarquinius Superbus, under whom Pythagoras flourished.

If therefore he came into Italy in the reign of Tarquinius Superbus,[125] the opinion of Cicero is to be received. That he was there when Lucius Brutus freed his country; and upon the expulsion of

Tarquinius Superbus, Brutus and Lucius Collatinus were made the first consuls. At which time the dominion of the Romans extended not any way above six miles from their city; and the southern parts of Italy were chiefly inhabited by the Grecians, who at several times had there planted diverse colonies, whereof we shall only mention those which were more particularly concerned in the actions of Pythagoras.

The most ancient of these is Metapontum, seated in the Bay of Tarentum between Heraclea and Tarentum, built by Nestor and the Pylians, a people of Peloponnesus.[126] Long after were founded:

Catana, a city on the east side of Sicily, between Messena and Syracuse, built by a colony of Chalcideans, in the eleventh Olympiad [ca. 736 B.C.].[127]

Tarentum in Italy, in the eighteenth Olympiad [ca. 708 B.C.],[128] built by the Parthenians.[129] These were children of the Lacedaemonian women, born in the absence of their husbands at the Messanian wars. They were therefore called Parthenians in reproach; which not brooking, they conspired against the Lacedaemonian people; but being betrayed and banished, came hither.

Crotona, a city in the Bay of Tarentum,[130] built in the nineteenth Olympiad [ca. 704 B.C.],[131] by a colony of Achaeans under the conduct of Miscellus. By whom it was named Crotona at the command of Hercules, in memory of Croto, his host, whom he, having unwittingly slain, buried there. This city, for being built by the command of Hercules, engraved his figure in their coins. [See illustration next page.]

Sybaris is a city distant from Crotona 200 furlongs according to Strabo's account—but as others conceive, more than twice so much—built at the same time by a colony of Troezenians, under the conduct of Iseliceus, between the two rivers Crathis and Sybaris.[132]

Locri in Italy was built in the twenty-fourth Olympiad [ca. 684 B.C.], by the Locrians, a people of Achaea.[133]

Agrigentum,[134] an Ionian colony, built by the Geloans 108 years after their own foundation. Gela[135] was built in the forty-fifth year after Syracusa in the eleventh Olympiad [ca. 736 B.C., forty-five years later would be 691 B.C.]: Agrigentum therefore in the forty-ninth [687 B.C.].[136]

To these add, of less certain time, Rhegium in Calabria built by the Chalcedeans, and Nimgra and Tauromenium in Sicily, colonies of the Zancleaans. Indeed so generally was the Pythagorean doctrine received in these parts, that Iamblicus affirms, all Italy was filled with philosophical persons; and whereas before it was obscure, afterwards by reason of Pythagoras, it was named Μεγάλη Ελλὰς , Magna Graecia ["Greater Greece"].[137]

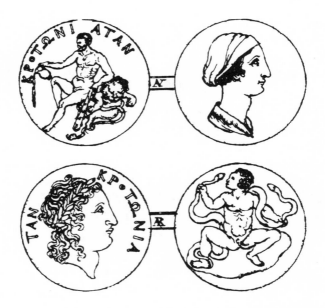

Crotonian coins with images of Hercules. Antique woodcut showing coins of the ancient city of Croton. The top image is a product of the imagination, whereas the second is a reasonably faithful representation of a known coin type of the 4th century B.C.
From Thomas Stanley, *The History of Philosophy*

CHAPTER 11

His Arrival at Crotona, and Upon
What Occasion He First Became Eminent There

He came at first to Crotona, the state of which city in particular was this. At the beginning, the Crotonians joining with the Sybarites and the Metapontines, determined to expel the rest of the Grecians out of Italy. They first took the city Syrus. And taking it ill that at their besieging of Syrus, the Locrians assisted the adverse party, raised a war against them, related thus by Justin:[138]

The Locrians being terrified, recur to the Spartans for refuge, and beg their aid. They, oppressed with a long war, bade them seek help of Castor and Pollux. Neither did the ambassadors sleight the advice of the associate city, but going into the next Temple, they sacrificed, and implored the help of the Gods. Having offered victims and obtained, as they thought, what they requested—no less joyful than as if they were to carry the Gods themselves along with them—they made couches for them in the ship, and by a fortunate voyage brought comfort, instead of relief to their countrymen. This known, the Crotonians also sent ambassadors to the Oracle at Delphi, praying for victory, and a happy success of the war. Answer is made, that enemies must be overcome in vows first, before in arms. They vowed to Apollo the tenths of the spoil.

The Locrians understanding the vow of their enemies, and the answer of the God, vowed the ninths, and kept it secret less they might be outdone in vowing. Being drawn forth into the field, the Crotonian army consisting of 120,000 soldiers; the Locrians beholding how small a number they were (for they had but 15,000), gave over all hope of victory, and unanimously resolved to die. And so great courage did every man take from desperation that they conceived they should be conquerors if they did not die unwillingly. But while they sought to die honorably, they overcame more fortunately; neither was there any other cause of that victory, than that they despaired of it. While they were in fight, an eagle never left the Locrian army but flew about it all the while, until they had gained the victory. In the wings of the army also, two young men, armed after a fashion different from all the rest, of extraordinary bigness, upon white horses, in crimson mantles, were seen to fight; and, after the fight, were seen no more. This wonder was increased by the incredible swiftness of same; for the very same day that this fight happened in Italy, the victory was reported at Corinth, Athens, and Lacedaemon. After this, the Crotonians used no military exercise, nor minded arms. For they hated what they had taken up unsuccess-fully, and would have changed their life into luxury had it not been for Pythagoras the philosopher.

As soon as Pythagoras arrived in Italy and came to Crotona, Dicaearchus says that upon the coming of a person who was a great traveler and excellent—and through a peculiar advantage of nature, prosperously guided by fortune (for he was of a free presence, tall, graceful in his speech and gesture, and in all things else)—the citizens of Crotona were taken with him.[139] Having won the affections of the old men, who were the magistrates of the city, he made an excellent and large discourse to the young men. He then, by command from the magistrates, made a second exhortation to the young men, and afterwards to the boys, who came flocking out of the school to hear him; and lastly to the women, assembled to that purpose. The occasion and manner mentioned, by Plutarch and Porphyry, is related thus by Iamblichus.[140]

At this time, walking from Sybaris to Crotona, upon the sea side, he lighted upon some fishermen; and while their net was yet at the bottom loaden, he told them exactly the number of fishes that they should draw up. The men, undertaking to do whatsoever he should command them if it fell out accordingly, he required them to turn back again the fishes alive after they had exactly numbered them. And, which is more wonderful, not one of all the number of the fishes, while they were out of the water, died. He being present, and giving the fishermen the price of the fish, departed to Crotona. But they divulged what was done, and, learning his name of the boys, declared it to everyone; which they hearing, desired to see the stranger, which was opportune to him. For he was of such an aspect, that whosoever saw him could not but admire him, and conceive him to be the person that he really was.

CHAPTER 12

His Oration to the Young Men

Some few days after, he went into the public school, and the young men flocking to him, it is said that he made discourses to them wherein he exhorted them to respect their elders, declaring the following: [141]

That in the world, and in life, and in cities, and in nature, that which is precedent in time is more honorable than that which is subsequent: as the east than the west, the morning than the evening, the beginning than the end, generation than corruption, natives than strangers. In like manner: in colonies the leader and planner of cities; and generally the gods than daemons, daemons than semi-gods, heroes than men—and of these (men), the cause of generation than the younger.

This he said by way of induction, to make them have a greater esteem of their parents, to whom he said they had as much obligation as a dead man might owe to him that should raise him again to life. Moreover, that it was just to love above all, and never to afflict, the first and those who have done us greatest benefits. But parents only, by the benefit of generation, are the first. And predecessors are the causes of all things that succeed rightly to their successors; showing, that they are nothing less beneficial to us than the gods, against whom it is not possible to offend in so doing.

And the gods themselves cannot but in justice pardon those who reverence their parents equal to them; for it is from them that we learn to worship the deity; whence Homer gives the king of the gods the same style, calling him, Father of Gods and Mortals. And many other fabulous writers have delivered that the chief of the gods was ambitious to make up the divided love of children by a new conjunction of parents. And for this end, making a new supposition of father and mother, Jupiter brought forth Minerva, Juno, and Vulcan, of a contrary sex to their own, that they might participate of that love which was more remote.

Now all persons granting the judgment of the gods to be strongest, he demonstrated this particularly to the people of Croto. Because that Hercules was of affinity with them, therefore they ought willingly to obey the injunctions of their parents, since they understood that this god, in obedience to another elder than himself, underwent his labors and presented to his father, as the song of victory of his actions, the Olympic Games.

He declared likewise that in their conversation to one another, they should so behave themselves that they might hereafter never become enemies to their friends, but might soon become friends to their enemies; as to their friends, they should never become enemies, but to their enemies quickly become their friends.[142] And that they should study in their behavior towards their elders, their reverence towards their parents, and in their love to one another, their community towards their brethren.

Furthermore he discoursed concerning Temperance, saying, that young men should make trial of their nature at that time in which they have their desires vigorous. Then he advised them that it was worth their observation that this only virtue was convenient both for children, and maids, and women, and old men, but especially for young men. Further, this virtue only declares that they understand the goods of the body and soul, seeing it preserves health, and a desire to the best studies. This is manifest from the contrary: for the Barbarians and the Grecians contending about Troy, both parties for the intemperance of one man fell into extraordinary calamities; those in the war, these in their voyage home. And God appointed ten years, and a thousand years—only for the punishment of this injustice; foretelling by oracle the taking of Troy, and the sending of the virgins by the Locrians to the temple of Minerva the Ilian.

He likewise exhorted the young men to love learning—telling them how absurd it was to judge learning to be the most advantageous of all things, and to wish for it above all things, yet to bestow no time or pains in that exercise. Especially, seeing that excessive attention to the care of our bodies is like evil friends (which soon forsake us); but that the pursuit of Instruction like the good, which stay with a man till death—procuring to some immortal glory after death.

He framed many other things—partly out of history, partly out of doctrines—showing, that learning was a common nobility of those who were first in every kind, for their inventions were the education of the rest. Thus is this naturally advantageous: that of some commendable things, it is not possible to communicate to another—such as strength, beauty, health, courage. Of other commendable things, whosoever imparts them to another cannot retain them himself—such as riches, government, and the like. But for education, you may receive it of another, and yet the giver have nothing the less of it.

Moreover, some a man cannot gain if he would. He may receive training if he will. Then he may apply himself to the affairs of his country, not upon self-confidence, but institution. For by education, men differ from beasts, Greeks from Barbarians, freemen from slaves, philosophers from the vulgar. Further, he said that those who have in general this advantage are rare. That as of those who run swifter than others, there had been seven out of this their own city at one celebration of the Olympic Games. But of such as did excel[143] in wisdom, there had been found but seven in the whole world. And in the following times in which he lived, there was but one who did excel all others in philosophy. For he called himself by that name (philosopher) instead of Sophos, a wise man.

His Oration to the Senators

Thus he discoursed to the young men in the school. But they, relating to their Fathers what he had said, the thousand men summoned Pythagoras to the court. They commended him for the advice he had given to their sons, and commanded him, that if he had anything which might benefit the people of Crotona, he should declare it to the magistrates of the commonwealth.[144] The Crotonians (says Valerius Maximus) did earnestly entreat him that he would permit their Senate, which consisted of a thousand persons, to use his advice.[145]

Hereupon he first advised them to build a Temple to the Muses, that they might preserve their present concord.[146] For these goddesses have all the same appellation, and have a reciprocal communication and delight, chiefly in honors common to them all;[147] and the chorus of the Muses is always one and the same. Moreover, concord, harmony, rhythm, all those things which procure unanimity, are comprehended. He likewise showed them, that their power did not only extend to the excellent, but to the concord and harmony of beings.

Further, he said they ought to conceive they received their country as a deposit from their people. Wherefore they ought so to manage it as being hereafter to resign up their trust with a just account to their own children. That this will certainly be if they be equal to all their citizens and excel other men in nothing more than in justice; knowing that every place requires justice. He showed it out of the mythology: that Themus has the same place with Jupiter, as Dice with Pluto, and law among cities. So that he who did anything unjustly in things under his charge seemed to abuse the whole world, both above, below, and on earth.

That it is convenient in courts of judicature that none attest the gods by oath, but rather always speaks such things as that he may be believed without oath.[148]

Moreover, that everyone should so govern his family as that they should refer themselves to their own house as to a court of justice. And that they should be naturally affectionate to such as are descended of them, as having only of all creatures received the sense of this affection. And that they should converse with the woman that is partner of their life. For as some men making contracts with others wrote them in tables and pillars; those with wives are in the children. And that they should endeavor to be beloved of those which come from them—not by nature, of which they are not the cause—but by election, for that kindness is voluntary.

That they should likewise take care, that they know no women but their wives; and that the wives do not adulterate the race through the carelessness and wickedness of their husbands.

Further, they must consider they take the wife from the altar with libations, as a Votaress in the sight of the gods. And so to go in unto her. And that she become in order and temperance a pattern to those that live in the house with her, and to the women of the city.

And that they should see carefully that none transgress, lest, not fearing the punishments of law such as do unjustly lie hid; but having a respect to honestly in their carriage, they may be incited to justice.

Further, he commanded, that in all their actions they should avoid idleness; for there is no other good than the opportunity in every action.

He asserted that it is the greatest of Injustices to separate children and parents from each other.

That he is to be thought the greatest person who can of himself foresee what is advantageous. The next in greatness is he who by those things which happen to other men, observes what is good for himself. The worst is he who stays to learn what is best by the experience of suffering ill.

He said that they who are desirous of glory shall not do amiss if they imitate those who are crowned for running. For they do no harm to their adversaries, but desire that they themselves may obtain the victory. And it is suitable to magistrates not to be rigid to those who contradict them, but to benefit those who obey them.

He likewise exhorted everyone that aimed at true glory to be indeed such as he desired to appear to others. For it is not so sacred a thing to be advised by another as to be praised for what is done; for one is only requisite to men, the other much more used by the gods.

In conclusion, he said that their city chanced to be built by Hercules. When he drove Gerion's oxen through Italy, being injured by Laecinius, Croto came to help him. Hercules, not knowing Croto by reason of the night, and thinking him to be one of his enemies, slew him. And then he promised at his grave that he would build a city which should bear his name, if ever he came to be a god. In gratitude for the kindness of Hercules, Pythagoras said it behooved them to govern their commonwealth justly.

They hearing this built a temple to the Muses, and put away the concubines which they used to keep; and entreated him to discourse severally in the temple of Pythian Apollo to the boys, and in the temple of Juno to the women.[149]

His Oration to the Boys

He, being persuaded by them, discoursed to the boys in this manner:[150]

That they should neither begin abusive and insulting behavior, nor return such to the reproachers. And concerning παιδεία (proper training and moral instruction), which is the same name as the time of their youth, he commanded them diligently to pursue it; adding that to a well-disposed youth it is easy to preserve honesty throughout all his life. To him that is not well-disposed, it is hard at that time to continue it; but more difficult from an ill beginning to run to the end. Moreover he declared, that boys are most beloved of the gods. And for that reason, in times of dearth they are sent forth to pray to the gods for rain, as if the deity would soonest hear them. And they only, being always sanctified, had leave to live in the temple.

For the same reason, the gods that are most kind to men—Apollo and Cupid—are by all painters represented, as having that age (of boys). It is likewise acknowledged that the crowned games were instituted for the sake of boys. The Pythian, upon the conquest of Pytho by a boy that in name; for a boy likewise, and that in Isthmus, upon the death of Archemorus and Melicertus.

Besides all this, at the building of the city Crotona, Apollo told the leader of the colony that he would give him a progeny if he conducted his colony to Italy. Whence they ought to reflect that Apollo has a particular providence for the generation—and over youth—even of all the gods. Wherefore they ought to study to be worthy of their love, and employ themselves in hearing, that they may be able to speak. Moreover, if they would live to be old themselves, they should obey their elders and not contradict them; for by that means they will become esteemed worthy, and not to be injured by those that are younger then themselves.

His Oration to the Women

It is said, that he discoursed to the women concerning sacrifices.[151]

First, that as when another man were to pray for them, they would have him to be honest and good, because the gods hearken to such men; in like manner ought they, above all things, so to behave themselves as that they may indeed have the gods attentive to their prayers.

Next, that they must present the gods with such things as they themselves make with their own hands. And without the help of servants, offer them at the altar; as cakes, wax and incense. But that they present not the deity with slaughter and death; nor that they offer so much at one time, as if they were never to come thither again.

As concerning their conversation towards their husbands, he commanded them to consider that fathers did yield to their daughters, that their husbands should be more beloved by them than their parents. Wherefore it is fit that either they contradict their husbands in nothing, or then think they have the victory when they are over-ruled by them.

Moreover he spared that well-known apothegm concerning coition: that for her who rises from her own husband, it is lawful to go to the temples the same day; but for her who rises from him that is not her husband, never.

He exhorted them likewise, throughout their whole lives to speak well of others, and to take care that others speak well of them; and that they destroy not that good report which is given. He cautioned them not to confute those mythographers, who (seeing the justice of women—that they lend their garments without witness when any has need of them, and that they made no bargains and engagements) feigned three women who made use of one eye amongst them because of their readiness to communicate. Which if applied to men, as if when one had received anything he should restore presently or communicate to his neighbor, everyone would say there is no such thing, it being contrary to their nature.

Further, he who is said to be the wisest of all persons, who disposed the language of men and invented all names—whether he were a god, or a daemon, or some divine man—upon consideration, because the female sex is most addicted to piety, made every degree of age synonymous with some god. He called the unmarried woman Core; she who is given to man Nympha; she who has children Mother; she who has children's children, in the Doric dialect, Maija; to which respect of their devotion it agrees that the oracles at Dodona and Delphi are delivered by women.[152]

Having thus commended their devotion, he converted his discourse to speak of decency of habit: that none should presume to wear any sumptuous cloths, but offer them all at Juno's temple (which amounted to) many millions of garments.

He is reported also to have said thus: that throughout the country of the Crotonians, the virtue of a man towards his wife was much celebrated. Ulysses refused Immortality at Calypso's hands rather than to forsake Penelope. Let it be the part of the wives to express their virtuous loyalty towards their husbands, that this praise may be reciprocal.[153]

HIS INSTITUTION OF A SECT IN PRIVATE AND PUBLIC

By this discourse, Pythagoras gained no small honor and esteem in Crotona, and by means of that city, throughout all Italy.[154]

At the first oration that he made in Crotona,[155] he attracted many followers. Insomuch that it is said he gained 600 persons, who were by him not only won to the philosophy which he professed, but following his rules, became as we call it *Caenobii*; and these were they who studied philosophy.[156] They did put their estates into one common stock, and kept silence five years, only hearing his discourses, but not seeing him until they were fully proved; and then they became of his family and were admitted to him. There were the same 600 persons, who Laertius says, came to his nocturnal *discourse*, perhaps meaning the lectures through a screen during their probation. For he adds that if any of them were thought worthy to see him, they wrote of it to their friends as having obtained a great matter. This society Laertius calls his "system," which Cassiodorus interprets as "college," and Aulius Gellius his "family."

Besides these, there were many auditors called *Acousmatics*,[157] whereof he gained, as Nicomachus relates,[158] two thousand by one oration which he made at his first coming into Italy. That they need not live at home, they erected a large *Homacoceion*,[159] which Clement of Alexandria interprets to be the same as *Ecclesia*, "Church," with us. Here were admitted also boys and women. They built cities, and inhabited all that part of Italy which is called Magna Graecia, and received laws and statutes from Pythagoras as divine precepts, without which they did not anything. They lived together unanimously, praised by all, and applauded as happy for such as lived round about them.

Thus Pythagoras distinguished those whom he admitted according to their several merits. For it was not fit that all should partake alike, being not of a like nature. Nor was it fit that some should receive all the learning, others none; for that would have been contrary to his community of all and to his equality. He therefore, of the discourses which he made, communicated to everyone that part which was proper for him; and distributed his learning so that it might benefit everyone according to his capacity. He observed the rules of Justice in giving to everyone that share of the discourse which they deserved; calling upon this account, some *Pythogoreans* (those of the system), and some *Pythagorites* (those of the *Homacoceion*), as we call some *Attics*, some *Atticists*.

Dividing them thus aptly into two names, he appointed one part to be γνησίους† ("Genuine"), the other he ordered to be Imitators of them. As to the Pythagoreans he decreed, that all their estates should be in common, and that they should lead their whole lives together in community; but the others he ordered to keep their estates to themselves, yet to meet together. Thus was this succession of both parties constituted by Pythagoras. The discipline which was observed by the more genuine—the Pythagoreans—we shall remit, together with his doctrine to the end of his life.

His Authority in Civil Affairs

Whatsoever cities in his travels through Italy and Sicily he found subjected to one another (whereof some had been so of a long time, others of late), he infused into them a passion for liberty through his disciples—of whom he had some in every city—and he restored them to liberty.[160] Thus he freed Crotona, Sybaris, Catana, Rhegium, Himera, Agrigentum, Tauromenium, and some others, to whom he sent laws by Charondas the Catanaean, and Zaleucus the Locrian, by means whereof they lasted a long time well governed, and were deservedly envied by their neighbors.

He wholly took away dissension, not only from among his disciples and their successors for many ages after, but also from all the cities of Italy and Sicily, both internal and external dissension. For he did frequently pronounce to all manner of persons everywhere, whether many or few, an apothegm which resembles an admonitory oracle of God, which was a kind of epitome or recapitulation of all that he taught. The apothegm was this:

That we ought to avoid with our utmost endeavor, and to amputate with fire and sword and all other means: from the body, sickness; from the soul, ignorance; from the belly, luxury; from a city, sedition; from a family, discord; from all things, excess.

By which he did indulgently put everyone in mind of his best doctrines.

Yet is he reported to have been the occasion of the war between the Sybarites and the Crotonians, which ended in the total Subversion of the Sybarites. The manner is thus related by Diodorus Siculus, and Iamblichus.

* * *

When the Grecians built Sybaris in Italy,[161] it soon came to pass that through the goodness of the soil (though Athaeneus deny it to be fertile[162]), the city became in a short time very rich. For being seated between two rivers, Crathis and Sybaris (from which it took

its name), and the citizens possessing a large country, they soon gathered together great riches; and admitting many to be free of their
country, they arrived to such height that they seemed far to excel
all the rest of the inhabitants of Italy. Yet, they were so luxurious
that they became infamous even to a proverb; and no less addicted
to all other vices, insomuch that they, out of insolence, put to death
thirty ambassadors of the Crotonians, and threw their bodies from
the walls to be devoured by beasts.[163]

The city was so populous, that it contained no less then 300,000
persons. At that time Telys was chief magistrate, who, accusing the
greatest men, procured of the Sybarites to banish 500 of the richest
citizens, and to confiscate their goods. These banished men went to
Crotona, and there, after the manner of suppliants, fled to the Altars
erected in the Forum. Hereupon Telys sent ambassadors to the Crotonians to declare, that they should either deliver up the banished
men or expect war. (These Sybarite ambassadors had been instrumental in the murder of some friends of Pythagoras, perhaps some of
the thirty Crotonians whom they slew.[164]) Amongst them, one there
was who had killed some of the ambassadors with his own hands;
another was son to one of the same murderers who had since died.
Moreover, he was of those kinds of persons, who, being oppressed
with want, stir up sedition that they may take occasion thereby to
fall on the goods of others.

These Sybarites came to Pythagoras and blamed him; and one
of them (which was he that had a hand in the death of his friends)
demanding a reason of his reproof, he said that he did not give Laws.
Whereupon they accused him as if he had made himself Apollo,
and especially for that before, upon a question being asked, "Why
these things were so," he asked him that propounded the question,
whether, when Apollo delivered his oracles, he would require him to
render a reason? The other deriding, as he thought, those discourses
in which Pythagoras declared the return of the soul, and telling him
that when he went into the other world, he would give him a letter
to carry to his father, and desired him to bring an answer of it when
he came back. "I shall not," replied Pythagoras, "go to the place of
the wicked, where murderers are punished."

The ambassadors having thus reviled him, and he going to the

seaside, and washing himself, many followed him. One of those
who advised the Crotonians said—when he had sufficiently spoken
against all the other things that they did—at last he accused them
especially for offering to oppose and abuse Pythagoras, of whom
when heretofore, as fables report, beasts could speak, no one of them
durst ever speak an ill word.

Diodorus says that a council being called,[165] and it being put to
the question whether they should deliver up the Italiotes to the Sybarites, or undergo a war with an enemy more powerful than themselves,[166] the Senate and people made some doubt. The people first
inclined to the delivery of the suppliants rather than endure the war.
But afterwards, Pythagoras the philosopher advising them to protect
the suppliants, they changed their opinion and determined to fight
in their defense.

The Sybarites came into the field, with an army of 300,000; the
Crotonians had but 100,000. They were led by Milo, the wrestler,
who at the first onset himself put to flight that wing of the army
which was opposite to him; for he was of invincible strength. This
man having courage answerable to his strength, had been six times
victor at the Olympic Games. And when he began this fight, he was
crowned with Olympic wreaths, wearing like Hercules a lion's skin
and carrying a club; and obtaining the victory for his countrymen,
was much admired by them.

The Crotonians likewise made use of a stratagem, whereby they
got the day. The Sybarites were so much addicted to luxury, that
they taught their horses to dance at feasts.[167] This the Crotonians
knowing, as Aristotle relates, in the midst of the fight they commanded some pipers, whom to that purpose they had brought along
with them, to play dancing tunes. The horses, as soon as they heard
the music, not only fell a dancing but carried their riders violently
over to their enemies. Thus the Sybarites being put to flight, the
Crotonians spared none that they took, but put all to the sword,
whereby the greater part of the army was slain, and the city, after a
dishonorable surrender, laid waste. This according to Diodorus, happened sixty-three years before the second of the eighty-third Olympiad [ca. 443 B.C.], which falls upon the first year of the sixty-eighth
Olympiad [ca. 504 B.C.].

Agrigentum was also by the counsel of Pythagoras freed from the tyranny of Phalaris in this manner. Pythagoras was detained by Phalaris,[168] a most cruel tyrant with whom he stayed six months.[169] Abaris the Hyperborean, a wise person, came to converse with him and asked him questions—particularly concerning sacred rites, images, divine worship, providence of the gods, as well of those in heaven, as conversant about the earth, and such like demands. Pythagoras, as being highly inspired, answered him with much truth and persuasion, insomuch as he drew the standers by to his opinion. Whereupon Phalaris, seeing the people taken with him, was angry with Abaris for praising Pythagoras. He grew fierce against Pythagoras himself, and at last came to that height as to speak all blasphemies against the gods as were possible for such a kind of person. But Abaris acknowledged himself thankful to Pythagoras for the things he learned of him: that all things depend upon heaven and are disposed of from thence, which he collected as from many other things, so especially from the efficacy of sacrifices. Far therefore was he from thinking that Pythagoras, who taught him these things, was a deceiver; but he rather admired him, as a person supernaturally inspired. Phalaris, in answer hereunto, denied plainly and openly all things that were done in sacred rites.

Whereupon Abaris transferred his discourse from these things to such as appear manifestly to all men, and by the divine operations which are in all extremities—as in extraordinary wars, and in incurable diseases, destruction of fruit, transmission of pestilence from country to country. By these difficult irremediable causes, he endeavored to prove that there is a divine providence which overrules all human hope and power. But Phalaris impudently opposed it.

Hereupon Pythagoras, knowing that this day would be fatal to Phalaris, spoke very freely; and looking upon Abaris, said, that there is a passage from heaven to the aerial and terrestrial parts; and did likewise discourse scientifically, concerning the dependence of all things upon Heaven; and did irrefragably demonstrate the free power of the soul; and proceeded to show the perfect operation of the reason and of the mind. Then he spoke boldly concerning tyranny, and all excess of fortune, all injustice, all covetousness, strongly maintaining that they are all worth nothing. After this, he made a divine

exhortation concerning the best life, and made a resolute opposition
against the worst, and did most plainly deliver the doctrine concerning the power and passions of the soul. And what was more then all
these, he demonstrated that the gods are not the causes of ills; and
that diseases and passions are seeds of the intemperance of the body.
And he reprehended mythographers and poets for such things as
they had falsely delivered; and sharply reproved Phalaris, and showed
what the power of heaven is, and how great, by its operations.

As concerning infliction of punishment by law, he gave many
instances thereof, and clearly showed the difference between man
and other living creatures. He likewise scientifically discoursed
concerning intrinsical and enunciative reason, and concerning the
mind, and the knowledge proceeding from it, with many other moral
documents dependent thereon. He treated of what things are useful in life, making an exhortation to the pursuit of the useful, and
condemning the hurtful. And that which is most of all, he made a
distinction between the things done according to fate, and according to the mind, and of those which are done according to necessity,
and according to decree. Moreover he discoursed concerning daemons, and the immortality of the soul, much and wisely (whereof
we shall have occasion to speak elsewhere). He showed that these
things do confer most to fortitude, seeing that he himself in the
midst of all dangers, did with a constant mind discourse philosophy
and arm himself against Fortune; as also for that he slighted and condemned the person that attempted to hurt him, and despised the fear
of death, and all human contingencies; nor was he at that instant at
all concerned for them.

Indeed (continues Iamblichus) it is manifest, that he was nothing
troubled with the fear of death, but had a far more noble design—
the freeing of Sicily from the oppression of tyranny. That it was he
who did it is manifest from the oracle of Apollo, which declared
that Phalaris, when his subjects grew better and more unanimous,
should lose his authority; which they did at the coming of Pythagoras through his exhortations and Instructions. But a clearer evidence
hereof is from the time: for that very day that Phalaris went about
to bring Pythagoras and Alaris into danger of death, he was himself
slain. The manner is thus related by Tzeizes.[170]

It chanced, that a hawk pursued a great flight of pigeons; which Phalaris seeing, said to those that stood by him, "Behold friends, how much an ignoble fear can do; for if but one of all these pigeons would turn again, it would presently give a stop to the pursuer." This speech an old man that was present no sooner heard, when taking up a stone he threw it at Phalaris; and the rest, following his example, did the like. Some say they stoned him to death; others, that they put him into chains, and wrapped him in a sheet of lead, wherein he died miserably.

To the Locrians, besides Charondas and Zeleucus already mentioned, he sent Timaratus also to make laws for them.[171] To the Rheginenses, he sent upon the same employment Theatetus, Helicaon, Aristrocrates and Phytius.[172]

Thus, as Porphyry says, Pythagoras and his friends were for a long time so much admired in Italy, that many cities committed themselves to be governed by them.[173]

CHAPTER 18

WONDERS RELATED OF HIM

If we may credit (says Porphyry, and from him Iamblichus[174]) what is related of Pythagoras by ancient and creditable authors, his commands had an Influence even upon irrational creatures. For he laid hold of the Daunian bear which did much hurt to the people thereabout, and having stroked her awhile, and given her **mazza** and fruits, and sworn her that she never more touch any living creature, he let her go. She straightaway hid herself in the hills and woods, and from thenceforward never assaulted any living creature.

Seeing an ox at Tarentum in a pasture wherein grew several things, munching on green beans, he came to the shepherd and counseled him to speak to the Ox that he should abstain from the beans.[175] But the shepherd mocked him, and said he could not speak the language of oxen. Pythagoras himself went up to the ox and whispered in his ear. The animal not only refrained immediately from Beans at that time, but from thenceforward would never touch any. He lived many years after about Juno's temple at Tarentum till he was very old; and called the sacred ox, eating such meats as everyone gave him.

At the Olympic Games, as Pythagoras was by chance discoursing to his friends concerning auguries, omens, and divine signs, and that there are some messages from the gods to such men as have true piety towards them, an eagle flew over his head. He is said by certain words to have stopped her, and to have caused her to come down.[176] After he had stroked her awhile, he let her go again.[177] This perhaps was that white eagle that Iamblichus reports he stroked at Croto, and she endured it quietly. For the Crotonians instituted games, which they called Olympic in emulation of the Grecians.

There is also the story of a river (which Porphyry calls Caucasus;[178] Apollonius, Ποταμον κατὰ Σαμον ["a river near Samos"]; Laertius and Iamblichus, Nessus; Aelian, Cosa; St. Cyril, Causus). As he passed over it with many of his friends, the river spoke to him and said with a plain clear voice, χαῖρε Πυθαγόρα, "Hail Pythagoras."

In one and the same day, almost all affirm, that he was present at Metapontum in Italy, and at Tauromenium in Sicily, with the friends which he had in both places. He discoursed to them in a public convention, when as the places are distant many **stadia** by sea and land, and many days journeys asunder.[179] Apollonius relates this as done at Croto and Metapontum.

At the public solemnity of the Olympic Games, he stood up and showed his golden thigh;[180] as he did in private to Abarus, to confirm him in the opinion that he was Hyperborean Apollo, whose priest Abarus was.[181]

A ship coming into the harbor, and his friends wishing they had the goods that were in it, Pythagoras told them, "Then you will have a dead body." And, when the ship came at them, they found in it the body of a dead man.[182]

To one who much desired to hear him, he said that he would not discourse until some sign appeared.[183] Not long after, one coming to bring news of the death of a white bear in Caulonia, he prevented him and related it first.

They affirm, he foretold many things and that they came to pass.[184] Insomuch that Aristippus the Kyrenaean, in his book on Physiology, says he was named "Pythagoras" from speaking things as true as Pythian Apollo.[185] He foretold an earthquake by the water which he tasted out of a well; and foretold, that a ship, which was then under sail with a pleasant gale, should be cast away.

At Sybarus, he took in his hand a serpent of deadly biting and let it go again. And at Tyrrhenia, he took a little serpent and biting it, killed it with his teeth.

A thousand other more wonderful and divine things are related constantly, and with full agreement, about him; so that, to speak freely, more was never attributed to any, nor was any more eminent. For his predictions of earthquakes most certainly are remembered, and his immediate chasing away of the pestilence. And his suppression of violent winds and hail, and his calming of storms—as well in rivers as upon the sea for the ease and safe passage of his friends— from whom Empedocles, Epimenides, and Abaris learning it, often performed the like, which their poems plainly attest. Besides,

Empedocles was surnamed *Alexanemos*, the Chaser away of Winds;
Epimenides, *Cathartes*, the Lustrator; Abaris, *Aethrobates*, the walker
in the air (for, riding upon an arrow of Hyperborean Apollo which
was given him, he was carried in the air over rivers and seas and
inaccessible places, which some believed to have been done by
Pythagoras when he discoursed with his friends at Metapontum and
Tauromenium upon the same day).

To these add his trick with a looking glass, as the scholiast of
Aristophanes calls it, who describes it thus. The Moon being in the
full, he wrote whatsoever he pleased in blood upon a looking glass.
And telling it first to the other party, stood behind him, holding the
letters towards the Moon; whereby he who stood between him and
the Moon, looking steadfastly upon her, read all the letters which
were written in the looking glass in the Moon, as if they were written in her.[186]

But these things, some even of the ancients have imputed to
Goetic Magic, as Timon, who terms Pythagoras, Γέντα, a Magician.† Others impute these to imposture, as appears by this relation
of Hermippus and the scholiast of Apollonius. They say that when
he came into Italy he made a vault underground, and charged his
mother to give out that he was dead, and to set down in a table-book
all things that happened, expressing the times punctually. Then he
went down and shut himself up in the vault, and his mother did as
he ordered her, until such time as he came up again. After a while,
Pythagoras came up lean and withered. Approaching the congrega-
tion, he declared that he was returned from the Infernal Regions,[187]
and related to them what was done there, and told them many pro-
digious stories concerning the Reborn, and the things of the Infernal
Regions; telling the living news of their dead friends with whom he
said he met in the Infernal Regions.[188] Hieronymus relates that he
saw there the soul of Hesiod bound with brass to a pillar, screeching;
and that of Homer hung up on a tree, encompassed by serpents, for
the fables which he had raised concerning the gods. Those likewise
were tormented who used not the company of their own wives.[189]

For this he was much honored by the Crotonians. They being
much moved at what he said, wept and lamented, and hereupon con-

ceived such an esteem of Pythagoras as being a divine person, that they sent their wives to him to be instructed in his doctrine, which women were called "Pythagoreans." Thus says Hermippus. The scholiast adds that hereby he raised an opinion concerning himself: that before the Trojan War he was Aethalides, the son of Mercury; then Euphorbus; then Hermotimus; then Pyrrhus, a Delian; lastly, Pythogoras.[190] And, as Laertius says in his writings, he reported of himself that he had come from the Infernal Regions to men 207 years since. Of this, more in the Pythagoran Doctrine, see Part 3, The Transmigration of the Soul [page 256].

His Death

The time of the death of Pythagoras has been formerly touched. It was, according to Eusebius, in the fourth year of the seventieth Olympiad [ca. 493 B.C.], after he had lived, as Justin says, at Crotona for twenty years.[191]

The occasion is differently related by Laertius, who says Pythagoras died in this manner: As he sat in counsel together with his friends, in the house of Milo, it happened that the house was set on fire by one who did it out of envy, because he was not admitted. Some affirm the Crotonians did it out of fear of being reduced to a tyranny. Pythagoras, running away, was overtaken when, coming to a field full of beans, he made a stop saying, "It is better to be taken than to tread, and better to be killed than to speak." So the pursuers slew him. In the same manner died most of his disciples, about forty in number. Some few only escaped, of whom were Archytas the Tarentine, and Lysis, of whom we spake before.

Dicaearchus says that Pythagoras fled to the Temple of the Muses at Metapontum, and died for want of food, having lived there forty days without eating. Heraclides, in his Epitome of the *Lives of Satyrus*, relates that having buried Pherecydes, he returned to Italy where, finding the faction of Cyclo prevalent, he departed to Metapontum and there starved himself, not willing to live any longer. Hermippus says that the Agrigentines and Syracusians warring against one another, Pythagoras with his friends went to the Agrigentines and was head of them. But they being vanquished, and he flying to a field of beans, was there slain; the rest (being thirty five) were burned at Tarentum for intermeddling with the governors and rule of the commonwealth.

Iamblichus, from Aristoxenus and others, gives a more particular account. There were, says he, some who opposed these men and rose up against them. That this conspiracy happened in the absence of Pythagoras is acknowledged by all; but they disagree concerning his journey. Some say he was gone to Pherecydes, the Syrian; others to Metapontum. The causes of this conspiracy are diversely related also.

One is said to have proceeded from the men who were called Cylonians. Cylo, a Crotonian—who in race, honor, and wealth excelled
all the rest of the citizens, but was otherwise of a harsh, violent, tur-
bulent, and tyrannical humor—was exceedingly desirous to participate in the Pythagorean institution. Coming to Pythagoras, who was
now very old, he was repulsed for the reasons aforesaid. Hereupon
there arose a great contest, Cylo and his friends opposing Pythagoras
and his friends. And so eager and violent was the malice of Cylo
and his party, that it extended even to the last of the Pythagoreans.
Pythagoras therefore for this reason departed to Metapontum where
it is said that he died.

The Cylonians (so called) continued to exercise their hatred
and enmity towards the Pythagoreans, and the kindness of the cities
(which was so great as to be governed by them) was prevalent. But at
last, they so plotted against the Pythagoreans, that surprising them
assembled in the house of Milo at Crotona consulting about military
affairs, they burned them all except two, Archippus and Lysis, who
being youthful and strong escaped out of doors.

This falling out, and the cities not taking any notice of the misfortune, the Pythagoreans gave up their business. This happened
from two causes: as well by reason of the unconcernment of the cities
(for they had no regard of the murder, to punish the authors hereof),
as by reason of the death of the most excellent persons—two only
of them were saved, both Tarentum. But Lysis, out of hatred of the
neglect they had received from the cities, departed into Greece and
lived at Achaea in Peloponnesus. Thence, upon a particular design,
he removed to Thebes, where Epimanondas heard him, and called
him Father, and there he died.

The rest of the Pythagoreans, all but Arthitas the Tarentine, forsook Italy and assembling at Rhegium, they lived there together. But
in progress of time, the management of public affairs decayed. The
most eminent of these were Phanto, and Echecrates, and Polymnastus, and Diocles (both Phliasians), and Xenophilus, a Chalcidean
of Chalcis in Thrace. These preserved the customs and doctrines
from the beginning, but with the sect itself, at last they were wholly
extinguished. This is related by Aristoxenus.

Nicomachus agrees in all things with this relation. Except in that he says this Insurrection happened at the time Pythagoras was gone to Delos to visit Pherecydes, who was sick of a Phthiriasis. Then were they stoned and burned by the Italiotes and cast forth without burial. Hitherto Iamblichus.

With these also agrees the relation of Neanthes, thus delivered by Porphyry.[192]

Pythagoras and his friends, having been a long time so much admired in Italy, many cities committed themselves to them. At last they became envied, and a conspiracy was made against them in this manner. Cylo was a Crotonian, who in extract, nobility, and wealth exceeded all the rest of the citizens, but otherwise was of a violent, rigid, and tyrannical disposition, and one that made use of the multitude of his friends to compass his unjust ends. As he esteemed himself worthy of all excellent things, so most particularly to partake of the Pythagorean philosophy, he came to Pythagoras and much extolled himself and desired his conversation. But Pythagoras presently observing the nature and manners of the person, and perceiving by the signs which he observed in the bodies of such as came to him what kind of disposition he was of, bade him depart and go about his business. Hereat Cylo was not a little troubled, taking it for a great affront, being of himself a person of a rough violent spirit. Therefore, calling his friends together, he began to accuse Pythagoras and to conspire against him and his disciples. Whereupon, as some relate, the friends of Pythagoras were gathered together in the house of Milo the wrestler. Pythagoras himself was absent for he was gone to Delos to visit Pherecydes, the Syrian, formerly his master, who was desperately fallen sick of a Phthiriasis, and to attend on him. Cyclo's men set the house on fire, and burned and stoned them all, except two who escaped the fire, Archippus and Lysis, as Neanthes relates, of whom Lysis went into Greece to Epimanondas, whose master he had formerly been.

But Dicaerchus and other more accurate authors affirm that Pythagoras himself was there present when this conspiracy was perpetrated; for Pherecydes died before he left Samos.[193] Of his friends, forty being gathered together were beset in a house; most of them going dispersedly to the city were slain. Pythagoras, his friends being taken, first escaped to the Caulonian haven, thence went to the Locrians. The Locrians sent some old men to the borders of their country who gave him this answer, "We have heard, Pythagoras, that thou art a person wise and of great worth; but we have nothing in our laws that is reprehensible, and therefore we will endeavor to preserve them. Go to some other place, taking of us whatsoever you have need of." Hereupon leaving the city of the Locrians, he sailed to Tarentum, where receiving the same entertainment he had at Crotona, he went to Metapontum. For great seditions were raised against him in every part which are remembered by the inhabitants to this day. They recount the seditions against the Pythagoreans, as they call them, for all that faction which sided with Pythagoras were called Pythagoreans. In the Metapontine faction, Pythagoras is said to have died, flying to the Temple of the Muses and staying there forty days, through want of necessaries.[194]

Others relate that when the house wherein his Friends used to meet was fired, his friends threw themselves into the fire to make a way for their master, spreading their bodies like a bridge upon the first; and that Pythagoras, escaping out of the burning, destitute of all his friends, for grief ended his days.

With these men, oppressed with this calamity, failed their knowledge also—which till then they had preserved secret and concealed, except some things difficult to be understood, which the auditors that lived without the screen, repeated by heart. Lysis and Archippus escaping, and as many as were at that time in other parts, preserved some little sparks of philosophy, obscure and difficult to be found out. For being not left alone, and much grieved at the perpetration of that wickedness, fearing lest the name of Philosophy should be quite extinguished amongst men, and that for this reason the gods would be angry with them, they made some summary commentaries. And having rendered the writings of the ancients, and those which they remembered into one body, everyone left them in the place where they died, charging their sons, daughters, and wives that they should not communicate them to any outside their own family. Thus privately continuing it successively to their successors, they observed it a long time. And for this reason, says Nicomachus, we conjecture that they did purposely avoid friendship with strangers; and for many ages they preserved a faithful constant friendship amongst themselves.

Moderatus says that this Pythagorean philosophy came at last to be extinguished. First, because it was enigmatic. Next, because their writings were in the Doric dialect which is obscure; and by which means the doctrines delivered in it were not understood, being spurious and misapprehended. Because moreover, they who published them were not Pythagoreans.[195] Besides, Plato, Aristotle, Speusippus, Aristoxenus, and Xenocrates, as the Pythagoreans affirm, vented the best of them as their own, changing only some few things in them. But the more vulgar and trivial, and whatsoever was afterwards invented by envious and calumnious persons to cast a contempt upon the Pythagorean school, they collected and delivered as proper to that sect.

But forasmuch as Apollonius gives a different account of these things, and adds many things which have not yet been spoken, let us give his narration also concerning the insurrection against the Pythagoreans.[196] He says that the Pythagoreans were envied from their very childhood; for the people, as long as Pythagoras discoursed with all that came to him, loved him exceedingly; but when he applied himself only to his disciples, they undervalued him. That he should admit strangers, they well enough suffered; but that the natives of the country should attribute so much to him, they took very ill, and suspected their meetings to be contrivements against them. Besides, the young men being of the best rank and estate, it came to pass that after a while they were not only the chief persons in their own families, but governed even the whole city. They becoming many as a society (for they were above 300 persons), but being a small part as to the city, which was not ordered according to their manners and institutions. Notwithstanding, as long as they possessed the place they were in only, and Pythagoras lived there, the city followed the original government thereof, though much perplexed, and watching for an opportunity for change.

But after they had reduced Sybaris, and that he departed, and they distributed the conquered country into colonies as they pleased; at length, the concealed hatred broke forth, and the multitude began to quarrel with them. The leaders of this dissension were those who had been nearest allied to the Pythagoreans. Many things had in the past grieved them, according as they were particularly affected. But one of the greatest was that Pythagoras only should be thought incapable of disrespect. For the Pythagoreans used never to name Pythagoras; but while he lived, they called him "Divine"; after death, "the Man," as Homer introduces Eumaeus mentioning Ulysses:

I to pronounce his name, though absent, fear;
So great is my respect, and he so dear.

In like manner, dissenters were disturbed by the disciplines of the Pythagorean community. Not to rise out of bed after the Sun is up, nor to wear a ring whereon the image of God is engraved; but to observe the Sun that they may adore his rising, and not to wear a ring lest they might chance to have it on at a funeral or carry it into any unclean place. Likewise, not to do anything without premeditation, nor anything whereof they could not give a good account; but that in the morning they should consider what they were to do, and at night they should make a recollection thereof, as well to ponder the things themselves as to exercise the memory. Likewise, if anyone of that community had appointed to meet another in any place, he should stay there day and night until the other came. The Pythagoreans likewise accustomed themselves to be mindful of what is said, and to speak nothing rashly. But above all things, as an inviolable precept to be kept even until death, he advised them not to reproach, but always to use good words as at sacrifices.

These things much displeased all in general, as I said, forasmuch as they admitted men to be educated in this singularity amongst them. But in that the Pythagoreans reached forth the hands to fellow members only, and not to any of their own family except their parents; likewise, in that they had their estates in common, wholly alienated from their own domestics; hereat their allies were much displeased. And they, beginning the dissension, the rest readily joined themselves and engaged in it.

And at the same time, Hippasus, Diodorus, and Theages said that it was fit everyone should partake of the public government and convention; and that the magistrates, being chosen by lot, ought to give account. But on the other side, the Pythagoreans Alcimachus, Dimachus, Meto, and Democedes opposed it, and forbid that the government of the country should be abrogated. These taking the part of the commons, got the better. But afterwards, many of the common people understood that there was a division in the public convention. The orators Cylo and Nino framed an accusation against the Pythagoreans: the first was one of the best quality; the other of the vulgar sort. To this effect, a long discourse being made by Cylo, the other continued it, pretending that he had found out the greatest secrets of the Pythagoreans. But indeed having forged and wrote such things as thereby he might chiefly traduce them; and having delivered the book to a notary, had him read it. The title was *The Sacred Discourse*. The sum whereof was this: That friends ought to be reverenced as the gods themselves, but all other men tyrannized over like beasts. That the same sentence of Pythagoras himself reduced to verse, was thus rehearsed by his disciples:

> Friends equal with the gods he did respect,
> All others (as of no account) neglect.

And that Pythagoras chiefly praised Homer for saving Ποιμένα λάων ("the shepherd of the people"†), he tacitly implied that the rest of mankind were but beasts. That he affected oligarchy, and was an enemy to unmarried persons, as those who had been chief in election of magistrates by lot. That he affected tyranny, inasmuch as he says, "It is better to be a bull though but one day, than an ox all our lifetime." That he praised the laws and customs of other people, and commanded that whatsoever was decreed by them should be used.

In fine, Nino declared that their philosophy was a conspiracy against the people, and advised them that they should not hearken to the voice of their consultations—but rather think of forbidding them to meet in counsel at all, if they alleged that they had a settled assembly consisting of a thousand voices. Wherefore it was not fit that they should, as far as in them lay, give ear to prohibited persons and permit them to speak; but to esteem their right hand, which they held from them hostile, when they should offer to put in a stone for voting. He conceived it an unworthy thing that 300,000 men who all lived about the river Tetrais, should be oppressed by seditions and overcome by the thousand part of them in that city. This calumny so much exasperated the hearers, that some few days after, as the Pythagoreans were sacrificing in the Temple of Pythian Apollo, the people ran in tumultuously to do violence to them. But the Pythagoreans, being informed beforehand thereof, fled to the public hall.

Democedes, with the young men, went to Platea. But they, dissolving the laws, used decrees—whereby accusing Democedes of stirring up the young men to tyranny, they proclaimed, that whosoever did kill him should have in recompence three talents. And there being a fight, wherein he by the means of Theages was overcome, they gave him three talents out of the public treasury. But there arising many misfortunes in the city and country, the banished persons were called to judgment, and the examination thereof was committed to three cities (Tarentum, Metapontum, and Caulonia). Those who were put in commission thought good, as appears by the Crotonian records, to banish them. So they banished the whole generation, saying that the children ought not to be separated from their parents, and seized their estates.

But after many years, Dimachus and his friends being slain in another fight, and Litago also who was head of this faction, they took compassion on them, and resolved to call home those who were left. Wherefore sending for their ambassadors from Achaea, they made an agreement with the banished men, and hung up the copies of their oaths in the Temple of Delphi. The Pythagoreans who returned, were about threescore, besides those who were very aged, of whom some addicted themselves to medicine and cured the sick, and so became masters of that which is called "method." Those who were restored grew into great favor with the people at that time, in which it was proverbially said in opposition to those who violate the laws, "These are not under the government of Nino."

CHAPTER 20

His Person and Virtues

His person, Iamblichus describes, to have been in his youth extraordinary beautiful.[197] He was, as mentioned, called "The fair haired Samian."[198] And at fifty-six years of age, of a more comely and divine presence. Laertius says he is reported to have been of a most awful aspect, insomuch as his disciples thought him Hyperborean Apollo.[199] He adds that Timon takes notice of the awfulness of his presence in his *Silli*, though he alleged it in disparagement of him.[200]

> Pythagoras skilled in the Goetic Laws,
> Who courts by grave discourse human applause.

So great an impression he made upon those with whom he conversed, that a young man being sharply reprehended by him, immediately went and hanged himself. Whereupon Pythagoras ever after forbore to reprove any person.

Lycon, in the *Life of Pythagoras*, says that he used a spare diet.[201] Athenaeus says that he drank very little, and lived so moderately that he was often content only with honey.[202] By his moderate diet he preserved his body in the same constant state, not sometimes sick, sometimes well, sometimes fat, sometimes lean. It appeared by his countenance that the same constancy was in his soul also. He was not subject to joy (as Cicero likewise observes) or grief, no man ever saw him rejoice or mourn. Neither did any ever see him *alvum exonerantem, coeuntem* [purging his stomach, having sexual intercourse], or drunk. He refrained wholly from derision, obsequiousness or servility, scoffs, and detractive speeches. He never punished any in anger, neither servant nor free person.[203]

He wore a white and clean stole (or gown), and used white woolen blankets (for as yet linen was not known in those parts),[204] and a gold crown and breeches.[205]

Diogenes, discoursing of his daily conversation, says he had morning exercises at his own house, composing his soul to the lyre, and singing some old paeans of Thales.[206] He likewise sung some verses of Homer and Hesiod, whereby he rendered his mind more sedate. Moreover, he used some dances, which he conceived to conduce to agility and bodily health. His walks he used not with many promiscuously, but with two or three in the temples or groves, making choice of such places as were most pleasant and remote from noise.

Having purchased the estate of Alcaeus, who after his embassy to Lacedaemon died, he was no less admired for his economy than philosophy.[207]

Besides this Pythagoras the philosopher, there were many others of the same name, the most ancient a Laconian, contemporary with King Numa.[208]

Laertius reckons four, all about the same time, or at least not long distant from one another. For (besides the philosopher) there was one a Crotonian, a tyrannical person. Another was a Phliasian σωμασκητής ["One that practices bodily exercises"], ἀλειπτης ("Exercitator"† as Pliny renders it[209]), one who professed to teach corporeal exercises, and to diet and order the body with them. This seems to be the same Pythagoras, son of Eratocles, who wrote *Aleiptic Commentaries*, and advised the wrestlers instead of figs to eat flesh, both of which are ascribed by some to Pythagoras the philosopher.[210] The third, a Lacynthian, to whom are ascribed the doctrines of philosophy which it was lawful to divulge, and the proverbial αὐτὸς ἔφη ["He said it himself"]†; both of which were proper to Pythagoras the philosopher. Some reckon another Pythagoras of Rhegium, a statuary, who invented rhythm and symmetry; and another of Samos, a statuary also (perhaps the same whom Pliny places in the sixty-seventh Olympiad [ca. 508–505 B.C.][211]); and another an orator of no reputation; another a physician who wrote of σκίλλη, the sea onion† (ascribed by Pliny to the philosopher[212]) and concerning Homer; and another who wrote of the history of the Doreans, as Dioysius relates. Hitherto Laertius. To these add Pythagoras the Ephesian,[213] who lived before Cyrus; another of the same name, Praefect under Ptolemy;[214] a third, a painter.[215]

His Wife, Children, and Servants

He took to wife Theano. Some affirm, she was a Crotonian;[216] but Porphyry, a Cretan, daughter of Pythanax, or Pythonax.[217] After the death of Pythagoras, she took upon her the tuition of their children and the government of the school,[218] marrying Aristaeus, who succeeded him in that dignity.[219] Laertius says there were some writings extant under her name; whereof Suidas instances philosophical commentaries, apothegms, and a poem in hexameter verse. Of her apothegms are remembered these:

Being demanded how soon after coition a woman is pure, she answered, "If with her own Husband, at the same instant; if with a strange person, never." She advised every woman, when she goes to bed to her husband to put off her modesty with her clothes, and when she rises to put it on again with them. Being asked—upon occasion perhaps of some ambiguous word, ποια ["what?"]†— which of the two she meant, she answered, "That for which I am called a woman."[220] To one, admiring her beauty and saying, "How white an arm!" she answered, "But not common."[221]

Laertius, who affirms she was daughter to Brontinus, a Crotonian, adds that according to some, Theano was wife to Brontinus and disciple to Pythagoras. And with this second, it seems the former was frequently confounded. This is so particularly in the first of the precedent apothegms, which Iamblichus affirms to have been spoken by Theano, the wife of Brontinus; though attributed by some (of whom Laertius is one) to Theano the wife of Pythagoras.

Of the sons of Pythagoras by Theano are remembered Telauges and Mnesarchus.[222] Mnesarchus seems to be the same whom Plutarch calls Mamercus;[223] for both these names are given to the father of Pythagoras, from whom that of his son doubtless was derived. (By some, he seems to be called Damo, if there be no mistake occasioned by Pythagoras having a daughter of the same name.[224]) These two, Telauges and Mnesarchus, were, upon their father's death, bred up under their mother Theano. Afterwards they governed the school, as Iamblichus attests of Mnesarchus, Laertius of Telauges, who adds that he taught Empedocles as some conceive. Hippobotus cites out of Empedocles himself, this:

> Noble Telauges[225] from Theano sprung.
> And great Pythagoras—

But of Telauges there is no writing extant. Thus says Laertius, who yet elsewhere cites an epistle of Telauges to Philolaus. And Iamblichus affirms that some ascribed to Telauges the sacred discourse, which went under the name of Pythagoras.

To these two sons, add (upon the authority of Duris the Samian, in his second *Book of Hours*[226]) Arimnestus, master to Democritus. Returning from banishment, he suspended a brazen tablet in the Temple of Juno, the diameter whereof was nigh two cubits, bearing this inscription.

> Me Arimnestus, who learning traced,
> Pythagoras beloved son here placed.

His daughters were Sara, Maya, Arignota (whose Pythagorean writings Porphyry mentioned as extant in his time), and Damo. With her, Pythagoras left his writings at his death, charging her not to communicate them to any that were not within the family. Whereupon she, though she might have had much money from the books, would not accept it, preferring poverty with obedience to her father's command before riches.[227] One of his daughters Pythagoras gave in marriage to Meno of Crotona, whom he had educated so well that, when a virgin, she went foremost in the company of the virgins; and when a wife, foremost among the married women. The Crotonians made of her house a temple to Ceres. The street on which she lived, they called *Museum*.

Of his servants are particularly remembered two, Astraeus and Zamolxis. Of the first, thus says Diogenes in his treatise of *Incredible Things Beyond Thule*:[228] Mnesarchus, the father of Pythagoras, being a Tyrrhenian by extract of those Tyrrhenians who inhabited Lemnus, Imber, and Scyrus, went from thence and traveled to many countries and cities. He found an infant lying under a large tall poplar, and coming to it, he perceived that it lay with his face towards the sky, looking steadfastly upon the Sun without winking. In its mouth was put a little slender reed like a pipe. And seeing to his great wonder that the child was nourished with the drops that distilled from the tree, he took the child away, believing it to be of a divine race.

This child when he grew up was entertained by Androcles, a native of that country, who adopted him into his own family and committed the management of his affairs to his trust. Mnesarchus afterwards growing very rich, brought up the child, naming him Astraeus, together with his own three sons, Eunostus, Tyrrhenus, and Pythagoras. Androcles put Astraeus under the tutelage of Lutenilt, a wrestler and a painter; but as soon as he was grown up, he sent him to Miletus to Anaximander, to learn geometry and astronomy. Mnesarchus gave Astraeus to Pythagoras—who receiving him, and considering his physiognomy, and examining the motions and restings of his body, instructed him. For he first found out the way of discerning the nature of every man; neither did he entertain any as his friend or disciple, before he had examined by physiognomy his disposition.

He had likewise another servant whom he entertained in Thrace named Zamolxis—for that as soon as he was born, they wrapped him in a bear's skin which the Thracians call Zalmus. Pythagoras felt friendship toward him and instructed him in sublime speculations, and concerning sacred rites, and the worship of the gods. Some affirm he was called Thales. The Barbarians worshipped him instead of Hercules. Dionysiphanes says he was servant to Pythagoras, and falling into the hands of thieves, and being branded by them, when Pythagoras was disturbed by seditious factions and banished, he bound his forehead about because of the scars. Some say, that the name Zamolxis signifies a strange person. Hitherto Diogenes. To this Zamolxis (says Laertius) the Getes sacrifice, as Herodotus relates, conceiving him to be Saturn. But Herodotus, having delivered the tradition of the Grecians (that he served Pythagoras at Samos, bought out his freedom at a great rate, and returning to his country, reformed their manners), concludes with his own opinion that Zamolxis lived many years before Pythagoras.[229]

His Writings

Some there are who hold, that Pythagoras left not anything in writing. Of this opinion are Plutarch,[230] Josephus,[231] Lucian,[232] Porphyry,[233] Ruffinus,[234] and others. But Laertius says that all such as affirm he wrote nothing do but jest. For Heraclitus, the natural philosopher, said expressly that Pythagoras, son of Mnesarchus, was skilful in history above all men; and selecting those writings, made up his own wisdom and variety of learning and art.[235] To which citation, perhaps, Clement of Alexandria refers who says, Heraclitus being later than Pythagoras, mentioned him in his writings.[236]

The books attributed to Pythagoras are these:

Three treatises: *Education*, *Politics*, and *Physic*, to which Laertius[237] refers the foresaid testimony of Heraclitus—forasmuch as Pythagoras, in the beginning of his physical treatise says, "Neither by the air that I breathe; nor by the water that I drink, shall I not bear the blame of this discourse."[238]

Six treatises are reckoned by Heraclides, son of Serapion, in his *Epitome of Solion*. One concerns the universe in verse. The second entitled, *The Sacred Discourse*, beginning thus: [239]

Young men in silence entertain all these.

To the same book perhaps belongs this:

Wretched, thrice wretched, beans forebear to eat,
Your parents' heads as well may be your meat.

And this cited by Eustathius:[240]

Which way to Orcus souls descend; which way
Return, and the Sun's cheerful light survey.

The third book, of the soul. The fourth, of piety. The fifth concerning Helothales, father of Epicharmus. The sixth, Crotona and others.

Two treatises, a discourse concerning nature, and another concerning the gods; both of which he, in a short time, taught Abaris through Hyperborean.[241] The first may possibly be the same as the physical treatise mentioned by Laertius. The second, as Iamblichus says, is entitled also *The Sacred Discourse* (but it is not the same as that *Sacred Discourse* which Heraclides ascribes to him; for that was in verse, this in prose). It is described as being collected out of the most mystical places of Orpheus. Most hold that it was written by Pythagoras. However, some eminent and creditable persons of that school assert that Telauges collected commentaries left by Pythagoras with Damo, his daughter, sister of Telauges. After her death, they report these to have been given to Bitale, daughter of Damo, and to Telauges, son of Pythagoras, husband to Bitale. [This is unclear as written—Ed.] What Iamblichus cites out of this work (see hereafter in the Doctrine of Pythagoras) is cited also by Hierocles,[242] Syrianus, and others.

An *Oration to Abaris* is mentioned by Proclus. *Orpheus*, a poem, is affirmed by Ion the Chian in *Triagmis* (Laertius).[243] *The Scopiads*, beginning thus, Μὴ ἀναίδου μηδένί ["behave not shamelessly to anyone"] (Laertius). *Hymns*, out of which Proclus brings these verses:

—Sacred Number Springs
From th' uncorrupted Monad, and proceeds
To the Divine Tetractys, she who breeds
All; and assigns the proper bounds to all,
Whom we the pure immortal Decad call.

Arthmetic is mentioned by Isidore, who affirms Pythagoras was the first that wrote upon this subject amongst the Grecians, which was afterward more copiously composed by Nicomachus.[244]

Prognostics, of which thus Tzetzes:[245]

> Pythagoras Samian, Mnesarchus son,
> Not only knew what would by fate be done,
> But even for those who futures would perceive,
> He of Prognostics several Books did leave.

Of the Magical Virtues of Herbs, frequently cited by Pliny, who says that though some ascribe it to Cleemporus, a physician, yet pertinacious fame and antiquity vindicate it to Pythagoras. And this very thing gives authority to the volumes. (Pliny asked if anyone thought Cleemporus could have written it, seeing that he put forth other things in his own name.[246]) To this work seems to belong that volume, which Pythagoras wrote concerning the sea onion, cited also by Pliny; but by Laertius ascribed to another Pythagoras, a physician.

The Golden Verses of Pythagoras, or as others, of the Pythagoreans. But indeed their author, as Suidas says, is not certainly known, though some ascribe them to him. Of these is Proclus who styles him, "Father of the Golden Verses."[247] Even the verses themselves seem to confirm it, there being amongst them some which Pythagoras is known to have repeated to his disciples by the testimonies of Laertius, Porphyry, and others.

> Nor suffer sleep at night to close thy eyes,
> Till thrice they acts that day thou hast ore-run;
> How slipped? What deeds? What duty left undone?

Others, such as Chrysippus, attribute them to his disciples;[248] some particularly to Lysis the Terentine; some to Philolaus. St. Hierom [i.e., Jerome—Ed.] conceives that the sentences and doctrines were of Pythagoras, but reduced to verse succinctly by Archippus and Lysides, his disciples, who had their schools in Greece and at Thebes, and having the precepts of their master by heart, made use of their own ingenuity instead of books. Or they might be compiled by Epicarmus, of whom Iamblichus says, coming to Syracusa in the reign of Hiero, he forbore to profess philosophy openly, but did reduce the opinions of the Pythagoreans into verse, thereby in sportive manner venting the doctrine of Pythagoras.[249]

Epistles; of which are extant two only, one to Anaximenes, the other to Hiero.

Pythagoras to Anaximenes.

And thou, O best of men, if thou didst not excel Pythagoras in extract and honor, wouldst have left Miletus. But now the honor of this country detains thee, and would also detain me, were I like Anaximenes. But if you, who are the most considerable persons, should forsake the cities, their glory would be lost and they become more infested by the Medes. Neither is it fit to be always busied in astrology; but better to take care of our country. Even I myself bestow not all my time in study, but sometimes in the wars, wherein the Italians are engaged one against another.

This epistle seems to have been written in answer to that of Anaximenes to Pythagoras, already produced in the *Life of Anaximenes.*

Pythagoras to Hiero.

My life is secure and quiet, but yours will no way suit with me. A moderate and self-denying person, needs not a Sicilian table. Pythagoras, wheresoever he comes, has all things sufficient for the day; but to serve a Lord is heavy and insolvable, for one unaccustomed to it. αυτάρκεια, self-sufficiency, is a great and safe thing. For it has none that envies or conspires against it; whence that life seems to come nearest God. A good habit is not acquired by venereal pleasures nor high feeding, but by indigence, which leads to Virtue. Various and intemperate pleasures enslave the souls of weak persons, but especially those which you enjoy, inasmuch as you have given yourself over to them. For you are carried in suspense, and cannot be safe; because your reason opposes not itself to those things which are pernicious. Therefore, write not Pythagoras to live with you; for physicians will not fall sick to bear their patient's company.

These are mentioned as the genuine writings of Pythagoras; others there were accounted spurious, such as the following:

The Mystic Discourse, which (says Laertius) they affirm to have been written by Hippasus, in detraction from Pythagoras. Many writings of Asto, a Crotonian, were likewise ascribed to Pythagoras;[250] as were also *Aliptic Commentaries,* written indeed by another of that name, son of Eratacles.[251]

The dialect used by Pythagoras and his disciples was the Doric, which some, such as Metrodorus cited by Iamblichus, conceive chosen by them as the most excellent. Epicharmus, says he, and before him Pythagoras, regarded the Doric as the best of dialects as it is also the best musical harmony. For the Ionic and Aeolic partake of the **Chromatic**; the Attic is much more participant of the Chromatic; but the Doric dialect is **Enharmonic**, consisting of full sounding letters.

The antiquity of the Doric dialect is testified by fable. Deucalion (son of Prometheus) and Pyrrha (daughter of Epimetheus) begot Hellen, father of the whole Hellenic race. (In the Babylonian sacred records, Hellen is said to be the son of Jupiter.) Hellen had three sons: Dorus, ancestor of the Dorians; Aeolus, father of the Aeolians; and Xanthus, father of Io, from whom descend the Ionic races. Now it is not easy to speak exactly concerning the ancients to those of later times, yet is it acknowledged that the Doric is the most ancient of these dialects. (Orpheus, the most ancient of poets, used the Doric dialect.) A fourth dialect, the Attic, was founded by Creusa daughter of Erechtheus, so named three ages after the rest according to the Thracians, and the rape of Orithuia which many histories declare.

But perhaps the true reason is because it was the dialect of the country. For the Pythagoreans admonished all persons to use the language of their own country, what Grecians soever came into their community. For to speak a strange language, they approved not.[252] The Doric dialect was common throughout Magna Grecia. Crotona and Sybaris were colonies of the Achaeans, Syracuse of the Corinthians; both of which were originally Doric, as being of Peloponnesus. Thucydides alleged this as a motive which induced the Athenians to war with the Sicilians, lest being Doreans they should at some time or other assist the Doreans by reason of their affinity, and

being a colony of the Peloponnesians, should join with the Peloponnesians.[253] Hence to the stranger in Theocritus, his *Adoniazousai*[254]
reproving the Syracusian women thus:

> Peace foolish babbling women, leave your place;
> Your wide mouth'd Doric here is out of date.

One of them answers,

> Gup, whence are you? What is our talk to thee?
> Correct your maids, not us of Sicily.
> I would you knew it, we are from Corinth sprung,
> As was Bellerophon, our mother tongue
> Peloponnesian is, nor is it scorn
> That they speak Doric who are Doric born.
> For (says the Scholiast) the Syracusians were originally
> Corinthians: Peloponnesus was inhabited by the Doreans,
> together with the Heraclidae.[255]

CHAPTER 23

His Disciples

Many were the persons, who from several parts, resorted to Pythagoras, to be his disciples and live with him in that condition. Of these there were, as Aristoxenus relates, Leucanians, Messapians (or, as Laertius, Peucepetians), and Romans.[256]

Simichus, tyrant of the Centoropians (a people of Sicily, the town itself being called Centorpa), having heard him, laid down his command and distributed his riches, part to his sister, part to his citizens. [257]

Abaris, also of Scythia, a Hyperborean came hither. He being unacquainted with the Greek language, and not initiated, and withal advanced into years, Pythagoras would not introduce him by various theorems; but instead of the silence, and the long attention, and other trials, he made him presently fit to receive his doctrines, and taught him in a short time to understand those two books concerning nature, and concerning the gods.[258] For Abaris now in years, came from the Hyperboreans, a priest of Apollo there; and converting the wisest things concerning religion from Greece to his own country, that he might lay up the collected gold to his god's use in his temple among the Hyperboreans.

He came by the way into Italy, and saw Pythagoras, and likened him to the god whose priest he was, and believed he was no other, not a man like him but very Apollo himself, both by his gravity, and by some marks and tokens which he knew. He gave Pythagoras an arrow which he had brought from the temple as necessary for his journey, through so many different contingencies, and such a long travel. For riding upon that, and so passing over places that were otherwise impassible—such as rivers, lakes, marshes, mountains, and the like—and coming to any place, as they say, he made purifications, and expelled pestilences and storms from those cities that desired his assistance. We are informed, that Lacedaemon being purged by him, never had the pestilence afterwards, whereas it was formerly very subject to that sickness, by reason of want of free passage of the air. (The Taygetan Mountains, amongst which it is built, penning it up. For those hills lie above it, as Gnossus to Crete.) And other such signs of the power of Abaris are reported.[259]

But Pythagoras, accepting the arrow and not looking strangely upon it, or asking the cause why he gave it him; but, as if he were himself the true god, taking Abaris aside he showed him his golden thigh, as an assured mark that he was not mistaken. And then, reckoning every particular of all those that were in the temple, proved that he did not guess amiss. He added that he came for the benefit of men, and for this reason was in man's shape, that they might not be astonished at one so far above them, and so fly his doctrine. And he commanded Abaris to stay there, and to join with him in instructing them who came to him. As for the gold which Abaris had gathered for his god, Pythagoras commanded him to give it to those whom he had assembled; insomuch that he actually confirmed the sentence, "All things are common amongst friends."

Abaris thus staying with him (as we said), he gave him the epitome of physiology and theology. And instead of the art of guessing by sacrifices, he taught him that kind of Prognostic which is by numbers, as thinking that more sacred and divine, and more agreeable to the celestial numbers of the gods. And other doctrines he taught Abaris, such as were proper for him.

Milo of Crotona, the most eminent wrestler of those times, was another disciple to Pythagoras.[260] He, when in the hall of the college a pillar begun to yield, went under it; and by that means saved all the scholars, and at last got away himself. It is probable that this confidence in his great strength was the occasion of his death. For they report that as he was going through a thick wood far from any way, finding a great tree with wedges in it, he set his hand and feet to it, trying to split it asunder; whereupon the wedges fell out, and he being caught, became a prey to the wild beasts. In his house it was that the Pythagoreans were surprised and burned by the Cylonians.

Calliphon of Crotona, is mentioned by Hermippus as an intimate friend of Pythagoras, who reported when Calliphon was dead, that his soul was continually present with him. He also said that the soul commanded him that he should not pass the place where his ass fell; and that he should abstain from impure water, and avoid ill-speaking.[261]

We only mention these here as being most particularly interested in the relation of Pythagoras and his life: a more perfect account of the rest, we will add in the following catalogue.

Sport competitions of many kinds were popular with the ancient Greeks, and wrestling was among the most important. Pythagoras' disciple Milo of Crotona, famed as a wrestler, would have engaged in contests like the one shown on the obverse of this silver stater of c.420–370 B.C., isued by the city of Aspendus in Asia Minor.
Photo courtesy of Numismatica Ars Classica

CHAPTER 24

THE SUCCESSION OF HIS SCHOOL

The successor of Pythagoras is by all acknowledged to have been Aristaeus, son of Damophon, a Crotonian who lived in the time of Pythagoras seven generations above Plato. Nor did he succeed in the school only, but in breeding the children of Pythagoras and in the marriage with Theano, for his eminent understanding of his opinions. He is said to have taught the doctrine of Pythagoras forty years together lacking one, living in all, near an hundred. Pythagoras assigned the school to Aristaeus as being the oldest.[262]

Next him Mnesarchus, son of Pythagoras. He delivered it to Bulagoras, in whose time the city of Crotona was sacked. He was succeeded by Tidas, a Crotonian, returning from travels he began before the war. But he died with grief for the calamity of his country; whereas it was a common thing to others, when they were very old, to free themselves from the fetters of the body. Afterwards they took one of the Lucanians, saved by some strangers, to be the President of the school. To him came Diodorus the Aspendian, who was taken by reason of the scarcity of men in their college.

At Heraclea, Clinias and Philolaus. At Metapontum, Theorides and Eurytus. At Tarentum, Archytas. One of the external listeners to his discourse was Epicharmus, who was not of the College. Coming to Syracusa in the time of the tyranny of Hieron, he forbare publicly to profess philosophy; but he reduced the opinions of those men (the Pythagoreans) into verse, sportively divulging the abstruse doctrines of Pythagoras.

Of the Pythagoreans it is likely that many were obscure; the names of such as were eminent, are these:

Crotonians: Hippostatus Dymas, Aegon, Aemon, Silius, Cleosthenes, Agelas, Episylus, Phyciadas, Ecphanius, Timaeus, Buthius, Eratus, Itanaus, Phodippus, Bryas, Evander, Millias, Antimedon, Aegas, Leophron, Agylas, Onatus, Hipposthenes, Cleophron, Alcmaeon, Damocles, Milon, Meton.

Metapontines: Brontinus, Parmiscus, Arestadas, Leo, Damarmenos, Aeneas, Chilas, Melisias, Aristeas, Laphaon, Evander, Agesidamus, Xenocides, Euriphemus, Aristomenes, Agesarchus, Alcias, Xenophantes, Thraseos, Arytus, Epiphron, Eiriscus, Megistaes, Leocydes, Thrasymides, Euphemus, Proclus, Antimedes, Lacritus, Damotages, Pyrrhon, Rhexibius, Alopecus, Astylus, Dacydus, Aliochus, Lacrates, Glucinus.

Agrigentine: Empedocles.

Velian: Parmenides.

Tartentines: Philolaus, Arytus, Archytas, Theodorus, Aristippus, Lycon, Estiaeus, Polemarchus, Asteas, Caenias. Cleon, Eurymedon, Arceas, Clinagoras, Archippus, Zopyrus, Euthynus, Dicaearchus, Philonides, Phrontidas, Lysis, Lysibius, Dinocrates, Echecrates, Paetion, Acusiladas, Iccus, Pisicrates, Clearatus, Leonteus, Phrinichus, Simicheas, Aristoclides, Clinias, Abroteles, Piserrydus, Brias, Evander, Archemachus, Mimnomachus, Achmondas, Sicas, Caraphantidas.

Sybarites: Metopus, Hippasus, Proxenus, Evanor, Deanax, Menestius, Diocles, Empedus, Timasius, Polemaeus, Evaeus, Tyrsenus.

Parians: Aetius, Phenecles, Dexitheus, Alcimachas, Dinarchus, Meton, Timaeus, Timesianax, Amcaerus, Eumaridias.

Locrians: Gyptius, Xenon, Philodamus, Euetes, Adicus, Sthenonidas, Sosistratus, Euthynus, Zaleucus, Timares.

Posidonians: Athamas, Simus, Proxenus, Cranius, Mayes, Bathylaus, Phaedo.

Lucanians: Ocellus and Ocylus (brethren), Oresander, Cerambus, Dardaneus, Malias.

Aegeans: Hippomedon, Timosthenes, Euelthon, Thrasydamus, Crito, Polyctor.

Laconians: Antocharidas, Cleanor, Eurycratus.

Hyperborean: Abaris.

Rhegians: Aristides, Demosthenes, Aristocrates, Phytius, Helicaon, Mnesibulus, Hipparchides, Athosion, Euthycles, Opsimus.

Selinuntian: Colaes.

Syracusians: Leptines, Phintias, Damon.

Samians: Melissus, Lacon, Archippus, Glorippus, Heloris, Hippon.

Caulonians: Callibrotus, Dicon, Nastas, Drymon, Xentas.

Phliasians: Diocles, Echecrates, Polymnastus, Phanton.
Sicyonians: Paliades, Demon, Sostratius, Sosthenes.
Kyrenaeans: Prorus, Melanippus, Aristangelus, Theodorus.
Cyzicenes: Pythodorus, Hipposthenes, Butherus, Xenophilus.
Catanaean: Charondas.
Corinthian: Lysiades.
Tyrrhene: Chrysippus.
Athenian: Nausitheus.
Of Pentus: Neocritus, Lyramnus.

In all, 213.[263]

The eminent Pythagorean women, are:

Tymicha, wife of Millius the Crotonian.
Philtes, daughter of Leophron, a Crotonian, sister of Bindaecus.
Oecelo and Eccelo, of Luca.
Chilonis, daughter of Chilo the Lacedaemonian.
Theano, wife of Brontinus the Metapontine.
Muya, wife of Milo the Crotonian.
Lasthenia of Arcadia, daughter of Abroteles the Tarentine.
Echecrates, a Phliasian.
Tyrsenes of Sybaris.
Pysirronde of Tarentum, daughter of Nistiades.
Salacera.
Bio of Argos.
Babelyma of Argos.
Cleaechma, sister of Authocharides, a Lacedaemonian.

In all, 17, thus Iamblichus.

Laertius says his system (or as Cassiodorus called it, his college) continued for nineteen generations. For the last of the Pythagoreans, whom Aristoxenus saw, were Xenophilus the Chalcidean of Thrace, and Phanton a Phliasian, and Echecrates, and Diocles, and Polymnestus, who also were Phliasians. They heard Philolaus and Eurytus, both of Tarentum.

Part Two

The Discipline and Doctrine
of the Pythagoreans

The Greeks believed a mysterious race of people lived in Hyperborea, a land
they placed beyond Scythia, where this gold stater was struck at Panticapaeum
between c.340 and 325 B.C. It shows on its obverse the head of a satyr (or the god
Pan), and on its reverse the mythical griffin with a spear in its beak.
Photo courtesy of Classical Numismatic Group, Inc.

THE GREAT AUTHORITY AND ESTEEM OF PYTHAGORAS AMONGST HIS DISCIPLES

Pythagoras, to render his disciples capable of Philosophy, prepared them by a discipline so strict and severe as might seem incredible to have been undergone by free persons—were it not founded upon the great authority and reputation which he had amongst them.

The credit of their opinions they conceived to be this: that he who first communicated them was no ordinary person, but a god.[264] The disciples, or *Acousmata*, believed him to be a god: indeed, Hyperborean Apollo.[265] In confirmation thereof they instance those wonders related in his life. They say that these stories being acknowledged to be true—and it being impossible they should all be performed by one man—they conceive it manifest that these relations are to be ascribed, not to a human being, but to something above mankind. This they acknowledge, for amongst them is a saying:

Two-footed Man,[266] and Bird
Is, and another Third.

By the "Third," they meant Pythagoras. And Aristotle, in his book on Pythagorean philosophy, relates, that such a division as this was preserved by the Pythagoreans amongst their ineffable secrets.[267] Of rational animals, one kind is God; another, man; a third between both these, Pythagoras.

They esteemed Pythagoras in the next place to the gods, as some good genius indulgent to mankind: some affirming that he was Pythian; others Hyperborean Apollo. Some said he was one of those genie which dwell in the Moon; others, one of the celestial deities appearing at that time in human shape for the benefit and direction of mortal life, that he might communicate the wholesome illumination of beatitude and philosophy to mortal nature. They affirmed a greater good can never come, nor shall ever come, than that which was given by the gods through the means of Pythagoras.[268] Whence to this day the proverb of the fair-haired Samian is used for a most reverend person.

Porphyry says they reckoned him amongst the gods.[269] Therefore, whenever they went to deliver to others any excellent thing out of the secrets of his philosophy—whence many physical conclusions might be deduced—they swore by the Tetractys. And calling Pythagoras, as some God to witness, they said:

> Who the Tetractys to our Souls express'd,
> Eternal Nature's Fountain I attest.

Which oath they used as forbearing through reverence to name him; for they were very sparing in using the name of any god.[270]

So great indeed was the respect they bore him, that it was not lawful for anyone to doubt of what he said, nor to question him further concerning it. They acquiesced in all things that he delivered as if they were oracles.[271] And when he went abroad to cities, it was reported he went not to teach, but to cure.

Hence it came to pass, that when they asserted anything in dispute, if they were questioned why it was so, they used to answer, *Ipse dixit* ("He said it")—"he" being Pythagoras.[272] This αὐτὸς ἔφα ["He said it"]† was amongst them the first and greatest of doctrines—his judgment being a reason free from and above all examination and censure.[273]

The Two Sorts of Auditors: and First of the Exoteric, How He Explored Them

The Auditors of Pythagoras (such, I mean, as belonged to the family) were of two sorts, exoteric and esoteric. The Exoterics were those who were under probation, which if they performed, they were admitted to Esoterics. For of those who came to Pythagoras, he admitted not everyone, but only those whom he liked: first, upon choice, and next by trial.

The Pythagoreans are said to have been averse to those who sell learning, and open their souls, like the gates of an Inn, to everyone that comes to them. And if they find not a vent or sale in this manner, then they run into cities and ransack the gymnasia, and exact a reward from dishonorable persons. Whereas Pythagoras hid much of his speeches; so only they who were purely initiated might plainly understand them.[274] But the rest, as Homer said of Tantalus, grieve, for that being in the midst of learning, they cannot taste of it. Moreover they said that they who for hire teach such as come to them, are meaner then statuaries and chariotmakers. For a statuary, when he would make a Mercury, seeks out some piece of wood fit to receive that form; but these, of every disposition, endeavor to make that of virtue.[275]

When (therefore) any friends came to him, and desired to learn of him, he admitted them not till he had made trial and judgment of them.[276] First, he enquired how they did heretofore converse with their parents and friends; next, he observed their unseasonable laughters, and unnecessary silence or discourse. Moreover, what their inclinations were (whether possessed with passion and intemperance, whether prone to anger or unchaste desires, or contentious or ambitious, and how they behaved themselves in contention and friendship[277]). As likewise what friends those were with whom they were intimate, and their conversation with them, and in whose society they spent the greatest part of the day; likewise upon what occasions they experienced joy or grief.[278]

Moreover he considered their presence and their gait, and the whole motion of their body. And physiognomizing them by their symptoms, he discovered by manifest signs the occult dispositions of their souls.[279] For he first studied that science concerning men, thereby discovering of what disposition everyone was. Neither did he admit any into his friendship and acquaintance before he had physiognomized the man, what he was.[280] This word (says Aulus Gellius, upon the same occasion) signifies to make enquiry into the manners of some by some kind of conjecture—of the wit by the face and countenance, and by the air and habit of the whole body.[281]

If upon exact observation of all these particulars, he found them to be of good dispositions, then he examined whether they had good manners, and were docile. First, whether they could readily and ingeniously follow that which he told them; next, whether they had any love to those things which they heard.[282] For he considered what disposition they were as to being made gentle. This he called κατάρτυσιν ["culture"]; for he accounted roughness an enemy to his way of teaching. Because roughness is attended by impatience, intemperance, anger, obtuseness, confusion, dishonor, and the like; but mildness and gentleness by their contraries.

Likewise in making the first trial of them, he considered whether they could ἐχεμυθεῖν ["restrain their speech"] (that was the word he used). And he examined whether if they could learn that which they heard, they were able to be silent and keep it to themselves.[283]

PURIFICATORY INSTITUTION BY SUFFERINGS

The chief goal that Pythagoras proposed was to deliver and free the mind from the engagements and fetters in which it is confined from her first infancy. Without which freedom, none can learn anything sound or true, nor can perceive by what that which is unsound in sense operates.[284] For the mind (according to him) sees all, and hears all; the rest are deaf and blind.

This he performed by many exercises which he appointed for purification of the mind, and for the probation of such as came to him, which endured five years before they were admitted.

If upon this examination (which we declared) he judged any person capable, he then remitted him for three years to be despised, making a test of his constancy and true love to learning, and whether he were sufficiently instructed as to despise glory, to condemn honor, and the like.[285]

He conceived it, in general, requisite that they should take much labor and pains for the acquisition of arts and sciences. To that end he appointed for them some torments of cauterizing and incision, to be performed by fire and steel, which none that were of an ill inclination would undergo.[286]

CHAPTER 4

SILENCE

Moreover, he imposed upon those that came to him silence for five years, making trial how firmly they would behave themselves in the most difficult of all contingencies; for such is the government of the tongue, as is manifest from those who have divulged mysteries.[287]

This πενταετὴς σιωπή, a quinquennial silence,† was called ἐχεμυθία ["restraining speech"], and sometimes, but less frequently, ἐχερημοσύνη ["keeping silent"], ὑπὸ τοῦ ἔχον ἕν ἑαυτῷ τὸν λόγον, from keeping our speech within ourselves.†[288]

The reason for this silence was that the soul might be converted into herself and away from external things—from the irrational passions in her, and from the body, even unto her own life, which is to live forever.[289] Or as Clement of Alexandria expresses it, that his disciples, being diverted from sensible things, might seek God with a pure mind.[290] Hence Lucian, to the demand how Pythagoras could reduce men to the remembrance of the things which they had formerly known (for he held science to be only reminiscence), makes him answer, "First, by long quiet and silence, speaking nothing for five whole years."[291]

Yet Aulus Gellius affirms that he appointed not the same length of silence to all, but different periods to several persons according to their particular capacities.[292] And Apuleius says that for the graver sort of persons this taciturnity was moderated by a shorter space; but the more talkative were punished, as it were, by exile from speech five years.

He who kept silence heard what was said by others, but was not allowed either to question, if he understood not, or to write down what he heard.[293] None kept silence less than two years. Agellius adds that those within the time of silence and hearing were called *Acoustici*. But when they had learned these things (the most difficult of all to hold their peace and to hear) and were now grown learned in silence, which they called ἐχεμυθίαν ["restraining speech"]— then they were allowed to speak, and to question, and to write what they heard and what they conceived. At this time they were called

Mathematici, from those arts which they then began to learn and to mediate. Thus says Agellus, although how rightly I question. For *Mathematici* and *Acousmatici* were distinctive appellations of the Pythagoreans, not in probation but after admission, as we shall see hereafter.

Thus Apuleius says Pythagoras taught nothing to his disciples before silence. And that the first meditation for one who meant to become a wise man was wholly to refrain the tongue of words—those words which the poets call "winged," to pluck off the feathers and to confine them within the walls of our teeth.[294] This was the first rudiment of wisdom, to learn to meditate, and to unlearn to talk.

CHAPTER 5

Abstinence, Temperance, and Other Ways of Purification

Moreover, he commanded them to abstain from all foods that had life, and from certain other meats also which obstruct the clearness of the understanding.[295] And for the same end (viz. in order to aid the inquisition and apprehension of the most difficult theorems), he likewise commanded them to abstain from wine; to eat little; to sleep little; to show a careless contempt of honor, riches, and the like; to offer an unfeigned respect towards kindred—sincere equality and kindness towards such as were of the same age, and a propensity to further the younger without envy.

In fine, he procured to his disciples a conversation with the gods by visions and dreams—which never happen to a soul disturbed with anger or pleasure, or any other unbefitting transportation, or with impurity, or rigid ignorance.[296] He cleansed and purified the soul divinely from all these; and enkindled the divine part in her and preserved her; and directed in her that intellectual divine eye which is better, as Plato says, than a thousand eyes of flesh. For by the help of this only, truth is apprehended.[297] After this manner he procured purification of the intellect. And such was his form of institution as to those things.

Diodorus says they had an exercise of temperance that worked in the following manner.[298] There being prepared and set before them all sorts of delicate food, they looked upon it a good while; and after their appetites were fully provoked by the sight thereof, they commanded it to be taken off and given to the servants.[299] They themselves went away without dining. This they did, says Iamblichus, to punish their appetite.

CHAPTER 6

COMMUNITY OF ESTATES

In this time, all that they had (that is their whole estate) was made common, that is, put together communally.[300] They brought forth, says Aulus Gellius, whatsoever they had of stock or money and constituted an inseparable society, as being that ancient way of association which truly is termed κοινόβιον ["life in community"].[301] This was given up to such of the disciples as were appointed for that purpose. These were called *Politici* and *Economici*, as being persons fit to govern a family and to give laws.

This was conformable to the precepts of Pythagoras (as Timeus affirms): first κοινα τὰ φὶλων εἶνας, all common amongst friends; and φιλότης, ἰσότης, friendship, equality;[302] and, esteem nothing your own. By this means he exterminated all propriety and increased community even to their last possessions. He sought thus to eliminate possessions as a cause of dissension and trouble; for, since all things were common amongst them, no man had a propriety to anything.[303]

But what Aulus Gellius terms an "inseparable society" is to be understood only conditionally. If someone misliked this community, he took again his own estate, and more than that which he brought into the community, and departed.[304]

ADMISSION OR REJECTION

They who appeared worthy to participate of his doctrines—judging by their lives and moderation after their five years silence—were made *Esoterics* and admitted to hear Pythagoras within the screen and to see him.[305] But before that time, they heard him discourse, being on the outside of the screen, and not seeing him—given a long time experiment of their proper manners by hearing only.

But if they were rejected, they received their estate double, and a tomb was made by the disciples as if they had been dead. For so all that were about Pythagoras spoke of them; and when they met them, behaved themselves towards them as if they had been some other persons; but the men themselves they said were dead.

CHAPTER 8

DISTINCTION

Whatsoever he discoursed to those that came to him, he declared either plainly or symbolically (for he had a twofold form of teaching). And of those who came to him, some were called *Mathematici*, others *Acousmatici*.[306] The Mathematici were those who learned the fuller and more exactly elaborate reason of science. The Acousmatici were they who heard only the chief heads of learning without more exact explication.

Thus, as there were two kinds of Philosophy, so were there two sorts of those who studied philosophy.[307] The Acousmatici did confess that the Mathematici were Pythagoreans. But the Mathematici did not acknowledge that the Acousmatici were Pythagoreans; for they had their learning, not from Pythagoras, but from Hippasus; who, some say, was of Crotona, others of Metapontium.

The philosophy of the Acousmatici consists of doctrines without demonstrations and reasons; rather being told that this is how it must be done and the like. These they were to observe as so many divine doctrines, and they did esteem those amongst them the wisest who had most of these *Acousmata*. Now Acousmata were divided into three kinds: some tell what something is; others tell what is most such a thing; the third sort tell what is to be done and what not.

Those that tell what a thing is are of this kind: as what is the Island of the Blessed? The Sun? the Moon? What is the Oracle at Delphi? The Tetractys? What is the Music of the Syrens?

Those which tell what is most such as: What is most just? To sacrifice. What is the wisest? Number, and in the next place that which gave names to things. What is the wisest amongst us? Medicine. What the most beautiful? Harmony. What the most powerful? Reason. What the best? Beatitude. What the truest? That men are wicked. For which (they say) he commended Hippodamas, a Poet of Salamis, who said,

O Gods! whence are you? How so good? so Blessed?
O Men! whence are you? How with ill possessed?

These, and such like, are the Acousmata of this kind. For every one of these tells what is most. The same it is with that which is called the "wisdom of the seven sages." For they enquired not what is good, but what is most good; not what is difficult, but what is most difficult (which is to know ourselves); not what is facile, but what is most facile (which is the custom of nations). Those Acousmata seem to follow this kind of wisdom for those sages were before Pythagoras.

The Acousmata which tell what is to be done, or what is not to be done, are thus: As that we ought to beget children, for we must leave behind us such as may serve the gods in our stead; or, that we ought to put off the right shoe first; or, that we ought not to go in the common road, and the like. Such were the Acousmata. But those which have had the most said about them are concerning sacrifices: at what times, and after what manner they are to be performed; and concerning removal from our place of habitation; and concerning sepulture, how we must bury the dead.

For some, there is a reason given. As that we ought to get children, that we may leave in our room another servant of the gods. But of others there is no reason. And in some, that which follows the precept seems to be allied to the words; but in others is wholly distant. An example is that we ought not to break bread, because it conduces to judgment in Hell. But the reasons that are applied to these are not Pythagorean, but given by some other who studied Pythagorean learning, endeavoring to apply some probable conjecture to them. As of the last mentioned, that bread is not to be broken, some say: He who gathers together, ought not to dissolve. For anciently all friends used after a barbarous manner to meet at one loaf; others, that you must not give so bad an omen as when you are going about anything to break it off.

But there was one Hippomedon, an Agrinean,[308] a Pythagorean of the Acousmatic rank, who said that Pythagoras gave reasons and demonstrations of all these things. But because they were delivered by tradition through many, and those still growing more idle, that the reasons were taken away, and the problems only left.

Now the mathematical Pythagoreans grant all this to be true, but the occasion of the difference they say was this. Pythagoras went from Ionia and Samos, during Polycrates's reign, to Italy, which was then in a flourishing condition, and where the chief persons of the cities became conversant with him. To the most ancient of these, and such as had least leisure (because they were taken up with public employments, so that it would be very hard for them to learn mathematics and demonstrations), he discoursed barely. He conceived it did nothing less advantage them, even without the causes, to know what they had to do—as patients, not enquiring why such things are prescribed them, nevertheless obtain health. But to the younger, who were able to act and learn, he imparted by demonstrations and mathematics. The Mathematici professed that they came from these; the Acousmatici from the others, chiefly from Hippasus who was one of the Pythagoreans. But because Hippasus published their doctrine and first wrote of the sphere of twelve pentagons, he died in the sea as an impious person, not obtaining the same at which he aimed.

CHAPTER 9

How They Disposed the Day

We shall next speak concerning those things which he taught them in the day. For according to his directions, thus did they who were taught by him.[309]

These men performed their morning walks by themselves, and in such places where they might be exceeding quiet and retired. These were temples and groves and other delightful places. For they thought it was not fit they should speak with anyone till they had first composed their souls and fitted their intellect—and that such quiet was requisite for the composure of their intellect. For as soon as they arose, to intrude among the people they thought a tumultuous thing. Therefore all the Pythagoreans ever made choice of the most sacred places.

After their morning walk, they came to one another chiefly in the temples, or in some such places. They made use of these times for doctrines and disciplines, and rectifications of their manners.

After they had studied awhile, they went to their morning exercises. The greater part used to anoint themselves and run races; the fewer, to wrestle in orchards and in groves. Some by throwing sledges, or by grappling hands, to make trial of their strength—choosing such exercises as they judged most convenient for them.

At dinner they used bread and honey. Wine after meals they drunk not. The time after dinner they employed in political affairs—as well foreign as domestic, according to the injunction of their laws; for they endeavored to manage everything in the afternoons.

As soon as the evening came, they betook themselves again, not singly as in their morning walks, but two or three walked together, repeating the doctrines they had learnt and exercising themselves in virtuous employments. After their walks, they used baths and washing. Having washed, they met together to eat; but they did not eat together more than ten persons. As soon as they who were to come together were met, they used libations and sacrifices of meal and frankincense. Then they went to supper, that they might end it before the Sun were set. They used wine, and grain, and bread, and broth, and herbs, both raw and boiled. They likewise set before them the flesh of such beasts as used to be sacrificed. They seldom ate broths of fish, because some of them are in some respects very hurtful; likewise (seldom) the flesh of such creatures as use not to hurt mankind.

After supper they offered libations, then had lectures. Their custom was that the youngest amongst them should read, and the eldest should, as president, order what and how he should read. When they were to depart, he who filled the wine poured forth to them in libation. And during the libation, the eldest of them declared these things: that none should hurt or kill a domestic plant or fruit; besides, that they should speak well and think reverently of the gods, daemons, and heroes; likewise to think well of parents and benefactors; to assist law and oppose rebellion. This said, everyone departed to his house.

They wore a white and clean garment; they had also coverlets—white and clean—of linen; for they used not any of skins, because they approved not the exercise of hunting.[310]

These were the traditions that were delivered to that society of men, partly concerning diet (of which hereafter more particularly), partly concerning the course of life.

CHAPTER 10

How They Examined Their Actions
Morning and Evening

These and all other actions of the day they contrived in the morning before they rose, and examined at night before they slept; thus, by a twofold act, exercising the memory.[311] They conceived that it was requisite to retain and preserve in memory all which they learned; and that lessons and doctrines should be so far acquired as they are able to remember what they have learned; for that is it which they ought to know and bear in mind. For this reason they cherished memory much, and exercised it, and took great care of it; and in learning they gave not over until they had gotten their lesson perfectly by heart.

A Pythagorean rose not out of bed before he had called to mind the actions of the day past, which recollection he performed in this manner. He endeavored to call to mind what he first had either heard or given in charge to his servants as soon as he rose; and what in the second place, and what in the third, and so on in the same order. And then for his going forth, whom he met first, whom next; and what discourses he had with the first, what with the second, what with the third, and so of the rest; for he endeavored to repeat in memory all that happened throughout the whole day in order as it happened. And if at their up-rising they had more leisure, then after the same manner they endeavored to recollect all that happened to them for three days before. Thus they chiefly exercised the memory.[312] For they conceived that nothing conduces more to science, experience, and prudence than to remember many things.

This was conformable to the institution of Pythagoras. For he advised to have regard chiefly to two times: that when we went to sleep, and that when we rose from sleep. At each of these we ought to consider what actions are past, and what to come.[313] Of the past, we ought to require an account of ourselves; of the future, we ought to have a providential care. Wherefore he advised everyone to repeat to himself these verses as soon as he came home or before he slept.[314]

> Nor suffer sleep at night to close thine eyes,
> Till thrice thy acts that day thou hast reviewed,
> How slipped? what deeds? what duty left undone?

And before they arose, these:

> As soon as thou wakest, in order lay
> The actions to be done that following day.

To this effect, Ausonius has a Pythagorean Discourse as he terms it.

> A good wise person, such as hardly one
> Of many thousands to Apollo known,
> He his own judge strictly himself surveys,
> Nor minds the Noble's or the Common's ways:
> But, like the world itself, is smooth and round,
> In all his polished frame no blemish found.
> He thinks how long Cancer the day extends,
> And Capricorn the night. Himself perpends
> In a just balance, that no flaw where be,
> Nothing exuberant, but that all agree;
> Within that all be solid, nothing by
> A hollow sound betray vacuity.
> Nor suffer sleep to seize his eyes, before
> All acts of that long day he has run o're;
> What things were missed, what done in time, what not;
> Why here respect, or reason there forgot;
> Why kept the worse opinion? when reliev'd
> A beggar; why with broken passion griev'd;
> What wish'd which had been better not desir'd;
> Why profit before honesty requir'd?
> If any by some speech or look offended,
> Why nature more than discipline attended?
> All words & deeds thus searched from morn to night,
> He sorrows for the ill, rewards the right.

CHAPTER 11

SECRECY

Besides the quinquennial silence, πενταετὴς ἐχεμυθία,† of the Pythagoreans while they were Exoterics, there was another termed παντελὴς ἐχεμυθία, a perpetual or complete silence (or secrecy) proper to the Esoterics—not amongst one another, but towards all such as were not of their society.

The principal and most efficacious of their doctrines they all kept ever amongst themselves as not to be spoken, with exact **Echemythia** towards extraneous persons; continuing them unwritten and preserved only by memory to their successors, to whom they delivered them as mysteries of the gods. By which means, nothing of any moment came abroad from them.[315] What had been taught and learned for a long time, was only known within the walls; and, if at any time there were any extraneous, and as I may say, profane persons amongst them, the Men (so commonly were the Pythagoreans termed) expressed their meaning to one another by Symbols.

Hence Lysis, reproving Hipparchus for communicating the discourse to uninitiated persons void of mathematics and theory, says:

> They report, that you teach philosophy in public to all that come, which Pythagoras would not do, as you, Hipparchus, learned with much pains.[316] But you took no heed after you had tasted (O noble person) the Sicilian delicacies, which you ought not to have tasted a second time. If you are changed, I shall rejoice. If not, you are dead to me; for he said, "We ought to remember, that it is pious, according to the direction of divine and human exhortations, that the goods of wisdom ought not to be communicated to those whose soul is not purified so much as in dream."
>
> For it is not lawful to bestow on everyone that which was acquired with so much labor, nor to reveal the mysteries of the Eleusian goddesses to profane persons. For they who do both these are alike unjust and irreligious. It is good to consider without ourselves, how much time was employed in

taking away the spots that were in our beasts, that after five years we might be made capable of his discourses. For as dyers first wash and wring out the clothes they intend to dye— that they may take the dye so as that it can never be washed out or taken away—in like manner the divine prepared those who were inclined to philosophy, lest he might be deceived by those of whom he hoped that they would prove good and honest.

For he used no adulterate learning, nor the nets where- with many of the Sophists entangle the young men; but he was skillful in things divine and human. Whereas they, under the pretence of his doctrine, do many strange things, invei- gling the young men unbeseemingly, and as they meet them, whereby they render their auditors rough and rash. For they infuse free theorems and discourse into manners that are not free but disordered. As if into a deep well full of dirt and mire we should put clear transparent water. It troubles the dirt and spoils the water. The same is it as to those who teach and are taught; for about the minds and hearts of such as are not initiated, there grow thick and tall coverts which darken all modesty and meekness and reason, hindering it from increas- ing there.

Hence spring all kinds of ills, growing up and hindering the reason, and not suffering it to look out. I will first name their mothers, *Intemperance* and *Avarice,* both exceedingly fruitful. From intemperance spring up unlawful marriages, lust, drunkenness, perdition, unnatural pleasures, and cer- tain vehement appetites leading to death and ruin. For some have been so violently carried away with pleasures that they have not refrained from their own mothers and daughters; but violating the commonwealth and the laws, tyrannically imprison men, and carrying about their Jalles[317] (or stocks) violently, hurry them to destruction.

From avarice proceed rapines, thefts, parricides, sacrileges, poi- sonings, and whatsoever is allied to these. It behooves therefore first to cut away the matter wherein these vices are bred with fire and sword, and all arts of discipline—purifying and freeing the reason from these evils—and then to plant something that is good in it.

Thus Lysis. Neither is that expression, "If you are not changed, you are dead to me," to be understood simply. For this, Hipparchus, because he communicated and publicly set forth by writing the Pythagorean doctrines, was expelled from the school, and a tomb was made for him as if he were dead (according to the custom formerly mentioned).[318] So strict were the Pythagoreans in observance of this secrecy.

Part Three

The Doctrine of Pythagoras

Among the earliest coins of the Greek colonists in Southern Italy, this silver stater of Croton dates to the late 6th century B.C. *It shows on its obverse the tripod of Apollo and the abbreviated name of the city, and on its reverse the incuse impression of that same design, less the inscription.*
Photo courtesy of Numismatica Ars Classica

Section I. Mathematics

THE MATHEMATICAL SCIENCES PREPARATIVE TO PHILOSOPHY

The mind being purified by discipline ought to be applied to things that are beneficial.[319] These Pythagoras procured by some contrived ways, bringing it by degrees to the contemplation of eternal incorporeal things which are ever in the same state. He began this in an orderly manner from the most minute—lest by the suddenness of the change, it should be diverted and withdraw itself through its so great and long habit of perverse mental nutriment.

To this end, he first used the mathematical sciences, and those speculations which are intermediate between corporeals and incorporeals (for they have a threefold dimension like bodies, but they are impassible like Incorporeals) as degrees of preparation to the contemplation of the things that are. They divert, by an artificial reason, the eyes of the mind from corporeal things (which never are permanent in the same manner and estate), never so little to a desire of aliment. By means whereof, introducing the contemplation of things that are, he rendered men truly happy. This is the use he made of the mathematical sciences.

Hence it was that Justin Martyr, applying himself to a Pythagorean eminently learned, desirous to be his disciple, the teacher demanded whether he were versed in music, astronomy, and geometry. "Or do you think," says he, "you may be able to understand anything that pertains to beatitude without having first learned these, which abstract the soul from sensibles, preparing and adapting her for her intelligibles? Can you without these contemplate what is honest and what is good?" Thus, after a long commendation of these sciences, he dismissed him, for that he had confessed himself ignorant of them.[320]

Mathematics, Its Name and Parts

These sciences were first termed Μαθήματα ["mathematics"] by Pythagoras, upon consideration that all mental discipline is

Reminiscence. This comes not extrinsically to souls, as the phantasies, which are formed by sensible objects in the Imaginal world. Nor
are they an advantageous accepted knowledge, like that which is
placed in opinion. But it is excited from phenomena, and perfected
intrinsically by the cogitation converted into itself.[321]

The whole science of mathematics, the Pythagoreans divided
into four parts—attributing one to multitude, another to magnitude,
and subdividing each of these into two.[322] For multitude either sub-
sists by itself, or is considered with respect to another. Magnitude
either stands still, or is moved. Arithmetic contemplates multitude
in self; music with respect to another; geometry, unmovable magnitude; and trigonometry, moveable.

These sciences consider not multitude and magnitude simply,[323]
but in each of these, that which is determinate. For sciences consider this abstracted from infinite; that they may not in vain attempt
in each of these that which is infinite.[324] When therefore the wise
persons say thus, we conceive it is not to be understood of that multitude which is in the sensible things themselves, nor of that magnitude which we perceive in bodies. For the contemplation of these,
I think, pertains to Physic, not to mathematic. But the Maker of all
things took union and division, identity and otherness, and station
and motion, to complete the soul—and framed it of these kinds, as
Timaeus teaches.

We must conceive therefore that the intellect—consisting
according to the diversity thereof, and the division of proportions and
multitude, and knowing itself to be both one and many—proposes
number to itself; and produces them and the arithmetical knowledge
of them. According to the union of multitude and communication
with itself, and conjunction, it brings to itself music. For which reason, arithmetic excels music in antiquity, the soul itself being first
divided by the Maker, then collected by proportions. And again,
establishing the operation within itself according to its station, it
produces geometry out of itself, and one figure, and the principles
of all figures. But according to its motion, trigonometry: for she is
moved by circles. It consists always in the same manner according to
the causes of those circles, the straight and the circular. And for this

reason, likewise geometry is precedent to Trigonometry, as station is to motion.

But forasmuch as the soul produced these sciences—not looking on the excitation of Ideas, which is of infinite power, but upon the boundary of that which is limited in their several kinds[325]—therefore they say that they take infinite from multitude and magnitude, and are conversant only about finite. For the mind has placed in herself all principles both of multitude and magnitude; because being wholly of like parts within herself, and being one and indivisible, and again divisible and producing the world of ideas; it does share essential finiteness and infiniteness with the things which it does understand. But it understands according to that which is finite in them, and not according to the infiniteness of its life. This is the opinion of the Pythagoreans, and their division of the four sciences. Hitherto Proclus.

Of these four methods, which is that which ought necessarily to be learned the first (viz. that which is by nature pre-existent to the rest and chief, being as it were principle and root, and mother of the rest)?[326] The answer is Arithemetic. Not only because it is pre-existent before the rest in the Intellect of the efficient God, as an ornative and exemplary reason—according to which the Maker of the Universe caused all things to be made out of matter to its proper end, as after a προκεντημα ["a thing pricked," i.e. "traced out beforehand"]† and archetypal pattern. But also because being naturally first generated,[327] it together takes away the rest with itself, but is not taken away with them. Thus animal is first in nature before man. For taking away animal, we take away man; but not in taking away man, do we take away animal. (Of this Nicomachus discourses more largely.)

As concerning Arithmetic, Timaeus affirms that Pythagoras addicted himself chiefly to it.[328] Stobaeus says that he esteemed it above all others, and brought it to light, reducing it from the use of trading.[329] Hence Isidore and others style him the inventor of arithmetic,[330] affirming he was the first who wrote upon this subject amongst the Greeks, which was afterwards more copiously composed by Nicomachus. He studied this science exceedingly, and so much did he prefer it above all the rest, that he conceived the ultimate good of man to consist in the most exact science of numbers.[331]

Number, Its Kinds:
The First Kind, Intellectual in the Divine Mind

Number is of two kinds, the Intellectual (or immaterial) and the Sciential.[332] The intellectual is that eternal substance of number which Pythagoras, in his discourse concerning the gods, asserted to be the principle most providential of all Heaven and Earth and the nature that is between them.[333] Moreover, it is the root of divine beings, and of gods, and of daemons. This is that which he termed the principle, fountain, and root of all things. He defined it to be that which before all things exists in the Divine Mind;[334] from which and out of which all things are digested into order, and remain numbered by an indissoluble series.[335]

For all things which are ordered in the world by nature—according to an artificial course in part and in whole—appear to be distinguished and adorned by Providence and the All-creating Mind according to number. The exemplar is established by applying (as the reason of the principle before the impression of things) the number pre-existent in the intellect of God, Maker of the world. This only in intellectual, and wholly immaterial, really a substance according to which as being the most exact artificial reason, all things are perfected—Time, Heaven, Motion, the Stars—and their various revolutions.

THE OTHER KIND OF NUMBER:
SCIENTIAL, ITS PRINCIPLES

Sciential number is that which Pythagoras defines as the extension and production into act of the seminal reasons which are in the Monad, or a heap of Monads, or a progression of multitude beginning from Monad, and a regression ending in Monad.[336]

The Pythagoreans affirmed the expositive terms whereby even and odd numbers are understood to be the principles of Sciential numbers.[337] For example, of three insensible things, the Triad; of four Insensibles, the Tetrad; and so of other numbers.

They make a difference between the Monad and One, conceiving the Monad to be that which exists in intellectuals. One exists in numbers.[338] (Or as Moderatus expresses it, Monad amongst numbers, One amongst things numbered, one body being divisible into infinite. Thus numbers and things numbered differ, as incorporeals and bodies.[339])

In like manner is two amongst numbers. The Duad is indeterminate. Monad is taken according to equality and measure, Duad according to excess and defect. Mean and measure cannot admit more and less, but excess and defect (seeing that they proceed to infinite) admit it. Therefore they call the Duad indeterminate, holding number to be infinite.[340] Not that number which is separate and incorporeal, but that which is not separate from sensible things.[341]

The Two Kinds of Sciential Number, Odd and Even

Of sciential numbers, Pythagoras asserted two orders: one bounded, Odd; the other infinite, Even.[342] Even number (according to the Pythagorean definition) is that which at once admits division into the greatest and the least; into the greatest magnitudes (for halves are the greatest parts); the least in multitude (for two is the least number) according to the natural opposition of these two kinds.[343] Odd is that which cannot suffer this, but is cut into two unequals.

Herein the Pythagoreans differ from the Platonists, in that they hold not all number to be infinite, but only the Even. For even number is the cause of section into equal parts, which is infinite, and by its proper nature generates infinity in those things in which it exists.[344] But it is limited by the Odd; for that being applied to the Even, hinders its dissection into two equal parts.

Odd number is said to have been found by Pythagoras to be of Masculine virtue,[345] and proper to the Celestial Gods (to whom they sacrificed always of that number),[346] and to be full and perfect.[347] Even number is indigent, and imperfect, and Female, and proper to the subterranean deities, to whom they sacrificed Even things.[348]

Moreover, whatever is generated of Odd number is male, whatsoever of Even is female; for Even number is subject to section and passion. Odd is void of both, and is efficacious. Wherefore they call one the Male, the other the Female.[349] A number, which arises out of the power and multiplication of Even and Odd, is called ἀρρενόθηλυς, Hermaphrodite.[350]

This opinion Pythagoras seems to have derived from Zaratas, his Master. He called Duad the Mother of number, Monad the Father; and therefore they said that those numbers which resemble Monad (viz. the Odd), are the best.[351]

Odd Numbers they called Gnomons, because being added to Squares, they keep the same figures; so Gnomons do in Geometry.[352]

Symbolic Numbers

The Pythagoreans, using the mathematical sciences as degrees of preparations to the contemplations of the things that are, were studiously addicted to the business of numbers for this reason. (So says Moderatus of Gades, who learnedly comprised their opinions in eleven books.[353])

Seeing they could not clearly explain the first forms and principles in discourse (those being the most difficult to understand and express), they had recourse to numbers for the better explication of their doctrine, imitating geometricians and such as teach to read. For as these, going about to explain letters and their powers, recur to marks—saying that these are, as it were, the first elements of learning—nevertheless, afterwards they tell us that they are not the elements, but that the true elements are known by them. And as the geometricians, not being able to express incorporeal forms in words, have recourse to the description of figures saying, "This is a triangle"; yet not meaning that this which falls under the sight is a triangle, but that which has the same figure and which is by the help thereof, and represents the knowledge of a triangle to the mind.

The same did the Pythagoreans in the first reasons and forms. For seeing they could not in words express incorporeal forms and first principles, they had recourse to demonstration by numbers. And thus they called the reason of unity and identity, and equality, and the cause of amicable conspiration, and of sympathy, and of the conservation of the universe which continues according to the same, and in the same manner, ONE. For the One which is in particulars, is united to the parts and conspiring by participation of the first cause.

But the two-fold reason of diversity and inequality, and of every thing that is divisible and in mutation, and exists sometimes one way, sometimes another, they called DUAD. For the nature of the Duad in particular things is such.

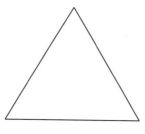

The Triangle

These reasons are not only according to the Pythagoreans, and not acknowledged by others; but we see that other philosophers also have left certain unitive powers, which comprise all things in the Universe. And amongst them there are certain reasons for equality, dissimilitude, and diversity. Now these reasons—that the way of teaching might be more perspicuous—he called by the names of Monad and Duad. But it is all one amongst them if it be called biform, or aequaliform, or diversiform.

The same reason is in other numbers, for everyone is ranked according to some powers. In the nature of things exists something which has beginning, middle and end. To such a form and nature they attributed the number Three, saying that whatsoever has a middle is triform; so they called every perfect thing. And if anything be perfect, they affirm it makes use of this principle and is adorned according to it; which, since they could not name otherwise, they made use of the term TRIAD to express it. And when they endeavor to bring us to the knowledge thereof, they lead us to it by the form of this triad. The same in other numbers.

These, therefore, are the reasons according to which the aforesaid numbers were placed. But these that follow are comprehended under one form and power, which they call *Decad quasi Dechad.*[354] Wherefore they say that ten is a perfect number, even the most perfect of all numbers; comprehending in itself all difference of numbers, all reasons, species, and proportions. For if the nature of the universe be defined according to the reasons and proportions of numbers—

and that which is produced, and increased, and perfected, proceeds according to the reasons of numbers—and the Decad comprehends every reason of number, and every proportion, and all species: Why should not nature itself be termed by the name of Ten, the most perfect number? Hitherto Moderatus.

Thus, from the symbolical use of numbers proceeded a multiplex variety of names, attributed to them by Pythagoras and his followers. Of which we shall now speak more particularly, beginning with the Monad.

CHAPTER 5

The Monad

The Monad is a quantity, which in the decrease of multitude, being deprived of all number, receives mansion and station. For below quantity, Monad cannot retreat.[355] The Monad therefore seems to be so called, either from standing; or from remaining (μένειν) always in the same condition; or from its separation (μεμονῶσθαι†) from multitude.

To the Monad are attributed these names:

Mind,[356] because the mind is stable, and every way alike, and has the preeminence.[357]

Hermaphrodite,[358] because it is both male and female, odd and even.[359] It partakes of both natures; being added to the even, it makes odd, to the odd, even.[360]

God, because it is the beginning and end of all, itself having neither beginning nor end.[361]

Good, for such is the nature of one.[362]

Matter, receptacle of all,[363] because it produces Duad, which is properly matter.[364]

Chaos, Confusion, Contemperation, Obscurity, Chasm, Tartarus, Styx, Horror, Impermanence, Subterranean Gulf, Lethe, Rigid Virgin, Atlas, Axis, Sume, Pyralios, Morpho.[365]

Tower of Jupiter,[366] *Custody of Jupiter, Throne of Jupiter.*[367] From the great power which the center has in the universe, being able to restrain the general circular motion, as if the custody of the Maker of all things were constituted therein.[368]

Seminal Reason,[369] because this one only is one to the Retractors and is alone; and the rest are procreated of it, and it is the only seminary of all numbers.[370]

Apollo Prophet.[371]

Prometheus, as being author of life.[372]

Geniture, because without it no number has being.[373]

Substance,[374] because substance is primary.[375]

Cause of Truth, Simple Exemplar, Constitution of Symphony.[376]

In greater and lesser, *Equal;* in intention and remission, *Middle;* in multitude, *Mean.*[377] In time, *Now,* the present[378] because it consists in one part of time which is always present.[379]

Ship, Chariot, Friend, Life, Beatitude.[380]

Form (or *Species*), because it circumscribes, comprehends, and terminates,[381] and because it produces the rest of the effects.[382]

Jupiter,[383] because he is father and head of the gods,[384] whence the Pythagorean verse:

Hear noble number, sire of gods and men.

Love, Concord, Piety, Friendship, because it is so connected, that it cannot be divided into parts.[385]

Proteus, as containing all forms.[386]

Mnemosyne.[387]

Vesta, or *Fire.*[388] For the nature of Monad, like Vesta, is seated in the midst of the world and keeps that seat, inclining to no side.

Polyonymous.[389]

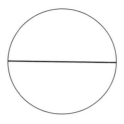

The Duad

The names of the Duad are these:

Genius, Evil.[390]

Darkness, Sinister, Unequal, Unstable, Moveable.[391]

Boldness,[392] *Fortitude,*[393] *Contention,*[394] because it proceeds to action, and first separates itself from the Monad.[395]

Matter,[396] because indefinite. Indeterminate Duad proceeds from Monad as matter. The cause of tumour and division.[397]

Cause of Dissimilars.[398]

Partition between Multitude and Monad.[399]

Equal, because in composition and permission, this only makes equality.[400] Two and two are equal to twice two.

Unequal, Defect, Superfluity,[401] according to the motion of matter.[402]

Only Inform, Indefinite, Indeterminate.[403] Because from a triangle and triad, polygons are actually procreated to infinity; in Monad they exist all potentially together; but of two right lines or angles is made no figure.[404]

Only Principle of Purity, yet not even, nor evenly even, nor unevenly even, nor evenly uneven.[405]

Erato,[406] because through love applying itself to Monad, as the species it procreated the rest of the effects.[407]

Harmony.[408]

Tolerance,[409] because it first underwent separation.[410]

Root, but not in act.[411]

Feet of Fountain-abounding Ida.[412]

Top, Phanes.[413]

Justice, because of its two equal parts.[414]

Isis, Nature, Rhea, Jove's mother, Fountain of Distribution, Phrygia, Lydia, Dindymene, Ceres, Eleusinia.[415]

Diana,[416] because the Moon takes many settings from all the Fixed Stars, and because she is forked, and called half-moon.[417]

Love, Dictinna, Aeria, Asteria, DiSamos, Station, Venus, Dione, Micheia, Cythereia, Ignorance, Ignobility, Falsity, Permission, Otherness, Contention, Diffidence, Fat, Death,[418] *Impulse*.[419]

Opinion, because it is true and false.[420]

Motion, Generation, Mutation, Division.[421] (Meursius reads δια-´κρεσις,† *Judgment*) *Longitude*,[422] or rather, *First Longitude*,[423] *Augmentation, Composition, Communion*.[424]

Misfortune, Enduring, because it first suffered separation,[425] *Discord*.[426]

Imposition.[427]

Marriage, Juno; Juno being both Wife and Sister to Jupiter.[428]

Soul, from motion hither and thither.[429]

Science, for all demonstration, and all credit of Science, and all Syllogism collects from some things granted, the thing in question, and easily demonstrates another; the comprehension of which things is Science.[430]

Maia.[431]

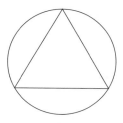

The Triad

The Triad is the first number actually odd: the first perfect number. It is middle and proportion.[432] It causes the power of the Monad to proceed to act and achieve extension. It is the first and proper joining together of unities.[433] For which reason Pythagoras said, Apollo gave oracles from a tripod; and he advised to offer libation three times.

The Names of the triad are these:

First Latitude, not simply Latitude.[434]

Saturnia, Latona, Cornucopiae, Ophion, Thetis, Harmonia, Hecate, Erana, Charitia, Polyhymnia, Pluto, Arctus, Helice. Not descending to the Ocean, *Damatrame, Dioscoria, Metis, Tridume, Triton, President of the Sea, Tritogenia, Achelous, Naclis, Agyiopeza* (perhaps ἀργυροπεζα, "silver-footed,"† as before, Thetis), *Curetis, Crataeis, Symbenia, Mariadge, Gorgonia, Phorcia, TriSamos, Lydius.*[435]

Marriage, Friendship, Peace, Concord,[436] because it collects and unites, not similars, but contraries.[437]

Justice.[438]

Prudence, Wisdom; because men order the present, foresee the future, and learn Experience by the past.[439]

Piety,[440] *Temperance.*[441] All Virtues depend upon this number, and proceed from it.

It is the *Mind*. It is the *Cause of Wisdom and Understanding*. It is *Knowledge* which is most proper to number.

It is the *power and composition of all music*, and much more of *geometry*. It has all *power in Astronomy*, and the nature and knowledge of celestials, containing and impelling it to the production of substance.

The cube of this number, Pythagoras affirmed to have the power of the lunar circle, inasmuch as the Moon goes round her orb in twenty-seven days, which the number Ternio, in Greek Τριάς , the triad gives in its cube.[442]

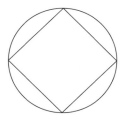

Chapter 8

The Tetrad

The Tetrad was much honored by the Pythagoreans.[443] It was esteemed the most perfect number,[444] the primary and earliest formed, which they called the root of all things, and the fountain of nature.[445]

The Tetrads are all intellectual and have an emergent order. They are, for that reason, the empyreal prefecture; they go round about the world as the Empyrean passes through all.[446]

Even God himself Pythagoras expressed by the Tetrad.

How God is a Tetrad, you will clearly find in the sacred discourse ascribed to Pythagoras, wherein God is described as the number of numbers.[447] For if all beings subsist by his eternal counsel, it is manifest, that number in every species of beings depends upon their causes. The first number is there, from thence derived hither. The determinate stop of number is the Decad, for he who would reckon further, must return to one, two, three, and number a second Decad. In like manner, a third to make up thirty, and so on; till having numbered the tenth Decad, he comes to a 100. Again, he reckons from 100 in the same manner, and so may proceed to infinite by revolution of the Decad.

Now the Tetrad is the power of the Decad; for, before we arrive at the perfection of the Decad, we find a united perfection in the Tetrad—the Decad being made up by addition of one, two, three, and four.

Moreover, the Tetrad is an arithmetical mean between one and seven, equally exceeding and exceeded in number. It wants three

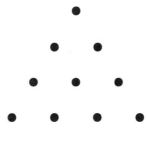

The Tetractys

of seven, and exceeds one by three. Monad, as being the mother of numbers, contains all their powers within itself.

The Hebdomad [i.e., the number seven]—as being motherless, and a virgin—possesses the second place in dignity. For it is not made up of any number within the Decad—as four is of twice two; six of twice three; eight of twice four; nine thrice three; and ten of twice five. Neither does it make up any number within the Decad— as two makes four; three makes six; five makes ten.

But the Tetrad, lying between the unbegotten Monad and the motherless Hebdomad, comprehends all powers, both of the productive and produced numbers. For this of all numbers under ten is made of a certain number, and makes a certain number; the Duad doubled makes a Tetrad, the Tetrad doubled makes eight.

Besides, the first solid figure is found in a Tetrad. For a point is correspondent to Monad, a line to Duad (because drawn from one point to another), a **superficies** to Triad (because it is the most simple of all rectilinear figures). But a solid properly agrees with the Tetrad. For the first pyramid is in a Tetrad; the base is triangular, so that at the bottom is a three, at the top one.

Furthermore, the judicative power in things is four: mind, science, opinion, and sense. For all beings are determined to be either mind, science, opinion, or sense. For which reason Pythagoras affirmed the soul of man to consist of a Tetrad.[448]

Finally, the Tetrad connects all beings, elements, numbers, seasons of the year, **Coaevous** society. Neither can we name anything which depends not on the Tetractys as its root and principle. For it is, as we have said, the maker and cause of all things—intelligible God, author of celestial and sensible good. The knowledge of these things was delivered to the Pythagoreans by Pythagoras himself. Hitherto Hierocles.

For this reason the word "Tetractys" was used by Pythagoras and his disciples as a great oath. They, likewise, out of respect to their master, forbearing his name, did swear by the person that communicated the Tetractys to them.

> Eternal Nature's Fountain I attest,
> Who the Tetractys to our Soul express't.

But Plutarch interprets this Tetractys (which he says was also called κόσμος, World) to be thirty-six, which consists of the first four odd numbers, thus:[449]

$$
\left.\begin{matrix} 1 \\ 2 \end{matrix}\right\} 3 \quad \left.\begin{matrix} 3 \\ 4 \end{matrix}\right\} 7 \quad \left.\begin{matrix} 5 \\ 6 \end{matrix}\right\} 11 \quad \left.\begin{matrix} 7 \\ 8 \end{matrix}\right\} 15 \quad \left.\begin{matrix} 3 \\ 7 \\ 11 \\ 15 \end{matrix}\right\} 36
$$

The names of the Tetrad are these:

Another Goddess, Multideity, Pantheos, Fountain of Natural Effects.[450]

Key-keeper of Nature: because the universal constitution cannot be without it. To these sciences it confers constitution and settlement, and reconciles them. Yea, it is nature itself and truth.[451]

Nature of Aeolus[452] from its various property.[453]

Hercules, Impetuosity, Most Strong, Masculine, Ineffeminate, Mercury, Vulcan, Bacchus, Soritas, Maiades, Erinnius, Socus, Dioscorus, Bassarius, Two-mother'd, of Feminine Form, of Virile performance, Bacchation.[454]

Harmony[455] because it has a **sesquitertia**.[456]

Urania the Muse.[457] *World*.[458]

Body: as a Point is one, a Line two, a Superficies three.

Soul, because it consists of mind, science, opinion and sense.[459]

First Profundity, as it is a body.[460]

Justice. The property of justice is compensation and equality. This number is the first evenly even. And whatsoever is the first in any kind is most that thing. This, they said, was the Tetrad, because being quadrate, it is divided into equals and is itself equal.[461]

CHAPTER 9

THE PENTAD

The Pentad is the first combination of both kinds of number, even and odd—two and three.[462] Its names are these:

Ἀνεικία, *Reconciliation*,[463] because the fifth element, Aether, is free from the disturbances of the other four.[464]

Alteration, Light, because it changed that which was separated three-fold into the Identity of its Sphere, moving circularly and engendering light.[465]

Justice,[466] because it divides ten into two equal parts.[467]

The least and top of livelihood.[468]

Nemesis,[469] because it distributes conveniently celestial, divine, and natural elements.[470]

Bubastia,[471] because worshipped at Bubastus in Egypt.[472]

Venus, Gamelia, Androgynia, Cytherea, Zoneia,[473] *Marriage,*[474] because it connects a masculine and feminine number:[475] consisting of two (the first even), and three (the first odd).[476]

Κυκλιοῦχος , *President of Circles.*[477]

Semi-Goddess,[478] not only as being the half of ten (which is divine), but for that it is placed in the middle.[479]

Tower of Jupiter.

Didymaea, or Twin,[480] because it divides ten into two.[481]

Firm Axis.[482]

Immortal, Pallas, implying the fifth essence.[483]

Καρδίατις , *Cordial*[484] from similitude with the heart.[485]

Providence, because it makes unequals equal.[486]

Τροφος, *Sound,* the fifth being the first **diasteme**.[487]

Nature: because multiplied by itself, it returns into itself. For as Nature, receiving wheat in seed—and introducing many forms by altering and changing it—at last returns it wheat at the end of the whole mutation, restoring the beginning; so, while other numbers multiplied in themselves are increased and end in other numbers; only five and six multiplied by themselves, represent and retain themselves.[488]

This number represent all superior and inferior beings. For it is either the supreme God, or the mind-born of God, wherein are contained the species of all things; or the Soul of the World, which is the fountain of all souls, or celestials, down to us; or it is terrestial nature. And so the Pentad is replete with all things.[489]

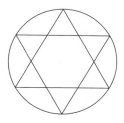

CHAPTER 10

THE HEXAD

The Pythagoreans held the number Six to be perfect, respecting (as Clement Alexandrinus conceives) the creation of the world according to the Prophet.

The names of the Hexad, are these:

Form of Form, Articulation of the Universe, Maker of the Soul, Harmony,[490] because it has the power to produce a vital habit. Whence it is called *Hexad,* ἀπὸ τῆς ἕξεως ; and *Harmony,* because all Souls are Harmonic.[491]

Regarding 'ουλομέλεια,† *Perfection of Parts,*[492] the Pythagoreans called it thus, imitating Orpheus—either as being the only number under ten which is whole and equal in its parts; or because the whole Universe is divided into parts by it.[493]

Venus,[494] because it procreates harmony. Six to twelve is a **diapason concord.** Six to nine is a **hemiolius.** Six to eight is **epitrites,** that is a diatessaron concord. Whence it is named Venus, who was the Mother of Harmony.[495]

Ζύγια ["yoke"],[496] Γαμήλια ["wedding"],[497] Γάμος, *Marriage,*[498] because of the mixture of the first even and first odd.[499] For as marriage procreates by a male and female, so this number is generated of three (which is odd and called male), and of two (which is even and called female); for two times three make six.[500] It produces children like the parents.[501]

Ζυγίτης ["central oarsman"],† Φιλοτησία ["friendship"],[502] or Φιλέωσις, *Conciliation*, because it conciliates the male and female.[503]

Ὑγίεια, *Health*,[504] a triple triangle, which being alternately conjoined within itself constitutes a figure of five lines. They used it as a symbol to those of their own sect, and called it ὑγίεια, Health.[505]

Ἀκμὼν, *Anvil*;[506] quasi ἀκάματον, *unwearied;* because the principal triangles of the mundane elements have a share in it, being each of them Six, if measured by three perpendiculars.[507]

Ἑκατηβελέτις ["Hecate's missile"], being compounded of, and, as it were, Βολήσασαν ["hurled forth"],† the triad which is called Hecate.[508]

Trioditis: from the nature of that goddess; or because the Hexad first assumes the three motions of intervals, being divided into two parts, each of which is on each side.[509]

Διοχρονία, the distribution of all time, of things above the earth, and under the earth, which is done by the Hexad in the Zodiac. Or because Time is of the nature of the Triad, consisting of three parts, and the Hexad consists of two Triads.[510]

Persaea, Triform.[511]

Amphitrite;[512] because it has a triad on each side.[513]

Neighbor to Justice,[514] as being nearest to 5 (which is named Justice.[515])

Thalia, the Muse,[516] because of the harmony of the rest.[517]

Panacaea,[518] in respect to health mentioned already; or, a *Panarceia* (omni-sufficience, endued with parts sufficient for totality).[519]

Μεσευθὺς, *Middle-Right,* being in the midst between two and ten, equidistant from both.[520]

World, because the world, as the Hexad, is often seen to consist of contraries by harmony.[521]

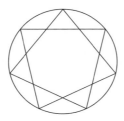

The Heptad

The Heptad was so called, quasi σεπτὰς, σεβα σμοῦ ἄξιος, worthy of veneration;[522] for Pythagoras held this number to be most proper to religion.[523] He also held that it is perfect.[524] And thence it was, as the Pythagoreans conceived, that creatures born in the seventh month live.[525]

The names of the Heptad, are these.

Fortune, Occasion,[526] because it occurs casually and opportunely to everything.[527] Whatsoever is best amongst sensible things, by which the seasons of the year and their periods are orderly complete. Participates of the Hebdomad,[528] the Moon having seven days, measures all time.[529]

Ἀμήτωρ, *Motherless, Virgin,*[530] *Minerva,* as being a virgin, unmarried, not born of a mother (odd number), nor of a father (even number); but out of the crown of the father of all, Monad.[531]

Mars,[532] Ἀκρεωσις ["citadel"].[533]

Ageleia,[534] an epither of Minerva.[535]

Ἀτρυτόνη ["The Unwearied"]†.[536]

Φυλακιτὶς, *Custody,*[537] because the stars which guard the universe are seven.[538]

Ὀβριμοπάτρα, *Tritogenia*, Γλαυκῶπις ["Blue-eyed"],† Ἀλαλκο-μένεια ["Protectress"],† Παντευχία ["in full armor"], Ἐργάνη ["worker"],† Πολυαρήτη ["much desired"], Οὐλομέλεια ["sound of limbs"],† *Stock of Amalphea, Aegis, Osiris, Dream, Voice, Sound, Clio the Muse, Judgment, Adrastia.*[539]

Τελέσφορος, *leading to the end*†;[540] because by it all are led to the end.[541]

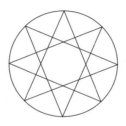

CHAPTER 12

THE OGDOAD

The Ogdoad, they said, was the first cube, and the only number evenly even under ten.[542]

The Names of it are these:

Panarmonia,[543] because of its excellent convenience.[544]

Cadmaea, Mother, Rhea, Θηλύποιος ["making weak"],† *Cibele, Dindymens,* Πολιοῦχος ["guardian of the city"],† *Love, Friendship, Council, Prudence, Orcia, Themis, Law,* Ἡλιτόμηνα ["untimely born"],† *Euterpe* the Muse, Ἀσφάλεια ["stability"],† Ἕδρασμα ["placing in position"],†[545] *Neptune*.[546]

Justice, because it is first resolved into numbers, especially equal.[547]

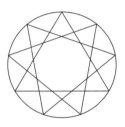

CHAPTER 13

The Ennead

The Ennead is the first square of an odd number. Its names are these:

Ocean, Horizon, because number has nothing beyond it, but it revolves all within it.[548]

Prometheus, because it suffers no number to exceed it, and justly being a perfect ternary.[549]

Concord,[550] *Perasia,*[551] *Halius,*[552] because it does not permit the consent of number to be dispersed beyond it, but collects it.[553]

Ἀνεικεία ["reconciliation"]† because of the revolution to Monad.[554]

Ὁμοίωσις ["similitude"], because it is the first odd triangle.[555]

Vulcan, because to it, as fellow ruler and relation, there is no return.[556]

Juno, because the sphere of the Air has the ninth place.[557]

Sister and Wife to Jupiter, from conjunction with unity.[558]

Ἑκάεργος ["far-darting"],† because there is no shooting beyond it.[559]

Paean, Nysseis, Agyica, Ennalios, Agelia, Tritogegenia, Suada, Curetis, Proserpina, Hyperion, Terpsichore the Muse.[560]

Τελέσφορος ["bringing to the end"],† Τέλειος ["perfection"], because nine months complete the infant.

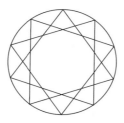

CHAPTER 14

THE DECAD

Ten, according to the Pythagoreans, is the greatest number—as well for that it is the Tetractys, as that it comprehends all arithmetical and harmonical proportions.[561] Pythagoras said that ten is the nature of number: because all nations, Greeks and Barbarians, reckon to it; and when they arrive at it, return to the Monad.[562]

Names of the Decad:

World, because according to the Decad all things are ordered in general and particular.[563] The Decad comprehends all numbers, the world all form;[564] for the same reason it is termed also Sphere.[565]

Heaven,[566] because it is the most perfect term of number, as heaven is the receptacle of all things.[567] The Decad being a perfect number, the Pythagoreans desired to apply to it those things which are contained in Heaven—where finding but nine (the orbs, the seven planets, and the heaven of Fixed Stars, with the earth), they added an Antichthon (another earth opposite to this) and made Ten; by this means they accommodated them to the Decad.[568]

Fate,[569] because there is no property neither in numbers nor beings, according to the composition of number, which is not seminally contained in the Decad.[570]

Age.[571]

Power,[572] from the command it has over all other numbers.[573]

Faith, Necessity.[574]

Atlas, for as Atlas is fabled to sustain heaven with his shoulders, so the Decad holds all the spheres as the diameter of them all.[575]

Unwearied, God, Phanes, Sun, Urania, Memory, Mnemosyne.[576]

First Square, because it is made of the first four numbers: one plus two plus three plus four.[577]

Κλειδοῦχος ["key-bearer"], as the magazine and confinement of all proportions,[578] or Κλαδοῦχος ["branch-bearer"], because other numbers branch out of it.[579]

Παντέλεια ["the absolute"], because it perfects all number, comprehends within itself all the nature of even and odd, moved and unmoved, good and ill.[580]

CHAPTER 15

DIVINATION BY NUMBERS

Upon the near affinity which Pythagoras (following Orpheus) conceived to be between the gods and numbers, he collected a kind of Arithmancy. This he not only practiced himself, but communicated to his disciples—as is manifest from Iamblichus, who cites this fragment of the Sacred Discourse, a book ascribed to him.

"Concerning the gods of Pythagoras, son of Mnesarchus, I learned this when I was initiated at Libeth in Thrace, Aglaophemus administering the rites to me. Orpheus, son of Calliope, instructed by his mother in the Pangaean mountain, said that number is an eternal substance, the most provident principle of the universe: heaven, and earth, and middle nature; likewise the root of divine beings, and of gods and daemons."[581]

Hence (says Iamblichus) it is manifest that Pythagoras received from the traditions of Orpheus the doctrine that numbers hold the determinate essence of the gods. By these numbers he framed a wonderful system of divination and service of the gods. This had the closest affinity to numbers, as may be evinced from hence (for it is requisite to give an instance for confirmation of what we say).

The student of Pythagoras, Abaris, performed those kinds of sacrifices to which he was accustomed, and diligently practiced divination after the ways of the Barbarians by victims (principally of cocks,whose entrals they conceived to be most exact for inspection). Pythagoras, not willing to take him away from his study of truth; yet, in order to direct him by a safer way, without blood and slaughter (moreover esteeming the cock sacred to the Sun), taught Abaris to find out all truth by the science of arithmetic.[582] Thus says Iamblichus, who writes elsewhere that Pythagoras, instead of the art of divining by sacrifices, taught that kind of prediction which is by numbers, conceiving that to be more sacred and divine, and more agreeable to the celestial nature of the gods.

This hint some have taken to impose upon the world, under the name of Pythagoras, an **Onomantic** kind of arithmetic—assigning particular numbers to the letters of the alphabet, to the planets, to the days of the week, and to the signs of the Zodiac. They thereby resolve questions concerning nativities, victory, life or death, journeys, prosperity or adversity. Such a system is set down by Fludd,[583] who adds that Apollonius has delivered another way of divination according to the Pythagorean doctrine; affirming that future things may be prognosticated by virtue of a wheel invented by Pythagoras. Hereby is treated of life and death, of fugitives, of litigious business, of victories, of the sex of children unborn, and infinite others of the like kind. But concerning the exposition of the wheel, and the true position of numbers, therein the ancient authors have written very inconstantly. So that the truth of its composition cannot be comprehended otherwise than by conjecture. What ancient authors he means I know not. The citation of Apollonius I doubt to be no less an assumption than the wheel itself, which Trithemius and others acknowledge to be an invention of later times.[584]

MUSIC

The Pythagoreans define music as an apt composition of contraries, a union of many, and consent of differents.[585] For it not only coordinates rhythms and modulation, but all manner of systems. Its end is to unite, and aptly conjoin. God is the reconciler of things discordant, and his chief work—according to music and medicine—is to reconcile enmities. In music consists the agreement of all things, and the aristocracy of the universe. For what is harmony in the world, in a city is good government, in a family temperance.

Of many sects (says Ptolemy) that were conversant about harmony, the most eminent were two: the Pythagorean and Aristoxenian.[586] Pythagoras judged it by reason, Aristoxenus by sense.[587] The Pythagoreans, not crediting the relation of hearing in all those things wherein it is requisite, adapted reasons to the differences of sounds, contrary to those which are perceived by the senses. So that by this criterion (reason), they gave occasion of calumny to such as were of a different opinion.[588]

Hence the Pythagoreans named that which we now call Harmonic, "Canonic"; not from the canon or instrument, as some imagine, but from rectitude—since reason finds out that which is right by using harmonic canons or rules.[589] Even of all sorts of instruments framed by harmonic rules (pipes, flutes, and the like), they call the exercise canonic; which, although it be not canonic, yet is so termed because it is made according to the reasons and theorems of canonic. The instrument therefore seems to be so denominated from its canonic affection.

A follower of canonic doctrine is a "harmonic" who is conversant by ratiocination about that which consists of harmony. Musicians and harmonics differ. Musicians are those harmonics who begin from sense; but canonics are Pythagoreans, who are also called harmonics. Both sorts are termed by the general name, Musicians.

Voice, Its Kinds

Of human voice, those of the Pythagorean school said that there are (as of one genus) two species. One they properly named Continuous, the other Diastematic (intermissive), framing appellations from the accidents pertaining to each. The diastematic they conceived to be that which is sung and rests upon every note, and manifests the mutation which is in all its parts. It is free from confusion and divided and disjoined by the magnitudes which are in the several sounds, as accumulated but not mixed up. The parts of the voice, being applied mutually to one another, may easily be separated and distinguished, and are not destroyed together. Such is the musical kind of voice, which to the knowing, manifests all sounds of what magnitude everyone participates. For if a man use it not after this manner, he is not said to sing, but to speak. [590]

The other kind they conceived to be continuous, by which we discourse one to another, and read. We are not constrained to use any manifest distinct tensions of sounds, but to connect the discourse till we have finished that which we intended to speak. For if any man, in disputing or apologizing or reading, makes distinct magnitudes in the several sounds, taking off and transferring the voice from one to another, he is not said to read but to sing.

Human voice, having in this manner two parts, they conceived that there are two places which each in passing possesses. The place of continuous voice—which is by nature infinite in magnitude— receives its proper term from that wherewith the speaker began until he ends; that is the place from the beginning of his speech to his conclusive silence; so that the variety thereof is in our power. But the place of diastematic voice is not in our power, but natural. And this likewise is bounded by different effects. The beginning is that which is first heard, the end that which is last pronounced. For from thence we begin to perceive the magnitude of sounds, and their mutual commutations, from whence first our hearing seems to operate.

Whereas it is possible there may be some more obscure sounds perfected in nature which we cannot perceive or hear. As for instance, in things weighed there are some bodies which seem to have no weight, such as straws, bran, and the like. But when, as by the adding together of such bodies some beginning of ponderosity appears, then we say they first come within the compass of static. So, when a low sound increases by degrees, that which first of all may be perceived by the ear we make the beginning of the place which musical voice requires.

First Music in the Planets

The names of sounds, in all probability, were derived from the seven stars, which move circularly in the heavens and compass the earth.[591] (The circular motion of these bodies must of necessity cause a sound, for air being struck from the intervention of the blow sends forth a noise. Nature herself constraining that the violent collision of two bodies should end in sound.[592])

Now (say the Pythagoreans) all bodies which are carried round with noise—one yielding and gently receding to the other—must necessarily cause sounds different from each other, in the magnitude and swiftness of voice and in place. These, according to the reason of their proper sounds, or their swiftness, or the orbs of repressions, in which the impetuous transportation of each is performed—are either more fluctuating, or on the contrary, more reluctant. But these three differences of magnitude, celerity, and local distance, are manifestly existent in the planets. These planets are constantly with sound circling around through the aetherial diffusion, whence every one is called ἀστὴρ [star], as void of στάσις, station; and ἀεὶθέών, always in course; whence God and Aether are called Θεὸς and Ἀεθηρ.[593]

Moreover the sound which is made by striking the air induces into the ear something sweet and musical, or harsh and discordant. For if a certain observation of numbers moderates the blow, it effects a harmony consonant to itself; but if it be haphazard and not governed by measures, there proceeds a troubled unpleasant noise which offends the ear.[594] Now in heaven nothing is produced casually or randomly; but all things there proceed according to divine rules and settled proportions. Whence it may be irrefutably inferred that the sounds which proceed from the conversion of the Celestial Spheres are musical. For sound necessarily proceeds from motion—and the proportion, which is in all divine things causes the harmony of this sound. This Pythagoras, first of all the Greeks, conceived in his mind. He understood that the Spheres sounded something concordant because of the necessity of proportion which never forsakes celestial beings.

From the motion of Saturn, which is the highest and furthest from us, the gravest sound in the **diapason concord** is called **Hypate**, because ὕπατον signifys highest. From the Lunary, which is the lowest and nearest the earth, **neate**, for νέατον signifys lowest.[595] From those which are next these, viz. from the motion of Jupiter who is under Saturn, **parypate**; and of Venus, who is above the Moon, **paraneate**. Again, from the middle, which is the Sun's motion, the fourth from each part, **mese**, which is distant by a **diatessaron** in the **Heptachord** from both extremes according to the ancient way; as the Sun is the fourth from each extreme of the seven planets, being in the middle. Again, from those which are nearest the Sun on each side: from Mars who is placed between Jupiter and the Sun, **hypermese**, which is likewise termed **lichanus**; and from Mercury who is placed between Venus and the Sun, **paramese**.

Pythagoras, by Musical proportion, calls that a Tone by how much the Moon is distant from the Earth; from the Moon to Mercury the half of that space; and from Mercury to Venus almost as much. From Venus to the Sun **sesqidulple**; from the Sun to Mars a tone (that is as far as the Moon is from the Earth); from Mars to Jupiter half; and from Jupiter to Saturn half; and thence to the Zodiac sesquiduple. Thus there are made seven tones: which they call a Diapason harmony, that is an universal concord, in which Saturn moves in the **Doric** mood, Jupiter in the **Phrygian**, and in the rest the like.[596]

The sounds made by the seven planets and the Sphere of Fixed Stars, and that which is above us (termed by them Antichthon), Pythagoras affirmed to be the Nine Muses. But the composition and symphony, and, as it were, connection of them all—whereof as being eternal and unbegotten, each is a part and portion—he named Mnemosyne.

The Octochord

Now Pythagoras, first of all, left the middle sound by conjunction, being itself compared to the two extremes, should render only a diatessaron harmony, both to the neate and to the hypate. But that we might have greater variety, the two extremes making the fullest concord each to other, that is to say the concord of diapason, which consists in a double proportion.[597] Inasmuch as it could not be done by two Tetrachords, he added an eighth sound, inserting it between the mese and paramese—setting it from the mese a whole tone, and from the paramese a semitone. So that which was formerly the paramese in the Heptachord is still the third from the neate, both in name and place. But that which was now inserted is the fourth from the neate, and has a harmony unto it of diatessaron—which before, the mese had unto the hypate.[598]

But the tone between them, that is the mese, and the inserted called the paramese, instead of the former, to whichever Tetrachord it be added, whether to that which is at the hypate, being of the lower; or to that of the neate, being of the higher; will render diapente concord. This is either way a system consisting both of the Tetrachord itself, and the additional tone; as the diapente-proportion (viz. **sesquialtera**) is found to be a system of **sesquitertia**, and **sesquioctava**; the Tone therefore is sesquioctava.[599] Thus the interval of four chords, and of five, and of both conjoined together, called diapason, and the tone inserted between the two Tetrachords, being after this manner apprehended by Pythagoras, were determined to have this proportion in numbers.

CHAPTER 4

The Arithmetical Proportions of Harmony

Pythagoras is said to have first found out the proportion and concord of sounds one to another: the Diatessaron in sesquitertia, the Diapente in sesquialtera, the Diapason in duple.[600] The occasion and manner is related by Censorinus,[601] Boethius,[602] Macrobius,[603] and others; but more exactly by Nicomachus[604] thus:

Being in an intense thought, whether he might invent any instrumental help for the ear, solid and infallible—such as the sight has by a compass, and a rule, and by a diopter; or the touch by a balance, or by the invention of measures—as he passed by a smith's shop, by a happy chance he heard the iron hammers striking upon the anvil, and rendering sounds most consonant one to another in all combinations except one. He observed in them these three concords: the diapason, the diapente, and the diatessaron. But that which was between the diatessaron and the diapente, he found to be a discord in itself, though otherwise useful for the making up of the greater of them (the diapente).

Apprehending this to come to him from God as a most happy thing, he hastened into the shop. By various trials he found the difference of the sounds to be according to the weight of the hammers—and not according to the force of those who struck, nor according to the fashion of the hammers, nor according to the turning of the iron which was in beating out. Having taken exactly the weight of the hammers,[605] he went straightaway home. He tied four strings of the same substance, length, swiftness, and twist [606] to a beam on one side of the room, and then extended and fastened the other end of the strings to the wall on the other side of the room (lest any difference might arise from thence, or might be suspected to arise from the properties of several beams). Upon each of them he hung a different weight, fastening it at the lower end, and making the length of the strings altogether equal. Then striking the strings by two at a time interchangeably, he found out the aforesaid concords, each in its own combination.

For that which was stretched by the greatest weight, in respect of that which was stretched by the least weight, he found to sound a diapason. The greatest weight was of twelve pounds, the least of six. Thence he determined that the diapason did consist in double proportion, which the weights themselves did show. Next he found that the greatest to the least but one, which was of eight pounds, sounded a diapente. Whence he inferred this to consist in the proportion called sesquialtera, in which proportion the weights were one to another. But unto that which was less than itself in weight, yet greater than the rest, being of nine pounds, he found it to sound a diatessaron. He discovered that proportionably to the weights, this concord was sesquitertia, which string to nine pounds is naturally sesquialtera to the least. For nine to six is so (viz. sesquialtera) as the least but one, which is eight, was to that which had the weight six, in proportion sesquitertia. And twelve to eight is sesquialtera. And that which is in the middle between diapente and diatessaron, whereby diapente exceeds diatessaron, is confirmed to be in sesquioctava proportion, in which nine is to eight. The system of both was called Diapente, that is, both of the diapente and diatessaron joined together, as duple proportion is compounded of sesquialtera and sesquitertia, such as are two, eight, six. Or on the contrary, of diatessaron and diapente, as duple proportion is compounded of sesquitertia and sesquialtera, as twelve, nine, six being taken in that order.

Applying both his hand and ear to the weights which he had hung—and by them confirming the proportion of the relations—he did ingeniously transfer the common result of the strings upon the cross-beam, to the bridge of an Instrument, which he called Χορδο-τόνος ["Stretched with strings"]. And as for stretching them proportionably to the weights, he did transfer that to an answerable screwing of the pegs. Making use of this foundation as an infallible rule, he extended the experiment to many kinds of instruments: cymbals, pipes, flutes, monochords, triangles, and the like. And he found, that this conclusion made by numbers was consonant without variation in all.

That sound which proceeded from the number six, he named hypate; that which from the number eight, mese, being sesquitertia to the other; that from nine, paramese, being a tone sharper than

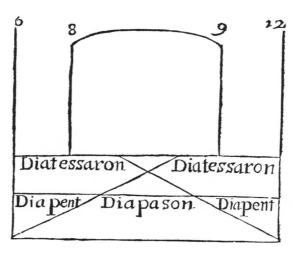

Arithmetical proportions of harmony
From Thomas Stanley, *The History of Philosophy*

the mese, viz. sesquioctave; that from twelve, neate. And supplying the middle spaces according to the diatonic kind, with proportional sounds, he so ordered the Octochord with convenient numbers: duple, sesquialtera, sesquitertia, and (the difference of these two last) sesquioctava.

Thus he found the progress by a natural necessity from the lowest to the highest according to the diatonical kind; from which again he did declare the Chromatic and Enharmonic kinds.

CHAPTER 5

The Division of the Diapason,
According to the Diatonic Kind

This Diatonic kind seems naturally to have these degrees and pro-gresses: **hemitone**, tone and tone (half-note, whole note, and whole note). This is the system Diatessaron, consisting of two tones, and that which is called a hemitone. Then another tone being inserted, Diapente is made, being a system of three tones and a hemitone. Then, in order after this, there being another diatessaron, that is to say, another sesquitertia. So that in the more ancient Heptachord, all fourths from the lowest sound a diatessaron one to another: the hemitone taking the first, second, and third place, according to the progression in the Tetrachord. The Pythagorean Octochord is a con-junction of a system of the Tetrachord and the Pentachord, and that either jointly of two Tetrachords, or disjointly of two Tetrachords, separated from one another by a tone. Here, the procession will begin from the lowest. So that every fifth sound will make a diap-ente, the hemitone passing into four places, the first, the second, the third, and the fourth.

CHAPTER 6

The Canon of the Monochord

Pythagoras, as Timaeus says, discovered the Canon of one Chord—that is the rule of the Monochord.[607] Aristides relates that a little before he died, he exhorted his friends to play on the Monochord; thereby implying that the height which is in Music is to be received rather by the Intellect through numbers, than by the sense through the ears.[608]

Duris (cited by Porphyry) mentions a brazen tablet set up in the temple of Juno by Arimnestus, son of Pythagoras, on which were graven, besides other arts, a Musical canon. This was afterwards taken away by Simon, a musician, who arrogated the canon to himself and published it as his own.[609]

The division of the canon, says Theon, is made by the Tetractys in the Decad, which consists of a Monad, a Duad, a Triad, and a Tetrad—one, two, three, four.[610] For it comprehends a sesquitertia, a sesquialtera, a duple, a triple, and a quadruple proportion. The section of the Pythagorean canon according to the intention of Pythagoras himself, not as Erastosthenes misunderstood it, or Thrasyllus (whose operation Theon sets down), but as Timaeus the Locrean (whom Plato also follows) to twenty-seven.[611] Nicomachus mentions it, as intending to deliver it in his larger Treatise of Music.[612] See also Euclid,[613] Aristides Quintilianus,[614] and others.

CHAPTER 7

INSTITUTION BY MUSIC

Conceiving that the first institution of men was to be made by sense—so that a man might see those fair figures and forms, and might hear the most excellent music—he first began teaching music by songs and rhythms. By these, the cures of manners and passions were made, and the harmonies of the faculties of their souls were reduced to their primitive dispositions, and cures of distempers, both of body and mind, were invented by him.[615]

And that music which was most worthy to be taken notice of, he reserved for his disciples—those which were called ἐξαρτύσεις ["preparations"] and ἐπαφὰς ["contact, touch"],† both by weight and by sound—he composed them harmonically in a strange way. He made commixtures of those tones which are called Diatonic, Chromatic, and Enharmonic. By means of these, he changed all the passions of the mind which were newly raised in them without reason— and which did procure griefs, angers, pities, unseemly loves, fears, all kind of desires, vexations, appetites, softnesses, idlenesses, and impetuosities— correcting and directing every one of these towards virtue, by convenient harmonies, as by certain effectual medicines.

And at night when his disciples went to sleep, he delivered them from all the noises and troubles of the day, and purified the perturbations of their minds, and rendered their sleeps quiet with good dreams and predictions. And when they rose again from their beds, he freed them from the drowsiness of the night, from faintness and sluggishness, by certain proper songs, either set to the Lute or some high voice.

As for himself, he never played on an instrument or anything. But he had it within him; and by an inconceivable kind of divinity, he applied his ears and mind unto the harmony of the world, which he alone did understand. And he understood the universal harmony and consent of the spheres, and those stars that move in them, which make a more full and excellent music than mortals. This they do by reason of their motion, and of unequal and differing swiftnesses and bignesses, overtaking one another, all of which are ordered and disposed in a most musical proportion one towards another. Being beautified with various perfections wherewith he was endowed, as having likewise the command of an orderly mind, as we may say, exercising it—he framed some representations of these sounds to exhibit them as much as was possible, imitating (that music) chiefly by instruments or the voice alone.

For he conceived that to himself only, of all upon the earth, were intelligible and audible the universal sounds from the natural fountain and root. And he thought himself worthy to be taught and to learn, and to be assimilated by desire and imitation to the celestials, as one that was organized in the parts of the body by the deity which begot him. But it was sufficient for other men that they, always looking upon him, and such things as they received from him, be benefited by images and examples; since they were not able to lay hold on the first clear archetypes of all things. As to them who cannot look upon the Sun by reason of its splendor, we show the eclipse either in a pond of water, or by some bored pitched thing, or by some dark-colored glass, searing the weakness of their eyes, and framing another way of perception instead of looking on it, to those who love such things, though something inferior.

This, Empedocles seems to imply, concerning the extraordinary and divine constitution of Pythagoras above others, when he said:

> Amongst these was one in things sublimest, skilled
> His mind with all the wealth of learning filled.
> He sought whatever Sages did invent;
> And while his thoughts were on this work intent,
> All things that are, he easily surveyed,
> And search through ten or twenty ages made.

Intimating by sublimest things, he surveyed all things that are. And the wealth of the mind and the like, the exquisite and accurate constitution of Pythagoras was beyond others, both for body and mind, in seeing, hearing, and understanding.

CHAPTER 8

MEDICINE BY MUSIC

Pythagoras conceived that music contributed much to health if used properly; for he was accustomed to make use of this purification, not perfunctorily.[616] This he called medicine by music, which kind of melody he exercised about the springtime. He seated him who played on the lute in the midst, and those who could sing sat round about him; and so he playing, they made a consort of some excellent pleasant verses, wherewith they seemed exhilarated and decently composed.

They likewise at another time made use of music as of a medicine; and there were certain pleasant verses framed tending much against the affections and diseases of the mind, and against the dejections and corrodings of the same. Moreover, he composed other music against anger and malice, and all such disorders of the mind. There was also another kind of music and song invented, against unlawful desires. He likewise used dancing. He used no musical instrument but the lute. Wind-instruments he conceived to have an ignoble sound, and to be only fit for the common people, but nothing generous.

He likewise made use of the words of Homer and Hesiod for the rectifications of the mind. It is reported that Pythagoras, by a spondaic verse out of the works[617] (perhaps of Hesiod, whose poem bears that title, ἔργα ["work"]†), by a player on the flute, assuaged the madness of a young man of Tauromenium. He, being drunk, and having employed all the night lasciviously with his mistress, was going about to burn the door of his rival's house; for he was exasperated and enflamed by the Phrygian mood. But Pythagoras, who was at that time busied in observing the stars, immediately appeased and reclaimed him by persuading the piper to change his air into the spondaic mood. Whereupon the young man being suddenly composed went quietly home—who but a little before would by no means hear the least exhortation from Pythagoras, but threatened and reviled him. In like manner Empedocles, when a young man, drew his sword upon Anchitus his host (for that he had in public judgment condemned his father to death). Empedocles was about to have killed him, when Pythagoras straightway changing his tune, sung out of Homer:

Nepenthe calming anger, easing grief.

And by that means freed Anchitus his host from death, and the young man from the crime of murder; who from thence forward became one of his disciples, eminent amongst them.

Moreover the whole school of Pythagoras made that which is called ἐξάρτησις ["preparedness"], and συναρμογὴ ["musical combination"], and ἐπαφὴ ["contact"],† by certain verses suitable thereto and proper against the contrary affections, profitably diverting the constitutions and dispositions of the mind. For when they went to bed and resigned themselves to rest, they purified their minds from the troubles and busy noises of the day by some songs and proper verses, whereby they rendered their sleeps pleasant and quiet, and little troubled with dreams. And those dreams which they had were good. In the morning, when they arose from the common relief of sleep, they expelled drowsiness and sleepiness of the head with other songs.

Sometimes also without pronouncing verses, they expelled some affections and diseases and brought the sick to health, ἐπᾴδοντες, by charming them.† And from hence it is probable that the word "Epode" [an incantation] came to be used. After this manner, Pythagoras instituted a most profitable correction of manners and life by music. Hitherto Iamblichus.

All of which is ratified by other testimonies. That they had verses against the affections of the mind—grief, anger, lust—is related also by Seneca, who says that Pythagoras composed the troubles of his soul by the lute.[618] And Cicero, that the Pythagoreans used to deliver verses and some precepts, and to reduce the mind from intensity of thoughts to tranquility by songs and instruments.[619] To which effect Aelian relates to Clinias the Pythagorean, that if at any time he perceived himself inclining to anger, before it took full possession of him, he played upon the lute; and to those who asked him why he did so, he answered, "Because I am calmed."[620]

That Pythagoras danced, Porphyry confirms, saying he danced some dances, which he conceived to confer agility and health to the body.[621]

That he disallowed flutes and wind-instruments appears in Aristides Quintilianus, who says he advised his disciples to refrain from permitting their ears to be defiled with the sound of the flute; but on the contrary, to purify the irrational impulsions of the soul by solemn songs on the lute.[622]

That he made use of Homer and Hesiod for rectification of the mind is thus related by Porphyry.[623] He had morning exercises at his own house, composing his soul to the lute, and singing some old paeans of Thales.[624] He likewise sung some verses of Homer and Hesiod whereby the mind seemed to be rendered more sedate.

The story of the young man is confirmed by Ammonius.[625] By Cicero, this is related: Whenas some young men being drunk, and irritated by the music of flutes, would have broken open the door of a modest matron's house, Pythagoras had the woman-piper play a spondaic tune; which as soon as she did, their raging petulancy was allayed by the slowness of the mood, and solemness of the tune.[626] St. Basil relates another story to the same purpose: that Pythagoras meeting with some that came from a feast drunk, bid the piper (the musician at that feast) to change his tune, and to play a Doric air; wherewith they were so brought to themselves that they threw away their garlands, and went home ashamed.[627]

That evening and morning his disciples used music to compose their minds is affirmed by many others. Quintilian wrote, "It was the custom of the Pythagoreans as soon as they waked, to excite their souls with the lute, that they might be the readier for action; and before they went to sleep, to soften their minds by it."[628] Plutarch says, "The music of the lute the Pythagoreans used before they went to sleep, thereby charming and composing the passionate and irrational part of the soul."[629] Censorinus wrote that Pythagoras, so that his mind might be continually seasoned with divinity, used (as they say) to sing before he went to sleep and as soon as he waked.[630]

As for the several moods which in musical compositions were observed by the Ancients for moving particular passions, there is a remarkable fragment of Damon the musician cited by Aristides.[631]

Geometry

Pythagoras (says Iamblichus) is reported to have been much addicted to Geometry, for amongst the Egyptians, of whom he learned it, there are many geometrical problems.[632] The most learned Egyptians were continually, for many ages of gods and men, required to measure their whole country by reason of the overflowing and decrease of the Nile—whence it is called Geometry.[633]

Some there are who ascribe all theorems concerning Lines jointly to the Egyptians and the Chaldeans; and all these, they say, Pythagoras took, and augmenting the science, explained them accurately to his disciples. Proclus affirms that Pythagoras first advanced the geometrical part of learning into a liberal science, considering the principles more sublimely (than Thales, Ameristus, and Hippias, his predecessors in this study) and thoroughly investigated the theorems immaterially and intellectually.[634] Timaeus says that he first perfected geometry, the elements whereof (as Anticlides affirms), were invented by Moeris.[635] Aristoxenus says that Pythagoras first introduced measures and weights amongst the Grecians.[636]

OF A POINT, LINE, SUPERFICIES AND SOLID

Pythagoras asserted a Point to be correspondent in proportion to a unit; a Line to two; a Superficies to three: a Solid to four. [637]

The Pythagoreans define a Point as a Monad having Position. [638]

A Line, being the second, and constituted by the First Motion from indivisible nature, they called Duad. [639]

A Superficies they compared to the number three, for that is the first of all causes which are found in figures: for a circle, which is the principle of all round figures, occultly comprises a triad in center, space, and circumference. [640] But a triangle, which is the first of all rectilinear figures, is manifestly included in a ternary, and receives its form according to that number.

Hence the Pythagoreans affirm, that the triangle is simply the Principle of Generation, and of the formation of things generable. Whereupon Timaeus says that all proportions, natural as well as of the constitution of elements, are triangular; because they are distant by a threefold interval and are collective of things every way divisible. Triangles are variously permutable and are replenished with material infinity, and represent the natural conjunctions of bodies dissolved. As triangles are comprehended by three right lines, they also have angles which collect the multitude of lines, and give the additional property of an angle and conjunction to them. [641]

With reason therefore did Philolaus dedicate the angle of a triangle to four gods: Saturn, Pluto, Mars, and Bacchus—comprehending in these the whole quadripartite ornament of elements coming down from heaven or from the four quarters of the Zodiac. For Saturn constitutes an essence wholly humid and frigid; Mars wholly fiery; Pluto comprises all terrestrial life; Bacchus predominates over humid and hot generation, of which wine is a sign being humid and hot. All these differ in their operations upon second bodies, but are united to one another, for which reason Philolaus collected their union according to one angle.

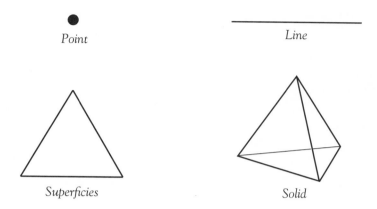

Point

Line

Superficies

Solid

But if the differences of triangles conduce to generation, we must justly acknowledge the triangle to be the principle and author of the constitution of sublunary things. For the right angle gives them essence, and determines the measure of its being; and the proportion of a rectangle triangle causes the essence of generable elements; the obtuse angle gives them all distance, the proportion of an obtuse-angled triangle augments material forms in magnitude, and in all kinds of mutation; the acute angle makes their nature divisible, the proportion of an acute-angled triangle prepares them to receive divisions into infinite; and, simply, the triangular proportion constitutes the essence of material bodies, distant and every way divisible. Thus much for triangles.

Of quadrangular figures, the Pythagoreans hold that the square chiefly represents the Divine Essence, for by it they principally signify pure and immaculate order; for rectitude imitates inflexibility, equality firm power; for motion proceedeth from inequality, rest from equality.[642] The gods therefore—who are authors in all things of firm consistence, pure incontaminate order, and inevitable power—are not improperly represented by the figure of a square.

Moreover Philolaus, by another apprehension, calls the angle of a square the angle of a Rhea, Ceres, and Vesta. Seeing that the

Square constitutes the Earth and is the nearest element to it (as Timaeus teaches), but that the Earth itself receives genital seeds and prolific power from all these gods, he not unaptly compares the angle of a square to all these life-communicating deities. For some call the Earth and Ceres herself, Vesta; and Rhea is said wholly to participate of her, and that in her is all generative causes. Whence Philolaus says the angle of a square, by a certain terrestrial power, comprehends one union of these divine kinds.

The Greek understanding of geometry can be observed in many surviving remants of the ancient world, including coinage. This silver stater issued on the island of Aegina c.480–457 B.C. pairs a sea turtle with a square incuse punch divided into five sections.
Photo courtesy of Numismatica Ars Classica

CHAPTER 2

Propositions

Of the many Geometrical theorems invented by Pythagoras and his followers, these are particularly known as such.

Only these three Polygons fill up the whole space about a point: the equilateral Triangle, the Square, and the Hexagon equilateral and equiangle.[643] The equilateral triangle must be taken six times, for six two-thirds make four right angles; the hexagon must be taken thrice, for every six angular angle is equal to one right angle, and one third; the square four times, for every angle of a square is right. Therefore six equilateral triangles joined at the angles, complete four right angles, as do also three hexagons and four squares. But of all other polygons whatsoever, joined together at the angles, some exceed four right angles, others fall short. This Proclus calls a Celebrious Theorem of the Pythagoreans.

Every triangle has the internal angles equal to two right angles.[644] This theorem, Eudemus the Peripatetic ascribes to the Pythagoreans. For their manner of demonstration see Proclus.

In rectangle triangles, the square which is made of the side opposite the right angle [the hypotenuse], is equal to the squares which are made of the sides containing the right angle.[645]

This theorem Pythagoras found out; and by it he showed how to make a gnomon or square (which the carpenters cannot do without much difficulty and uncertainty), not mechanically, but according to rule. For if we take three rulers: one of them being three feet long, the second four feet, the third five feet, and put these three so together that they touch one another at the ends in a triangle, they make a perfect square. Now if to each of these rulers be ascribed a square, that which consisted of three feet will have nine; that which of four will have sixteen; that which of five will have twenty-five. So that how many feet the areas of the two lesser squares of three and four make, so many will the square of five make.[646]

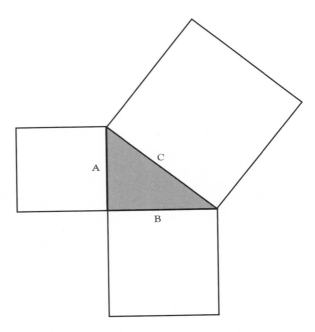

Illustration of the Pythagorean Theorem ($a^2+b^2=c^2$)

Apollodorus the Logician,[647] and others relate that upon the invention of this Theorem, Pythagoras sacrificed a **Hecatomb** to the Muses,[648] in confirmation whereof they alleged this epigram,

> That noble Scheme Pythagoras devis'd,
> For which a Hecatomb he sacrific'd.

Plutarch says, it was only one ox[649] and even that is questioned by Cicero as inconsistent with his doctrine, which forbade bloody sacrifices.[650] The more accurate therefore relate (says Porphyry), that he sacrificed an ox made of flower; or, as Gregory Nazianzen says, of clay.[651]

But Plutarch doubts whether it was for the invention of the fore-mentioned proposition that Pythagoras sacrificed an ox, or for the problem concerning the area of a Parabola.[652] Indeed, the application of spaces or figures to lines is (as his follower Eudemus affirms), an invention of the Pythagorean Muse: Parabola, Hyperbola, Ellipsis.[653] From them, the later writers taking these names, transferred them to conical lines, calling one parabola, another hyperbola, another, ellipsis. Whereas those ancient divine persons, the Pythagoreans, signified by those names the description of places applied to a determinate right line. For when a right line being proposed, the space given is wholly adequate to the right line, then, they say the space is applied (παραβάλλειν). But when you make the length of the space greater than that of the right line,[654] then they say it exceeds (ὑπερβάλλειν). But when less, so as the space being described there is some part of the right line beyond it, then it falls short (ἐλλεί-πειν†). In this sense Euclid uses parabola, Liber I, prop. forty-four, and hyperbola and ellipsis, in the sixth book.

How He Determined the Stature of Hercules

Plutarch, in his treatise discussing how great difference there is in the souls and bodies of men as to ingenuity and strength, relates that Pythagoras reasoned curiously and subtly in finding out and collecting the extraordinary stature and length of the body of Hercules.[655] For it being manifest that Hercules measured with his feet the running course of Olympian Jupiter at Pisa, and that he made it 600 feet long, and that all the other running courses in Greece instituted afterward by others were 600 feet long, yet shorter than this; Pythagoras easily understood the measure of Hercules's foot. He determined that it was proportionably as much longer than that of other men as the Olympic course he established was longer than all others. And having comprehended the size of Hercules's foot, he considered what length of body did suit with that measure, according to the natural proportion of all the members one to another. He concluded that Hercules was so much taller in body than others, by how much the Olympic course was longer than the rest which were made after the same number of feet.

Neither did the Pythagoreans superficially consider the speculation of celestial things, in which Pythagoras was also exquisite, as appears by these few remains.[656]

Although only a demi-god, Hercules (Heracles to the Greeks) was as familiar as any of the Olympian deities. He is shown holding a drinking vessel (a rhyton) and his club on this electrum stater struck in about 380 B.C. at the city of Cyzicus on the southern shore of the Propontis.
Photo courtesy of Numismatica Ars Classica

The System of the Spheres

The word Oὐρανὸς, Heaven, is taken three ways: first, for the Sphere of Fixed Stars; second, for all that is between the Sphere of Fixed Stars and the Moon; lastly, for the whole world, both Heaven and Earth.[657]

The anonymous writer of the life of Pythagoras affirms that Pythagoras said there are twelve orders in Heaven. The first and outmost is the fixed Sphere; next to this is the star of Saturn; and then the other six planets, Jupiter, Mars, Venus, Mercury, Sun, and Moon; next these, the Sphere of Fire, then that of Air, then of Water, last of all the Earth.[658]

But they who seem more strictly to follow the mind of Pythagoras and his disciples, aver that they held the celestial Spheres to be ten—whereof nine only are visible to us (the fixed Sphere, the seven planets, and our Earth). The tenth is Antichthon, an Earth above, or opposite to ours.[659] This Antichthon they added to make up the number of the moving bodies.[660] For they considered that the affections and proportions of music consist in numbers; that all other things appear to be assimilated to numbers; that numbers are the first of all nature; and that the elements of numbers are the elements of all beings. They therefore asserted that all Heaven is harmony and number, and that the affections and parts of Heaven are correspondent to number. And collecting these, they adapted them to the composition of the whole; wherein if anything were wanting they supplied it, that the whole might be alike compacted. Thusly, because the Decad seems to be perfect and to comprehend the whole nature of numbers, they asserted the celestial spheres to be ten. Now there being nine only visible to us, hereupon they conceived the tenth to be Antichthon, an Earth opposite to ours.

As concerning the order and system of these, the Pythagoreans held, that in the middle of the world is Fire.[661] Or, as Stobaeus says,[662] in the midst of the four elements is the fiery globe of unity which they term Vesta and Monad.[663] Simplicius says that they who

understand this thing more intimately state that this fire is the pro-
creative, nutritive, and excitative power which is in the midst of
the Earth. But Simplicius himself seems not to have apprehended
the right meaning of the Pythagoreans—who by this fire, or fiery
globe of unity, meant nothing else but the Sun seated in the midst of
the universe, immoveable, about which the other parts of the world
are moved. This opinion Pythagoras seems to have derived from the
Egyptians, who hieroglyphically represented the Sun by a beetle.
They chose this symbol because the beetle, having formed a ball of
cow dung, and lying upon its back, rolls it about from claw to claw;
so the other parts of the world are moved and rolled by and about
the Sun.[664]

By this immovable fire in the midst of the Universe, they understood not (as Simplicius conceives) that the Earth is manifest. Forasmuch as they further held that the Earth is not immovable,[665] nor
seated in the midst of the globe, but suspended, as being one of the
stars carried about the fire which is in the middle; and that thereby
it makes day and night.[666] The reason why the Earth ought not to
have the middle place is because the most excellent body ought to
have the most excellent place. Fire is more excellent than Earth, and
the center more excellent than all places without it; therefore they
conceived that not the Earth, but the Fire is placed in the midst.[667]
Moreover, because that which is the most excellent of the universe,
ought principally to be preserved, and the middle is such, therefore
they term the Fire Διὸς φυλακὴν,† the custody of Jupiter.

The same they held of the Antichthon also, that like our Earth
it is suspended, as being one of the stars carried about the Fire, and
thereby makes day and night.[668] By this Antichthon, Clemens says
they understood Heaven. Simplicius says the Moon, as being a kind
of aetherial Earth—as well for that it eclipses the light of the Sun
which is proper to the Earth, as for that it is the bound of celestials,
as the Earth of sublunaries. But the contrary is manifest, as well from
the completing of the number ten (in respect whereof this Antichthon was imagined). For they held it is not visible to us by reason
that following the motion of this Earth, it is always opposite to, or
beneath us, and the bigness of our Earth hinders us from seeing it.[669]

And Aristotle affirms there were some who conceived the Antich-thon to be the cause why there are more eclipses of the Moon than of the Sun, which may likewise happen by reason of many other bodies invisible to us.

Laertius, who, says Philosaus, was the first who conceived the Earth to have a circular motion, seems to mean no more than that he first committed this opinion of Pythagoras to writing and first made it public.[670] For Eusebius expressly affirms that he committed to writing the dissertations of Pythagoras. His opinion, as delivered by Plutarch and Stobaeus, is exactly the same: for he placed fire in the midst, which he called the genius of the universe, and the man-sion of Jupiter, and the mother of gods, and altar, and ward, and measure of nature. He conceived that the ten celestial bodies move about it—Heaven, the Sphere of Fixed Stars, the five planets, the Sun, the Moon, the Earth, and lastly the Antichthon.

From the same fountain seems Aristarchus the Samian to have derived this hypothesis, though some ascribe the invention thereof to him. For he supposed that the Sun and planets move not, but that the Earth moves round about the Sun which is seated in the middle.[671] Plutarch adds that Plato in his old age repented for that he had placed the Earth in the midst of the universe, and not in its proper place.[672]

This opinion was of late revived by Nicolaus Copernicus, who considering how inconvenient and troublesome it is to understand and maintain the motions of the Heavens and immobility of the Earth, explained it with admirable ingenuity after the mind of the Pythagoreans. According to whose hypothesis, the Sun, as we said, is settled in the midst of the world, immovable. The Sphere of Fixed Stars in the extremity or outside of the world is immovable also. Between these are disposed the planets, and amongst them the Earth as one of them. The Earth moves both about the Sun, and about his proper axis. Its diurnal motion by one revolution, makes a night and a day; its annual motion about the Sun, by one revolution makes a year. So as by reason of its diurnal motion to the east, the Sun and other stars seem to move to the west; and by reason of its annual motion through the Zodiac, the Earth itself is in one sign, and the

Sun seems to be in the sign opposite to it. Between the Sun and the Earth they place Mercury and Venus. Between the Earth and the Fixed Stars are Mars, Jupiter, and Saturn. The Moon, being next the Earth, is continually moved within the great orb between Venus and Mars, round about the Earth as its center. Its revolution about the Earth is completed in a month; about the Sun (together with the Earth) in a year.

THE MOTIONS OF THE PLANETS

As concerning the course and revolution of the planets, they affirm the great year to be the revolution of Saturn. For the rest of the planets complete their periods in a shorter time; but Saturn in no less then thirty years. Jupiter in twelve years; Mars in two; the Sun (speaking according to the phenomenon) in one; Mercury and Venus as the Sun (or to speak more exactly, Mercury in three months, Venus in eight); the Moon as being next the Earth, soonest, in a month.[673]

According to this inequality appears the motion of the planets to our sight, by reason that the eye is out of the center of the orb. But in the whole course of Astronomy (says Geminus) are supposed the motions of the Sun, Moon, and five planets, equal and circular; contrary to the diurnal revolution of the world. The Pythagoreans, first applying themselves to these disquisitions, supposed circular and equal motions of the Sun, the Moon, and five planets. For they admitted not such irregularity in eternal and divine bodies, that sometimes they should move swifter, sometimes slower, and sometimes stand still (as the stationary points in the planets). Neither in any sober, well-tempered person could we admit such irregularity of pace. Indeed, the necessities of life often cause men to move faster or slower; but in the incorruptible nature of the stars, there cannot be alleged any cause to swiftness and slowness. Wherefore the Pythagoreans proposed this question, how the phenomena's might be salved by circular and equal motions.

That Pythagoras himself observed these irregularities and the ways to assuage them, appears from Iamblichus, who says he communicated a revelative right knowledge of all manner of motion of the spheres and stars, ἐπιπροσθήσεών τε καὶ ὑπολείψεων καὶ ἀνωμαλιῶν ἐκκεντρότητών τε καὶ ἐπικύκλων ["their oppositions, their eclipses, inequalities, eccentricities and epicycles"]. Ἐπιπρόσθησις ["oppositions"] is the anticipation of any planet, either in respect to some other planet or to the Fixed Stars. Ὑπόλειψις ["eclipses"] is the falling later of any planet, either in respect to some other planet, or to the Fixed Stars. Ἀνωμαλία, Inequality,† is when the same planet moves slower and faster according to its distance from the Sun in the Pythagorean hypothesis (or from the Earth in the Ptolemaic), slower in its aphelion, faster in its perihelion.

The two ways of solving these phenomena are by eccentrics or by epicycles. For a **homocentric** with an epicycle (as Eudoxus first demonstrated), is equipollent to an eccentric. Eccentricity is when the center of their equal motion is distant from the center of their apparent motion. Both these Iamblichus ascribes to Pythagoras,[674] from whom perhaps they were communicated to Eudoxus, to whose invention others ascribe them.[675]

The Intervals and Harmony of the Spheres

Pythagoras (says Censorinus) asserted that this whole world is made according to musical proportion; and that the seven planets between Heaven and the Earth, which govern the nativities of mortals, have a harmonious motion. And they have Intervals correspondent to musical Diastemes, and render various sounds according to their several heights so consonant that they make most sweet melody. But to us these sounds are inaudible by reason of the greatness of the noise, which the narrow passage of our ears is not capable to receive.[676]

For as Eratosthenes determined that the largest circumference of the Earth is 252,000 stadia; so Pythagoras declared how many stadia there are between the Earth and every star. In this measure of the world, we are to understand the Italic *stadium*, which consists of 625 feet. (For there are others of a different length, such as the Olympic of 600 feet, and the Pythic of 500.) From the Earth therefore to the Moon, Pythagoras conceived to be about 12,600 stadia. And that distance, according to musical proportion, is a tone. From the Moon to Mercury (who is called στίλβων ["twinkling"]) half as

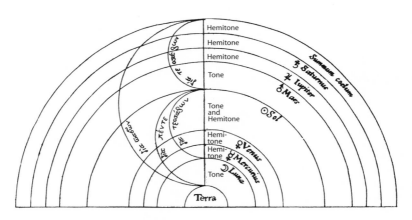

Intervals and harmony of the spheres
From Thomas Stanley, *The History of Philosophy* (slightly modified)

much, as it were a hemitone. From thence to Phosphorus, which is the star Venus, almost as much, that is, another hemitone. From thence to the Sun, twice as much, as it were a tone and a half. Thus the Sun is distant from the Earth three tones and a half, which is called diapente; from the Moon, two and a half, which is diatessaron. From the Sun to Mars, who is called Πυροεις ["Fire"], there is the same interval as from Earth to the Moon, which makes a tone; from thence to Jupiter, who is called Φαέθων ["radiant"], half as much, which makes a hemitone. From there to the Supreme Heaven where the signs are is a hemitone also. So that the diasteme from the Supreme Heaven to the Sun is diatessaron, that is, two tones and a half: from the same Heaven to the top of the Earth six tones, a diapason concord. Moreover he referred to other stars many things which the masters of music treat of, and showed that all this world is Enharmonic. Thus Censorinus. But Pliny, delivering this opinion of Pythagoras, reckons seven tones from the Earth to the Supreme Heaven; for whereas Censorinus accounts for a hemitone from Saturn to the Zodiac, Pliny makes it sesquiduple.[677]

CHAPTER 4

OF THE PLANET VENUS

Next to the Sun (says Pliny), there is a great star called Venus, alternately errant in names, emulating both the Sun and Moon.[678] For presenting and rising before morning, he takes the name of Luci-fer, as another Sun bringing on day. On the other side shining at Sunset, it is called Vesper, as suspending light and performing the office of the Moon. This is its nature, which Pythagoras the Samian first found out about the forty-second Olympiad [ca. 608 B.C.], which was of Rome the 147th year. In magnitude, Venus exceeds all the other stars, and is of so great splendor that this star only casts a shadow. Whence it has a diversity of names: some call it Juno; oth-ers, Isis; others, Mother of the gods. By the nature hereof, all things are generated upon Earth. For at rising, it scatters prolific dew, sup-plying not only the conceptions of Earth, but likewise stimulating all living creatures. It performs the revolution of the Zodiac in 348 days, never receding from the Sun more than forty-six parts, according to Timaeus. Thus Pliny.

That there is a mistake in the time has been already shown; but the thing itself is confirmed by Laertius, who affirms Pythagoras first said that Vesper and Lucifer are the same star. Yet elsewhere Laertius adds that some ascribe this to Parmenides. But that it was a doctrine of the Pythagoreans, appears from this account given by Timaeus. The star Juno many call Venus and Lucifer. All person are not skill-ful in the rules of sacred Astronomy, and in the sciences of rising and setting. For the same star is sometimes *Hesper* when it follows the Sun in such manner that it is conspicuous to us when the Sun is set; and sometimes *Eous* when it goes before the Sun and rises before Sun-rising.

Section II: Philosophy

Philosophy, Its Name, Definition, Parts, Method

The Pythagoreans, being adorned with these studies of Science, from thence ascended to perfect the Works of the World and the Principles of Nature.[679]

Pythagoras first gave the name to Philosophy defining it as, "A longing and love of wisdom."[680] Wisdom is the science of truth in things that are. Things that are, he called *immaterials*, *eternals*, and *sole agents*, which are the *incorporeals*; the rest are equivocally called such by participation with these: viz. *corporeals*, *materials*, and *corruptibles*, which indeed are not.

Now wisdom is the science of those things which are, but not of those which are equivocally. For corporeals are not capable of being taught, nor admit certain knowledge, being infinite and not comprehensible by science. And things which (as it were) are not—according to the difference of all things—neither can be rightly described by any definition. Of those whose nature is such as that they cannot be known, it is impossible to frame a science. Wherefore neither is it likely that there can be a love of a science which is not. But rather of that which is conversant about those things which properly are, and continue always the same, and are like themselves, and co-exist always with a true appellation—upon the knowledge of these follows that which is of equivocal things (though not sought after), as the science of particulars follows the science of universals. For as Archytas says, "They who know universals well, will plainly see what particulars are."

Wherefore things that are, are not of one kind only and simply, but of many and various kinds—intelligibles and incorporeals, whose appellation is τὰ ὄντα, "things that are." Corporeal things, subject to sense, are those which exist by participation of those that are. Concerning all these, he delivered most proper sciences, leaving nothing unexcused; and delivered also to men the common sciences—such as the demonstrative, the definitive, and the divisive—as is manifest from the commentaries of the Pythagoreans.

Hereupon he defined philosophy as the knowledge of things that are; and the knowledge of things divine and human; as also the meditation of death,[681] daily endeavoring to free the soul from the prison of the body; and the resemblance of God as far as is possible for man.[682]

For the scope of philosophy is to free the mind, the divine part of the soul which is planted in us, and to set it at liberty. Without which liberty none can learn or perceive anything solid or true by the help or benefit of sense. For the mind, according to him, sees all things and hears all things. All things else are deaf and blind.[683]

Thus it is that philosophy is of two kinds: practical and theoretical. The practical, according to the method of the Pythagoreans, precedes the theoretical. The reason is thus explained by Hierocles.

Philosophy is the purification and perfection of human life—purification from material irrationality and the mortal body; perfection from the recovery of its own excellent life, reducing it to the divine resemblance. Virtue and truth are chiefly able to effect these by taking away excess of passions. This (rightly) induces the divine form.[684]

First are laid down the instructions of practical virtue: for to begin with, we must compose the Irrationality which is in us, and then (so prepared) apply ourselves to the knowledge of the more divine things. For as it is not possible for the eye, being full of dirt and not cleansed, to look upon things very bright, so neither can the soul, not possessing virtue, gaze upon the beauty of Truth. For that which is not pure is not capable of touching that which is pure. Practical philosophy produces virtue; theoretical, truth. As in these Golden Verses of Pythagoras we find the practical philosophy called human virtue, but the theoretical celebrated as divine virtue when closing the instructions in civil virtue,

> These labor (says he) study these, and these affect;
> To divine Virtue, these thy steps direct.

First therefore a man must be made good, then a god. The civil virtues render a man good, but the sciences conducing to the divine virtue divinize. But to those who ascend, the lesser things precede the greater. For which reason in the Pythagorean precepts, the rules of virtue are first delivered, teaching us to ascend from the greatest use of life to the divine resemblance.

Three ways, say they, man may become better than himself. First by conversation with the gods. For it is necessary that he who addresses himself to them, at that time, sequester himself from all evil, assimilating himself as near as he can to God. Secondly, by well doing, for that is proper to God, and therein he imitates God. Thirdly, by death. For if the soul in this life, being a little separated from the body, becomes better and begins to divine in dreams, by visions, and the altered states of mind brought on by diseases, it will be much better when it shall be wholly separated from the body.[685]

Hence he affirmed that the most considerable of all things human is to inform the soul concerning good and ill.[686] He taught that men have perfect felicity[687] when they have a good soul;[688] or that the knowledge of the perfection of the virtues of the soul is the chief felicity. Further, that every man is appointed by God to know and to contemplate;[689] that virtue is a harmony, and so is all good, even God himself;[690] and that the end or chief good is to resemble God. Whence he expressly said, "Follow God, not visible to the eye, but intelligible to the understanding, by the harmony of the World."[691] That the most excellent things given by the gods unto men are: to speak truth, and to benefit others [theoretical and practical virtue], and that each of these resembled the works of God.[692] To the latter Strabo alludes when commending those who said men imitate the gods most when they benefit others.[693] The former is confirmed by Porphyry when he advised above all things to speak truth, for that only is able to make men like to the gods.[694] For God himself in his body resembles light, in his soul truth, as he learned of the Persian Magi who term God Ahura Mazda. This is that Θειότης (divinity) which Iamblichus[695] reckons last in his recapitulation of the same with which the Golden Verses conclude, thus:

Then stripped of flesh up to free Aether soar,
A deathless God, divine, mortal no more.

Practical Philosophy: Its Parts; and First of Education

Practical philosophy seems to have been the invention of Pythagoras, for Aristotle affirms that he first undertook to discourse concerning virtue. That Socrates is generally esteemed the author thereof perhaps is only because, as Aristotle adds, coming after Pythagoras he discoursed better and more fully thereupon.

To this part of philosophy alluded this sentence of Pythagoras: That the discourse of that Philosopher is vain by which no passion of a man is healed. For as there is no benefit of medicine if it expel not disease out of bodies, so neither is there of philosophy if it expel not ill out of the soul.[696]

Virtues being of two kinds—private, which respect ourselves, and public, which have reference to others—Pythagoras seems to have comprehended the first under Education, the second under Politics. Laertius affirms he wrote three treatises: Education, Politics, Physic.[697] The heads of Education, according to the general recapitulation of Iamblichus, seem to have been these: Institution, Silence, Abstinence from Flesh, Fortitude, Temperance, Sagacity.

INSTITUTION, SILENCE, ABSTINENCE

Concerning Instruction or Institution, there are these sentences and precepts of Pythagoras, preserved by Stobaeus and others.

We ought to make choice of the best course of life; for custom will make it pleasant.[698] Wealth is a weak anchor, glory a weaker: The body, magistracies, honors—all these are infirm and unable. What are then able anchors—wisdom, magnanimity, fortitude. These no tempest shakes. This is the law of God: that virtue only is solid; all else are but trifles.

To take away bitterness from wormwood and liberty from speech are both alike.[699]

Endeavor not to conceal thy faults with words but to amend them by reproof.[700]

It is not so hard to offend as to not reprove an offending person.[701]

As the sickness of the body if hid or praised, is not healed, so the soul cherished in its ways or concealed is not reformed.[702]

Rejoice more in reprovers than in flatterers: fly from flatterers as enemies.[703]

We ought either to be silent or to speak things that are better than silence.[704]

It is better to throw a stone at random than an idle word.[705]

Comprehend not few things in many words but many things in few words.[706]

We must faithfully restore to him that entrusts us the deposit,
not only of money, but of words.[707]

Of opinion, the Pythagoreans said thus. Is the part of a man void
of understanding to adhere to all men's opinions, especially to that
which is maintained by the greatest number? For to conceive and
judge aright is proper to few; it only belongs to the knowing who
are not many. This power therefore extends not to many.[708] On the
other side, it is no less madness to condemn all conception and opinion. Such a person must be unlearned and unrectifiable. For it is
necessary that he who is ignorant learn those things whereof he is
ignorant; and that he who learns, addict and resign himself to his
teacher. In a word, they said it is necessary that such young men as
would be preserved, should addict themselves to the conceptions
and opinions of their elders and such as lead a good life.

Now in the whole course of human life, there are certain distinct ages which are not recklessly to be connected—for they are
expelled by one another, unless a man be well and rightly ordered
from his birth. It is requisite, therefore, that from the institution of
a little child in goodness, temperance, and fortitude, a great part be
transmitted to his youth when he arrives at that age. Likewise of his
youth instituted in goodness, fortitude and temperance, a great part
be transmitted to his manly estate.

Herein the course ordinarily taken is ridiculous. For most think
that children ought to be well-ordered, instructed in temperance,
and to abstain from all things odious and undecent. But when they
come to be youths, most leave them to their own management, to do
what they please; whereas at that age, they are subject to both sorts
of vices—of children and of men. To shun study and order, and to
follow play and wantonness, the vice of childhood, is likewise most
proper to youth again. Vehement desires, ambition, and the like, the
affections of manhood, insinuate into youth. For which reason, this
age requires care above all the rest. In fine, a man should never be so
given over as to do whatsoever he pleases, but there should always be
some overseer, a president over the rest, a legitimate sitting magistrate whom every citizen ought to obey. For a living creature, as soon
as ever it is neglected, falls into ill and wickedness.

They affirm, that they have often enquired and examined for what reason we give children food at set times and moderately. The ordinary answer is that order and moderation are good; their contraries, disorder and immoderateness, ill—as is manifest, inasmuch as to be a glutton or a drunkard is esteemed a great reproach. For if none of these were useful and beneficial to us when we arrive at man's estate, it were needless to accustom ourselves, while children, to such order. It is the same in other habits. We see it manifest also in all other kinds of living creatures, which are taught by man from the very beginning as whelps and the like, those things which they are required to practice when they are come to full growth. Thus Iamblichus. Of silence, abstinence, and the whole course of his Institution, we have formerly treated.

FORTITUDE

The greatest argument of the Pythagoreans for fortitude was that they fully persuaded themselves that of all human chances, nothing ought to happen unexpectedly to any, but that they should expect all things which were not within their own power. Precepts of Pythagoras, tending to this virtue, are these.[709]

> Do those things which you judge to be good, although after you have done them you shall be not be esteemed; for the vulgar is an ill judge of all good things. As you despise their praise, so despise their dispraise.[710]

He forbade to forsake the protection and station of this life without the command of our Supreme Lord.[711]

CHAPTER 3

Temperance and Continence

He often gave the following apothegms, or aphorisms, to all his auditors whether many or few.

We must avoid with our utmost endeavor, and amputate with fire and sword, and by all other means: from the body, sickness; from the soul, ignorance; from the belly, luxury; from a city, sedition; from a family, discord; from all things, excess.[712]

It is better to live lying on the ground with a settled conscience than to have a golden bed and be troubled.[713]

Temperance is the strength of the soul; for it is the light of the soul, clear from Passion.[714]

To serve passions is more grievous than to serve tyrants.[715]

It is impossible he can be free who serves passions and is governed by them.[716]

No man is free who does not command himself.[717]

The labor of continence precedes all excellent things.[718]

To possess continence is the best strength and wealth.[719]

It is better to die than to cloud the soul by intemperance.[720]

He said that drunkenness is a little madness; or that it is the study of madness; or, as Laertius, that it is the canker of the flower of the mind.[721]

The voice of the flesh is, no hunger, no thirst, no cold.[722]

He admonished all men to shun ambition and vainglory, because these chiefly excite envy.[723]

He discouraged all excess, saying that we ought not to exceed a due proportion in labor and food.[724]

We must consider that there are three kinds of things which deserved to be pursued and acquired. The first is of those which are honorable and virtuous; the second those that assist life; the last, pleasures. Not the vulgar enchanting pleasure—for that he allowed not—but the solid and grave, free from blame.[725] He said there are two kinds of pleasure. Whereof that which indulges to the belly and to lasciviousness by profuseness of wealth, he compared to the murderous songs of the Sirens. The other, which consists in things honest and just, as also in the necessaries of life is sweet, as well as the first, and withal it is not followed by repentance. Hither perhaps alludes Clemens, who says Pythagoras advised to esteem the Muses sweeter than Sirens; teaching that we should study learning not with delight; whereby he condemned the other delight of the mind, which is fallacious.[726]

Pythagoras said, upon seeing one that made himself fat by exercising and eating, "This man will not cease to make a stricter prison for himself."[727]

The Pythagoreans exhorted such as came into their society to shun pleasure as much as anything that ought to be avoided; for nothing so deceives us, and draws into sin, as this passion.[728] In general, as it seems, they endeavored not to do anything which might tend to pleasure, this scope being for the most part indecent and hurtful; but that they should aim at what is good and decent, to do what they ought. In the next place, to discern what is convenient and beneficial requires a more than ordinary judgment.

As to that which is called desire, they said thus: desire is an impulsion and appetite of the soul, either of some gluttonous habit, or derogation of some things belonging to sense, or the sensitive affection. This passion is various, and the most multiplicative of all that belong to man. Of human desires, many are acquired and framed by the persons themselves; wherefore this passion requires the greatest care and observation and corporeal exercises, more than ordinary. For the body, when its aliment is evacuated, to desire repletion is natural; and again, being replete, to desire evacuation is natural also. But to desire superfluous aliment, or superfluous and sumptuous raiment and lodging, or superfluous and various household stuff, and utensils, and cups, and servants, and herds of cattle, bred for diet— in a word, of all human passions, this is most such that it never is at a stay, but proceeds to infinite. Wherefore from our very childhood, care must be taken that we desire such things as are needful, and shun vain and superfluous desires, being undisturbed and clear from such appetites, and condemning those who deserve contempt, being fettered by their desires.

It is of most concern to observe the vain, hurtful, superfluous desires of those who are transported by their power; there is nothing so absurd, whereto the souls of such persons—children, men, and women—are not transported. The most various is that of meats. Infinite is the multitude of fruits, infinite of roots, used by mankind. Besides this, all sorts of flesh, making it their business to find, of terrestrial, volatile, and aquatile creatures, wherewith to satisfy their taste; and all variety of dressing them, with the mixture of all kind of juices, whereby mankind is really prophetic and multiform as to the motion of the soul; for every several sort of meat is the cause of a peculiar constitution. Now men behold that these produce great alteration, as excess of wine to such a degree exhilarates; further, causes frenzy and disorder. But those things which discover not so much their force and efficacy, they are ignorant of; notwithstanding that whatsoever food we take is the cause of some peculiar constitution. Wherefore it is a great part of wisdom to know and understand, what kind and quantity of meat is requisite for nourishment. This science was first communicated by Apollo and Pan, afterwards by the Aesculapians.

Concerning generation, he said thus. We ought principally to observe that which is called προφερὲς, precocious†: for neither too forward plants nor animals before the due season when they are in their full strength.[729] Youths therefore and virgins ought to be educated in labor and exercises, and actions conducing to fortitude, using food convenient thereto, and in a laborious, temperant and tolerant life. Of the things in human life, there are many in which to be late conversant is best; of this kind is coition. A youth ought so to be educated, as not to addict himself thereto before twenty years of age; and when arrived at those years, to use it seldom is best, if we esteem a good habit of body; for intemperance and good rarely meet in the same person.

They recommended the rites and laws of the ancients in Greek cities: not to lie with mothers, or daughters, or sisters, nor in a temple, nor in public. For this is evil, and to procure all possible impediments thereof is very profitable.

They were of opinion, that all unnatural ignominious generations ought to be taken away, and those only preserved which were according to nature, with temperance, and lawful.

They conceived, that such as go about to beget children ought to have much providence of their future issue. The first and greatest providence is to prepare himself for that action by a temperate healthful life, not eating too much at unreasonable times, nor using such meats as deprave the habits of the body; but above all things, not to perform it when drunk. For they thought that by ill, and discordant, and disturbed temperament, the seed became adulterate. They also thought him a foolish, inconsiderate person who being desirous of children, and taking a wife to that end, should not with utmost study foresee by what means his issue might be most advantaged.

They who love dogs, are very careful of their breed, as of which they shall breed, and when, and accordingly the whelps prove. The like do they who love birds. But though it be well known that they who breed any other kind of living creature use their utmost endeavor to procure a generous race, yet men have no respect to their own offspring, but beget them inconsiderately and bring them up negligently. This is the chief and most manifest cause that so many men are evil and wicked, the greatest part begetting their children like beasts without any consideration.

Finally, Pythagoras as discoursing concerning the benefit of venereal pleasures, advised in the summertime to abstain wholly from coition; in the winter to use it but rarely. For it is generally hurtful, and the continual use thereof causes debility and is most pernicious.[730] Laertius says, He advised, that in the winter and spring it should not be used at all, in summer and autumn but sparingly. For at all times it is pernicious and prejudicial to the health. And being asked, "At what time a man should use it," he answered, "When he has a mind to be weaker."

CHAPTER 4

Sagacity and Wisdom

To Wisdom (the last general head of Education) belong these sentences of Pythagoras.

The strength, wall, and armor of a wise man is wisdom.[731]

Call to mind that most men acknowledge wisdom to be the greatest good, but few endeavor to possess this greatest good.

The sacrifices of fools are the food of fire; their donations, the subsistence of sacrilegious persons.[732]

A horse is not to be guided without a bridle, nor riches without wisdom.[733]

He conceived the imposition of names on things to be the highest part of wisdom.[734]

OF POLITICS:
THE OTHER PART OF PRACTICAL PHILOSOPHY

The heads of Politics (according to Iamblichus) are these: common conversation, friendship, worship of the gods, piety to the dead, and lawmaking.[735]

They hold Pythagoras to be the inventor of all political discipline. He used to say that amongst beings nothing is pure, but everything partakes of some other—as Earth of Fire, Fire of Water and Air. In like manner, honest partakes of dishonest, just of unjust, and the like. Hence it is that reason is carried away to either side. There are two motions: one of the body, the other of the mind; one irrational, the other elective. Commonwealths he compared to a Right Triangle, wherein one side consists of three parts, the base of five, the other side of the mean between them, of four. In the coincidence of these lines with one another, and their squares, we behold delineated the best form of a commonwealth, and of Justice.

COMMON CONVERSATION

To common conversation belong these maxims of Pythagoras.

A just stranger is to be preferred, not only before a country-man, but before a kinsman.[736]

Esteem as a great part of good education to be able to suffer the want of education in others.[737]

Desire that they who converse with you should rather respect than fear you. For admiration accompanies respect; hatred, fear.[738]

There being a justice in the mutual conversation of men, one towards another, of this also the Pythagoreans delivered this manner.[739] There is in the common conversation of men one opportune, another importune. They differ in diversity of age, in dignity, in nearness of affinity, beneficence, and if there be anything like these in mutual differences. For there is a kind of conversation which appears to the younger towards the younger not to be importune; but towards the elder, it is importune. For no kind—neither of anger, nor of menacing, or boldness, but all such kind of importunity ought diligently to be avoided by the younger toward the elder. In like manner is the reason of dignity; for coming to a person endowed with true worth and virtue, it is neither decent nor opportune to speak much, or to commit any of the aforementioned things. Like these also are those which concern such as have obliged and deserved well of others.

There is a various and multiple use of opportunity. For of those that are angry and incensed, some do it opportunely, others importunely. And again, of those who covet, and desire, and have appetite, it may be opportune for some to pursue those things, not for others. The same reason there is of other affections, actions, dispositions, conversations, intercessions, and discourses. But opportunity is of such a nature that it is capable of being taught, and undeceivable, and capable of act, and generally and simply having nothing of all those in it. But the consequences are of such a kind that they together—decent, and convenient, and the like—attend the nature of opportunity.

They held that there is a primacy in everything, and that everywhere there is one thing which is best. In science, in experience, in generation, likewise in a family, a city, an army, and in all such like constitutions: but it is difficult to discern and understand the nature of the primacy in all the aforesaid things. For in sciences, it is the part of more than ordinary intelligence, by clear intuition, to discern and judge the parts of the thing which is the primacy of them. But there is a great difference, and almost of the whole and general a hazard, in not rightly taking the primacy. For in a word, nothing can afterwards be right if the true primacy be not known. The same manner and reason is in other kinds of primacy. For neither can a family be well governed where there is not a true master and voluntary government; for it is requisite that both these be voluntary in the prefecture, as well he who is chief as those who are subject to him. As learning is then right when there is such conformity between the masters and the scholars that they will teach, these will learn; for if either he refractory, it cannot be rightly performed. In this manner he conceived it to be fit for inferiors to obey superiors, disciples their masters.

FRIENDSHIP

Pythagoras evidently demonstrated that there is a friendship of all unto all: of gods towards men by piety and religious worship; of doctrines to one another; of the soul to the body; of the rational part to the irrational by philosophy and its theory; of men towards one another; between countrymen by right observation of laws; between strangers by right physiology; of a man to his wife, or children, or brethren, and servants, by unperverted communion.[740] In a word, of all towards all. Moreover of some irrational creatures by justice and natural affinity and communion; of the body, in itself mortal, a conciliation and combination of the contrary faculties, by health and wholesome diet, and temperance, in imitation of the good composure in the elements. In all these, of one and the same, according to comprehension of the name friendship, Pythagoras is acknowledged to be the inventer and lawgiver. And so admirable a friendship did he deliver to those who enquired of him, that unto this day (says Iamblichus), we say of those who are intimately joined together by friendship, they are of the Pythagoreans.

We must add the Institution of Pythagoras herein, and the exhortations he used to his Disciples. They were advised to take away all contention and love of controversy out of true friendship; if possible out of all. But if that be not possible, at least out of that which is our own country, and generally that towards elders. Likewise out of that towards benefactors; for to become antagonists or contest with such when we are fallen into anger, or some other passion, is not consistent with the preservation of the amity we have with them. They said that in friendship there ought to be least scratches and cuts; and, if any happen, we should slay and subdue anger. It were best that both should do so, but chiefly the younger, and that those exercises which they called παιδαρτάσεις ["admonitions"],† ought to be made from the elder towards the younger with much commendation and benevolence. That there appear much care and tenderness in those who give the correction; for by this means, the correction shall be profitable. That we do not destroy friendship, neither in jest nor in earnest; for it is not easy to heal the friendship between men, if once a falsehood has incurred into the manners of those who call themselves friends.

That we must not renounce friendship for adversity, or any other impotence which happens in life. That renunciation of friendship only is commendable which is made by reason of some great wickedness, and misdemeanor. But that we must not take away our friendship from them unless they become absolutely wicked. And before we renounce a friend, we must ingeniously pause to see if by challenging him he may be diverted from this ill habit and become rectified. We must fight, not in words, but actions; the fight is lawful and pious. Though difference of power be not a just ground for one man to fight with another, yet this is a just ground, even the most just that is possible.

They said that to a friendship that will prove true, are required many definitions and rules; these must be well discerned, and not confused. Moreover, it ought to be accommodated to the disposition of others that no conversation be made negligently and vainly, but with respect and right order. Neither that any passion be excited vainly and wickedly and sinfully, such as concupiscence or anger. The same of the other passions and habits.

Much more admirable are those things which they defined concerning the community of the divine good, and those concerning the unanimity of the mind, and those concerning the Divine Mind. For they mutually exhorted one another, that they should not tear asunder the god which is in them. Thus their study of friendship by words and actions had reference to some divine temperament, and to union with God, and to unity with the mind, and the divine soul. Thus Iamblichus.

He conceived the extremity (or end) of friendship, to be the making one of two. Man ought to be one.[741] This sentence (says Clemens) is mystic.[742] He first said, κοινὰ φέλων ["friends share in common"], and φιλιαν ισότητα ["friendship is equality"].†[743]

WORSHIP OF THE GODS

The principles of worshipping the gods proposed by Pythagoras and his followers, are these.[744]

That all which they determine to be done, aim and tend to the acknowledgment of the deity. This is the principle, and the whole life of man consists in this: that he follow God. This is the ground of philosophy. For men do ridiculously who seek that which is good anywhere else than from the gods. They do as if a man in a country, governed by a king, should apply his service to some citizen of inferior magistry and neglect the supreme governor. In the same manner conceive they that such men do; for since there is a God, we must confess that good is in his power. Now all, to those whom they love and delight in, give good things; and to the contrary to these, their contraries. Therefore it is manifest, that such things are to be done in which God delights.

Thus he defined particularly of all things. To believe of the divinity that it is; and that it is in such manner as to mankind; that it overlooks them not and neglects them not—such beliefs the Pythagoreans, taught by him, conceived to be profitable. For we have need of such a government, as we ought not in anything to contradict; such is that which proceeds from the divinity. For the divinity is such that it merits the dominion of all. Man they affirmed to be, rightly speaking, a creature reproachful and fickle as to his appetites, affections, and other passions. He therefore has need of such government and guidance, from which proceeds moderation and order. Now they conceived that everyone, being conscious of the fickleness of his own nature, should never be forgetful of sanctity and service towards the Divinity, but always have the Divinity in their mind; how it overlooks and observes human life.

In fine, they say that Pythagoras was an imitator of the Orphean constitutions—worshipping the gods after the manner of Orpheus, placed in brazen images, not representing the forms of men but of the gods themselves, who comprehending and foreseeing all things, resemble in nature and form the whole. He declared their purifications and rites, which are called τελεταὶ ["Rites of Fulfillment"],† having the most exact knowledge of them.

Moreover they affirm, he made a composition of the divine philosophy and service: part whereof he had learned from the Orpheans; part from the Egyptian priests; some from the Chaldeans and Magi; some from the Eleusinian Rites; and those in Imber, and Samothracia, and Delos, and the Celtae, and Iberians.

Amongst the Latins also is read the sacred discourse of Pythagoras. Not to all, but to such as are admitted to the doctrine of excellent things, and are not addicted to ought that is dishonest.

It prescribes that men offer libation thrice; and Apollo gives oracles from a tripod, because number first consists in a triad.

That we must sacrifice to Venus on the sixth day, because that is the first common number of the number of universal nature. Now after all ways, the thing divided in like manner assumes as well the power of those things which are taken away as of those which are left.

That to Hercules we ought to sacrifice on the eighth day of the month, in respect of his being born at the end of seven months.

It says also, that we ought to enter into a temple having a pure garment, and in which none has slept the sleep of slothfulness; black and russet, testifying purity in ratiocinations of equality and justice.

It commanded, that if blood be shed unwillingly in a temple, that it be either taken up in a dish or scattered into the sea; for that is the first element, and most estimable of all creatures.

It says likewise, that a woman ought not to be brought to bed in a temple, for it is religious; that the divinity of the soul should be annexed to the body in a temple.

It commanded that upon holy days we cut not our hair, nor pare our nails; intimating that the increase of our goods ought not to be preferred before the empire of the gods.

That we must not kill a flea in the temple, because to the deity we ought not to offer any superfluous things, or vermin. But that the gods are to be worshipped with cedar, laurel, cypress, and myrtle, etc.

He said piety and religion are chiefly conversant in our minds, at such time as we attend the divine rites.[745]

He taught that the gods and heroes are not to be worshipped with equal honors.[746] But that the gods must always be worshipped with applause (or silence at the celebration of their rites), we being white and pure. Heroes are to be worshipped only from noon. He advised that such as sacrifice should present themselves to the gods, not in rich, but in white and clean garments; and that not only the body be clear from all blemish, but that they bring also a pure mind.[747] Purity is acquired by expiations, and bathings, and sprinklings; and by refraining from murder, and adultery, and all pollution; and by abstaining from the flesh of things that die of themselves, and from mullets, and **melanures**, and sheep, and oviparous creatures, and beans, and all other things which are commanded by those who have the care of sacred rites.

He permitted not that any man should pray for himself, because none knows what is good for himself.[748]

An Oath is just, and therefore Jupiter is surnamed Ὅρκος ["of oaths"]†.[749] He commanded his disciples to be very backward and cautious in taking an Oath; but that when they have taken it, they should be very forward and diligent to keep it.[750]

CHAPTER 4

PIETY TO THE DEAD

Piety to the dead was a part, not the least, of the Pythagorean doctrine. Whence Cicero, speaking of the immortality of the soul: "More prevalent with me," says he, "is the authority of the ancients, or our ancestors, who afforded the dead religious rites—which certainly they had not done if they had conceived that nothing pertains to them; or of those who were in this country and instructed Magna Graecia (which now is abolished but then flourished), with their institutions and precepts."[751]

Pythagoras allowed not the bodies of the dead to be burned, herein imitating the Magi, as not willing that any mortal should participate of divine honor.[752] The Pythagorean custom, as described by Pliny, was to put the dead into earthen barrels amongst leaves of myrtle, olive, and black poplar.[753]

To accompany the dead at funerals in white garments he conceived to be pious; alluding to the simple and first nature, according to number, and the principle of all things.[754]

The Crotonians delighted in burying their dead sumptuously. One of the Pythagoreans told them he had heard Pythagoras discoursing of divine things thus:

> "The celestial gods respect the affections of the sacrificers, not the greatness of the sacrifice. On the contrary, the terrestrial gods, as to whose share the lesser things belong, delight in banquets, and mournings, and funeral litations, and costly sacrifices. Whence Hades (the Infernal Regions), from its making choice of entertainment, is named Pluto. Those who pay honors to him most sparingly he permits to continue longest in the upper world. But of those who are excessive in mourning, he brings down ever and anon one, that thereby he may receive the honors which are paid in memory of the dead."

By this discourse he wrought a belief in his Auditors that they who do all things moderately upon such adverse occasions further their own safety; but as for those who bestow excessive charge, they will all die untimely.[755]

They forbore to make tombs of Cypress, forasmuch as Jupiter's scepter was of that wood, as Hermippus, in his second book of Pythagoras, affirms.[756]

CHAPTER 5

Reverence of Parents, and Obedience to the Law

Next to gods and daemons, we ought to reverence parents and the law; and to render ourselves obedient to them, not falsely, but really.[757] Or as Porphyry says, "He commanded to think and to speak reverently of gods and daemons, to be kind to parents and benefactors, and to obey the law."[758]

They held (says Iamblichus) that we ought to believe, there is no greater ill than anarchy; for a man cannot be safe, where there is no governor.[759] They held also that we ought to persevere in the customs and rites of our own country, though they be worse than those of other countries. To revolt easily from settled laws, and to be studious of novelty, they conceived to be neither advantageous nor safe.

Seeing that contumelies, pride, and contempt of law often transport men to unjust actions, he daily exhorted, that the law should be assisted and injustice opposed.[760] To which end he alleged this distinction: The first of ills, which insinuates itself into houses and cities, is pride; the second, insolence; the third, destruction. Everyone therefore ought to expel and extirpate pride, accustoming himself from his youth to a temperate masculine life, and to be free from slanderous repining, contentious reproaching, and hateful scurrility.

Wickedness disobeys the Divine Law, and therefore transgresses.[761]

A wicked man suffers more torment in his own conscience than he who is punished in body and whipped.[762]

CHAPTER 6

LAWMAKING

Moreover, says Iamblichus, he constituted another excellent kind of Justice, the legislative part, which commands that which ought to be done, and forbids that which ought not to be done. This is better than the judicative part. For the judicative resembles that part of medicine which cures the sick, but the legislative suffers them not to fall sick, but takes care afar off of the health of the soul.

Varro affirms that Pythagoras delivered this discipline (of governing states) to his auditors last of all—when they were now learned, now wise, now happy. For he saw so many rough waves therein, that he would not commit it but to such a one as was able to shun the rocks; or if all failed, might stand himself as a rock amidst those waves.[763]

They who punish not ill persons would have the good injured.[764]

Theoretical Philosophy: Its Parts
And First of the Science Concerning Intelligibles

We come next to the theoretical part, to which more particularly belongs that saying of Pythagoras: that by philosophy be had this advantage—to admire nothing. For philosophical discourse takes away wonder—which arises from doubt and ignorance—by knowledge and examination of the facility of everything.

Theoretical philosophy seems to have been divided by the Pythagoreans into two parts, they first (says Iamblichus) delivered the science of intelligibles and the gods; next which, they taught all Physic. To the science of intelligibles belong these heads, wherewith Iamblichus begins his recapitulation of the gods, of heroes, and of daemons.[765]

CHAPTER I

Of the Supreme God

Pythagoras defined what God is thus: a Mind which penetrates in all directions, and is diffused through every part of the World and through all Nature; from whom all animals that are produced receive life.[766]

God is one.[767] He is not (as some conceive) out of the world, but entire within himself, in a complete circle surveying all generations. He is the Temperament of all ages, the Agent of his own powers and works, the Principle of all things; one in heaven luminary, and father of all things; mind and animation of the whole, the motion of all circles.

God (as Pythagoras learned of the Magi, who term him Ahura Mazda) in his body resembles Light, in his soul, Truth.[768] He said that God only is wise.[769]

He conceived that the first being (God) is neither sensible nor susceptible to sensation or emotion; but is invisible and intelligible.[770]

CHAPTER 2

OF GODS, DAEMONS, HEROES

Next to the supreme God, there are three kinds of intelligibles: gods, daemons, heroes. That Pythagoras thus distinguished them is manifest from his precept that we must in worship prefer gods before daemons, heroes before men.[771] But in Iamblichus, he seems either to observe a different method, or to confound the terms; teaching first of gods, then of heroes, last of daemons; which order perhaps is the same with that of the Golden Verses.[772]

> First, as decreed, th' immortal Gods adore,
> Thy Oath keep: next great Heroes, then implore
> Terrestrial Daemons with due sacrifice.[773]

By Terrestrial Daemons seems to be understood not Princes (as Hierocles) but the daemons themselves, confined to several offices upon earth; For,

"All the air is full of souls, which are esteemed daemons and heroes. From these are sent to men dreams and presages of sickness and of health; and not only to men, but to sheep also, and to other cattle. To these pertain expiations, and the warding off of evil, and all divinations, **Cledons** and the like."[774]

CHAPTER 3

OF FATE AND FORTUNE

All the parts of the world above the Moon, are governed according to Providence and firm order, and εἱμαρμένη, the Decree of God† which they follow. But those beneath the Moon by four causes: by God, by fate, by our election, by fortune.[775] For instance, to go aboard into a ship or not is in our power; storms and tempests to arise out of a calm is by fortune; for the ship, being underwater to be preserved, is by the providence of God. Of fate there are many manners and differences. It differs from fortune as having a determination, order, and consequence; but fortune is spontaneous and casual—as to proceed from a boy to a youth, and orderly to pass through the other degrees of age, happens by one manner of fate. (Here the text seems deficient.)

Man is of affinity with the Gods, by reason that he participates of heat, wherefore God has a providential care of us.[776] There is also εἱμαρμένη, a Fate of all things in general and in particular, the cause of their administration.†

DIVINATION

For as much as by daemons and heroes all divination is conveyed to men, we shall here add what Pythagoras held and practiced therein. Iamblichus says that he honored divination not the least of the sciences.[777] For what things are agreeable to God cannot be known unless a man hear God himself, or the gods, or acquire it by divine art. For this reason, they diligently studied divination, as being the only interpretation of the benevolence of the gods. It is likewise an employment most suitable to those who believe there are gods. But whoever thinks either belief in the gods or divination a folly, to him the other is such also.

Pythagoras approved all kinds of divination, except that which is performed by the sacrifice of living creatures.[778]

He first used divination by frankincense.[779] This was the only burnt offering by which he divined.[780]

He also used divination by Cledons,[781] and by birds, which Cicero confirms, saying that he would himself be an augur;[782] and that the Pythagoreans observed not only the voices of the gods, but of men also, which they call omens.[783] Cledons are observations of occurrent speeches, collecting from what is accidentally said upon some other occasion, the effect of what is sought: an instance whereof, see in the Epigram of Callimachus upon Pittacus.[784]

The interpretation of dreams, Porphyry says, he learned of the Hebrews. He communicated it also to his disciples; for Iamblichus relates he used means to procure them quiet sleeps with good and prophetic dreams. For this reason, some conceive, it was that he forbade flatulent and gross meats, for that they obstruct the serenity which is requisite thereto. Such apparitions he held not to be fantastic but real (not ὄναρ "a dream" but ὕπαρ "in reality"), as is manifest from one who told him that he dreamed he had talked with his father who was dead, and asked him what it portended. "Nothing," says he, "for you did really talk with him. As my speaking now to you portends nothing, nor did that."[785]

He was skillful likewise in judicial Astrology, if we credit Apuleius, who affirms the Chaldeans showed him the science of the stars, the number of the planets, their stations, revolutions, and the various effects of both in the nativities of men.[786]

Varro relates him skillful in Hydromancy,[787] which (says he) came from Persia, and was practiced by Numa, and afterwards by Pythagoras; wherein they used blood, and invocation of daemons.

Eustathius says the Pythagoreans affirm that all brass does sound by some diviner spirit, for which reason a tripod of that metal is dedicated to Apollo. And when the winds are all laid, the air calm, and all things else quiet, yet the hollow brass caldrons seem to quake.[788] The same may be the meaning of Pythagoras when he says, "The sound which is made by brass, is the voice of the voice of the Daemon enclosed in the brass."[789] (Reading, perhaps, ἐναπειλημμένην†.)

For so Psellus describes a kind of hydromancy practiced by the Assyrians: They take a basin full of water convenient for the daemons to glide into the bottom. The basin of water seems to make a noise as if it breathed. The water in the basin in substance differs nothing from other water—but through the virtue infused thereinto by charms is much more excellent, and made more ready to receive a prophetic spirit. This is a particular daemon, terrestrial, attracted by compositions. As soon as he glides into the water, he makes a little sound inarticulate, which denotes his presence. Afterwards the water running over, there are certain whispers heard with some prediction of the future. This kind of spirit is very wandering, because it is of the solar order, and this kind of daemons purposely speak with a low voice, that by reason of the indistinct obscurity of the voice, their lies may be less subject to discovery. Hitherto Psellus.

PHYSIC

The general heads of Physic are these: of the world, and of all things in the world, of Heaven, and of Earth, and of the natures between them.[790] The defect of the fragments concerning these, we shall endeavor to supply by adding the Treatise of Timaeus the Locrian upon the same subject. [See page 301]

The brass tripod of Apollo appears on the reverse of this silver stater of Croton, struck c.420 B.C. The obverse shows young Heracles seated before an altar, and among his accouterments. The reverse shows Apollo's tripod decorated with hanging fillets, amidst a scene of Apollo preparing to discharge an arrow into the serpent Python.
Photo courtesy of Numismatica Ars Classica

CHAPTER I

PRINCIPLES

The most learned of the Naturalists (says Sextus Empericus) attributed so great power to numbers, that they thought them to be the principles and elements of all things.[791] These were the disciples of Pythagoras. For, say they, such as treat of philosophy aright imitate those who study a language. They first examine words, because language consists of words; then, because words consist of syllables, they next consider syllables; and because syllables consist of letters, they next examine letters. In like manner, say the Pythagoreans, natural philosophers, when they make enquiry into the universe, must first examine into what the universe is resolved.

Now to affirm that something apparent to sense is the principle of all things is repugnant to Physic. For whatsoever is apparent to sense must be compounded of things not apparent. Whereas a principle is not that which consists of any thing, but that of which the thing consists. Therefore things apparent cannot be said to be principles of the universe, but those of which things apparent consist, themselves not being apparent.

They who maintain atoms, or **Homoeomeries**, or bulks, or intelligible bodies, to be the principles of all things were partly in the right, partly not. As conceiving the principles to be unapparent, they are in the right; as holding them to be corporeal, they err. For as intelligible unapparent bodies precede the sensible, so must incorporeals precede intelligible bodies. The elements of words are not words; nor of bodies, bodies. But they must either be bodies or incorporeal; therefore they are wholly incorporeal.

Neither can we say that Atoms are eternal, and therefore though corporeal, the principles of all things. For first they who assert Homoeomeries, and bulks, and leasts, and indivisibles, to be elements, conceive their substance eternal; so as in that respect, Atoms are no more elements than they. Again, though it were granted that atoms were eternal, yet they who conceive the world to be unbegotten and eternal, enquire by an imaginary way the principles whereof it first consists. So we (say the Pythagoreans), treating of Physic, consider in an imaginary way of what things these eternal bodies, comprehensible only by reason, consist.

Thus the Universe consists either of bodies or incorporeals. We cannot say bodies, for then we must assign other bodies whereof they consist; and so proceeding to infinite, we shall remain without a principle. It rests therefore to affirm that intelligible bodies consist of incorporeals, which Epicurus confesses, saying, "By collection of figure, and magnitude, and resistance, and gravity, is understood a body."

Yet it is not necessary that all corporeals preexistent to bodies be the elements and first principles of beings. Ideas (according to Plato) are incorporeals, pre-existent to bodies, and all generated beings have reference to them; yet they are not the principles of being. For every Idea, singly taken, is said to be one; when we comprehend others with it, they are two, or three, or four. Number therefore is transcendent to their substance, by participation whereof, one, two, or more, are predicated of them. Again, solid figures are conceived in the mind before bodies, as having an incorporeal nature; yet they are not the principles. Superficies precede them in our imagination, for solids consist of superficies. But neither are superficies the elements of beings, for they consist of lines; lines precede them; numbers precede lines. That which consists of three lines, is called a Triangle; that which of four, a Quadrangle. Even line itself, simply taken, is not conceived without number—but being carried on from one point to another, is conceived in two. As to Numbers, they all fall under the Monad. For the Duad is one Duad, the Triad one Triad, and the Decad one summary of number.

This moved Pythagoras to say, that the principle of all things is the Monad, by participation hereof, every being is termed One. And when we reflect on a being in its identity, we consider a Monad. But when it receives addition by the other, it produces indeterminate Duad, so called in distinction from the Arithmetical determinate Duads, by participation whereof all Duads are understood as Monads by the Monad. Thus there are two principles of beings, the first Monad, and the indeterminate Duad.

That these are indeed the principles of all things, the Pythagoreans reach variously. Of beings (say they), some are understood by

Difference, others by **Contrariety,** others by **Relation.** By difference
are those which are considered by themselves subjected by their
proper circumscription: as, a man, a horse, a plant, earth, water, air,
fire; each of these is considered absolutely without any comparison.
By contrariety are those which are considered by one to the other: as
good and ill, just and unjust, profitable and unprofitable, sacred and
profane, pious and impious, moving and fixed, and the like. By relation are those which are considered by relation to others: as right to
left, upwards to downwards, double to half. For right is understood by
a relative habit to left, and left by a relative habit to right; upwards
to downwards, and downward to upwards; and so on of the rest.

Those which are understood by contrariety differ from those
that are understood by relation. In contraries, the corruption of the
one is the generation of another: as of health, sickness, motion, rest.
The induction of sickness is the expulsion of health, and the induction of health is the expulsion of sickness; the same in grief and joy,
good and ill, and all things of contrary natures. But the relative exist
together, and perish together. For right is nothing unless there be
left; double is nothing unless we understand the half whereof it is the
double. Moreover, in contraries there is no mean, as between health
and sickness, life and death, motion and rest. But between relatives
there is a mean—as between greater and lesser, the mean is equal;
between too much and too little, sufficient; between too flat and too
sharp, concord.

Above these three kinds—absolute, contrary, relative—there
must necessarily be some Supreme Genus; every genus is before
the species which are under it. For if the Genus be taken away, the
species are taken away also; but the removal of the species takes
not away the genus; the species depending on the genus, not the
genus on the species. The transcending genus of those things which
are understood by themselves (according to the Pythagoreans) is
the One. That exists and is considered absolutely, so they say. Of
contraries, equal and unequal, holds the place of a genus; for in
them is considered the nature of all contrarieties. By example, of
rest in equality, it admits not intension and remission; of motion or
inequality, it admits intension and remission. In like manner, natural
inequality is the instable extremity; preternatural inequality admits

intension and remission. The same of health and sickness, straightness and crookedness. The relative consists of excess and defect as their genus; great and greater, much and more, high and higher, are understood by excess: little and less, low and lower, by defect.

Now forasmuch as absolutes, contraries, and relatives appear to be subordinate to other genera (that is, to one, to equality and inequality, to excess and defect), let us examine whether those genera may be reduced to others. Equality is reducible to one, for one is equal in itself; inequality is either in excess or defect; of unequals, one exceeds, the other is deficient. Excess and defect are reducible to the indeterminate Duad; for the first excess and defect is in two, in the **excedent** and the deficient. Thus the principles of all things appear above all the rest in the first Monad and the indeterminate Duad.

Of these are generated the Arithmetical Monad and Duad. From the first Monad, one; from the Monad and the indeterminate Duad, two. The Duad, being not yet constituted amongst Numbers, neither was there two before it was taken out of the indeterminate Duad. From the indeterminate Duad, together with the Monad, was produced the Duad which is in Numbers. Out of these, in the same manner proceeded the rest of the Numbers: one continually stepping forward, the indeterminate Duad generating two, and extending Numbers to an infinite multitude.

Hereupon they affirm that, in principles, Monad has the nature of the efficient cause, Duad of passive matter. And after the same manner as they produced Numbers, which consists of them, they composed the world also and all things in it.

A Point is correspondent to the Monad. The Monad is indivisible, so is the Point; the Monad is the principle of Numbers, so is the Point of Lines. A Line is correspondent to the Duad; both are considered by transition. A line is length without breath, extended between two points. A Superficies corresponds to the Triad. Besides length, whereby it was a Duad, it receives a third distance, breadth. Again, settling down three points: two opposite, the third at the juncture of the lines made by the two, we represent a superficies. The solid figure and the body (as a pyramid) answer the Tetrad. If we lay down, as before, three points, and set over them another point—

behold the pyramidical form of a solid body, which has three dimensions, length, breadth, thickness.

Some there are who affirm that a body consists of one point; the point by fluxion makes a line; the line by fluxion makes a superficies; the superficies moved to thickness makes a body in three dimensions. This sect of the Pythagoreans differs from the former. They held that of two principles—the Monad and the Duad—were made Numbers; of Numbers were made Points, Lines, Superficies, and Solids. These hold that all things come from one point—for of it is made a line, of the line a superficies, of the superficies a body.

Thus are solid bodies produced of numbers precedent to them. Moreover, of them consist Solids, Fire, Water, Air, Earth, and in a word, the whole World; which is governed according to Harmony— as they affirm again—recurring to Numbers which comprise the proportions that constitute perfect Harmony.[792] Harmony is a system consisting of three concords: the Diatessaron, the Diapente, the Diapason; the proportions of these three concords are found in the first four numbers: one, two, three, four. The Diatessaron consists in a sesquitertia proportion. The Diapason is in sesquialtera. The Diapente is in duple. Four being sesquitertius to three (as consisting of three and one third) has a Diatessaron proportion; three being sesquialter to two (as containing two and its half), a Diapente; four being the double of the Monad of two, a Diapason. The Tetractys affording the analogy of these concords, which make perfect harmony, according to which all things are governed, they styled it:

The root and fountain of eternal nature.

Moreover, whatsoever is comprehended by man (say they) either is a body or incorporeal; but neither of these is comprehended without the notion of numbers. A body, having a triple dimension, denotes the number three. Besides of bodies, some are by connection: as ships, chains, buildings; others by union comprised under one habit: as plants and animals; others by aggregation: as armies and herds. All these have numbers, as consisting of plurality. Moreover of bodies: some have simple qualities, others multiplex. Examples include an apple, various colors to the sight, juice to the taste, odor to the smell; these also are of the nature of numbers. It is the same of incorporeals. Time, an incorporeal, is comprehended by number: years, months, days, and hours. The like of a Point, a Line, a Superficies, as we said already.

Likewise to numbers are correspondent both naturals and artificials. We judge everything by criteria, which are the measures of numbers. If we take away number, we take away the cubit, which consists of two half-cubits, six palms, twenty four digits. We take away the bushel, the balance, and all other criteria, which, consisting of plurality, are kinds of number. In a word, there is nothing in life without it. All art is a collection of comprehensions. Collection implies number; it is therefore rightly said:

To number all things reference have.

That is to determinative reason, which is of the same kind with numbers, whereof all consists. Hitherto Sextus.

The sum of all (as said by Alexander in his Successions, extracted out of the Pythagorean commentaries) is this: the Monad is the principle of all things.[793] From the Monad came the indeterminate Duad. As matter subjected to the cause, Monad; from the Monad and the indeterminate Duad came Numbers. From Numbers came Points. From Points came Lines; from Lines, Superficies; from Superficies, Solids; from these, solid bodies. Solid bodies are composed of four elements: Fire, Water, Air, Earth; of all which, transmutated and totally changed, the world consists.

CHAPTER 2

Of the World

The World, or comprehension of all things, Pythagoras called Κόσμος ["order"], from its order and beauty.[794]

The world[795] was made by God,[796] in thought, not in time.[797] He gave it a beginning from fire and the fifth element. For there are five figures of solid bodies which are termed mathematical. Earth was made of a Cube; fire of a Pyramid or Tetrahedron; Air of an Octahedron; Water of an Icosahedron; the Sphere of the Universe of a Dodecahedron. In these, Plato follows Pythagoras.

The world is corruptible in its own nature, for it is sensible and corporeal.[798] But it shall never be corrupted, by reason of the providence and preservation of God.[799] Fate is the cause of the order of the universe and all particulars.[800] Necessity encompasses the world.

The world is animate, intelligible, spherical, enclosing the earth in the midst of it.[801]

The Pythagoreans affirm[802] that what is without heaven is infinite; for beyond the world there is a Vacuum, into which, and out of which, the world respires.[803]

The right side of the world is the east, whence motion begins; the left is the West.[804]

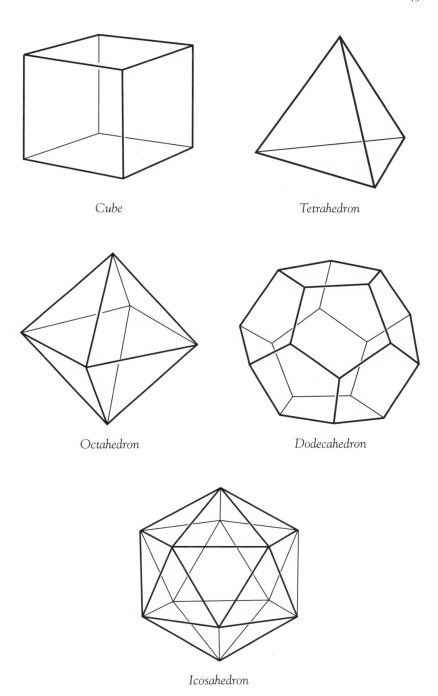

Cube

Tetrahedron

Octahedron

Dodecahedron

Icosahedron

Of the Superior or Aetherial Parts of the World

Pythagoras first called heaven Κόσμον ["order"],† as being perfect in all kinds of animals and adorned with all kinds of pulchritude.[805]

In the fixed sphere resides the first Cause: whatsoever is next him, they affirm to be best, and firmly compounded and ordered; that which is furthest from him, the worst.[806] There is a constant order observed as low as the Moon, but all things beneath the Moon are moved promiscuously.

For the air which is diffused about the earth is unmoved and unwholesome, and all things that are in it are mortal. But the air which is above is perpetually in motion, and pure, and healthful; and all that are in it are immortal, and consequently divine.[807]

This they call, the free Aether (immediately above the Moon). Aether, they perceived, as being void of matter and an eternal body; free, because it is not obnoxious and filled with material disturbances.[808]

Hence it follows that the Sun, Moon, and the rest of the stars, according to Pythagoras, are gods.

The Pythagoreans held that every star is a world in the infinite Aether, which contains earth, air, and Aether. This opinion was also held by the followers of Orpheus, that every star is a world.[809]

The Sun is spherical, eclipsed by the Moons coming under him.[810]

The body of the Moon is of a fiery nature; she receives her light from the Sun.[811] The eclipse of the Moon is a reverberation or obstruction from the Antichthon.

The Pythagoreans affirm that the Moon seems earthly because she is round-about inhabited as our earth. But the creatures are larger and fairer, exceeding us in size fifteen times, neither have they any excrements, and their day is so much longer.[812]

Some of the Pythagoreans affirm that a comet is one of the planets that appears not in heaven but after a long time, and is near the Sun, as it happens also to Mercury. For because it recedes but little from the Sun, often when it should appear, it is hid; so as it appears not but after a long time.[813] Or, as Plutarch expresses it, a comet is one of those stars which are not always apparent, but rise after a certain period. Others hold that it is the reflection of our sight on the Sun, like images in glasses.[814]

The rainbow he asserted to be the splendor of the Sun.[815]

Celestial bodies frequently appear in ancient art. This silver denarius was issued by Juba II and his wife Cleopatra Selene, the only daughter of Marc Antony and Cleopatra VII, who were made co-rulers of the Kingdom of Mauretania by Rome's first emperor, Augustus. It represents Juba II with his portrait on the obverse and Cleopatra Selene with a star above a crescent (alluding to the goddess Selene) on its reverse.

Photo courtesy of Classical Numismatic Group, Inc.

Of the inferior sublunary parts of the world, the anonymous Pythagorean places first the sphere of fire, then that of air, next that of water, last that of Earth.[816]

The bodies of all the elements are round, except that of fire, which is conical.[817]

Below the Moon all things move in a disorderly manner. Evil therefore necessarily exists about the region of the Earth; that being settled lowest as the basis of the world, the receptacle of the lowest things.[818]

The air, which is diffused about the Earth is unmoved and unwholesome, and all things in it are mortal.[819]

There, is generation and corruption. For things are produced by alteration, mutation, and resolution of the elements. Motion is a difference or diversity in matter.[820]

In the world, there is equally proportioned, light and darkness, heat and cold, dryness and humidity. When they are exuberant, the excess of heat causes summer; of cold, winter. When they are equal, then are the best seasons of the year: whereof that which is growing up is the spring, healthful; that which is decaying is autumn, unhealthful.[821] Even of the day, the morning is growing up, the evening decaying, and therefore more unwholesome.

Of Living, and Animate Creatures

There penetrates a beam from the Sun through the Aether which is cold and dry.[822] (They call the air, "cold aether," and the Sun and humidity, "gross aether.") This beam penetrates to the Abyss, and thereby all things vivificate. All things live inasmuch as they participate of heat (wherefore even plants are ζῶα, living creatures). But all things have not soul. The soul is a portion of aether, of heat, and cold, for it participates of cold aether. The soul differs from life. She is immortal, because that from which she is taken is immortal. Thus Alexander in his successions, out of the commentaries of the Pythagoreans.

CHAPTER 2

Of the Generation of Animate Creatures

Animate creatures are generated of one another by seed (but of earth nothing can be generated).[823] Seed is a distillation from the brain of the foam of the most useful part of the blood, the superfluity of the aliment, as blood and marrow. This being injected τῇ μήτρᾳ ["in the womb"], purulent matter, moisture, and blood issue from the brain, whereof flesh, nerves, bones, hair, and the whole body consists. (The power of seed is incorporeal as the motive mind; but the effused matter corporeal.) From the vapor comes the soul and sense; it is first compacted and coagulated in forty days. And being perfected according to harmonical proportions in seven, nine, or ten months (at the farthest), the Infant is brought forth, having all proportions of life; of which (aptly connected according to the proportions of harmony) it consists; all things happening to it at certain times. Thus Alexander, out of the Pythagorean commentaries.

The proportions themselves are more exactly delivered by Censorinus thus.[824] Pythagoras said that generally there are two kinds of births: one lesser, of seven months; which comes into the world the 207th day after the conception. The other greater, of ten months; which is brought forth in the 274th day. The first and lesser is chiefly contained in the number six. For that which is conceived of the seed (as he says) the six first days, is a milky substance; the next eight days, bloody; which eight with the six make the first concord, Diatessaron. The third degree is of nine days; in which time, it is made flesh. These to the first six are in sesquialtera proportion, and make the second concord, Diapente. Then follow twelve days more in which the body is fully formed. These to the same six consist in duple proportion, and make the Diatessaron concord. These four numbers, six, eight, nine, twelve, added together make thirty-five days; nor without reason is the number six the foundation of generation. For the Greeks call it τελείον, we perfect; because its three parts perfect it. Now as the beginnings of the seed and that milky foundation of conception is first completed by this number, so this is the beginning of the man now formed. And, as it were, another foundation of maturity which is of thirty-five days, being multiplied by six, makes 220 days in which this maturity is fulfilled.

The other (greater) birth is contained in the greater number seven. And as the beginning of the former is in six days, after which the seed is converted into blood, so that of this is in seven. And as there the members of the Infant are formed in thirty-five days; so here in about forty. These forty days being multiplied by the first seven, make 280 days, that is forty weeks. But forasmuch as the birth happens on the first day of the last week, six days are subtracted, and the 274th observed.

He held that mankind had ever been; and never had beginning.[825]

CHAPTER 3

The Soul: Its Parts
And First of the Irrational Part

The power of number, being greatest in nature,[826] Pythagoras defined the soul as a self-moving number.[827]

Of the Pythagoreans, some affirm that the soul is the motes in the air; others, that it is that which moves those motes.[828]

The soul is most generally divided into two parts, rational, and irrational, but more especially into three.[829] For the irrational they divide into irascible and desiderative. These are termed νοῦς ["intelligence"], φρὴν ["reason"], and θυμὸς ["passion"]. Νοῦς ["intelligence"] and θυμὸς ["passion"] are in other living creatures, φρὴν ["reason"] only in man.[830]

Yet, the souls of all animate creatures are rational, even of those which we term irrational. But they act not according to reason because of the ill temperament of the body and want of speech: as in apes and dogs, λαλοῦσι μὲν γὰρ οὗτοι, οὐ φράζουσι δέ, who talk but cannot speak.[831]

The beginning of the soul comes from the heat of the brain. That part which is the heart is θυμὸς ["passion"], but φρένες ["reason"] and νοῦς ["intelligence"] are in the brain. The senses are distillations from these: the rational part is immortal, the rest mortal. The soul is nourished by blood, and the faculties of the soul are spirits. Both the soul and her faculties are invisible, for Aether is invisible. The fetters of the soul are veins, arteries, and nerves. But when she is strong, and composed within herself, her fetters are reasons and actions.

Every sense is derived from its proper element. Sight is from Aether, hearing from air, smelling from fire, taste from water, touch from earth.[832]

Sense in general, and particulary sight, is a vapor very hot. For this reason we are said to see through air and through water, for the heat pierces the cold. For if that which is in the eyes were a cold vapor, it would fight with the air—which is like it hot. In some places, he calls the eyes the gates of the Sun; the same he determined concerning hearing and the rest of the senses.

Sight is the judge of colors.[833] Color they call the superficies of a body. The kinds of color are black, white, red, pale.[834] Or, as the anonymous writer delivers the opinion of Pythagoras, ten: black, white, and the rest between them, yellow, tawney, pale, red, blue, green, bright, grey.[835] The differences of colors are derived from the mixture of the elements, and, in living creatures, from variety of place and of air.

The image in a mirror is made by reflection of the sight.[836] This, being extended to the brass, and meeting with a thick smooth body, is pushed back and returns into itself, as when the hand is stretched forth and again brought back to the shoulder.[837]

Hearing is the judge of voice, sharp and flat.[838] Voice is incorporeal; for not air, but the figure and superficies of air, by a stroke becomes voice. But no superficies is a body.[839] And though it follows the motion of the body, voice itself has no body; as when a rod is bent, the superficies suffers nothing, the matter only is bent.

Smelling judges of odors, good and ill and the four between them: putrid, humid, liquid, vaporous.[840]

Taste judges of flavors, sweet, bitter, and the five between them. For they are in all seven: sweet, bitter, sharp, acid, fresh, salt, hot.

Touching judges many things: heavy, light, and those that are between them; hot, cold, and those that are between them; hard, soft, and those that are between them; dry, moist, and those that are between them. The other four senses are seated in the head only and confined to their proper organs. But touching is diffused through the head, and the whole body. It is common to every sense, but exhibits its judgment most manifestly by the hands.

CHAPTER 4

OF THE RATIONAL PART OF THE SOUL: THE MIND

According to Plutarch, Pythagoras defined the soul as, "A self-moving number," adding that he takes number to be the same as a mind.[841] The mind, νοῦς, is induced into the soul *ab extrinseco*, from without, by divine participation[842] (θεία μείρᾳ†), culled out as a small part of the universal Divine Mind.[843] For there is a soul intent and penetrating in all directions through the whole nature of things[844] from which our souls are plucked.[845] She is immortal, because that from which she is taken is immortal, yet not a god—but the work of the eternal God.[846] Thus Pythagoras confirmed the opinion of his master Pherecides, who first taught that the souls of men are sempiternal.

Our Souls (said he) consist of a tetrad: mind, science, opinion, sense. From this tetrad proceeds all art and science by which we ourselves are rational.[847] The mind therefore is a monad, for the mind considers according to a monad. By way of example, there are many men. These, one by one, are incomprehensible by sense and innumerable. But we understand this one man to which none has resemblance. And we understand one horse, for the particulars are innumerable. Thus every genus and species is according to monad, wherefore to everyone in particular they apply this definition—whether a rational creature or a neighing creature. Hence is the mind a monad, whereby we understand these things. The indeterminate duad is science. For all demonstration, and all belief of science, and likewise all syllogism from some things granted, infer that which is doubted. And they easily demonstrate another thing, the comprehension whereof is science. Therefore it is as the duad. Opinion is justly a triad, being of many. Triad implies a multitude, as, thrice happy Greeks—(The rest of the text is wanting.)

The Pythagoreans assert eight organs of knowledge: Sense, **Phantasie**, Art, Opinion, Prudence, Science, Wisdom, Mind.[848] Of these, we have in common with divine natures, art, prudence, science, mind. With beasts we share sense and Phantasie. Only opinion is proper to us. Sense is a deceitful knowledge through the body; Phantasie, a motion in the soul; art, a habit of operating with reason. We add, "with reason," for a spider also operates, but without reason. Prudence is a habit elective of that which is right in things to be done. Science is a habit of those things which are always the same and in the same manner. Wisdom is a knowledge of the First Cause. Mind is the principle and fountain of all good things.

CHAPTER 5

OF THE TRANSMIGRATION OF THE SOUL

What he delivered to his auditors (says Porphyry) none can certainly affirm, for there was a great and strict silence observed amongst them.[849] But the most known are these: First, he said that the soul is immortal; then, that it enters into other kinds of living creatures. (Or, as Laertius expresses it: He first asserted that the soul, passing through the circle of necessity, lives as several times in different living creatures.)[850] Moreover, that after some periods, the same things that are now generated are generated again; that nothing is simply new. And that we ought to esteem all animate creatures to be of the same kind with us.

These doctrines Pythagoras seems to have brought first into Greece. Diodorus Siculus affirms, he learned them of the Egyptians.[851] They were the first who asserted that the soul of man is immortal, and the body perishing, it always passes into another body. And when it has run through all things terrestrial, marine, volatile, it again enters into some generated human body. This circuit is completed in three thousand years. This opinion (adds Herodotus) some of the Greeks have usurped as their own—some more ancient, others later—whose names knowingly I omit.[852]

Pythagoras (says Theodoret), Plato, Plotinus, and the rest of that sect acknowledged souls to be immortal. They asserted that souls are preexistent to bodies, and that there is an innumerable company of souls. Those which transgress are sent down into bodies, so as being purified by such discipline, they may return to their own place. Those which while they are in bodies lead a wicked life, are sent down farther into irrational creatures, hereby to receive punishment and right expiation: the angry and malicious into serpents, the ravenous into wolves, the audacious into lions, the fraudulent into foxes, and the like.

Upon this ground (as some conceive) it was that he forbade to eat flesh.[853] For we ought to esteem all animals creatures to be of the same kind with us,[854] and to have common right with us, and to be allied (in a manner) to us.[855] Whence a bean is by Horace styled *cognata Pythagorae*, because he forbade it to be eaten upon the grounds that men and beans arose out of the same putrefaction.[856]

This assertion he defended by many instances, particularly of himself. Heraclides relates the following.[857] Pythagoras said he had been in former times Aethalides, esteemed the son of Mercury. (Aethalides was a powerful orator who wrote two treatises, the one mournful, the other pleasant.[858] Like Democritus and Heraclitus, he bewailed and derided the instability of life, and was said to die and live from day to day.) Pythagoras related that Mercury bade him (as Aethalides) request whatsoever he would, immortality only excepted. He desired that he might preserve the remembrance of all actions, alive and dead. Whereupon he remembered all things while he lived, and after death, retained the same memory. That afterwards he came to be Euphorbus and was slain by Menelaus.

Now Euphorbus said that he had been in former times Aethalides, and that he had received this gift from Mercury: to know the migration of the soul as it passed from one body to another; and into what plants and animals it migrated; and what thing his soul suffered after death; and what other souls suffered. Euphorbus dying, his soul passed into Hermotimus. Now Hermotimus, desiring to profess who he was, went to the Branchidae. Coming into the Temple of Apollo, he pointed to the shield which Menelaus had hung up there. He said, that upon his return from Troy, he had dedicated that shield to Apollo, it being then old, and nothing remaining but the Ivory stock. (But Porphyry and Iamblichus affirm it was dedicated, together with other Trojan spoils, to Argive Iano in her Temple at Mycenae.)

As soon as Hermotimus died, he became Pyrrhus, a fisherman of Delos, and again remembered all things: how he had been first Aethalides, then Euphorbus, then Hermotimus, and lastly Pyrrhus. When Pyrrhus died, he became Pythagoras, and remembered all that we have said.

Others relate that he said he had been first Euphorbus; secondly, Aethalides; thirdly, Hermotimus; fourthly, Pyrrhus; and lastly, Pythagoras.[859] Clearchus and Dicaearchus said that he had been first

Euphorbus; then Pyrander; then Calliclea; then a beautiful courtesan, named Alce.[860] For this reason, of all Homer's verses he did especially praise these, and set them to the harp, and often repeated them as his own funeral ode.

> As by some hand, a tender Olive set
> In a lone place, near a smooth Rivolet:
> Fair she shoots up, and, fan'd on every side
> By amorous winds, displays her blooming pride;
> Until some churlish unexpected gust
> Plows up her root, and buries her in dust.
> So by Alcides slain Euphorbus lay,
> Stretch'd on the ground, his Arms the Victor's prey.

Hence in his person, Ovid.[861]

> O you, whom horrors of cold death affright,
> Why fear you Styx? vain names, and endless night,
> The dreams of Poets, and feign'd miseries
> Of forged Hell? Whether last-flames surprise,
> Or age devours your bodies; they nor grieve,
> Nor suffer pains. Our souls for ever live:
> Yet evermore their ancient houses leave
> To live in new, which them, as guests receive.
> In Trojan Wars, I (I remember well)
> Euphorbus was, Pantheus son, and fell
> By Menelaus Lance: my shield again
> At Argos late I saw in Juno's fane.
> All alter, nothing finally decays;
> Hither and thither still the spirit strays,
> Guest to all bodies, out of beasts it flys
> To men, from men to beasts, and never dies.
> As pliant wax each new impression takes,
> Fixed to no form, but still the old forsakes,
> Yet is the same: so souls the same abide,
> Though various species their reception hide.

Then lest thy greedy belly should destroy
(I prophesy) depressed piety,
For bear t'expulse thy kindreds Ghosts with food
By death procur'd, nor nourish blood with blood.[862]

Neither did he instance himself only, but put many others also in mind of the accidents of their former life: how they had lived before their souls were confined the second time to the body.[863] This he did (adds Porphyry[864]) to those whose souls were rightly purified, such was Millias of Crotona, whom he caused to call to memory, that he had been Midas son of Gordias. Whereupon Millias went to Epire to perform some Funeral rites as he appointed.[865]

CHAPTER 6

The Separate Life of the Soul

The soul has a twofold life: separate from, and within the body. Her faculties are otherwise in anima, otherwise in animali.[866]

The soul is incorruptible; for when it goes out of the body, it goes to the soul of the world which is of the same kind.[867]

When she goes out upon the earth, she walks in the air like a body.[868] Mercury is the keeper of souls and for that reason is called called ποπεὺς ["the Escorter"], and πυλαῖος ["the keeper of the gate"], and χθόνιος ["of the underworld"], because he brings souls out of bodies in the earth and the sea—of which those that are pure he leads into a high place. The impure come not to them, nor to one another, but are bound by the Furies in indissoluble chains.

The Pythagoreans affirmed that the souls of the dead neither cast a shadow, nor wink; for that it is the Sun which causes the shadow.[869] But he who enters there is by the law of the place deprived of the Sun's light, which they signify in that speech.

Pythagoras held that earthquakes proceed from no other cause but the meeting of the dead.[870]

To physic we shall annex, as its immediate consequent, medicine. Apuleius affirms that Pythagoras learned the remedies and cures of diseases from the Chaldeans.[871] Laertius, that he neglected not medicine.[872] Aelian, that he studied it accurately.[873] Iamblichus, that the Pythagoreans esteem it not the least of the sciences.[874] Lastly, Diogenes relates of Pythagoras that whenever his friends fell into any indisposition of body, he cured them.[875]

Health Pythagoras defined as the consistence of a form. Sickness, the violation of it.[876]

DIETETICS

Of medicine, the Pythagoreans chiefly applied themselves to the Dietetic part, and were most exact in that. They endeavored first to understand the proportion, not only of labor, but likewise of food and rest.[877] Then concerning the dressing of such meats, they were almost the first who endeavored to comment and to define.

Forasmuch as diet does much conduce to good institution, being wholesome and regular, let us examine what he decreed therein. Of meats, he absolutely disallowed such as are flatulent and disorder the body. On the contrary, he approved and commanded those which confirm and unite the constitution—whence he judged millets to be a convenient food.

But he also wholly forbade such meats as are not used by the gods, because they separate us from the correspondence which we have with them.

Likewise he advised to abstain from such meats as are esteemed sacred, which deserve a respect, and are nothing convenient for the ordinary use of man.

Whatsoever meats obstructed divination, or were prejudicial to the purity and sanctity of the mind, or to temperance and habitual virtue, he advised to shun. As also those which are contrary to purity, and defile the Imaginations which occur in sleep, and the other purities of the soul, he rejected and avoided.[878]

These rules concerning diet he prescribed generally to all persons, but more particularly to philosophers who are most addicted to contemplation of the sublimest things.[879] He denied at once all superfluous meats as were unlawful to be eaten, not permitting them at any time to feed on that which had life, or to drink wine, or to sacrifice to the gods any living creature, or hurt any of them. But he commanded with all exactness to preserve the justice which belongs even to them. In this manner he lived himself, abstaining from the flesh of living creatures, and worshipping unbloody altars. He took care that others should not put tame beasts to death. And himself making the savage tame, and moderating and instituting them both by words and actions; but by no means would he punish or kill them.

He likewise commanded civil lawgivers to abstain from the flesh of living creatures, because it behooved them—who would make use of the height of justice—no way to injure living creatures which are of affinity with us. For how can they persuade other men to do just things, who themselves are transported by avarice to feed on living creatures—which are of affinity with us; allied in a manner to us; and, through the community of life, consisting of the temperament and commixture of the same elements.[880]

But to others whose life was not extraordinary pure, sacred, and philosophical, he prescribed a certain time for abstinence.[881] To those he decreed that they should not eat the heart, and that they should not eat the brain. And these are prohibited to all Pythagoreans: for they are leaders, and, as it were, seats and houses of wisdom and life. But these were consecrated by the nature of the divine word.

In like manner he prohibited mallows, as being the first messenger and interpreter of celestial affections, and (as I may say) compassions towards men.

Likewise he commanded to abstain from the melanure (a fish so called from the blackness of its tail) because it is peculiar to the terrestrial deities.

He forbade also the **Erythrine** for the like reasons.

Also to abstain from beans, for many reasons divine and natural, referring to the soul.

The Pythagoreans at dinner used bread and honey.[882] Wine they drank not between meals. At supper, wine, and grain, and bread, and broth, and herbs, both raw and boiled. They likewise set before them the flesh of sacrificed beasts. They seldom ate broths of fish, because some of them are in some respects very hurtful. Likewise seldom the flesh of such creatures as do not hurt mankind.

As concerning the diet of Pythagoras himself,[883] his dinner consisted of honeycombs or honey; his supper of bread made of millet. He ate bread with a relish or spread made of boiled or raw salads, very seldom of the flesh of sacrificed victims (and that not promiscuously of every part), and seldom of seafish.[884]

When he chose to go into the private places of the gods and to stay there a while, he used for the most part such meats as expelled hunger and thirst. For the expelling of hunger, he made a composition of the seed poppy, sesame, and the skin of the sea-onion—well-washed till it was quite drained of the outward juice; of the flowers of the daffadil, and the leaves of mallows, of barley and pea. Of all these, taking an equal weight, and chopping them small, he made up into a mass with Hymettian honey. Against thirst, he took of the seeds of cucumbers, and the fullest dried raisins (taking out the kernels), and the flower of coriander, and the seeds of mallows, and purselain, and scraped cheese, meal and cream; these he mixed up with wild honey.[885] This diet he said was taught to Hercules by Ceres when he was sent into the Lybian deserts.[886]

CHAPTER 2

THERAPEUTIC

The Therapeutic part Pythagoras practiced by Poultices, Charms, and Music. The Pythagoreans (says Iamblichus) treated chiefly by poultices; but potions they less esteemed. And of those they used only such as were proper against ulcerations; but incision, and cauterizing they absolutely disallowed.

Magical Herbs, says Pliny, were first celebrated in our part of the world by Pythagoras, following the Magi.[887] He first wrote a treatise on their virtues, assigning the invention and original to Apollo and Aesculapius, Immortal gods.

By **Coriacesia** and **Callicia**, says Pliny, Pythagoras affirms that water will be turned into ice. I find in others no more concerning this.[888]

He likewise speaks of Menais, which he also calls by another name "Corinthas." The juice whereof boiled in water, he says, immediately cures the biting of serpents when treating with moist heat the part therewith. The same juice being spilt upon the grass, they who tread upon it, or are besprinkled therewith, die irrecoverably: a strange nature of poison except against poison.[889]

There is an herb that Pythagoras called "Aproxis," the root whereof takes fire at distance, as does naptha, of which says Pliny, we have spoken in the wonders of the Earth.[890] The same Pythagoras relates: that if any disease shall happen to men when the Aproxis is in its flower, although they be cured, yet shall they constantly have some grudging thereof as often as it blows; and wheat, and hemlock, and violet, have the same quality. "I am not ignorant," adds Pliny, "that this book is by some ascribed to Cleemporus, the physician. But pertinacious fame and antiquity vindicate it to Pythagoras."

Pythagoras wrote also one volume concerning the sea onion, collecting the medicinal properties thereof, which Pliny professes to have taken from him.[891] And again, Pliny says Pythagoras affirms that a sea-onion, hung over the threshold of the gate, hinders all ill medicaments from entering the house.

Likewise, coleworts (as Pliny relates) were much commended by Pythagoras.[892] He adds that concerning the white kind of the Eringo (by the Romans called *centum-capita*), there are many vanities delivered, not only by the Magi, but by the Pythagoreans.[893]

Besides the Pharmaceutic, Pythagoras practiced two other ways of cure—one by music, the other by charm. Of the first we have already spoken. Of the second, Iamblichus relates that there is also a way, without the singing of birds, by which they expelled some passions, and sicknesses. As they say indeed by incantation. Whence it seems was derived the word επωδη, the way of cure by charm—which was, says the Greek etymologist,[894] of ancient use. Whence wrote Homer:

—And staid the black blood by a Charm![895]

and Pindar, speaking of Aesculapius,

ἀμφέπων ["tending them"] with soft charms.†

That Pythagoras made use of poetic incantations is also affirmed by Porphyry. He allayed, says he, the passions of the soul and body by rythms, verses, and incantations. And Diogenes, cited by Porphyry, said that if his friends fell into any indisposition of body, he healed them; if they were troubled in mind, he assuaged their grief—partly by charms and magic verses, partly by music.[896] For he had some verses proper to the cure of the indispositions of the body; by singing which he restored the sick to their former health. He had other verses that procured forgetfulness of grief, assuaged anger, and suppressed inordinate desires.

Of these charms we find an instance preserved by Pliny, who describes it as an invention of Pythagoras which seldom fails against lameness, or blindness, or the like accidents. He prescribes that it be applied to the injured part: if on the right side, an uneven number of vowels of impositive words; if on the left, an even.[897]

Section III: Symbols

CHAPTER I

PYTHAGORAS: HIS SYMBOLIC WAY OF TEACHING

Pythagoras had a two-fold manner of teaching: whatsoever he communicated to his auditors was delivered either plainly or symbolically.[898] We have hitherto treated of the plain way. We come now to the other, the symbolical.

He used by short sentences to prophesy an infinite, multiplex signification to his disciples after a symbolical manner.[899] No other than Apollo, by short answers, exhibits many imperceptible sentences. And nature herself, by small seeds most difficult, effects of this kind, such as the following:

—half is the whole's beginning.

This is an Apothegm of Pythagoras himself. Neither in that short verse only, but in others of the same kind, the most divine Pythagoras wrapped up sparks of truth for such as could enkindle them. He did so in a short way of speech, treasuring up concealed a most copious production of theory, such as this:

—to number all have reference.

And again φιλότης, ἰσότης, Friendship, Equality; and in the word κόσμος (World, or Heaven); and in the word Philosophy; and in στώη καίετων,†; and in that renowned word Tetractys. All these, and many more, did Pythagoras invent, for the benefit and rectification of such as conversed with him.

Some things likewise (says Porphyry) he spoke in a mystical way, that is symbolically, most of which are collected by Aristotle.[900] Such as when he called the Sea, a tear of Saturn;[901] the two Bears, the hands of Rhea; the Pleiades, the lutes of the Muses; the Planets, the dogs of Proserpina;[902] the eyes, the gates of the Sun.[903]

He made use of other symbols or aphorisms. For example: Go not over a balance; that is, shun avarice, etc. Thus Porphyry.[904] These are variously recited and interpreted by several authors. We shall begin with Iamblichus, as being herein of greatest credit.

Iamblichus, the Neoplatonist renowned for his work on Pythagorean philosophy, is said to have been the descendant of the priest-kings of Emesa. One such figure, Uranius Antoninus, led a revolt against the Romans in A.D. 253/4, while Iamblichus was a child. This gold aureus shows the portrait of Uranius Antoninus and the sacred stone of Emesa escorted in a chariot.
Photo courtesy of Numismatica Ars Classica

CHAPTER 2

The Symbols of Pythagoras According to Iamblichus.

The last way of exhortation to virtue, and dissuasion from vice, is that by symbols.[905] The first way of teaching being proper to the sect, not communicable to other Institutions; the second vulgar and common to them; the third is between both—neither absolutely public, nor wholly Pythagorean, nor quite different from either. Such are those they term symbols. As many as deserve commemoration, in our opinion, of the exhortatory form, we shall communicate and add a suitable interpretation. We conceive that hereby the exhortation to philosophy may be more prevalent on those that hear them, than if delivered more at large.

And forasmuch as we shall insert some Exoteric solutions common to all philosophy, it is to be understood as different from the meaning of the Pythagoreans. But inasmuch as we shall intermix some of the most particular opinions of the Pythagoreans consonant to each, this is wholly proper to them and dissonant from all other philosophers, but most fit to be alleged. This will insensibly lead us from the exoteric notions, bringing us to the others, and acquainting us with them. And to the exhortations framed according to this sect as a bridge or ladder by which we ascend from a depth to a great height, guiding the minds of those who addict themselves genuinely thereto.

For to this end it was framed, according to imitation of the things already mentioned. For the most ancient and such as were contemporary with and disciples to Pythagoras did not compose their writings intelligible, in a common vulgar style, familiar to everyone, as if they endeavored to dictate things readily perceptible by the hearer. But consonant to the silence decreed by Pythagoras concerning divine mysteries, which it was not lawful to speak of before those who were not initiated. They therefore clouded both their mutual discourses and writings by symbols; which—if not expounded by those that proposed them by a regular interpretation—appear to the hearers like old wives proverbs, trivial and foolish. But being rightly explained, and instead of dark, rendered lucid and conspicuous to

269

the vulgar, they discover an admirable sense no less than the divine oracle of Pythian Apollo, and give a divine inspiration to the philologists that understand them.[906]

That therefore their benefit may be known, and their exhortative use manifest, we will give the solutions of every symbol, both after the exoteric and by the method of discourse, not omitting those things which were preserved in silence, not communicable to uninitiated persons. The Symbols are these:

1. When you go to the Temple, worship, neither do nor say anything concerning life.
2. If there be a Temple in your way, go not in; no not though you pass by the very doors.
3. Sacrifice and worship barefoot.
4. Concerning the gods, disbelieve nothing wonderful, nor concerning divine doctrines.
5. Decline highways, and take the foot-path!
6. Abstain from the Melanure, for it belongs to the Terrestrial gods.
7. Above all things, govern your tongue, when you follow the gods.
8. When the winds blow, worship the noise.
9. Cut not fire with a sword.
10. Turn away from the self every edge.
11. Help a man to take up a burden, but not to lay it down.
12. Put on the shoe first on the right foot, but the left foot first into the basin.
13. Discourse not of Pythagorean things without light.
14. Pass not over a pair of Scales.
15. Travelling from home, turn not back; for the Furies go back with you.
16. Pass not Urine, being turned towards the Sun.
17. Wipe not a seat with a torch.
18. A cock keep, but not sacrifice; for it is consecrated to the Moon and the Sun.
19. Sit not upon a **Choenix**.
20. Breed nothing that has crooked talons.

21. Cut not in the way.
22. Receive not a swallow into your house.
23. Wear not a ring.
24. Grave not the image of God on a ring.
25. Look not in a glass by candlelight.
26. Be not taken with immoderate laughter.
27. At a sacrifice, pare not your nails.
28. Lay not hold on everyone readily with your right hand.
29. When you rise out of bed, disorder the coverlet, and deface the print.
30. Eat not the heart.
31. Eat not the brains.
32. Spit upon the cuttings of your hair, and the parings of your nails.
33. Receive not an Erythrine.
34. Deface the print of a pot in the ashes.
35. Take not a woman that has gold, to get children of her.
36. First honor the figure and steps, a figure and a Triobolus.
37. Abstain from beans.
38. Set mallows, but eat it not.
39. Abstain from living creatures.

CHAPTER 3

AN EXPLICATION OF THE PYTHAGOREAN SYMBOLS
BY IAMBLICHUS

All these symbols are in general exhortative to all virtue; and every one of them in particular conduces to some particular virtue, and part of philosophy, and learning; as the first are exhortative to devotion, and divine knowledge.

SYMBOL I
When you go to the temple, worship, neither do nor say anything concerning life. This exhortation observes the divinity after such manner, as it is in itself—pure and unmixed. He joins pure to the pure, and takes care, that no worldly business insinuate itself into the divine worship. For they are things wholly different and opposite to one another. Moreover, this conduces much to science; for we ought not to bring to the divine science any such thing as human consideration, or care of outward life. Thus nothing is hereby commanded, but that divine discourses, and sacred actions ought not to be intermixed with the instable manners of men.

SYMBOL II
To that is consonant the next symbol: *If a temple lie in your way, go not in, not though you pass by the very doors.* For if like is delightful to its like, it is manifest that the gods, having the chief essence of all things, ought to have the principal worship. But if any man does it upon occasion of any other thing, he makes that the second which is the first and chief of all; and by that means he subverts the whole order of worship, and science. The most excellent good ought not to be ranked in the latter place as inferior to human good; neither ought our own affairs to have the place of the chief end and better things either in our words or thoughts.

SYMBOL III
That which follows—*Sacrifice and worship barefoot*—is an exhortation to the same. For this signifies that we ought to serve the gods

and perform their knowledge decently and moderately, not exceeding the order in the earth. Another way that we ought to perform their service and knowledge is to be free and without fetters. This, the symbol commands to be observed not in the body only, but in the acts of the soul. That such acts be not restrained by passions, nor by the infirmity of the body, nor by our external generation, but all free and ready for communication with the gods.

SYMBOL IV

There is another symbol of this kind exhorting to the same virtue: *Concerning the gods, disbelieve nothing wonderful, nor concerning divine doctrines.* This rule is religious, and declares the superlative excellence of the gods, instructing us and putting us in mind that we ought not to estimate the divine power by our own Judgment. To us who are corporeal, and generated, and corruptible, and transitory, and obnoxious to several diseases, and to narrowness of habitation, and to aggravation of motion towards the center, and to sleepiness, and to indigence, and to abundance, and to imprudence, and to infirmity, and to impediment of soul and the like—some things will seem difficult, and impossible. Yet have we many excellencies by nature. But we are quite short of the gods. Neither have we the same power or ability. This symbol, therefore, chiefly advises to a knowledge of the gods, as of those who are able to do all things; whence it admonishs to disbelieve nothing concerning the gods. There is added, *nor concerning divine doctrines*, meaning those which are declared by the Pythagorean philosophy. Because, they being settled by mathematics and scientific speculation, will show by demonstration, strengthened by necessity, that there are true beings existent void of fallaciousness.

These may also exhort to the science concerning the gods and persuade that such a Science is to be acquired, as by which we shall not disbelieve[907] anything concerning the gods. The same may advise to divine doctrines and to proceed by mathematics; for they only clear the eyes and are illuminative of all beings to him that will behold them. For by participation of mathematics, one thing is constituted before all: that we disbelieve not anything, either concerning the nature of the gods, or their essence, or their power. Nor of those Pythagorean doctrines which seem monstrous to persons not initiated into mathematics. Thus "disbelieve not" is equivalent to "acquire and possess those things by means whereof you shall not disbelieve"—that is mathematics, and Scientific demonstrations.

SYMBOL V

The next symbol tends (as I conceive) to the same effect: *Declining highways, walk in pathways*. For it commands to leave the public popular course of life and to pursue that which is separate and divine. Likewise, that we despise the common opinions, and much esteem the private which are not to be divulged. And to condemn the pleasure which tends towards men; but to value exceedingly that felicity which is joined with the divine will. And to leave human customs as vulgar; but to apply ourselves to the worship of the Gods, which far excels the ordinary course of life. Allied to this, is that which follows.

SYMBOL VI

Abstain from the Melanure, for it belongs to the Terrestrial Gods. We shall say more upon this in our explication of the exhortative Symbols. It advises to make choice of the Heavenly Journey and to adhere to the Intellectual Gods. To withdraw ourselves from Material nature, and to direct our course to that life which is pure, void of matter, and to make use of the best way of Divine worship and that which is most suitable to the chief deities. These Symbols are exhortative to the knowledge and worship of the Gods.

SYMBOL VII

The following symbols exhort to Wisdom: *Above all things govern your Tongue, following the Gods*. For the first work of Wisdom is to revert our speech into itself, and to accustom it not to pass forth, that it may be perfect within ourselves, and in its conversion towards ourselves. Moreover in *following the Gods:* for nothing renders the mind so perfect as when a man, being reverted into himself, follows the Gods.

SYMBOL VIII

This symbol likewise, *When the winds blow, worship the noise,* is an exhortation to Divine Wisdom. For it implies that we ought to love the similitude of Divine Natures, and Powers. And when they make a reason suitable to their efficacies, it ought exceedingly to be honored and reverenced.

SYMBOL IX

The next symbol, *Cut not fire with a sword*, also exhorts to wisdom. For it excites in us a convenient knowledge that we ought not to give sharp language to a man full of fire and anger, nor to contest with him. For you may often by words exasperate and trouble a rude and unlearned person. Of this Heraclitus witnesses. To contest with anger (says he) is hard, for whatsoever it would have done, it will purchase, though at the expense of life. And he said truly: for many gratifying their own anger have exchanged their Souls and preferred death before them. But from continence of the tongue and peacefulness, this happens: that out of contention arises friendship, the wrathful fire being extinguished, and thou thyself wilt appear not to be void of reason. This symbol is confirmed by that which follows.

SYMBOL X

Turn away from thyself every edge; for towards whomsoever it shall be turned, it will hurt him. This symbol commands to use prudence, not anger. For that edge of the mind which we call anger is void of reason and prudence. For anger boils like a pot upon the fire, never dividing the mind to that which is past. You must therefore settle your mind in tranquility, diverting it from anger, and diligently controlling yourself—as a man makes brass sound not without touching it. This passion therefore must be suppressed by reason.

SYMBOL XI

This symbol, *Help to lay on a burden, but not to take it off*, advises to fortitude. For whosoever lays on a burden, signifies labor and action; but he who takes it off, rest and remissness. The meaning therefore of the Symbol is this. Be not the cause, either to thyself or any other, of negligence of mind and soft life; for every useful thing is acquitted by labor. This Symbol Pythagoras called Herculean, as being sealed by his labors. For while he lived amongst men, he passed frequently through fire and many difficulties, shunning idleness. From actions and labor proceed a right office, but not from sloth.

SYMBOL XII

Pluck off your right shoe first, but put your left foot first into the basin
exhorts to active prudence. That good actions, as right, are to be set
round about us; but the ill, as left, to be laid aside and rejected.

SYMBOL XIII

Discourse not of Pythagorean things without light is chiefly exhortatory
that the mind acquire prudence. For that resembles the light of the
mind which, being indefinite, limits and reduces it, as it were, out of
darkness into light. It is therefore chiefly requisite to look upon the
mind as the guide of all good actions in life. But in the Pythagorean
doctrines this is most particularly necessary. For it is not possible to
understand what they are without light.

SYMBOL XIV

Pass not over a balance, commands us to do justly. And above all
things to respect equality and mediocrity. And to know justice, the
most perfect Virtue which completes the rest, and without which the
rest profit nothing. Neither must we know it superficially only, but
by Theorems and Scientific Demonstration. This knowledge is the
work of no Art and Science, but only of the philosophy of Pythagoras, which prefers Mathematics before all things else.

SYMBOL XV

To the same purpose is this: *Travelling from home, turn not back, for
the furies go back with you.* This Symbol exhorts to Philosophy and
free action about the mind. It likewise manifestly teaches thus.
When you study philosophy, separate thyself from all corporeal and
sensible things intelligible, which are always the same and after the
same manner; proceeding (without turning back) by Mathematics,
conducing thereto. For as travel is the change of place, death is the
separation of the Soul from the Body. But we must so study philosophy as to make use of the pure mind sincerely—without the acts
of corporeal sense—to the comprehension of the truth which is in
things that are, which is acknowledged to be wisdom. But after you
have once applied yourself to study philosophy, turn not back, nor
be drawn back to the former corporeal things in which you were
bred up. For you will much repent hereof, being hindered from

sacred comprehensions by the darkness which is in corporeal things. Repentance they call *Erinys*, or Fury.

SYMBOL XVI

Pass not Urine while being turned towards the Sun admonishes that we offer not to do any bestial action—but to study and practice philosophy, looking upon Heaven and the Sun. And remember that in the study of Philosophy, you never bear a low mind; but by the contemplation of heavenly things, ascend to the gods and to wisdom. And having applied yourself to study philosophy and to the light of truth that is in it—purifying yourself and converting yourself wholly to that design: to Theology, and Physiology, and Astronomy, and Etiology which is above all the rest—do nothing irrational or bestial.

SYMBOL XVII

The same meaning is of the next: *Wipe not a seat with a Torch.* For not only because a torch is purificative, as partaking of much quick fire like sulphur, it advises that this ought not to be defiled—its nature being such as it dispels all things that defile. Nor ought we to oppose natural habitude by defiling that whose nature is repugnant to defiling. Much less ought we to join and mix things proper to wisdom with those which are proper to animality. For a torch in respect of its brightness is compared to philosophy; a seat in respect of its lowness to animality.

SYMBOL XVIII

The symbol—*Breed a Cock, but do not sacrifice it, for it is sacred to the Moon and the Sun*—admonishes us to nourish and cherish (and not to neglect so as to suffer them to perish and corrupt) the great evidences of the union, joining together, sympathy and conspiration of the World. It therefore advises to address ourselves to contemplation of the Universe, and to philosophy. For the truth of all things is by nature concealed, and hard to be found out, yet requisite to be sought and investigated by man chiefly through philosophy (for to do it by any other study is impossible). Philosophy receiving some little sparks from nature, blows them up and makes them greater and more perspicuous by its doctrines; it therefore ought to be studied.

SYMBOL XIX

This, *Sit not upon a Choenix,* may appear to be more Pythagorean
from what was already said. For because aliment is to be measured by
corporeity and animality, not by the Choenix, rest not, nor lead thy
life uninitiated into philosophy. But applying thyself thereto, take
greatest care of that in thee which is most Divine—the Soul. And
the aliment of the Soul, chiefly the mind, is not measured by the
Choenix, but by contemplation and discipline.

SYMBOL XX

This, *Breed nothing that has crooked talons,* advises to a thing which is
yet more Pythagorean. Be free and communicative, and endeavor to
make others such also, accustoming thyself to give and receive without grudging or envy; not to take all things insatiably and to give
nothing in return. For the natural condition of those Fowls which
have crooked talons is to receive and snatch readily and quickly, but
not easily to let go or impart to others, by reason of the tenacity of
their talons, being crooked. Such is also the nature of shrimps, that
they quickly lay hold of a thing but very hardly part with it unless
they be turned upon their backs. Now we having hands given us
by nature, proper to communicate, and straight not crooked fingers,
ought not to imitate those which have crooked talons, unlike us.
But rather mutually to communicate to and participate with one
another, as being excited thereto by those who first gave names to
things; who named the more honorable hand δεξιὰν, the right,
not only ἀπὸ τοῦ δέχεσθαι, from receiving; but likewise, ἀλλὰ καὶ
ἀπὸ τοῦ δεκτὴν ὑπάρχειν ἐν τῷ μεταδιδόναι, from being ready to
receive in communicating.† We must therefore do justly, and for
that reason philosophize; for Justice is a return and remuneration,
exchanging and supplying excess and defect.

SYMBOL XXI

This, *Cut not in the way,* expresses that truth is one, falsehood multiplex. Which is manifest from this—that what everything is, speaking plainly, is expressed but one way; but what it is not, is expressed
infinite ways. Philosophy seems to be a way. It therefore says, choose
that philosophy and that way to philosophy, in which thou shalt not

cut (or divide) nor establish contrary doctrines. But choose those which are constituted and confirmed by Scientific demonstration, by Mathematics and contemplation—which is to say, philosophize in a Pythagorean manner.

It may be taken also in another sense. Forasmuch as that philosophy which proceeds by corporeals and sensibles (with which philosophy the younger sort are satisfied, who conceive that God, and qualities, and the mind, and virtues—and in a word all the principal causes of things—are bodies) is easily subverted and confuted; as appears by the great disagreement amongst them who go about to say anything therein. But the philosophy which is of incorporeals, and intelligibles, and immaterials, and eternals—which are always the same in themselves, and towards one another, never admitting corruption or alteration—is firmly established and the cause of irrefragable demonstration. Now this precept advises us when we philosophize and perfect the way which is manifest, that we shun the snares and entertainments of corporeals and divisibles, and intimately apply ourselves to the substances of incorporeals—which are never unlike themselves by reason of the truth and stability which they naturally have.

SYMBOL XXII

This, *Receive not a Swallow into your house*, advises that you admit not a slothful person (who is not a constant lover of labor, neither will persevere to be a disciple) unto your doctrines—which require continual labor and patience by reason of the variety and intricateness of the several disciplines. He makes use of the swallow to represent sloth, and cutting off times, because this bird comes to us but in one season of the year and then stays but a short while with us; but is absent from us and out of our sight a much longer space.

SYMBOL XXIII

This, *Wear not a Ring*, is likewise exhortatory after the Pythagorean way thus. Forasmuch as a ring encompasses the finger of the wearer in the nature of a chain; but has this property—that it pinches not, nor pains, but is so fit as if it naturally belonged to that part—and the body is such a kind of chain to the soul. Wear not a ring signifies this: Philosophize truly, and separate your soul from the chain which goes round about it. For philosophy is the meditation of death, and separation of the soul from the body. Seriously and earnestly therefore apply yourself to the Pythagorean philosophy, which separates the soul by the mind from all corporeals, and is conversant about intellectuals and immaterials by theoretical doctrines. But untie and loose your sins, and all things that pluck you back and hinder philosophizing—diversions of the flesh, excessive eating, unreasonable repletion, which as it were, fetter the body, and continually breed infinite disease.

SYMBOL XXIV
This, *Grave not the image of God in a Ring,* advises thus: Philosophize, and above all things, think that the gods are incorporeal. This Symbol is beyond all others the Seminary of the Pythagorean doctrines. Of it all things (almost) are fitly adapted, and by it are they established to the end. Think not that they use forms that are corporeal, neither that they are received into material substance—fettered (as it were) to thy body—like other living beings. As we have said, the ring expresses a chain, and corporeity, and sensible form. The figures engraved in rings, as it were the figure of some animal perceptible by sight, are those from which we must absolutely separate the gods. The gods being eternal and intelligible and always the same in themselves and towards one another, as is largely discoursed in the treatise concerning God.

SYMBOL XXV
This, *Look not in a glass by candlelight,* advises in a more Pythagorean manner the following. Philosophize, pursuing not the phantasies of sense (which give a kind of light to comprehensions like a candle, neither natural nor true), but those which procure Science and are conversant in the mind. Seek those by which a most bright purity is constituted in the eye of the soul of all Notions and Intelligibles, and the speculation of them; but not of Corporeals and Sensibles. For such are in continual fluxion and mutation (as has often been shown). They are no way stable nor existing like themselves,

whereby they might uphold a firm and Scientific comprehension as the others do.

SYMBOL XXVI

This, *Be not seized with immoderate laughter,* shows that we should vanquish passion. Put thyself in mind of right reason; be neither blown up in good fortune, not cast down in bad; admitting no thought of change in either. He named laughter above all other passions, because that is most apparently shown in the face itself. Perhaps also because this is proper to man only of all living creatures; whence some define man as a risible living creature. This precept shows that we ought to take humanity only, as it were in our way, like guests. But to acquire the imitation of God, as far as we are able by Philosophising, secretly withdrawing ourselves from the property of men, and preferring the rational before the risible in distinction from other creatures.

SYMBOL XXVII

This, *At a Sacrifice pare not your nails,* is exhortative to friendship. For of domestics and allies, some being nearly related to us (such as brothers, children, parents) are like our limbs and parts which cannot be taken away without much pain and maim. Others who are allied to us at a great distance (as the children of uncles, or of cousins, or their children, or such like) resemble those parts which may be cut off without pain (as hair, nails, and the like). Intending therefore to signify those allies, whom by reason of this distance we at other times neglect, he uses the word "nails," saying, "Cast not those quite away." But in Sacrifices—though at other times neglected—carry them along with you and renew your domestic familiarity with them.

SYMBOL XXVIII

This, *Lay not hold on everyone readily with your right hand,* means: Give not your right hand easily. That is, draw not to you, nor endeavor to draw out, improper and uninitiated persons by giving them your right hand. Moreover, to such as have not been long tried by disciplines and doctrines, nor are approved as worthy to participate of temperance and of the quinquennial silence, and other trials, the right hand ought not to be given.

SYMBOL XXIX

This, *When you rise out of bed, wrap the coverlets together and confound the print of your body*, advises that having undertaken to philosophize, you should acquaint yourself with Intellectuals and Incorporeals. Therefore as soon as you rise from the sleep of ignorance and that darkness which resembles night; draw not to yourself any corporeal thing to the light of philosophy—which resembles the day. But blot out of your remembrance all prints of that sleep.

SYMBOL XXX

This, *Eat not the heart,* signifies that we ought not to tear asunder the unity and conspiration of the whole. Moreover it implies, Be not envious, but obliging, and communicative. Hereupon it exhorted to philosophy. For of all Arts and Sciences, only philosophy envies not the good of others, nor grieves thereat, nor rejoices in the ill of a neighbor. But it declares that all men are by nature allied to one another, and friends, and alike affected, and subjected alike to fortune, and alike ignorant of the future; and therefore commands them to commiserate and love one another as becomes a creature sociable and rational.

SYMBOL XXXI

Like that is this, *Eat not the Brain,* for this is the principal instrument of Wisdom. It signifies therefore that we ought not with reproaches to bite and tear in pieces things well intended and doctrines. Those are well intended which are exactly considered by the principal reason of mind, like to things comprehended by Science. For these are beheld not by the organs of the irrational soul—that is, by the heart and the liver—but by the pure rational part of the soul. Wherefore it is a folly to oppose them. This Symbol rather advises to worship the fountain of Minds, and next instrument of Intellection, by whose means we acquire Speculation and Science, and (in a word) all Wisdom, and truly philosophize; and not to confound and deface the prints that are therein.

SYMBOL XXXII

This, *Spit upon the cutting of thy Hair and parings of they Nails*, says thus. Those things are easily condemned which are born with thee, but are more distant from the Mind. As on the other side, those are more esteemed which are nearer to the mind. So having addicted thy mind to philosophy above all, reverence those things which are demonstrated by the soul and mind without the organs of sense by speculative Science. But condemn and spit upon those things which are seen without the light of the mind by the sensitive organs which are born with us—which are not capable of reaching the eternity of the mind.

SYMBOL XXXIII

This, *Receive not an Erythrine*, seems to respect the etymology of the word. Entertain not an impudent blushless person, nor on the other side one over-bashful, ready to fall back from the mind and firm intellection. Whence is understood also, Be not such yourself.

SYMBOL XXXIV

This, *Deface the print of a pot in the ashes*, signifies that he who applies his mind to philosophy, must forget the demonstrations of confusion and grossness (that is of corporeals and sensibles) and wholly make use of demonstrations of Intelligibles. By ashes are meant the dust or sand in Mathematical tables wherein the demonstrations and figures are drawn.

SYMBOL XXXV

Approach not her to get Children who has money, is not meant of a woman but of a Sect and philosophy which has in it much corporeity and gravity tending downwards. For of all things in the Earth, Gold is the most heavy and aptest to move towards the center which is the property of corporeal weight. To approach means not only coition, but to apply ourselves and to be assistant.

SYMBOL XXXVI

This, *In the first place honor the figure and the degrees, the figure and the **Triobolus***; advises to philosophize, and study Mathematics not superficially; and by them as by degrees of ascension, arrive at our proposed end; but despise those things which others prefer before these. And chiefly reverence the Italic philosophy which considers Incorporeals in themselves, before the Ionic which first looks upon bodies.

SYMBOL XXXVII

This, *Abstain from Beans*, advises to beware of everything that may corrupt our discourse with the gods and prescience.

SYMBOL XXXVIII

This, *Plant Mallows but eat it not*, signifies that such things are turned with the Sun. "Plant," that is, insisting on its nature and application to the Sun and Sympathy, neither abstain from it, nor wholly adhere to it. But transfer your mind and intellect, and transplant them, as it were, to plants and herbs of the same kind; and to animals which are not of the same kind; and to stones and rivers; and in a word to all natures. For thou wilt find that which designs the unity and conspiration of the World to be fruitful and full of variety and admirably copious, as if it sprung from a mallow root. Therefore not only eat not, nor deface such observations, but on the contrary increase them, and multiply them, as it were by transplantation.

SYMBOL XXXIX

This, *Abstain from living Creatures*, exhorts to Justice and respect of alliance by a like kind of life and the like.

By these is explained the Symbolical exhortative form—containing much that is common with the customs of the Ancients, and the Pythagoreans. Thus Iamblichus.

CHAPTER 4

The Same Symbols Explained by Others

Most of these Symbols are mentioned also by others, with different explications. The first, Olympiodorus ascribed to Philolaus, delivering it thus: *When you come into a Temple, turn not back.*[908] Iamblichus, in the life of Pythagoras, cites it in the same words, adding this exposition: "That we ought not to perform divine rites, cursorily and negligently."

Upon the second, *Adore not the gods, as it were, in passing by,* Plutarch says we ought to go from home with that express intent.[909] And for this reason the cryers used upon Festival days to go before the Priests, and commanded the people to forbear working.

The same exposition Iamblichus, in the life of Pythagoras gives of the third, *Sacrifice and go to sacred rites barefoot.*

To the fourth, *Concerning the gods, disbelieve nothing wonderful, and concerning divine Doctrines,* may be applied to what Iamblichus says in the life of Pythagoras. Many precepts were introduced into the practice of divine rites, forasmuch as they gave firm credit to these things, conceiving them not to be fantastic boasts, but to derive their beginning from some god.[910] All this the Pythagoreans believe to be true—as the fabulous reports concerning Aristaeus the Proconnesian, and Abaris the Hyperborean, and the like. And they did not only believe all these, but also endeavored themselves to frame many things that seem fabulous, derogating from nothing which relates to the Deity. In all such things he conceived not that the persons themselves were foolish, but those only who gave no belief to it. For they are not of opinion that the gods can do some things, others they cannot, as the Sophists imagine; but, that all things are possible. And the same is the beginning of the verses which they ascribe to Linus, but perhaps were made by Pythagoras.

Hope all things, for to none belongs despair;
All things to God easy and perfect are.

The fifth, *Decline highways,* is mentioned by many. Only Laertius delivers it quite otherwise: *Go not out of the highway.* But in the exposition differs not from the rest. That we ought not to follow the opinions of the vulgar, which are without judgment, and not indisputable; but those of the few and learned.

The sixth, *Abstain from the Melanure, for it belongs to the Terrestrial gods,* Plutarch interprets, as forbidding to converse with persons black in impiety.[911] Tryphon, as forbidding falsehood and lies which are black in their essence. The Melanure is a kind of fish so named from the blackness of its tail.

The ninth, *Cut not fire with a sword,* is one of those Symbols which are ascribed to Andocides the Pythagorean. Porphyry,[912] Plutarch,[913] Laertius,[914] and Athenaeus,[915] interpret it as advising not to exasperate an angry person, but to give way to him. Fire is anger, the sword, contention. St. Basil expounds it of those who attempt an impossibility.

The tenth, Laertius reads thus, *Turn away a sharp sword.* It is generally expounded, Decline all things dangerous.

The eleventh, *Help to lay on a burden, but not to take it off,* is expounded by Porphyry that we ought to further others, not in sluggishness, but in virtue and labor. Or as Iamblichus, that we ought not to be the cause of another's being idle. Laertius and Olympiodorus cite it thus: *Lay not burdens down together, but take them up together;* expounding it that we must work together in the course of life, and co-operate with others in actions, tending not to idleness but to virtue.

The twelfth which is cited by Suidas out of Aristophanes, in verse, thus:

Into the shoe first the right foot,
The left first in the basin put.

He expounds it not as a Symbol, but a Proverb of those who perform things dexterously.

The fourteenth, *Pass not over a balance*, is generally interpreted by Plutarch,[916] Laertius,[917] Clement of Alexandria,[918] Porphyry,[919] and others that we ought to esteem Justice, and not to exceed it. Athenaeus and Porphyry expound it as counseling against avarice, and advising to pursue equality.

The fifteenth, Laertius delivers thus: *When you go to travel, look not back upon the bounds*.[920] Plutarch thus, *When you come to the borders, return not back*. They both interpret it that when we are dying, and arrived at the bound or end of our life, we should bear it with an equal mind—without grief, nor to desire a continuance of the pleasures of this life. So also Porphyry.

The seventeenth Laertius reads thus, *Wipe not a seat with Oil*.

The eighteenth, Laertius and Suidas deliver thus: *Touch not a white Cock, for it is sacred to the Moon, and a monitor of the hours*.

The nineteenth, *Sit not upon a Choenix*, Plutarch and Porphyry interpret, that we ought not to live idly, but to provide necessaries for the future. For a Choenix, according to Laertius and Suidas, is the same which Clearchus calls "Hemorotrophen," a proportion of food daily spent. But Clement of Alexandria interprets it as advising to consider not the present day, but what the future will bring forth. To be solicitous, not of food, but prepared for death.

The twentieth, *Breed nothing that has crooked talons*, is ascribed to Andocydes the Pythagorean.

The twenty-first, Olympiodorus delivers thus: *Cleave not wood in the way*. Whereby, says he, the Pythagoreans advised not to disquiet life with excessive cares and vain solicitude.

The twenty-second is *Entertain not a swallow under your roof*. Plutarch interprets this as take not unto you an ungrateful and unconstant friend and companion. For only this bird, of all the lesser kind, is reported to prey upon flesh. [921] Clement of Alexandria and Porphyrius interpret it as forbidding to admit into our society a talkative person, intemperate of speech, who cannot contain what is communicated to him. [922]

The twenty-third, Plutarch alleged thus, *Wear not a straight Ring*. That is, says he, Follow a free course of life and fetter not yourself.[923] Or, as St. Hierom, That we live not anxiously, nor put ourselves into servitude, or into such a condition of life as we cannot free ourselves from when we should have a mind to do it.

The twenty-fourth, *Wear not the picture of the gods in Rings*, Porphyry expounds: Discourse not of the gods inconsiderately or in public. [924] Iamblichus, in the life of Pythagoras, delivers it thus: *Wear not the image of God in a Ring lest it be defiled; for it is the image of God*.[925] Clement of Alexandria affirms the meaning to be that we ought not to mind Sensibles but to pass on to Intelligibles.[926]

In the twenty-eighth, *Lay not hold on everyone readily with your right hand*, Plutarch omits ῥαδίως , Suidus παντί.† It is generally expounded thus, *Be not hasty and precipitate in contracting friendship with any*.

The twenty-ninth, *When you rise out of bed, wrap the coverlet together, and confound the print of your body*, Plutarch refers to the modesty and respect due to the bed. Clement of Alexandria says it signifies that we ought not in the daytime to call to mind any pleasures, even of dreams, which we had in the night.[927] Perhaps also, says he, it means, that we ought to confound dark phantasie with the light of truth.

The thirtieth and thirty-first, *Eat not the Heart and the Brains*, Iamblichus, in the life of Pythagoras, says he enjoined forasmuch as these two are the seats of life and knowledge.[928] Porphyry to the first, and Plutarch to the second, give one interpretation: Consume not yourself with grief nor afflict your mind with cares.

The thirty-second, Laertius delivers contrary to Iamblichus: *Upon the paring of your nails or cuttings of your hair, neither pass urine nor tread.*

The thirty-fourth, *Deface the print of a pot in the ashes*, Plutarch and Clement of Alexandria expound as advising that upon reconcilement of enmity, we utterly abolish and leave not the least print or remembrance of anger.

The thirty-sixth, *Honor the figure and the three oboli*, seems to have reference to the story related in the sixth chapter of his life.

Of the thirty-seventh, *Abstain from Beans*, there are alleged many different reasons.[929] Aristotle says he forbade them for that they resemble αἰδοῖα ["the genitals"], or the gates of the Infernal Region; or for that they breed worms (a little sort of maggot called "Midae"); or for that they resemble the nature of the Universe; or for that they are oligarchic, being used in suffrages. This last reason is confirmed by Plutarch, who explains this Symbol: Abstain from suffrages; which of old were given by beans.†[930]

Porphyry says He interdicted beans because the first beginning and generation being confused, and many things being commixed and growing by assimilation together, and putrifying in the earth by little and little, the generation and discretion broke forth together; and living creatures being produced together with plants, then out of the same putrefaction arose both men and beans; whereof he alleged manifest arguments. For, if anyone should chew a bean, and, having minced it small with his teeth, lay it abroad in the warm Sun, and so leaving it for a little time return to it, he shall perceive the scent of human blood. Moreover, if anyone at the time when beans shoot forth the flower, shall take a little of the flower which then is black, and put it into an earthen vessel, and cover it close, and bury it in the ground ninety days, and at the end thereof take it up and take off the cover—instead of the bean, he shall find either the head of an Infant or or γυναικὸς αἰδοῖον ["the vagina of a woman"].[931] The same reason Origen ascribes to Zaratus, from whom perhaps Pythagoras, being his student, received them.[932]

Hence it is that Pliny says he condemned beans, because the souls of dead are in them. And Porphyry elsewhere, because they most partake of the nature of a living creature. Some, including Cicero, say it was because beans disturb the tranquility of mind. Wherefore to abstain from them, says Porphyry, makes our dreams serene and untroubled. Aulus Gellius says he meant, from venereal delights.[933] And Plutarch says he forbade beans because they conduce thereto. On the contrary, Clement of Alexandria affirms they were prohibited out of no other reason than that women feeding on them became barren.[934]

For the thirty-ninth, *Abstain from the flesh of living creatures*, the most general reason is because they are of the same nature and temperament with us, and in a manner, allied unto us. But of this we spoke formerly.

CHAPTER 5

Other Symbols

To the foregoing Symbols collected by Iamblichus, may be added these:

Take not up what falls from the Table. Meaning that men should not accustom themselves to eat intemperately. Or alluding to some religious rite. For Aristophanes says that which falls so belongs to the Heroes, saying in his *Heroes:*

> Taste not what from the Table falls.[935]

Break not Bread. Divide not friends. Others refer it to the judgment in the Infernal places. Others, that it implies fear in War.[936]

Set down Salt. This is in remembrance of Justice. For Salt preserves all things, and is brought out of the purest thing, Water.[937]

Pluck not a Crown. That is offend not the Laws, for Laws are the crown of Cities.[938]

Offer libation to the gods just to the ears of the cup. This signifies that we ought to worship and celebrate the gods with Music, for that passes in at the ears.[939] And drink not of that libation.[940]

Eat not (which are unlawful) *generation, augmentation, beginning, end, nor that of which the first basis of all things consists.* Meaning, we must abstain from the loins, διδύμων αἰδοίων ["testicles (and) genitals"],† marrow, feet, and head of victims. He called the loins "Basis," because living creatures are settled upon them as their foundation, διδύμυς καὶ αἰδοῖα , Generation,† for without the help of these, no living creature is engendered. Marrow he called "Increase," it being the cause of augmentation in living creatures. The beginning, the feet; the head, the end; which have most power in government of the body.[941]

Eat not Fishes.[942] Some apply this to silence.[943] Others say he disapproved them because they are not used in sacrifice to the gods.

Put not meat in a Chamber-pot. Meaning, communicate nothing that is wise to a rude and foolish person.[944]

Sleep not at noon. For at that time the Sun shows its greatest force.[945] We ought not to shut our eyes against the light when it is most manifest.

Quit not your station without the command of your General. Our souls ought to be kept in the body, neither may we forsake this life without special leave from Him who gave it us, lest we seem to despise the gift of God.[946]

Roast not what is boiled. That is, change not meekness to anger.[947]

Heap not up Cypress. Of this wood they conceived the Scepter of Jupiter to be made.[948]

Sacrifice even things to the Celestial deities, odd to the Terrestrial. Of this, already in his Arithmetic.

When it thunders, touch the earth. This calls to mind our own mortality.[949] Or, when a King is angry, the offender ought to humble himself.

Eat not sitting in a Chariot.[950] Some expound it, that we ought to eat in quiet, or that we ought not to give ourselves to luxury in a time of business.

Go into the Temple on the right hand, go out on the left. Right and left seem to refer to the ceremonial numbers—as already discussed.

Where blood has been shed, cover the place with stones. That is, abolish the very remembrance of any war or dissension.[951]

Hurt not a mild plant.[952] Some expound it, Harm not the harmless.

Pray aloud. This implies not that God cannot hear such as pray softly, but that our prayers should be just.[953] They should be such as we need not care who hears.

Sail not on the ground. Signifying, that we ought to forbear raising taxes, and such revenues as are troublesome and unstable.[954]

Beget children. For it is our duty to leave behind us such as may serve the gods in our room.[955]

Neither dip in a basin, nor wash in a bath.[956]

Put not away thy wife. For she is a suppliant.[957]

Counsel nothing but what is best. For counsel is a sacred thing.[958]

Plant not a Palm.[959]

Lastly: Hither may be referred the Symbolic Letter Y. They said that the course of human life is like that letter, for everyone arriving at the first state of youth where the way divides itself into two, stands at a gaze, not knowing which to take. If he meets with a guide that leads to the better—that is, if he learn Philosophy, Oratory, or some honest art which may prove beneficial, but cannot be attained without much labor—they affirm that he shall lead an honorable and plentiful life. But if not lighting upon such a Master, he takes the left hand way which seems at first to be the better and to lead to virtue—that is if he gives himself over to sloth and luxury, which seem pleasant at first to him who is ignorant of true good—he shall e're long lose both his credit and estate, and live thence forward, ignominiously, and miserably. Thus Lactantius, perhaps alluding to the old verses.[960]

The Pythagorean Y
From Geoffroy Tory, *Champfleury*, 1529

The Pythagorean Letter two ways spread,
Shows the two paths in which Man's life is led.
The right hand track to sacred Virtue tends,
Though steep and rough at first, in rest it ends;
The other broad and smooth, but from its Crown,
On rocks the Traveller is tumbled down.
He who to Virtue by harsh toils aspires,
Subduing pains, worth and renown acquires:
But who seeks slothful luxury, and flys,
The labour of great acts, dishonour'd dies!

CHAPTER 6

The Golden Verses of Pythagoras

A Summary of the Pythagorean Doctrine is extant in verse entitled
The Golden Verses of Pythagoras; or as others, *of the Pythagoreans*. For,
says Hierocles, as Gold is the best and purest of Metals, so these are
the best and most Divine of verses. They are these:

> First, in their ranks, th' Immortal Gods adore,
> Thy Oath keep; next, great Heroes; then implore,
> Terrestrial Daemons with due sacrifice.
> Thy Parents reverence, and near Allies:
> Him that is first in Virtue make thy Friend,
> And with observance his kind speech attend:
> Nor (to thy power) for Light faults cast him by,
> Thy pow'r is neighbour to Necessity.

> These know, and with intentive care pursue;
> But anger, sloth, and luxury subdue.
> In sight of others or thyself forbear
> What's ill; but of thyself stand most in fear.
> Let Justice all thy words and actions sway;
> Nor from the even course of Reason stray:
> For know that all men are to die ordain'd,
> And riches are as quickly lost as gain'd.
> Crosses that happen by divine decree,
> (If such thy lot) bear not impatiently.
> Yet seek to remedy with all thy care,
> And think the Just have not the greatest share.
> 'Mongst men, discourses good and bad are spread,
> Despise not those, nor be by these misled.
> If any some notorious falsehood say,
> Thou the report with equal Judgment weigh.
> Let not men's smoother promises invite,
> Nor rougher threats from just resolves thee fright.

If ought thou wouldst attempt, first ponder it;
Fools only inconsiderate acts commit.
Nor do what afterwards thou may repent;
First learn to know the thing on which th' art bent.
Thus thou a life shalt lead with joy repeat.

Nor must thou care of outward health forget.
Such temp'rance use in exercise and diet,
As may preserve thee in a setled quiet.
Meats unprohibited, not curious chose,
Decline what any other may accuse.
The rash expence of vanity detest,
And sordidness: A mean in all is best.
Hurt not thyself: Before thou act, advise;
Nor suffer sleep at night to close thine eyes,
Till thrice thy acts that day thou hast ore-run,
How slipped? what deeds? what duty left undone?
Thus thy account summ'd up from first to last,
Grieve for the ill, joy for what good has past.

These study, practise these, and these affect;
To sacred virtue these thy steps direct.
Eternal Nature's fountain I attest,
Who the Tetractys on our soul imprest.
Before thy mind thou to this study bend,
Invoke the Gods to grant it a good end.
These if thy labour vanquish, thou shalt then
Know the connection both of Gods and men;
How everything proceeds, or by what staid,
And know (as far as fit to be survey'd)
Nature alike throughout: that thou mayest learn
Not to hope hopeless things, but all discern.
And know those Wretches whose perverser wills
Drawn down upon their head spontaneous Ills;
Unto the good that's nigh them deaf and blind:
Some few the cure of these misfortunes find.

This only is the Fate that harms, and rolls,
Through miseries successive, human souls.
Within is a continual hidden fight,
Which we to shun must study, not excite.
Great Jove? how little trouble should we know,
If thou to all men wouldst their Genius show?

But fear not thou. Men come of heav'nly race,
Taught by diviner Nature what t' embrace:
Which if pursu'd, thou all I named shalt gain,
And keep thy Soul clear from thy body's stain.
In time of Prayer and cleansing, meats denied
Abstained from; thy mind's reign let reason guide.

Then strip'd of flesh up to free Aether soar,
A deathless God, Divine, mortal no more.

Part Four

Pythagorean Commentators

Timaeus the Locrean
John Reuchlin

The supreme Greek god Zeus is honored on this silver stater of Locri Epizephyrii ('of the western wind'), struck c.400–350 B.C.*, with his portrait on the obverse and his animal familiar, the eagle, shown devouring its prey on the reverse.*
Photo courtesy of Classical Numismatic Group, Inc.

Timaeus the Locrian

Of the Soul of the World, and of Nature

Timaeus, the Locrian, in his *Principles*, said these things. There are two principles of all things: the Mind, of things effected according to reason; Necessity, of those which are by violence according to the powers of bodies. Of these one is of the nature of good, and is called God, and is the principle of the best things. The consequent and concausals are reduced to Necessity. For all things are the offspring of these: *Idea, Matter, Sensibles*. The *Idea* is ungenerated, immovable, permanent, of the nature of Identity, intellectual, the exemplar of things that are made, and immutable. *Matter* is the print, mother, nurse, and productrix of the third essence. For, receiving likeness into itself, and being, as it were, characterised by them, it perfects all productions. This matter he asserted to be eternal, but not immovable, in form of itself and without figure, but receiving all forms. In bodies it is divisible and of the nature of Otherness. They call Matter, "Place" and "Region." These two principles are contrary. Form, has the nature of male and father; Matter, of female and mother; the Third (*Sensibles*) is their offspring.

These being three are known three ways: Idea, by intellect, according to science; Matter, by spurious ratiocination, not being understood by direct comprehension but by analogy; their Offspring, by sense and opinion. Before Heaven was made, we must conceive that there was Idea, and Matter, and God, the maker of the better (viz. Idea). Now forasmuch as the elder is better than the younger, and the orderly than the disorderly—God, being good, and seeing Matter receive Idea and become totally changed, yet disorderly, saw also it was needful to bring it into order; and from indefinite transmutations to fix it determinately, that bodies might have proportionate distinctions and not receive promiscuous variations.

Of all this Matter he framed the World (making it the bound of the nature of Being since it comprehends all other things). He made it one, only begotten, perfect, animate, and rational (for these are better than inanimate and irrational), and a spherical body (that

being more perfect than other figures). Designing therefore to make
the best production, he made this God, generate, not corruptible
by any other cause but by the same God only which composed it, if
it should please him at any time to dissolve it. But he who is good,
will not be carried on to the destruction of the fairest production.
Wherefore it is permanent, and being such, incorruptible, imperishable, and blessed. It is the best of productions, being made by the
best cause; who looked not upon patterns made by hands, but upon
the Idea, the intellectual essence. After which, this being exactly
made, is the fairest of all and not to be demolished.

It is perfect, as to sensible things, for the exemplar comprehending in itself all intelligible creatures, left nothing out. It being the
perfect bound of Intelligibles, as the World is of sensibles; which
being solid, tactile, and visible, is divided into Earth, Fire, and
(between these) Air, and Water. It consists of perfect bodies which
exist entirely in it, so as no part remains beyond it, that the body of
the Universe might be self-sufficient, and not liable to dissolution by
any external accidents. For there are no other things besides these
and what are contained in them—they being, after the most excellent analogy, connected in equal power, neither predominating over
the other in any part, nor being predominated, that whereby some
might increase, others decrease. But it rests in an indissoluble harmonious concord, according to the best proportion.

For there being three bounds, and the intervals distant from
each other in the same proportion. The middle is that to the first
which the third is to it, and so reciprocally, according to disposition
of place and order. But to number these, without the help of another
thing equal to them, is absolutely impossible. It is well ordered both
for figure and motion. As to the first, being round, it is every way
like itself, and able to contain all other figures. As to its circular
motion, it keeps a perpetual tenor. For a Sphere only, whether in
rest or in motion, is so adapted to the same place as that it never
ceases nor removes—all its parts being equidistant from the Center.
Now its outward superficies being exactly smooth, it needs not the
weak organs which are bestowed on other living creatures for their
accommodation.

The Soul of the World God inkindled in the midst, but diffused beyond it, covering the Universe with it and tempering it with a temperament of indivisible Form and divisible Substance, so as these two make one temperament. With this he mingled two powers, principles of the two motions of Identity and Otherness; which (Soul), not easily capable of being mixed, was not without difficulty blended together.

All these proportions are mixed according to harmonious numbers, which proportions he cunningly divided, that it might be known of what and by what the Soul consists. This Soul God did not ordain (as we affirm) after corporeal substance (for that which is most honorable is first both in power and time). But He made it before the body, removing one, the first of four Monads, into eight Decads and three Centuries. Of this, the duple and triple is easily collected, the first being settled. All these, with their complements, and sesquioctaves, will amount to thirty-six. The whole sum will be 114,695. The divisions are 114,695. After this manner he divided the Soul of the Universe.

The Mind only sees the Eternal God, the Ruler and Father of all things.[961] That which is generated we behold with our eyes— this World and its parts. The Aetherial are twofold: some of the nature of Identity, others of Difference. Of these, some extrinsically carry about all that is within them from East to West by an universal motion. The rest, being of the motion of Diversity, intrinsically turn about from the West to the East, moved by themselves. They are carried round by accident, with the motion of Identity, having the greatest force in the World.

The motion of Diversity, divided according to harmonious proportions, is disposed into seven circles. The Moon being nearest the Earth, performs her course in a month. Next her, the Sun perfects his course in a year. There are two of equal course with the Sun— Mercury, and the Star Juno, which many call Venus, and Lucifer. (All persons not being skillful in the rules of sacred Astronomy and the observations of rising and setting). The same star is sometimes Hesper, when it so follows the Sun, that it is conspicuous to us when the Sun is set; sometimes Eous, when it go before the Sun, and rises before him. Lucifer, therefore, many times is the star Venus when she runs along with the Sun. And likewise are many of the Fixed Stars and planets. For any star of visible magnitude, ushering the Sun above the Horizon, foretells day. The other three, Mars, Jupiter, and Saturn, have peculiar velocities and unequal years. But they complete their course in certain and comprehensible regularities, and appearances, and occultations, and eclipses, and risings, and settings. They have, besides their phases, rising and setting in regard of the Sun.

The Sun makes day in performing his course from East to West; night, by motion from West to East; while he is carried about with the motion of Identity, a year, by his own proper motion. By these two motions the Sun performs a double course: one as being carried about with the general motion of Heaven, the other by an oblique motion. One distinguishes the times of the day and the seasons. The other, by which he is carried about after the rapid motion of the Fixed Stars, at every revolution makes night day. These are parts of time called Periods, ordained by God together with the World. For before the World there were no Stars, and consequently neither year nor seasons, by which this generable World is commensurated. This time is the image of that which is innate, called Eternity. For as this Universe was formed after the eternal exemplar of the Ideal World, so was this time ordained together with the World after its pattern, Eternity.

The Earth being established in the midst, the seat of the gods is the bound of night and day, of rising and setting, according to the section of Horizons, as they are circumscribed by the sight and by section of the Earth. It is the most ancient of all bodies in the Universe. For Water was not produced without Earth; nor Air without humidity; and Fire cannot subsist without humidity and matter which it kindles. So that the Earth is settled upon its own weight as the root and basis of all things.

The principle therefore of generated things, as to the subject, is Matter; as to the form, Idea. The productions of these are bodies— Earth, Water, Air, and Fire—whose generation is thus. Every body consists of superficies; a superficies of Triangles; of which this is a rectangled equal-legged semiquadrangle; the other unequilateral, having the greater angle in power, triple to the lesser. The least angle in it is one-third of a right angle. Double to this is the middle angle, consisting of two-thirds. The greatest is a right angle, sesquialter to the middle, triple to the least. Now this Triangle is a sesquiquadrangle to an equilateral Triangle, the perpendicular from the top to the bottom being divided into two equal parts. There are therefore in each two rectangled Triangles. But in one the two sides which include the right angle are equal; in the other, all the three sides are unequal. This figure is called "Scholion." This semiquadrangle is the principle of which the earth was constituted; for the Quadrangle is compounded of these four semiquadrangles.

Of the Quadrangle is generated the Cube, the firmest and most settled of all bodies, having six sides, eight angles. For this reason Earth is the most heavy body, and unapt for motion, and not transmutable into any other, as being incommunicable with any kind of Triangle. For the Earth only has a stable principle, which is the semiquadrangle, the element of the other bodies—Fire, Air, and Water. For the semiquadrangle being six times compounded, there arises an equilateral Triangle, of which a Pyramid with four bases and four equal angles is compounded, the form of fire most apt to motion and of rarest parts.

Next these is the Octahedron with eight bases and six angles, the element of Air. The third, Icosahedron, of twenty bases, and twelve angles is the element of Water, being fullest of parts, and heaviest. These being compounded of the same Element are transmutated into one another.

The Dodecahedron, he made the image of the Universe, as nearest to a Globe. Fire by reason of the rarity of its parts penetrates all things; Air all things but Fire; Water, all but Earth.

All things therefore are full, and admit no vacuity. They are carried about by the circumvolution of the Universe; and, by reason of their solidity, grate one upon another, rendering an unintermitted alteration to generation and corruption. These God used in framing the World—tactile by reason of Earth, visible by reason of Fire— the two extremes. By Air and Water, he connected it in a most firm band, proportion, capable to contain both itself and the things that are comprised in it. If then that which is connected be a superficies, one medium is sufficient; if a solid, it requires two. To the two mediums, he adapted the two extremes—Fire to Air, Air to Water, Water to Earth; and again Fire to Air, Air to Water, and Water to Earth; and again as Earth to Water, Water to Air, and Air to Earth; and reciprocally as Earth to Air, Water to Fire. And forasmuch as all these are equal in power, their proportions are equal likewise.

Thus is the World one, and by a happy connection, proportionable. Each of these four bodies has diverse species. The Fire is flame, light, splendor, by reason of the inequality of the Triangles in each of these. The Air is partly clear and dry, partly humid and cloudy. The Water is fluid and concrete, as snow, frost, hail, and ice. Of Humid, one sort is fluid as honey and oil; another compact, as pitch and wax. Of the compact are two kinds: one fusile, as gold, silver, brass, tin, lead; the other frangible, as sulphur, bitumen, nitre, salt, alum, and stones of that kind.

After he had made the World, he proceeded to the production of mortal creatures that it might be perfect and completely wrought according to its pattern.[962] Having blended together and distributed the Soul of Man by the same proportions and powers, he delivered it over to that nature which had the power of changing. She succeeding him in the producing of mortal transitory creatures and instilled their souls: some from the Moon, some from the Sun, some from the other Stars which wander in the Region of Otherness. Excepting one soul in the power of Identity which he mingled in the rational part, an image of wisdom to those who make use of good Fate. For of the human soul, one part is rational and intellectual, the other irrational and foolish. Of the irrational, the better is of the nature of Identity, the worse that of Diversity. Each of these is resident about the head, that all the other parts of the soul and body may be subservient to it according to the analogy of the body of the Universe. Of the irrational part: one is irascible placed about the heart; the other desiderative about the liver.

As for the body, the principle and root of marrow is in the brain, wherein is the hegemonic of the Soul. From the brain issues an emanation flowing down along the vertebra of the spine from whence it is distributed into seed and generative substance. The bones are the case of the marrow; the flesh is the covering of the bones; the joints he connected by nerves for motion. Of the inward parts, some were made for nourishment, others for conversation. Of the motions, those which come from without and flow into the apprehensive part are sensible; those which fall not under comprehension are insensible, whether by reason that the affected bodies are more earthy, or that the motions are weaker. Whatsoever motions change nature are painful; those that comply with her are named pleasures.

Of the senses, God enlightned our Sight for contemplation of Celestials and apprehension of Science. Hearing, he framed perceptive of Discourse and of Music. Of this sense, if any be destitute from his birth, he will also be incapable of Speaking. Whence we say Hearing is nearest allied to Reason. All that are termed affections of bodies are denominated with reference to the Touch and their inclination to a place. For the Touch determines vital faculties: warm, cold; dry, moist; smooth, rough; yielding, resisting; soft, hard. But heavy and light the Touch prejudges. Reason defines by inclination to move to the middle and from the middle. Below and the middle they affirm to be the same thing, for the center of a globe is below. Whatsoever is between that and the circumference is above.

Heat, seems to consist of rare parts, and disintegrates bodies; Cold, of more dense parts, and binds the pores. The Taste resembles the Touch in concretion and discretion, and in penetration of the pores, and in its objects, which are either harsh or smooth. Those which have a cleansing or scouring faculty stupify the tongue and are bitter. Those which are moderately purgative, salt. Those which inflame and pierce further into the flesh, acid. Contrary to these, are smooth and sweet. The kinds of odor are not distinct for they insinuate through narrow pores which are too solid to be contracted and dilated by putrefaction, and concoction of earth and earthly things. They are sweet or stinking.

Voice is a percussion in the air passing to the soul through the ears, whose pores extend to the liver. In the ears is a spirit whose motion is Hearing. Of voice and hearing some are swift, the sharp; some slow, the flat; the mean are incommensurable. Again, one is much and diffused, the loud; another small and contracted, the low;

one is ordered according to proportions, the harmonious; another disorderly and unproportionate, the inharmonious.

The fourth kind of Sensibles is most various and multiform—termed Visibles—comprising all colors, and innumerable colored things. The primary colors are four: White, Black, Bright, Purple. The rest are made by mixing these together. White disperses the sight. Black contracts it, as hot diffuses the touch. Cold contracts it. Bitter contracts the taste, and sweet dissipates it.

The bodies of creatures that breathe air are nourished by aliment, distributed by the veins through the whole frame defluxively, as by channels, and irrigated by the spirit which diffuses it to the utmost bounds. Respiration is made (there being no vacuity in nature) by influxion, and attraction of the air in the room of that which issued forth at invisible vents, out of which also sweat evaporates. Now something of it being wasted by the natural heat, it is necessary something be introduced to supply that which was consumed. Otherwise there would be a vacuity, which is impossible. For a living creature could not be restored by perpetual fluxion and entire, if the body were disjoined by vacuity. The like composition of organs is likewise in inanimate things with an analogical respiration. A cupping-glass and amber are resemblances of respiration. For the spirits evaporate through the body and enter again at the mouth and nostrils by respiration; then again, like Euripus, it is brought round into the body which by these effuxions is extended. The cupping-glass, the air being consumed by fire, attracts moisture; the amber, by emission of spirits, attracts the body that is like to it.

All aliment is taken into the body from the root of the heart, and the fountain of the ventricle; if the accession be more than the flowing down, it is termed Growth; if the contrary, Decay. The Acme consists in the confine between these two, and is conceived to be the equality of accession and emanation. When the ligaments of the constitution are dissolved, so as there is no passage for the breath, or distribution of aliment, the animal dies.

There are many things which are pernicious to life and cause death; whereof one is termed Sickness. The origins of sickness are the disproportions of the primary faculties. If the simple faculties—

Heat, Cold, Humidity, Dryness—abound, or are deficient, then follow mutations and alterations of the blood by corruption, and deprivations of the consumptive flesh. If according to the changes into Sharp, or Salt, or Acid (humours) the turnings of the blood, or consumptions of the flesh be caused; for hence are generated Choler and Phlegm. Unwholesome **Chyles** and putrefaction of Humours are inconsiderable except they be deep; but those whose causes lie in the bones are not easily cured; those which arise out of the marrow are painful. The extremities of Diseases are Wind, Choler, Phlegm, increasing and flowing into places not proper to them, or into the vital parts. For then obtaining a better place, they expel their neighbors and settle there, and afflicting the bodies, they resolve them into themselves.

These are the diseases of the body. Out of these arise many sicknesses of the soul, several of several faculties. These are: of the sensitive, stupidity; of the reminiscent, forgetfulness; of the desiderative, loathing and excessive appetite; of the pathetic, wild passions and furious frenzies; of the rational, indocility and indiscretion. The forces of vice are pleasures and griefs, desires and fears, raised out of the body, mingled with the soul, and expressed by various names: loves, desires, dissolute affections, impetuous angers, deep malices, various longings, inordinate delights. In a word, to behave ourselves amiss as to passions, or to subdue them, is the bound between virtue and vice. For to be excessive in them, or too hard for them, puts us in a good or bad condition.

To these inclinations, the temper of the body may contribute much. If vehement, abject, or anyway extraordinary, it transports us to melancholy and extravagant lusts. For the parts being overflown by these emanations make the constitution of the body rather turgid than sound, whence arise sadness, forgetfulness, folly, and consternation. The customs also whereunto a man has conformed himself in the city or family where he was born and bred, conduce much. This is also true of the daily course of life, whether softening or corroborating the soul. For living abroad, diet, exercise, and the manners of those with whom we converse, greatly avail to virtue or vice. And these occasions are derived rather from our parents and elements, than from ourselves. For they are not ineffectual; we are ourselves so easily receding from those actions which are good.[963]

To the well-being of an animal, it is requisite that the body have the virtues competent to it: Health, perfect Sense, Strength, and Beauty. The principles of Beauty are a symmetry of the parts amongst themselves and with the soul; for nature made the body as an instrument, obedient and accommodate to all the businesses of life. In like manner, the soul must be ordered to virtues answerable to those: to Temperance, as the body to Health; to Wisdom, as the body to perfect sense; to Fortitude, as the body to strength; to Justice, as the body to beauty.

The principles of these are from Nature; their means and ends from industry. Those of the body are attained by exercise and Medicine; those of the Soul by Institution and Philosophy. For these faculties nourish and strengthen both the soul and body by labor, exercise and pureness of diet—these by medicaments; those instituting the soul by chastisements and reprehensions. For they strengthen it, by exhortation, by exciting the inclination, and enjoining those things which are expedient for action.

The gymnastic art, and its nearest ally Medicine, are designed for the cure of bodies—reducing the faculties to the best harmony. They purify the blood and make the spirits flow freely, so that if anything unwholesome settle, the vigors of the blood and spirits being thus confirmed, overmaster it. Music, and its director Philosophy—ordained by the gods and by the laws for reformation of the soul—inure, compel and persuade the irrational part to obey the rational, and in the irrational mollify anger, and quiet desire; so they neither move nor rest without reason, the mind summoning them either to action or fruition.

The bound of temperance is obedience and fortitude. Now science and venerable philosophy, purifying the mind from false opinions, bring her to knowledge. And reducing her from great ignorance, raise her to contemplation of Divine things; wherein if a man be conversant with contentedness as to human things, and endeavor in a moderate way of living, he is happy. For he to whom God has allotted this estate is undoubtedly guided to a most happy life.

But if a man be stiff and refractory, he shall be pursued by pun-ishment according to the laws and those discourses which declare things Celestial and Infernal. For irremissible punishments are pre-pared for the unhappy dead and many other things; for which I com-mend the Ionic poet, who makes men religious by ancient fabulous Traditions. For as we cure bodies with things unwholesome when the wholesome agree not with them, so we restrain souls with fabulous relations when they will not be led by the true. Let them then— since there is a necessity for it—talk of these strange punishments: as if souls did transmigrate: those of the effeminate into the bodies of women given up to ignominy; of murderers into those of beasts for punishment; of the lascivious into the forms of swine; of the light and temerarious into birds; of the slothful, and idle, unlearned, and ignorant into several kinds of fishes. All these in the second period Nemesis decrees, together with the vindictive and Terrestrial Dae-mons, the overseers of human affairs to whom God, the disposer of all things, has committed the administration of the World—replen-ished with gods, men, and all other living creatures. All of which are formed after the best image of the ungenerate and eternal Idea.

An Explication of the Pythagorean Doctrine
By John Reuchlin[964]

CHAPTER I

OF PYTHAGORAS: HIS WAY OF TEACHING,
BY SILENCE AND SYMBOLS

The incommunicable and abstruse tradition of Mysteries and Symbols is not to be investigated by acuteness of human wit (which rather affects us with a doubtful fear than an adherent firmness). It requires ample strength of thinking and believing, and above all things, faith and taciturnity.[965] Whence Pythagoras taught nothing (as Apuleius says) to his disciples before silence; it being the first rudiment of contemplative wisdom to learn to meditate, and to unlearn to talk.[966] As if the Pythagorean sublimity were of greater worth than to be comprehended by the talk of boys. This kind of learning (as other things) Pythagoras brought into Greece from the Hebrews. That the disciple intending to ask some sublime question, should hold his peace; and being questioned, should only answer αὐτὸς ἔφα , "He said."† Thus the Cabalists answer אמרו הכמים, "The wise said"; and Christians, πίστευσον, "Believe."†

Moreover, all the Pythagorean philosophy (especially that which concerns divine things) is mystical, expressed by Riddles and Symbols.[967] The reasons are these: First, the Ancients used to deliver wisdom by Allegories. All their Philosophers and Poets are full of Riddles, avoiding by obscurity contempt of the vulgar. For the most apt interpreter of things not perceptible by human infirmity is Fable. That befits Philosophers which is declared under the pious veil of fictions, hidden in honest things, and attired in honest words. For what is easily found is but too negligently pursued. Secondly, it sometimes happens that we cannot express abstruse things without much circumlocution, unless by some short Parable. Thirdly, as generals use watch-words to distinguish their own soldiers from others, so it is not improper to communicate to friends some peculiar Symbols as distinctive marks of a Society. These, among the Pythagoreans, were a chain of indissoluble love. Pythagoras was studious of friendship; and if he heard of any that used his Symbols, he presently admitted him into his Society.[968] Hereupon all became desirous of them—as well thereby to be acceptable to their Master as to be known as Pythagoreans. Lastly, symbols may serve as memorial notes. For in treating of all things divine and human, the vastness of the subject requires short Symbols as conducing much to memory.

CHAPTER 2

The Triple World

The Pythagoreans reduce all Beings, subsistent or substantive, immediately to Ideas which truly are; and those to the Idea of Ideas.[969] Hereupon they asserted three Worlds—whereof the third is infinite, or rather not-finite—and that all things consist of Three. The Pythagoreans (says Aristotle) affirm that the whole and all things are terminated by three. Some are bodies and magnitudes, others keep and inhabit bodies and magnitude, others are the rulers and origins of the inhabitants. This we understand of the three Worlds: the Inferior, the Superior, and the Supreme.

The Inferior contains bodies, and magnitudes, and their appropriate Intelligences, movers of the Spheres, overseers, and guardians of things generable and corruptible, who are said to take care of bodies, each according to the particular task assigned him. By the Ancients, they are named sometimes Angels, sometimes gods, and (in respect of the anxious solicitude of things whereto they are confined) Daemons.

Next over it immediately shines the Superior World. This contains the superior Powers, incorporeal essences, divine exemplars, the seals of the inferior World, after whose likeness the faces of all inferior things are formed. These Pythagoras calls "Immortal Gods,"[970] as being the principles of things produced out of the Divine Mind, essential ἀρχαι. They are the causes of those forms which dwell in bodies, and inform the compounded substances of the lower World. There are also other gods, incorporeal beings, individual, differing not by material, but by formal number. These are spirits, void of matter, simple, unmixed, seated beyond the sensible Heaven, confined neither to time nor place, neither suffering age nor transmutation much less any alteration. In a word, not being affected with any passion, they lead a self-sufficient excellent life, and inhabit Eternity, which is ἀιων ἀει ὤν, always being, because it always was, is, and shall be intemporally in the Divine Mind. Yet by the energy of God it was created and placed beyond the convex of the visible Heaven, as being the lucid mansion of the blessed spirits (whom the Pythagoreans believe gods), placed in the highest region of Aether, of ever-lasting duration, invested in the immortal Eternity.

The third World, Supreme, containing all other Worlds, is that of the Deity, consisting of one divine Essence, existent before Eter-nity. For it is the Age of Ages, the preexistent entity and unity of existence, substance, essence, nature.

These three Worlds are called "Receptacles" in different respects: the first, of Quantity; the second, of Intelligences; the third, of Prin-ciples. The first, circumscriptively; the second, definitively; the third is not received, but receives, because it is everywhere, and is called a replenishing receptacle.

Through the Superior World is communicated—from the Tet-ractys to the inferior—life, and the being (not accidental, but sub-stantial) of every species; to some, clearly; to others, obscurely. This the Pythagoreans collect from those words of their Master:

—The Tetractys to our Souls did send,
The Fountain of Eternal Nature—[971]

The Tetractys is the Divine Mind communicating. The Foun-tain is the exemplar Idea communicated. And eternal Nature is the essential Idea of things received. Idea, considered as to God (say they), is his knowledge; as to the sensible World, exemplar; as to itself, Essence.

Now as in the Sensible World the Superior sphere has an influ-ence on all the Spheres beneath it, so in the Intelligible World. Not only every superior Chorus of Angels has an influence upon all the inferior, but the whole superior World has an influence upon the whole inferior. Whereby all things are reduced according to their capacities as far as possible: momentary to Eternal, inferior to supe-rior. But to the third World, nothing that is merely a creature can be reduced, incapable in its own nature of that sublimity which is proper only to God.

CHAPTER 3

The Supreme World

The Supreme World, being (as we said) that of the Deity, is one, divine, continual, constant Essence of Sempiternity, poised (as it were) with immoveable weight. It is termed παυρατορική ἕδρα, the all-governing Throne.[972] Not confined to genus, place, time, nor reason, it is the free unlimited president over all these; infinitely supreme in place, power, possession, excellence, above all Essence, Nature, Eternity, Age.

This Divine Mind, the receptacle of principles, Pythagoras symbolically terms Number; saying Number is the Principle of all things. (For none can believe so meanly of so wise a person, as that he should conceive the ordinary numbers by which we cast account, to be the Principles of all things—which are far from being antecedent to things, for they are consequential accidents.) So Plutarch: by Number Pythagoras understands the Mind, a Symbol not improper; in Incorporeals nothing more divine than the Mind; in Abstractions nothing more simple than Number.[973]

The divine Essence therefore—existent before Eternity and Age (for it is the Age of Ages), the preexistent entity and unity of existence, substance, essence, nature—was by Pythagoras called ἕν, ONE; by Parmenides ὄν, BEING, both upon a like ground. Because it is the super-essential Unit and Being, from which, by which, through which, in which, and to which all things are; and are ordered, and persist, and are contained, and are filled, and are converted.

Of this first one, and first **Ens**, Aristotle says thus: Plato and the Pythagoreans hold no other concerning Ens or One. But that this is their nature, their essence is the same, to be One and a Being. Xenophanes declared this One to be God, herein agreeing with Pythagoras, who asserted infinite, and one, and number, to be the first Principles of things. By "infinite" is signified the power, for nothing can be imagined before power, which in God is infinite, or rather it is infinite God. In him **Esse** and **Posse** are not distinct. He contains the essences, virtues, and operations of all producibles.[974]

With Pythagoras agrees Anaxagoras, for all things were together.[975] Democritus says all thing were in power. This also is the mixing of things mentioned by Empedocles and Anaximander. Not confusedly in Chaos, Erebus, or Night; but distinctly and orderly in full light, in the most perfect splendor of the divine light, intuitive knowledge. That is the IDEA (from ἔιδω γινώσκω ["seeing, *meaning* understanding"]†), whose power is being. It includes all, whether mental, rational, intelligible, sensible, vital, substantial, or adhesive; and is not only all things that are, but those that are not.

This is no other than the divine Essence—within which (before all things) one produced two. Two is the first number; one is the principle of Number; One is God. And the production of two is within the divine Essence (for number is constituted of itself, and next one is naturally only the number two). This two must necessarily be God also, for within God is nothing but God. Thus these three (One and Two) being the Principle and first, and not exceeding the Essence of God, are indeed one God. For his Essence is not divided by the production of two out of one. In like manner it often happens in corporeals, that one being moved to two, proceeds to three, the substance of things continuing. For example, as in a tree, of boughs and branches; in man, the body arms and fingers. Of one therefore in the Divinity producing, and two produced, arises a Trinity to which, if there be added an essence formally distinct from them, there will be a formal Quaternity. This is the infinite one and two, the Substance, Perfection, and end of all Number. One, two, three, four by a collective progression make Ten; beyond ten there is not anything. This Pythagoras meant, when he asserted that the Principle of all things is the Tetractys. He understood God by it; for he swore by it, and seems to have transferred the Hebrew Tetragammaton into Greek Symbol.

Thus the most apt symbol of the Principles of things is one and two. For when we make enquiry into the causes and origin of all things, what sooner occurs than one and two?[976] That which we first behold with our eyes is the same and not another; that which we first conceive in our mind is Identity and Diversity, One and Two. Alcmaeon (contemporary with Pythagoras) affirmed two to be many—

which he said were contrarieties (perhaps the same with Empedocles
Ἔρις ["strife"]†), yet unconfined and indefinite, such as white and
black, sweet and bitter, good and evil, great and small.

These multiplex diversities the Pythagoreans designated by the
number Ten: as finite and infinite, even and odd, one and many, right
and left, male and female, steadfast and moved, straight and crooked,
light and darkness, good and ill, square and oblong. These pairs are
two, and therefore contrary; they are reduced all into ten, that being
the most perfect number, as containing more kinds of numeration
than the rest: even and odd, square and cube, long and short, the
first uncompounded and first compounded. Nothing is more absolute than the number Ten, since in ten proportions, four cubic numbers are consummated, of which (according to the Pythagoreans)
all things consist. By this all nations reckon (not exceeding it) as
by the natural account of ten fingers. Heaven itself consists of ten
Spheres. Architas includes all that is in the number ten. In imitation of whom Aristotle names ten kinds of Ens, categories, reducible
to two, Substance and Accident, both springing from one Essence.
For ten so loves two that from one it proceeds to two, and by two it
reverts into one.

The first Ternary is of one and two, not compounded, but consistent. One having no position makes no composition; a unit while
a unit has no position, nor a point while a point. There being nothing before One, we rightly say one is first. Two is not compounded
of numbers but a co-ordination of units only. It is therefore the first
number, being the first multitude. It is not commensurable by any
number, only by unit, the common measure of all number. For one
two is nothing but two. So that the multitude which is called "Triad,"
Arithmeticians term the first number uncompounded, the Duad
being not an uncompounded number, but rather not-compounded.

Now the Triad, through its propensity to multiply and communicate its goodness to all creatures, proceeds from power to operation.[977] The Triad, beholding with a perpetual intuition that fecun-
dity of multitude which is in it—productive (as it were) of number
from number—and that essentiality which is one in it—the fountain
of all production, the beginning of all progression, the permanence

of all immutable substance—it reverts itself into itself, multiplying itself (as it were) by unity and duality, saying, "Once twice two, are four." This is the Tetractys, the Idea of all created things; for all progression is perfected in four.[978]

Hence arises the Decad, the ten most general kinds of all things. One, two, three, four, going out of Omnipotency to Energy (out of power to act) produce ten, the half whereof is five. Now in the midst put five, on the right hand the next superior number six, on the left hand, the next inferior four; these added together, make ten. Again, the next superior seven, and the next inferior three make ten. Again, the next superior eight, and the next inferior two make ten. Lastly, one and nine make ten.

This ten being carried up to twenty, comes again to one; and so on, in all the cardinal numbers to a hundred. For as twice one makes two, thrice one three, four times one four, and so forward; so twice ten makes twenty, thrice ten thirty, four times ten forty, and so on. The like in a hundred, a thousand, and forward. And because the Decad arises out of and ends in a Monad, the Greeks express ten by ἴ [iota]. The Hebrews express it by a Point, which mark (as well amongst the Barbarians, as in Latin) denotes One.[979] Hitherto allude the Pythagorean symbols One and Two. Zaratas (the Master of Pythagoras) used these as the names of propagation—one the father; two the mother. One and two (in the divine essence) producing four, the Tetractys, the idea of all things, which are consummated in the number Ten. This Pythagoras styles:

Eternal Nature's fountain—

This is the knowledge of things in the Divine Mind operating intellectually. From this fountain of Eternal Nature, flows down the Pythagorean numbers One and Two—which from Eternity, in the fountain of the immense Ocean, was, shall be, or rather always is, abundantly streaming. This One was by the Ancients termed Ζεὺς ["Zeus"], Jupiter; Two, Ἥρα ["Hera"], Juno, wife and sister to Jupiter, of whom writes Homer:

> Golden-thron'd Juno, with eyes full of love
> Beheld her spouse and brother, sacred Jove,
> Sitting on th' top of fount abounding Ide.[980]

In Ide, ἀπὸ τοῦ ἰδεῖν, from "prescience") Jupiter and Juno sat as one and two—in the streaming idea of the Tetractys, whence flow the principles of all things, Form and Matter.

CHAPTER 4

The Intelligible World

The Intelligible World proceeds out of the Divine Mind after this manner.[981] The Tetractys, reflecting upon its own essence as the first unit, productive of all things, and on its own beginning as the first product, says thus. Once one, twice two, immediately arises a Tetrad, having on its top the highest unit. It is a pyramid whose base is a plain Tetrad, answerable to a superficies, upon which the radiant light of the divine unity produces the form of incorporeal fire, by reason of the descent of Juno (Matter) to inferior things. Hence arises essential light, not burning but illuminating. This is the creation of the middle world, which the Hebrews call the Supreme, the world of the Deity, admitting no comparison. It is termed Olympus, ὁλολαμπρὰς, wholly lucid and replete with separate forms—where is the seat of the Immortal gods, whose top is Unity, wall Trinity, superficies Quaternity:

—*Deum domus alta* [the high house of the gods]

Number, emanating from the divinity by degrees, declines to the figure of creatures; instead of the Tetractys, a Tetragon. In each of its angles a point, for so many units, the unit at the top, which now begins to have position, elevated as much as is possible. Thus the former sides elevated will be four triangles, built upon their quadrangular latitude, and carried on to one high point. This is the Pyramid itself, the species of fire, of which a Pyramid having four bases and equal angles is compounded.[982] It is the most immovable and penetrant form, without matter essential separate light, next to God sempiternal life.

The work of the Mind is life; the work of God is immortality, eternal life. God himself is not this created light, but the Author of all light, whereof in the divine Trinity He contains a most absolute Pyramid, which implies the vigor of Fire. Whence the Chaldeans and Hebrews affirm that God is Fire. But the Pyramid which this divine Tetractys produces is the fiery light of the immaterial world, of separate intelligences, beyond the visible Heaven, termed αἰών, age, eternity, aether.

Having overcome these things (says Pythagoras), thou shalt know σύστασιν, the cohabitation, of the immortal gods, and mortal men.†[983] In which words are implied three properties of this middle world: *Condition, Chorus,* and *Order*. (Pythagoras terms the middle world "free Aether"; free, as being separated from the power of matter; Aether, as receiving ardor from God and heating all inferiors by an insensible motion.)

Condition: It is replenished with forms, simple, immaterial, separate, both universal and individual, containing all ideations of genus and species. The exemplars are imitated in lesser copies, their original being in the Divine Mind. Thus the world of the Deity is the absolute exemplar: in the intelligible world the abstract example; and in the sensible world, not example but contraction of exemplars, as seal, figure, and sealed wax.

Chorus: It is the infinite joy of the blessed spirits, their immutable delight, styled by Homer ἄσβεστος γέλως, inextinguishable laughter.† For what greater pleasure, than to behold the serene aspect of God; and next Him, the ideas and forms of all things, more purely and transparently, than secondarily in created beings? And to communicate these visions to inferiors, the office of the gods called θεοὶ ἀπὸ τῆς θέας, from speculation and vision. These are the Angels communicating their visions to others, not that we imagine them equal to the Supreme God who is ineffable. No Daemons, how good soever, are admitted into this chorus: so says Plotinus (the most exact follower of the Pythagorean Mysteries, as Porphyry and Longinus attest). The gods we conceive to be void of passion.[984] But to Daemons we adjoin passions, saying they are sempiternal in the next degree after the gods. It is better to call none in the intelligible world Daemon; rather, if a Daemon be placed there, to esteem him a god.

Order: It is thus explained by Pythagoras. If thou live according to right reason, grieving for what is ill done, and rejoicing in what is well done, and prayest the gods to perfect thy work:

Then stript of flesh, up to free Aether soar,
A deathless god, divine, mortal no more. [985]

This is the order in the acquisition of man's beatitude. The incorporeal Heaven of the middle world—the invisible Olympus of the blessed—admits nothing impure. Therefore vices are to be shunned and virtues to be embraced. The preservation of men is by the mercies of God. Therefore the Divinity is to be worshipped, and the superior powers to be invoked, that they would perfect our work. Lastly, nothing material, corporeal, or mixed is received there. Therefore we must die, and wholly put off the body, before we can be admitted to the society of the gods.

CHAPTER 5

THE SENSIBLE WORLD

We now come down to the sensible World.[986] Its exemplar is the world of the Deity; its example the intelligible world of Ideas, the ἀυθοπόστατον, subsistence of exemplars in itself. As One is the beginning of the intelligible world, so is Two of the corporeal. It would not be corporeal if it did not consist of these four: point, line, superfices, solidity—after the pattern of the Cube, made by one, two, three, four.

One, fixed by position, creates a point. A line, being protracted from one point to another, is made of the number two. A superfices arises from three lines. A solid contains four positions: before, behind, upwards, downwards. Two multiplied in itself produces four; retorted into itself (by saying twice two twice) makes the first Cube. Next five (the Tetragonical Pyramid, principle of the Intelligible World) is the cube of eight with six sides, architect of the Sensible World. Amongst principles, the Heptad has no place, being virgin, producing nothing, and therefore named Pallas.

This first cube is a fertile number, the ground of multitude and variety, constituted of two and of four. Zaratas termed two "the Mother"; we call the cube that proceedes from it "Matter," the bottom and foundation of all natural beings, the seat of substantial forms. Timaeus says: from the Tetragon is generated the Cube, the most settled body, steadfast every way, having six sides, eight angles.[987] The form immersed in this solid receptacle is not received loosely, but fixedly and singly. It becomes individual and incommunicable, confined to time and place, losing its liberty in the servitude of Matter. Thus the two principles of temporal things: the Pyramid and Cube, Form and Matter, flow from one fountain, the Tetragon, whose Idea is the Tetractys, the divine exemplar.

Now there is requisite some third thing to unite these two, Matter and Form. For they flow not into one another spontaneously or casually; the matter of one thing does not contingently receive the form of another. When the soul departs out of man, the body becomes not brass or iron, neither is wool made of a stone. There must then be a third thing to unite them. (Not privation: privation and power act nothing substantively. Nor motion: an accident cannot be the principle of a substance.) God is the uniter, as Socrates and Plato acknowledge.[988] They say there are three principles of things: God, Idea, and Matter—symbolized before by Pythagoras in these three secret marks: Infinite, One and Two. By Infinite, designing God; by Unity, Form; by Diversity, Matter. Infinite, in the Supreme world; One, or Identity, in the Intellectual; Two, or Diversity, in the Sensible, for Matter is the mother of Alteration.

The Tetragonal bases of these figures, joined together, make a Dodecahedron, the symbol of the Universe. Alcinous says God used the Dodecahedron in making the Universe this world.[989] If upon an octangle Cube we erect a Pyramid, by four equal-sided triangles, it makes a Dodecahedron, wherein the Cube is, as it were, mother, and the Pyramid, father. Thus Timaeus: Form has the nature of male and father; Matter of female and mother; the compositions are their offspring.[990]

Of these are produced all things in this world by their seminal faculties; which things appear in a wonderful variety by reason of the various commensuration of forms to their matter, and the admixture of innumerable accidents—by excess and defect, discord and amity, motion and rest, impetuosity and tranquility, rarity and density. Hence arise the Spheres, the Stars, the four Elements: out of which come forth hot, moist, cold, dry, and all the objects of sense, the transmutation of forms, and variety of colors in several things.

The gods are natural, the gods of gods supernatural. Those inhabit the inferior world, these the superior. The gods of gods are most simple and pure, as being nowhere. They are supercelestial as being everywhere. They are with us here strangers, there natives; never in our world, but when sent: Angels, messengers from heaven, appearing in what form they please, kind and beneficial to us. The inferior spirits never ascend to the super celestial, but are sent sometimes on embassy to us, whence termed Angels as the others.

God himself inhabits the lowest, the highest, and the middlemost intimately; so that there is no being without God. Moreover, the gods of this world are more excellent than the souls of men—though those assist, these inform bodies. Between them are placed Daemons and Heroes—Daemons next the gods, Heroes next souls—mentioned by Pythagoras in his Golden Verses, who assigns to each a peculiar worship.

Croesus (561–546 B.C.), the Lydian king so rich that his name became proverbial for wealth, issued this gold stater which shows the confronted foreparts of a lion and a bull. The reverse bears the impressions of two square punches of unequal size.
Photo courtesy of Numismatica Ars Classica

CHAPTER 6

THE STATE OF THE SOUL AFTER DEATH

Rational man is more noble than other creatures.[991] He is more divine. He is not content solely with one operation (as all other things drawn along by nature, which always act after the same manner), but imbued with various gifts, which he uses according to his free will. In respect of which liberty:

—Men are of heavenly race,
Taught by diviner Nature what t'embrace. [992]

By "diviner Nature" is meant the Intellectual soul. As to intellect, man approaches nigh to God; as to inferior senses, he recedes from God. Reason teaching us what to embrace, when it converts itself to the mind, renders us blessed. When perverted by the senses, wretched. For men often straying from the rule of right reason precipitate themselves into misery, αὐθαίρετα πήματ᾽ ἔχοντας, in Pythagoras's word, incurring ills voluntarily.†

Thus is man placed between Virtue and Vice, like the stalk between the two branches in the Pythagorean Y,† or young Hercules described by Prodicus. As therefore none can be called happy before his death (as Solon said to Croesus[993]), so none is to be esteemed unhappy while he is in this life. We must expect the last day of a man. If when he has put off his body, he remains burdened with vices, then begins he to be truly miserable. This misery after death Pythagoras divides into two kinds. The unhappy are either near Beatitude, which though at the present they enjoy not, yet are they not oppressed with extreme misery, being hereafter to be delivered from their punishment. Or wholly distant from Beatitude, in endless infinite pains. Thus there are two mansions in the *Inferi*: the Elysium, possesed by those that are to ascend into blessedness; and Tartarus, by those who endure infinite torments ὅθεν ουποτε ἐκβαίνουσιν. From these torments, Plato, imitating Pythagoras, says they never come out.† But when a man who has lived justly dies, his soul ascends to the pure Aether and lives in the happy realm of Eternity with the blessed, as a god with the gods.

Man is the image of the world. He, in many things, metaphorically receives the names of the world.[994] The mind of man (as the Supreme mind) is termed God by participation. The rational soul, if directed by the mind it incline the will to virtue, is termed the good Daemon or Genius; if by phantasie and ill affections it draws the will to vices, the evil Daemon. Whence Pythagoras desires of God to keep us from ill, and to show everyone the Daemon he ought to use.[995] Leaving the body, the soul if defiled with vices becomes an evil Daemon. Its life, δυσδαιμονέα, infelicity; but if having forsaken vice it retain a solicitous affection to the good exercises and virtues which it practiced in this life, it shall become a good Daemon. And in the amenity of that world live happily, reflecting with joy upon the good actions it has done, and retaining the same willingness to the right doing of them. This life is εὐδαιμονία, felicity, of which Virgil says:[996]

> —the same care
> Which heretofore, breathing this vital air,
> Of Chariots, Arms, and sleek-skin'd Steeds they
> Pursues them now in earth's cold bosom laid.

These souls the Ancients termed *Lemures*. Of these, that which lives in and takes care of any particular house is *Lar familiaris*. That which, for its demerits in this life, wanders up and down in the air, a terror, vain to good men, but to the bad hurtful is *Larva*. Those which are not certainly known to be *Larvae* or *Lares*, are called *Dii manes: Dii*, out of reverence, who having performed the course of their lives prudently and justly, died holy.

CHAPTER 7

OF THE PYTHAGOREAN TRANSMIGRATION

It is commonly averred that Pythagoras held the opinion that the souls of men after death informed the bodies of beasts. We cannot imagine this of so knowing a person. The suspicion of this Trans-animation seems rather to have been raised by such as were partly ignorant and partly envious of the Pythagorean mysteries. These included Timon, Xenophanes, Cratinus, Aristophon, Herippus, and others who have ascribed many things to Pythagoras which he never said nor wrote, and have perverted what he did say.[997]

Pythagoras held that the substantive unity of one number is not the unity of another number. That the Monads in the Duad are not connected to those in the Triad. That the participate essence of everything is One, which will not occupy the essence of another thing.

No animal (then) can transmigrate into the life of a different animal. But it must continue under the Law of its own nature in its proper office, ὥστε τὸ εἶδος εἴδες οὗ συνέρχεται, species not being coincident with species. One seal may make many impressions upon several pieces of wax, but one piece of wax cannot bear the form of many seals.

The seal of human form (the image of God) is not permitted to set an impression upon inferior nature—implied by Pythagoras in this Symbol, *We must not wear the image of God in a Seal-ring.*[998] The image of God (man's soul) cannot seal or form the other natures that are near it. So Hermes Trismegistus, "Of man, one part is simple, which we call the form of divine similitude." And again, "There are two images of God, the World and Man."

This is the meaning of Pythagoras concerning the transmigration of souls after death and their descent into life. Others thought that the soul is drawn forth out of the power of Matter; Pythagoras asserted it is infused by God into the body, and therefore before it, not in time but in purity and dignity. This infusion he termed, "The descent of the soul." This is not be be understood as its situation or its motion from the intellectual world, as interpreted by several who heard the elementary idea such as Proclus; but of the natural series or form—the rational soul being the ultimate perfection of the human body.

That Pythagoras said he was in times past Euphorbus, the meaning is this.[999] The Ancients called the inclinations and wills of men their Minds; whence such as are of one study, intention, inclination, motion, and sense are termed Unanimous. Thus the ancient Philosophers call the motive and sensitive faculty, the Soul. An animate differs from an inanimate (says Aristotle) chiefly in two things: Motion and Sense. Whosoever therefore are alike affected and moved by the same object are said to have the same Soul. The Metempsychosis then is nothing else but equal care, motion, and study of some dead person appearing in some living person. Thus Pythagoras might arrogate the soul of Euphorbus, Callicles, Hermotimus, Pyrrhus, Pyrander, Calidona, and Alce as having an inclination to the several excellencies that were in those persons.

Again, in saying he was Euphorbus, Pythagoras enigmatically taught not the transmigration of souls, but the transmutation of bodies out of first matter.[1000] It is not only susceptible, but covetous of all forms, continually desiring, never satiated with any. It is as if a comedy (to use the comparison of Aristotle) should say, "I was first a tragedy," because both tragedy and comedy are formed of the same letters and elements.[1001] Thus Apollonius, demanding of the Indian Brahmans what their opinion was concerning the Soul, Iarchus answered, "According as Pythagoras delivered to you, we to the Egyptians." Apollonius replies, "Will you then affirm you were one of the Trojan captains, as Pythagoras said he was Euphorbus?" Thespasion warily asks, whom he thought the most worthy of them? "Achilles," saith Apollonius, "if we believe Homer." Then Iarchis said, "Look on him as my progenitor, or πρόγονον σῶμα, progeniting body;† for such Pythagoras esteemed Euphorbus."[1002]

Or if he meant it historically, παλαιγενεσία, that is the soul, separate from the body, may by the power of God be brought again the same into the same body. The body in which Pythagoras was so often revived, though called by several names, was one and the same— not in quantity, but substance. As the sea is one and homogeneous in itself, yet is here called Aegean, there Ionian, elsewhere Myrtaean and Colsaean—so one man often reborn is named Aethalides, Euphorbus, Hermotimus, Pyrrhus, and lastly Pythagoras. These generations he ascribes not to the power of Nature but to the God Mercury. None can revive but by the Divine power of God, whom he acknowledges, ψύχωσις τῶν ὅλων, Animation of all things. He infuses soul into all men, and being infused takes it away—and being taken away, restores it, when and as often as he pleases.

GLOSSARY

Antichthon: The Pythagorean concept of an unseen counter earth, whose motion always keeps it at 180° from the earth, hidden from view by the sun.

Callicia: According to Pliny, Pythagoras ascribed to this plant the power of turning water into ice. (See Coriacesia.)

Ceraunian Stone: Refers to Ceraunite, "Thunder-stone," a meteorite mineral from which, it is said, Thunderbolts (such as that of Jupiter) were fashioned.

Choenix: A Greek dry measure, almost equal to a quart.

Chromatic: In Greek music, the name given to one of three kinds of tetrachords, the two others being Enharmonic and Diatonic. A scale which proceeds by semitones.

Chyles: Lymph that is milky from emulsified fat, most apparent during intestinal absorption of fats. Also, more broadly, the fluid in the intestines prior to absorption.

Cledon: An ancient Greek term for the phenomena in which unsuspecting people are used by the gods to convey messages to the inquirer. Stanley defines Cledons as, "observations of occurrent speeches, collecting from what is accidentally said upon some other occasion, the effect of what is sought." See page 235. From the Greek κληδών: rumor, report, fame; unknown. An omen or augury, particularly taken from a sound or word.

Coriacesia: According to Pliny, Pythagoras ascribed to this plant the power of turning water into ice. (See Callicia.)

Diapason: The interval of an octave; the consonance of the lowest and highest notes of the musical scale.

Diapason Harmony or Concord: The complete agreement or correspondence between the range of sounds in the scale.

Diapente: In ancient and medieval music, the consonance or interval of a fifth.

Diasteme: In ancient Greek music, an interval especially an interval forming a single degree of the scale.

Diatessaron: In Greek and medieval music the interval of a fourth.

Diatonic: In Greek music, the name of that genus or scale in which the interval of a tone was used, the tetrachord being divided into two whole tones and a semitone (see also Chromatic and Enharmonic).

Doric: (in Music) One of the ancient Greek modes of music, characterized by simplicity and serenity.

Duple: In music, a rhythm having two beats in the bar.

Echemythia: This word probably means using dissimulation, concealing truth by indulging in mythmaking.

Enharmonic: In Greek music, the name of that genus or scale in which an interval of two and a half tones was divided into two quarter tones and a major third. (See also Chromatic and Diatonic.)

Ens: Essence. That which has existence.

Epitrites: A term in Greek music signifying the ratio of four to three.

Epode: An incantation.

Erythrine: A rose-red mineral, crystallized and earthy, a hydrous arseniate of cobalt, known also as cobalt bloom. Also, a colorless crystalline substance extracted from certain red lichens, as the various species of Rocella. So called because of certain red compounds derived from it. Stanley discusses it thus: "Receive not an Erythrine, seems to respect the Etymology of the word. Entertain not an impudent blushless person; nor on the other side one over-bashful, ready to fall back from the mind and firm intellection." (p. 283)

Esse: In actual existence. Opposed to *Posse*, in potentiality.

Excedent: That which exceeds

Furlong: A measure of distance equal to 220 yards.

Hebdomad: The number seven viewed collectively as a group.

Hecatomb: An ancient Greek and Roman sacrifice of one hundred oxen or cattle.

Hemiolius: In medieval music, a perfect fifth, the ratio of one and a half to one.

Hemitone: A half-tone or semitone.

Heptachord: A seven-stringed instrument. A series of seven notes formed of two conjunct tetrachords. The interval of a seventh.

Homocentric: Having the same center, concentric. In old Astronomy, a sphere or circle concentric with another or with the Earth.

Homoeomery: The ancient Greek theory, propounded by Anaxagoras, that the ultimate particles of matter are homogenous or of the same kind. "Homoeomeries" refers to the homogenous particles themselves.

Hypate: The name of the lowest tone in the lowest two tetrachords of ancient Greek music.

Hypermese: In musical intervals, measured upwards above the mese.

Lichanus: In ancient Greek music, the name of one of the sounds of a tetrachord. It was next to the neate (nete).

Mazza (Meze): A term for Greek and Middle Eastern small food dishes, which can be hot or cold, and composed of various ingredients, comparable to a Scandinavian smorgasbord.

Melanure: A small fish of the Mediterranean; a gilthead; so named from the blackness of its tail, thus symbolizing negativity.

Mese: In ancient Greek music, the middle string of the seven-stringed lyre and its note; subsequently the key-note of any of the scales in use.

Monochord: A medieval musical instrument of one string used to teach intervals in singing schools. Also, an instrument to measure the mathematics of musical intervals.

Neate (Nete): A term in Greek music applied to the fourth, or most acute chord of each of the three tetrachords which followed the two first or deepest.

Nepenthe: A drink or drug supposed to bring forgetfulness of trouble or grief. Possessing sedative properties.

Obol, (obolus): (pl. obols, also oboli) A silver coin or unit of weight in ancient Greece equal to one sixth of a drachma, (approximately .5 gram). See *Trioboli*.

Octochord: Having eight strings. Also, relating to a scale of eight notes.

Olympiad: The Greek calendar was based on the four-year Olympiad, marking the Olympic Games instituted by Hercules in honor of his father Zeus. When Greek historians refer to dates, they most often refer to a year (i.e., first, second, third, fourth) of a four-year period or Olympiad. The first Olympiad began in 776 B.C.

Onomantic: Pertaining to divination from names or the letters of a name.

Oviparous: Producing eggs that hatch outside the body.

Paramese: The second sound of the second octave. The string next the middle; in ancient Greek music, the tone next above the mese; the lowest tone of the disjunct tetrachord.

Paraneate: In ancient Greek music, the note next below the nete (neate) in either the disjunct or the upper tetrachord.

Parypate: The second note of a tetrachord. (Parypate hypaton equals second note of lowest tetrachord; parypate meson equals second sound of the second tetrachord).

Pentachord: The interval of a fifth. Also, a musical instrument with five strings. A musical series of five notes.

Phantasie (fantasy): As used here when capitalized, refers to the imagination, the creation of mental images, the formation and perception of visionary notions,.

Phrygian: (in Music) One of the ancient Greek modes of music, characterized by a warlike nature.

Phthiriasis: A morbid condition of the body in which lice multiply excessively, causing extreme irritation.

Posse: In potentiality. Opposed to *Esse*, in actual existence.

Sesquialtera: Of a proportion that is as one and a half is to one. In music, a triple measure of three notes to two such like notes of the common time.

Sesquiduple: Involving a ratio of two and a half to one.

Sesquioctava: Applied to harmonic intervals producible by sounding four fifths, five sixths, etc. of a given string; rhythmic combinations of four notes against five, five notes against six, etc.

Sesquitertia: Denoting a ratio of one and one-third to one, that is four to three. An interval having this ratio, viz. the perfect fourth, a rhythm of three notes against four.

Stade: The length of the footrace taught to mankind by Hercules.

Stadia: An ancient measure of distance approximately 200 meters or one-eighth of a mile.

Superficies: In Geometry, the outside or exterior surface of any body, consisting of two dimensions, length and breadth, without thickness.

Tetrachord: An ancient Greek musical four-stringed instrument. Also, a scale-series of four notes being the half of an octave.

Trioboli (plural of *Triobolus*)**:** A half drachma coin; also, a trifle. See *Obol*.

Endnotes

1 Porphyry, *De Vita Pythagorae*, Chap. 1.

2 Plutarch, *Symposiac*, Liber VIII.

3 Porphyry, *De Vita Pythagorae*, Chap. 10.

4 Clement of Alexander, *Stromateis*, Liber I, Chap. 14.

5 Porphyry *De Vita Pythagorae*, Chap. 1.

6 Porphyry, *De Vita Pythagorae*, Chap. 5.

7 Josephus, *Contra Apionem*, Liber II, 2.

8 Justin, *Historiarum Philippicarum*, Liber XX, 4.

9 Diogenes Laertius, *De Vitis Philosophorum*, Liber VIII, Chap. 1.

10 Laertius, *De Vitis Philosophorum*, Liber VIII, Chap. 1; Suidas *Lexicon [Cf.* Πυθα-γόρας*]*; Apulleius, *Florida*, Chap. 15.

11 Porphyry, *De Vita Pythagorae*, Chap. 1.

12 Laertius, *De Vitis Philosophorum*, Liber VIII, Chap. 1.

13 Clement of Alexandria, *Stromateis*, Liber I, Chap. 14.

14 Iamblichus, *De Vita Pythagorica*, Chap. 2.

15 So read both here and afterwards, as appeareth by the Oracle, ἀντὶ Σάμης ["instead of Same"].†

16 Strabo, *Rerum Geographicarum*, Liber XIV.

17 Porphyry, *De Vita Pythagorae*, Chap. 2.

18 Cited also by Porphyry, *De Vita Pythagorae*, Chap. 2.

19 Porphyry, *De Vita Pythagorae*, Chap. 2 .[But Cf. Iamblichus, *De Vita Pythagorica*, Chap. 2—Ed.]

20 Adding, καὶ κυούσης αὐτὴν ἐκ μὴ οὕτως ἐχούσης καταστῆσαί.†

21 Porphyry, *De Vita Pythagorae*, Chap. 2.

22 Iamblichus, *De Vita Pythagorica*, Chap. 2.

23 Laertius, *De Vitis Philosophorum*, Liber VIII, Chap. 25.

24 St. Augustine, *Epistulae*. 3. ad Volusianus. [Augustine, Letter CXXXVII to Volusianus, Chap. 12—Ed.]

25 Porphyry, *De Vita Pythagorae*, Chap. 2.†

26 In Pythagoras. [i.e. Suidas *Lexicon*, the entry on Πυθαγόρας.—Ed.]

27 Iamblichus, *De Vita Pythagorica*, Chap. 2.

28 As once in Ritterhusius's Edition [of Iamblichus, *De Vita Pythagorica*] or perhaps τοῦ Κρεοφύλου.

29 Iamblichus, *De Vita Pythagorica*, Chap. 2.

30 Strabo, *Rerum Geographicarum*, Liber XIV, Chap. 18.

31 Apuleius, *Florida*, Chap. 15.

32 Iamblichus, *De Vita Pythagorica*, Chap. 2 continues.

33 Laertius, *De Vitis Philosophorum*, Liber VIII, Chap. 3.

34 Apuleius, *Florida*, Chap. 15.

35 Thebes.

36 Laertius, *De Vitis Philosophorum*, *Liber I*, 'Thaletis' [i.e Thales—Ed.].

37 Porphyry, *De Vita Pythagorae*, Chap. 55–56.

38 Salmasius, *Plinianae Excercitationes*.

39 Porphyry, *De Vita Pythagorae*, Chap. 15. Iamblichus, *De Vita Pythagorica*, Chap. 30. Laertius, *De Vitis Philosophorum*, Liber VIII, Chap. 21.

40 Laertius, *De Vitis Philosophorum*, Liber VIII, Chap. 12.

41 Porphyry, *De Vita Pythagorae*, Chap. 15.

42 Iamblichus, *De Vita Pythagorica*, Chap. 5. Laertius, *De Vitis Philosophorum*, Liber VIII, Chap. 12.

43 Iamblicus, *De Vita Pythagorica*, Chap. 3.

44 Reading ἐξαιρέτως ["principal"].†

45 Iamblicus, *De Vita Pythagorica*, continueth.

46 For μόνον τε ἐπιφθεγξάμενος , reading ἐπιφθεγξάμενος τε μῶν εἰς Ἀιγυπτον ὁ λους, etc.†

47 Iamblicus, *De Vita Pythagorica*, Chap. 3.

48 Porphyry, *De Vita Pythagorae*, Chap. 7, cited also by Laertius, *De Vitis Philosophorum*, Liber VIII, Chap. 3.

49 *Herodotus*, Liber 3.

50 Clement of Alexandria, *Stromateis*, Liber V, Chap. 7.

51 Clement of Alexandria, *Stromateis*, Liber I, Chap. 15.

52 Laertius, *De Vitis Philosophorum*, Liber VIII, Chap. 3.

53 Porphyry, *De Vita Pythagorae*, Chap. 12.

54 Clement of Alexandria, *Stromateis*, Liber V, Chap. 4.

55 Valerius Maximus, *Factorum et Dictorum Memorabilium*, Liber VIII, Chap. 7.

56 Iamblichus, *De Vita Pythagorica*, Chap. 4. continuing.

57 Laertius, *De Vitis Philosophorum*, Liber VIII, Chap. 3.

58 Clement of Alexandria, *Stromateis*, Liber I, Chap. 15.

59 Cf. *Herodotus*, Liber III, Chap. 10.

60 Pliny, *Naturalis Historiae*, Liber XXXVI, Chap. 9.

61 James Ussher, *Annales Veteris Testamenti* [Julian Year] 4167 [page 142.]

62 Iamblichus, *De Vita Pythagorica* , Chap. 4.

63 Clement of Alexandria, *Stromateis*, Liber I, Chapter 15., Laertius, *De Vitis Philosophorum*, Liber VIII, Chap. 4.

64 Cicero, *De Finibus Bonorum et Malorum*, Liber V, Chap. 29.

65 Apuleius, *Florida*, Chap. 15.

66 Eusebius, *Praeparatio Evangelica*, Liber X, Chap. 4.

67 Valerius Maximus, *Factorum et Dictorum Memorabilium*, Liber VIII. Chap. 7.

68 Lactantius, *Divinarum Institutionum*, Liber I, Chap. 2.

69 Gerard Johann Vossius. *De Philosophorum Sectis*, Vol 1. Chap. 6.

70 Iamblichus, *De Vita Pythagorica* , Chap. 4, continueth.

71 Valerius Maximus, *Factorum et Dictorum Memorabilium*, Liber VIII, 7, 2.

72 Apuleius, *Florida*, Chap. 15.

73 Porphyry, *De Vita Pythagorae*, Chap. 12.

74 Apuleius, *Florida*, Chap. 15.

75 [The reference is to Alexander Polyhistor's now lost "On The Pythagorean Symbols." This quote is from Clement of Alexandria, *Stromateis*, Liber I, Chapter 15—Ed.]

76 Suidas, *Lexicon*, *In voce* Pythagoras [i.e. in the name Πυθαγόρας —Ed.].

77 John Selden, *De Diis Syris Syntagmata II*, pp. 210-213.

78 Clement of Alexandria, *Stromateis*, Liber I, Chap. 15.

79 Porphyry, *De Vita Pythagorae*, Chap. 10.

80 Lactantius, *Divinarum Institutionum*, Liber IV, Chap. 2.

81 Eusebius, *Praeparatio Evangelica*, Liber X, Chapter 4.

82 James Ussher, *Annales Veteris Testamenti*, p. 151 [Julian Year 4189].

83 Josephus, *Contra Apionem*, Liber I, Chap. 22.

84 Origen, *Contra Celsum*, Liber I, Chap. 15.

85 Clement of Alexandria, *Stromateis*, 1, Chap. 22 & Eusebius, *Praeparatio Evangelica*, Liber XIII.

86 Clement of Alexandria, *Stromateis*, Liber I, Chap. 15.

87 Porphyry, *De Vita Pythagorae*, Chap. 12.

88 Clement of Alexandria, *Stromateis*, Liber I, Chap. 15.

89 Porphyry, *De Vita Pythagorae*, Chapter 6.

90 Josephus, *Contra Apionem*, *Liber I*, Chap. 22.

91 Gerard Johann Vossius. *De Philosophorum Sectis*, Vol 1. Chap. 6.

92 Iamblichus, *De Vita Pythagorica*, Chapters 2, 5 (for the Chapters are ill-distinguished).

93 Pliny, *Naturalis Historiae*, Liber XXXIII, Chap. 63.

94 Iamblichus, *De Vita Pythagorica*, Chap. 5 & 7.

95 Clement of Alexandria, *Stromateis*, Liber VII, Chap. 6.

96 Laertius, *De Vitis Philosophorum*, Liber VIII, Chap. 12.

97 Iamblichus, *De Vita Pythagorica*, Chap. 5.

98 Porphyry, *De Vita Pythagorae*, Chapter 16, Reading, δ᾽ ἐν τῷ καλουμένῳ Τρίοπι. [Cf.] Hesychius' *Lexicon*, "Τρίοψ, ὁ ὑπὸ τῶν Πυθάγορικῶν ἐν Δελφοῖς τρίπους".†

99 Laertius, *De Vitis Philosophorum*, Liber VIII, Chap. 5.

100 Justin, *Historiarum Philippicarum* Lib. XX, Chap. 4.

101 Iamblicus, *De Vita Pythagorica*, Chap 5.

102 Porphyry, *De Vita Pythagorae*, Chap. 17.

103 Laertius, *De Vitis Philosophorum*, Liber VIII, Chap. 3 [Cf. Apuleius, *Florida*, Chap. 15—Ed.]

104 Porphyry, *De Vita Pythagorae*, Chap. 17

105 Laertius, *De Vitis Philosophorum*, Liber VIII, Chap. 3

106 Valerius Maximus, *Factorum et Dictorum Memorabilium*, Liber VIII, Chap. 7, 2.

107 Laertius, *De Vitis Philosophorum*, Liber I, *Prooemium*, Chap. 8.

108 Ibid.

109 Laertius, *De Vitis Philosophorum*,, Liber VIII, Chap. 6.

110 Cicero, *Tusculum Disputationum*, Liber V, Chap. 3.

111 Laertius, *De Vitis Philosophorum*, Liber I, *Prooemium*, Chap. 8, and Iamblichus, *De Vita Pythagorica*, Chap. 8.

112 Iamblichus, *De Vita Pythagorica*, Chap. 5.

113 Porphyry, *De Vita Pythagorae*, Chap. 9.

114 Iamblichus, *De Vita Pythagorica*, Chap. 5 & 6 (for these also are ill-distinguished).

115 Livy, *Historiarum Ab Urbe Condita*, Decad. 4, Liber XL, Chap. 29.

116 Pliny, *Naturalis Historiae*, Liber XIII, Chap. 13.

117 Diodorus, *Excerpta Valesiana*, p. 241.

118 Clement of Alexandria, *Stromateis*, Liber I, Chap. 14.

119 Ptolemy, *Almagestum*, Liber V, Chap. 14.

120 Diodorus, *Excerpta Valesiana*, p. 241.

121 Strabo, *Rerum Geographicarum*, Liber XIV, Chap. 17.

122 Cicero, *Tusculum Disputationum*, Liber I, Chap. 4.†

123 Aulus Gellius, *Noctes Atticae*, Liber XVII, Chap. 21.

124 Pliny, *Naturalis Historiae*, Liber II, chap. 8.

125 Cicero, *Tusculum Disputationum*, Liber I, Chap. 4.

126 Solinus, *De Mirabilibus Mundi*, Liber II, Chap. 4.

127 Eusebius, *Chronicon*.†

128 Eusebius, *Chronicon*.

129 Strabo, *Rerum Geographicarum*, Liber VI, Chap. 3.

130 Eusebius, *Chronicon*.

131 Ibid.

132 Solinus, *De Mirabilibus Mundi*, Liber II, Chap. 4.

133 Eusebius, *Chronicon*.

134 Strabo, *Rerum Geographicarum*, Liber VI, Chap. 2.

135 Thucydides, *De bello Peloponnesiaco*, Liber VI, Chap. 4

136 Eusebius, *Chronicon*.

137 Iamblicus, *De Vita Pythagorica*, Chap. 29.

138 Justin, *Historiarum Philippicarum*, Liber XX, Chap. 2–4.

139 Porphyry, *De Vita Pythagorae*, Chap. 18.

140 Iamblichus, *De Vita Pythagorica*, Chap. 8.

141 Iamblichus, *De Vita Pythagorica*, Chap. 8 continueth. The beginning of this Oration is in Laertius, *De Vitis Philosophorum*, Liber VIII, Chap. 19 also.

142 This is also in Laertius, *De Vitis Philosophorum*, Liber VIII, Chap. 19.

143 Strabo, *Rerum Geographicarum*, Liber VI, Chap. 12.

144 Iamblichus, *De Vita Pythagorica*, Chap.9

145 Valerius Maximus, *Factorum et Dictorum Memorabilium*, Liber VIII, Chap. 15,1.

146 Μοῦσαι quasi μοῦσαι. Synessius in *Dion*, Chap. 5 & Cassiodorus, *Variarum*, Liber II, 40.†

147 Aristotle, *Analytica Priora et Posteriora*, Posterior Analytics Chap. 11. Ἐπικοινωνοῦσι δὲ πᾶσαι αἱ ἐπιστῆμαι ἀλλήλαις κατὰ τὰ κοινά. Cicero, *Oratio Pro Licinio Archia*, Oratio IX, "Quasi cognatione quadam" etc.†

148 To the same effect Laertius *De Vitis Philosophorum*, Liber VIII, Chap. 19.

149 Mentioned by Cicero and others.

150 Iamblichus, *De Vita Pythagorica*, Chap 10.

151 Iamblichus, *De Vita Pythagorica*, Chap 11.

152 So supply the text from Laertius, *De Vitis Philosophorum*, Liber VIII, Chap. 11, who cites something to the same purpose out of Timaeus.† Κόρη [Core], is a Name of Proserpina; Νύμφη, Bride, relates to the Nymphs; Μήτηρ [mother], to Cybele mother of the Gods Μαῖα, to Maja, mother of Mercury.

153 Iamblichus, *De Vita Pythagorica*, Chap. 12.

154 Porphyry, *De Vita Pythagorae*, Chap 18.

155 Iamblicus, *De Vita Pythagorica*, Chap. 5.

156 Laertius, *De Vitis Philosophorum*, Liber VIII, Chap. 15.

157 Iamblichus, *De Vita Pythagorica*, Chap 6.†

158 Porphyry, *De Vita Pythagorae*, Chap. 20.

159 Clement of Alexandria, *Stromateis*, Liber I, Chap. 15.†

160 Porphyry, *De Vita Pythagorae*, Chap. 21. And from him, Iamblichus, *De Vita Pythagorica*, Chap. 7.

161 Diodorus, *Bibliotheca Historica*, Liber XII, Chap. 3.

162 Athenaeus, *Deipnosophistarum*, Liber XII, Chap. 15.

163 Ibid, Liber XII, Chap. 21.

164 Iamblicus, *De Vita Pythagorica*, Chap. 30.

165 Diodorus, *Bibliotheca Historica*, Liber XII, Chap. 3. *Olympiad* 83. 2.

166 So were the Greeks that inhabited Italy called, not the Natives. The same difference between Siciliaotes and Sicilians.

167 Athenaeus, *Deipnosophistarum*, Liber XII, Chap. 19.

168 Iamblicus, *De Vita Pythagorica*, Chap. 32.

169 Tzetzes, *Chiliades*, V, 31.

170 Tzetzes, *Chiliades*, VI, 30.

171 Iamblichus, , *De Vita Pythagorica*, Chap. 30.

172 Ibid.

173 Porphyry, *De Vita Pythagorae*, Chap. 54

174 Porphyry, *De Vita Pythagorae*, Chap. 23. Iamblicus, *De Vita Pythagorica*, Chap. 13.

175 Porphyry, *De Vita Pythagorae*, Chap. 24 and Iamblichus, *De Vita Pythagorica*, Chap. 13.

176 Plutarch, *Numa*, Chap. 8.

177 Porphyry, *De Vita Pythagorae*, Chap. 25, and Iamblichus, *De Vita Pythagorica*, Chap. 13.

178 Porphyry, *De Vita Pythagorae*, Chap. 27.

179 Porphyry, *De Vita Pythagorae*, Chap. 27. and Iamblichus, *De Vita Pythagorica*, Chap. 28.

180 Plutarch, *Numa*, Chap. 8.

181 Laertius, *De Vitis Philosophorum*, Liber VIII, Chap. 9, and Porphyry, *De Vita Pythagorae*, Chap. 28.

182 Porphyry, *De Vita Pythagorae*, Chap. 28.

183 Iamblichus, *De Vita Pythagorica*, Chap. 28.

184 Anonymous, *De Vita Pythagorae* apud ["in the works of"] Photius.

185 Laertius, *De Vitis Philosophorum*, Liber VIII, Chap. 19.

186 Aristophanes, *Nubes*, 749–756.

187 Hermippus apud Laertius, *De Vitis Philosophorum*, Liber VIII, Chap. 21.

188 Laertius, *De Vitis Philosophorum*, Liber VIII, Chap. 4.

189 Laertius, *De Vitis Philosophorum*, Liber VIII, Chap. 19.

190 So read [Pyrrhus], not Pythius.†

191 Justin, *Historiarum Philippicarum*, Liber XX, Chap. 4.

192 Porphyry, *De Vita Pythagorae*, Chap. 55.

193 Porphyry, *De Vita Pythagorae*, Chap. 56.

194 σπάνει τῶν ἀναγκαίων, ill rendered, *amicorum inopia* ["lack of friends"].†

195 Porphyry, *De Vita Pythagorae*, Chap. 57.

196 Iamblichus, *De Vita Pythagorica*, Chap. 35.

197 Iamblichus, *De Vita Pythagorica*, Chap. 2.

198 Ibid, Chap. 2.†

199 Laertius, *De Vitis Philosophorum*, Liber VIII, Chap. 9.

200 Ibid, Chap. 20.

201 Athenaeus, *Deipnosophistarum*, Liber X, Chap. 13.

202 Porphyry, *De Vita Pythagorae*, Chap. 34.

203 Laertius, *De Vitis Philosophorum*, Liber VIII, Chap. 18.

204 Ibid. See also Iamblichus, *De Vita Pythagorica*, Chap. 21.

205 Aelian, *Varia Historia*, Liber XII, Chap. 32.

206 Porphyry, *De Vita Pythagorae*, Chap. 32.

207 Iamblichus, *De Vita Pythagorica*, Chap. 30.

208 Plutarch, *Numa*, Chap. 1.

209 Pliny, *Naturalis Historiae*, Liber XXIII, Chap. 7.

210 Iamblichus, *De Vita Pythagorica*, Chap. 5.

211 Pliny, *Naturalis Historiae*, Liber XXXIV, Chap. 19.

212 Pliny, *Naturalis Historiae*, Liber XIX, Chapter 30.

213 Suidas *Lexicon* [Πυθαγόρας Ἐφέσιος].

214 Pliny, *Naturalis Historiae*, Liber XXXVII, Chap. 9.

215 Ibid, Liber XXXIV, Chap. 19.

216 Suidas, *Lexicon*, In [voce] Theano [in the name Θεανώ —Ed.].

217 Ibid.

218 Theodoret, *Graecarum Affectionum Curatio*, Chap. 2.

219 Iamblicus, *De Vita Pythagorica*, Chap. 36.

220 Laertius, *De Vitis Philosophorum*, Liber VIII, Chap. 22.

221 Clement of Alexandria, *Stromateis*, Liber IV, Chap. 19.

222 Suidas, *Lexicon*. [in the name Θεανώ —Ed.]

223 Plutarch, *Numa*, Chap. 8.

224 Suidas, *Lexicon*. In [voce] Pythagoras [in the name Πυθαγόρας —Ed.]

225 Perhaps τήλαυγες κλυτὲ κοῦρε†; etc.

226 Porphyry, *De Vita Pythagorae*, Chap. 3.

227 Anonymous, *De Vita Pythagorae apud Photius*, Chap. 22.

228 Porphyry, *De Vita Pythagorae*, Chap. 10.

229 *Herodotus*, Liber IV. [Ζάμολξις, also found as Ζάλμοξις "Zalmoxis," and Σάλ-μοξις, "Salmoxis"—Ed.]

230 Plutarch, *De Fortuna Alexander* Liber I, Chap. 4.

231 Josephus, *Contra Apionem*, Liber I., Chap. 2.

232 Lucian, *Pro Lapsu Inter Salutandum*, 5.

233 Porphyry, *De Vita Pythagorae*, Chap. 57.

234 Rufinus, *Apologiae In Sanctum Hieronimum*, Liber II, Chap. 7.

235 [*De Vitis Philosophorum*, Liber VIII, Chap. 5]. κακοτεχνίην ["poor workman-ship"], *artes callidas* ["crafty art"] & *vafras* ["cunning"]. So is κακοτεχνως ["misch-evious art"] sometimes taken in a good sense; Gregory Nazianzus, *Adversus Julianus*, Oratio 4, ἐπεὶ καὶ οὗτοι μιμεῖσθαι μεν λέγονται τῶν ἀνθρωπίων τινὰ δελεασμα-᾿των μεν τοι κακοτέχνως προστιθεμένων τούτοις καὶ ἁλίσκονται, the text being so to be restored.†

236 Clement of Alexandria, *Stromateis*, Liber I, Chap. 21.

237 Laertius, *De Vitis Philosophorum*, Liber VIII, Chap. 5

238 κοτ᾿ οἴσω ["bear ill-will"],† the Interpreters both otherwise.

239 Laertius, *De Vitis Philosophorum*, Liber VIII, Chap. 5

240 Eustathius, *Ad Homeri Iliadem*, 2.

241 Iamblichus, *De Vita Pythagorica*, Chap. 19.

242 Hierocles of Alexandria, *Commentarius in Aurea Carmina*, 45–48.

243 [Ion of Chios, a dramatist, poet and philosopher of the 5th Century B.C. was the author of a work entitled *Triagmos* (or *Triagmoi*) of which fragments survive possibly indicating Pythagorean ideas. Laertius, *De Vitis Philosophorum*, Liber VIII, Chap.8, stated, "According to Ion of Chios in his *Triagmi* [Pythagoras] ascribed some of his own poems to Orpheus." Cf. also Clement of Alexandria, *Stromateis*, Liber I, Chap. 21 where this same statement occurs almost verbatim.—Ed.]

244 Isidore, *Etymologiae*, Liber III, Chap. 2

245 Tzetzes, *Chiliades* I, 58.

246 Pliny, *Naturalis Historiae*, Liber XXIV, Chap. 101.

247 Proclus, *In Platonis Timaeum*, Liber III.

248 Aulus Gellius, *Noctes Atticae*, Liber VII, Chap. 2.

249 Iamblichus, *De Vita Pythagorica*, Chap. 36.

250 Laertius, *De Vitis Philosophorum*, Liber VIII, Chap. 5.

251 Iamblichus, *De Vita Pythagorica*, Chap. 5.

252 Iamblichus, *De Vita Pythagorica*, Chap. 34.

253 Thucydides, *De bello Peloponnesiaco*, Liber VI, Chap. 4.

254 [From Ἀδωνιάζουσαι, in turn from Ἀδωνιάζω, "keep the Adonia" (mourning for Adonis). The 15th Idyll of Theocritus is named ΣΥΡΑΚΟΥΣΙΑΙ Η ΑΔΩΝΙΑΖ-

ΟΥΣΑΙ (The Syracuse Women, or the Adonis Festival). This Idyll was sometimes was sometimes simply called "Adoniazousai"—Ed.]

255 Mr. Sherburn. [Sir Edward Sherburn, cousin of Thomas Stanley, translator of *Theocritus*.—Ed.]

256 Porphyry, *De Vita Pythagorae*, Chap. 22.

257 Ibid, Chap. 21.

258 Iamblichus, *De Vita Pythagorica*, Chap. 19.

259 For τέχνη perhaps read εχνη.†

260 Strabo, *Rerum Geographicarum*, Liber VI, Chap. 12.

261 Josephus, *Contra Apionem*, Liber I, Chap. 22.

262 Iamblichus, *De Vita Pythagorica*, Chap. 36.

263 [Cf. Iamblichus, *De Vita Pythagorica*, Chap. 36, where the number is 218.—Ed.]

264 Iamblichus, *De Vita Pythagorica*, Chap. 28.

265 Ibid.

266 Read δίπος ["two-footed," i.e. "bipedal."] See *Etymologicon Magnum*.

267 Iamblichus, *De Vita Pythagorica*, Chap. 6.

268 Ibid.

269 Porphyry, *De Vita Pythagorae*, Chap. 20.

270 Iamblichus, *De Vita Pythagorica*, Chap. 28.

271 Aelian, *Varia Historia*, Liber IV, Chap. 17.

272 Cicero, *De Natura Deorum*, Liber I, Chap. 5

273 Gregory Nazianzen, *Adversus Julianus*, 102.

274 Iamblichus, *De Vita Pythagorica*, Chap. 34.

275 Apuleius in *Apologia* cites this sentence of Pythagoras.

276 Iamblichus, *De Vita Pythagorica*, Chap 17.

277 Ibid.

278 Ibid.

279 Iamblichus, *De Vita Pythagorica*, Chap. 20.

280 Porphyry, *De Vita Pythagorae*, Chap. 13.

281 Aulus Gellius, *Noctes Atticae*, Liber I, Chap. 9.

282 Iamblichus, *De Vita Pythagorica*, Chap. 20.

283 Ibid.

284 Porphyry, *De Vita Pythagorae*, Chap. 46.

285 Iamblichus, *De Vita Pythagorica*, Chap. 17.

286 Iamblichus, *De Vita Pythagorica*, Chap. 29.

287 Iamblichus, *De Vita Pythagorica*, Chap. 17.

288 Hesychius of Alexandria, *Lexicon* [under ἐχέμυθος —Ed.].

289 Simplicius, *Epicteti stoici philosophi Enchiridion*, Chap. 42.

290 Clement of Alexandria, *Stromateis*, Liber V, Chap. 11.

291 Lucian, *Vitarum Auctio*.

292 Aulus Gellius, *Noctes Atticae*, Liber I, Chap. 9.

293 Ibid.

294 Apuleius, *Florida*, Chap. 15.

295 Iamblichus, *De Vita Pythagorica*, Chap. 16.

296 Ibid.

297 For σωθῆνας reading, ὡς φῆναι κατὰ τὸν Πλάτωνα ["Thus, as said by Plato…"].†

298 Diodorus, *Excerpta Valesiana*, p. 245.

299 Iamblichus, *De Vita Pythagorica*, Chap. 31.

300 Iamblichus, *De Vita Pythagorica*, Chap. 17.

301 Aulus Gellius, *Noctes Atticae*, Liber I, Chap. 9.

302 Laertius, *De Vitis Philosophorum*, Liber VIII, Chap. 10.

303 Iamblichus, *De Vita Pythagorica*, Chap. 18.

304 Iamblichus, *De Vita Pythagorica*, Chap. 17.

305 Iamblichus, *De Vita Pythagorica*, Chap. 17.

306 Porphyry, *De Vita Pythagorae*, Chap. 37.

307 Iamblichus, *De Vita Pythagorica*, Chap. 18.

308 For ἄγριος Αἰνεὺς ["savage Aenean"], perhaps read Ἀγριανεύς ["Agrinean"].†

309 Iamblichus, *De Vita Pythagorica*, Chap. 20 and Chap. 21, for the chapters are here also confounded.

310 For ἱματιλινά , perhaps read καὶ ἱμάτια λινα ["and linen garment"]. Yet Laertius expressly says that linen was not as yet used in those parts.†

311 Iamblichus, *De Vita Pythagorica*, Chap. 29.

312 From Iamblichus restore Diodorus in *Excerpta Valesiana* page 245, reading οὐδὲν γὰρ μεῖζον πρὸς ἐπιστήμην και φρόνησιν, ἔπι δὲ τῶν πάντων ἐμπειρειαν, τοῦ δυνασθαι πολλὰ μνημονευειν.†

313 Porphyry, *De Vita Pythagorae*, Chap. 40.

314 Ibid.

315 Iamblichus, *De Vita Pythagorica*, Chap. 23.

316 Iamblichus, *De Vita Pythagorica*, Chap.17.

317 Ἀγῶνας.

318 Clement of Alexandria, *Stromateis*, Liber V, Chapter 9.

319 Porphyry, *De Vita Pythagorae*, Chap. 46.

320 Justin Martyr, *Dialogus cum Tryphone Judaeo*, Chap. 2.

321 Proclus, *In Primum Euclidis Elementorum*, Liber I, Chap. 15.

322 Ibid, Liber I, Chap. 12.

323 Τὸ καθ᾽ ἑκάτερον ὡρισμένον. Barocius renders it otherwise.†

324 Read ὡς οὐ τὴν καθ᾽ ἑκάτερον ἀπειρίαν γνώσει λαβεῖν κενόν.†

325 Read κατὰ γίνη.

326 Nicomachus, Ἀριθμετικῆς εἰσαγωγῆς ["Introduction to Arithmetic"] (so supply the Title, as a page. 30. 35. 44. 62. 76) Chap. 4.†

327 Read προγενέστερα υπαρχουσα, συναιρει etc. viz. η ἀριθμετικη.

328 Laertius, *De Vitis Philosophorum*, Liber VIII, Chap. 11.

329 Stobaeus, *Eclogarum Physicarum et Ethicarum*, Liber I, Chap. 2.

330 Isidore, *Etymologiae*, Liber III, Chap. 2

331 Isidore, *Etymologiae*, Liber III, Chap. 2 & Stobaeus, *Eclogarum Physicarum et Ethicarum*, Liber I, Chap. 2.

332 Nicomachus, *Introductionis Arithmeticae*, Chap. 6

333 Iamblichus, *De Vita Pythagorica*, Chap. 28.

334 Theon of Smyrna, *Mathematica*, Chap. 1.

335 Nicomachus, *Introductionis Arithmeticae*, Chap. 6.

336 Moderatus apud Stobaeus *Eclogarum Physicarum et Ethicarum*, Liber I, Chap. 41.

337 Theon of Smyrna, *Mathematica*, Chap. 4.

338 Anonymous, *De Vita Pythagorae* apud Photius, Chap. 3.

339 Stobaeus *Eclogarum Physicarum et Ethicarum*, Liber I, Chap. 1.

340 Themistius, *In Aristotelis Physica Paraphrasis*, Chap. 3.

341 Aristotle, *Physica*, Liber III, Chap. 4.

342 Eustratius, *Ethica Nicomachea*. 1 & Servius, *Incipit Expositio Primae Eclogae*, VIII.†

343 Nicomachus, *Introductionis Arithmeticae*, Chap. 6.

344 Themistius, *In Aristotelis Physica Paraphrasis*, Chap. 3.

345 Macrobius, *Saturnalia*, Liber I, Chap. 13.

346 Servius, *Grammatici in Virgilii Aeneidos*, 3.

347 Plutarch, *De Vita et Poesi Homeri*.

348 Servius, *Grammatici in Virgilii Aeneidos*, 3.

349 Ptolemy, *Mathematicus Tetrabiblios*, Liber 1, Chap. 15.

350 Anonymous, *Theologumena Arithmeticae*, 34.

351 Plutarch, *De Animae Procreatione in Timaeo*, Chap. 2

352 Simplicius, *In Aristotles Physicorum*, Liber III.

353 Porphyry, *De Vita Pythagorae*, Chap. 48.

354 Dechad (from comprehension).

355 Moderatus apud Stobaeus, *Eclogarum Physicarum et Ethicarum*, Liber I, Chap. 2.

356 Nicomachus, *Introductionis Arithmeticae*, Chap. 6, Photius apud Nicomachus, *Theologumena Arithmeticae*.

357 Alexander of Aphrodisias, *In Aristotelis Metaphysica Commentaria.*

358 Nicomachus, *Theologumena Arithmeticae* apud Photius.

359 Macrobius, *Ciceronis Somnium Scipionis*, Liber I, Chap. 6.

360 Aristoxenus in *Libro Pythagorico*, cited by Theon of Smyrna, *Mathematica*, Chap. 5.

361 Macrobius.

362 Porphyry, *De Vita Pythagorae*.

363 Nicomachus.

364 Anonymous, *Theologumena Arithmeticae*.

365 Nicomachus & *Theologumena Arithmeticae* apud Photius.

366 Nicomachus.

367 Simplicius *In Aristotelis De Coelo*.

368 Proclus, *In Platonis Timaeum*, Liber IV.

369 Proclus, *In Platonis Timaeum*, Liber IV.

370 Martianus Capella, *De Nuptiis Philologiae et Mercurii*, Liber VII.

371 Nicomachus.

372 Anonymous, *Theologumena Arithmeticae*.

373 Anonymous, *Theologumena Arithmeticae*.

374 *Theologumena Arithmeticae*.

375 Alexander of Aphrodisias, *In Aristotelis Metaphysica Commentaria*, I.

376 Anonymous, *Theologumena Arithmeticae*.

377 Anonymous, *Theologumena Arithmeticae*.

378 Anonymous, *Theologumena Arithmeticae*.

379 Macrobius, *Ciceronis Somnium Scipionis*, Liber I, 6.

380 Anonymous, *Theologumena Arithmeticae*.

381 Anonymous, *Theologumena Arithmeticae*.

382 Martianus Capella.

383 Anonymous, *Theologumena Arithmeticae* & Proclus, *In Platonis Timaeum*.

384 Martianus Capella.

385 Martianus Capella.

386 Anonymous, *Theologumena Arithmeticae*.

387 Anonymous, *Theologumena Arithmeticae.*

388 Plutarch in *Numa.*

389 Hesychius of Alexandria, *Lexicon.*

390 Plutarch, *De Placitis Philosophorum*, Liber I, Chap. 3.

391 Porphyry, *De Vita Pythagorae.*

392 Nicomachus.

393 Anonymous, *Theologumena Arithmeticae.*

394 Plutarch, *De Iside et Osiride.*

395 Anonymous, *Theologumena Arithmeticae.*

396 Nicomachus.

397 Simplicius, *In Aristotles Physicorum*, Liber I.

398 Nicomachus.

399 Nicomachus.

400 Nicomachus.

401 Nicomachus.

402 Anonymous.

403 Nicomachus.

404 Anonymous.

405 Nicomachus.

406 Nicomachus.

407 Anonymous.

408 Nicomachus.

409 Nicomachus.

410 Anonymous.

411 Nicomachus.

412 Nicomachus.

413 Nicomachus.

414 Anonymous, *Theologumena Arithmeticae &* Martianus Capella.

415 Nicomachus.

416 Nicomachus.

417 Anonymous.

418 Nicomachus.

419 Anonymous.

420 Anonymous. Alexander of Aphrodisias, in *Aristotelis Metaphysica Commentaria*, I & John Philoponus, *In Aristotelis Metaphisica.*

421 Anonymous.

422 Anonymous.

423   Simplicius, *In Aristotles De Anima.*

424   Anonymous.

425   Anonymous & Martianus Capella.

426   Plutarch, *De Iside et Osiride.*

427   Hesychius of Alexandria, *Lexicon.*

428   Martianus Capella & Favonius Eulogius, *Disputatio De Somnio Scipionis.*

429   John Philoponus, *In Aristotelis Metaphisica,* 1.

430   Plutarch, *De Placitis Philosophorum,* Liber I, Chap. 3.

431   Nicomachus, *Theologumena Arithmeticae* apud Photius.

432   Anonymous, *Theologumenis Arithmeticis.*

433   Iamblichus, *De Vita Pythagorica,* Chap. 28.

434   Simplicius, *In Aristotles De Anima.*

435   Nicomachus.

436   Nicomachus.

437   Anonymous.

438   Nicomaachus.

439   Anonymous.

440   Anonymous.

441   Anatolius.

442   Aulus Gellius, *Noctes Atticae,* Liber I, Chap 20.

443   Johannes Protospath, in Hesiod, *Opera et Dies.*

444   Lucian, *Pro Lapsu Inter Salutandum,* Chap. 5.

445   Irenaus, *Adversus Haereses,* Liber I, Chap. 1.

446   Simplicius, *In Aristotelis Physicorum,* Liber IV.

447   Hierocles of Alexandria, *Commentarius in Aurea Carmina.*

448   Plutarch, *De Placitis Philosophorum,* Liber I.

449   Plutarch, *De Animae Procreatione in Timaeo,* Chap. 30.

450   Nicomachus.

451   Nicomachus.

452   Nicomachus.

453   Anonymous.

454   Nicomachus.

455   Nicomachus.

456   Anonymous.

457   Nicomachus.

458   Plutarch.

459   Plutarch, *De Placitis Philosophorum,* Liber I, Chap. 3.

460 Simplicius, *In Aristotles De Anima*, 1.

461 Alexander of Aphrodisias, *In Aristotelis Metaphysica Commentaria*, 5.

462 Theon of Smyrna, *Mathematica*, Chap. 44.

463 Nicomachus.

464 Anonymous.

465 Anonymous.

466 Nicomachus.

467 Johannes Protospath, in Hesiod, *Opera et Dies*.

468 Nicomachus.

469 Nicomachus.

470 Anonymous.

471 Nicomachus.

472 Anonymous.

473 Nicomachus.

474 Anonymous.

475 Anonymous & Plutarch, *De E Apud Delphos*.

476 Alexander of Aphrodisias, *In Aristotelis Metaphysica Commentaria* & Johannes Protospath, in Hesiod, *Opera et Dies*.

477 Nicomachus.

478 Nicomachus.

479 Anonymous.

480 Nicomachus.

481 Anonymous.

482 Nicomachus.

483 Anonymous.

484 Nicomachus.

485 Anonymous.

486 Anonymous.

487 Plutarch, *De Animae Procreatione in Timaeo*.

488 Plutarch, *De E Apud Delphos*.

489 Macrobius, *Ciceronis Somnium Scipionis*, Liber I, Chap. 6.

490 Nicomachus.

491 Anonymous.

492 Nicomachus.

493 Anonymous.

494 Nicomachus.

495 *Martianus Capella*, 7.

496 Nicomachus.

497 Nicomachus.

498 Clement of Alexandria, *Stromateis*, Liber V, Chap. 14.

499 Plutarch, *De Animae Procreatione in Timaeo*.

500 Clement of Alexandria, *Stromateis*, Liber VI, Chap. 16.

501 Theon of Smyrna, *Mathematica*, Chap. 45.

502 Nicomachus.

503 Anonymous.

504 Nicomachus & Anonymous.

505 Lucian, *Pro Lapsu Inter Salutandum*.

506 Nicomachus.

507 Anonymous.

508 Anonymous, *Theologumena Arithmeticae*.

509 Anonymous.

510 Anonymous.

511 Nicomachus.

512 Nicomachus.

513 Anonymous.

514 Nicomachus.

515 Anonymous.

516 Anonymous.

517 Anonymous.

518 Nicomachus.

519 Anonymous.

520 Clement of Alexandria, *Stromateis*, Liber VI, Chap. 16.

521 Anonymous.

522 Nicomachus, *Theologumena Arithmeticae* apud Photius & Macrobius, *Ciceronis Somnium Scipionis*, Chap. 6.

523 Apuleius, *Metamorphoses*, Lib. XI.

524 Alexander of Aphrodisias, *Quaestiones Medicae et Problemata Physica*, Probl. 2. Quaest. 47.

525 Julius Paulus, *Receptarum Sententiarum*, Liber IV, Tit. 9.

526 Nicomachus.

527 Anonymous.

528 Philo Judaeus, *De Allegoriis Legum*, Chap. 5.

529 John Philoponus, *In Aristotelis Metaphisica*, 7.

530 Hierocles of Alexandria, *Commentarius in Aurea Carmina* & Nicomachus.

531 Anonymous & Chalcidius *In Platonis Timeus*, & Theon of Smyrna, *Mathematica*, Chap. 45.

532 Nicomachus & Anonymous.

533 Nicomachus.

534 Nicomachus.

535 Hesychius of Alexandria, *Lexicon*.

536 Nicomachus.

537 Nicomachus.

538 Anonymous.

539 Anonymous.

540 Anonymous.

541 Philo Judeus, *De Opisico Mundi*.

542 Anonymous.

543 Nicomachus.

544 Anonymous.

545 Anonymous.

546 Plutarch, *De Iside et Osiride*.

547 Macrobius, *Ciceronis Somnium Scipionis*, Liber I, Chap. 5.

548 Anonymous.

549 Anonymous.

550 Nicomachus & Anonymous.

551 Anonymous.

552 Nicomachus & Anonymous.

553 Anonymous.

554 Anonymous.

555 Anonymous.

556 Anonymous.

557 Anonymous.

558 Anonymous.

559 Anonymous.

560 Nicomachus & Anonymous.

561 Athenagoras of Athens, *Legatio Pro Christianis*, Chap. 6.

562 Plutarch, *De Placitis Philosophorum*, Liber I, Chap. 3.

563 Anonymous.

564 John Philoponus, *In Aristotelis Metaphisica*, 1.

565 Anonymous.

566 Nicomachus.

567 Anonymous.

568 George Pachymer, in *In Aristotelis Metaphisica*, 3.

569 Nicomachus.

570 Anonymous.

571 Nicomachus.

572 Nicomachus.

573 Anonymous.

574 Anonymous.

575 Anonymous.

576 Anonymous.

577 Chalcidius *In Platonis Timeus*.

578 Anonymous.

579 George Cedren.

580 Anonymous.

581 Iamblichus, *De Vita Pythagorica*, Chap. 28.

582 Iamblichus, *De Vita Pythagorica*, Chap 19.

583 Robert Fludd, *Microcosmi*, Tomus Secundus, Chap. 13.

584 Johannes Trithemius, *Antipalus Maleficiorum*, Liber I, Chap. 3.

585 Theon of Smyrna, *Mathematica*, Chap. 1.

586 Porphyry in *Ptolemaios' Harmonics*.

587 Plutarch, *De Musica*. Porphyry apud Ptolemy, *Harmonics* &c.

588 Porphyry in *Ptolemaios' Harmonics*, Chap. 2.

589 Ptolemaios loco citato apud Porphyry [*Ptolemaios' Harmonics*].

590 Nicomachus, *Harmonices Manualis*, Chap. 2.

591 Nicomachus, *Harmonices Manualis*, Chap. 3.

592 Macrobius, *Ciceronis Somnium Scipionis*, Liber II, Chap. 1.

593 Nicomachus, *Harmonices Manualis*, Chap. 3.

594 Macrobius, *Ciceronis Somnium Scipionis*, Liber II, Chap. 1.

595 Nicomachus, *Harmonices Manualis*, Chap. 3.

596 Pliny, *Naturalis Historiae*, Liber II, Chap. 22.

597 Nicomachus, *Harmonices Manualis*, Chap 5.

598 The Heptachord was made up of two Tetrachords, which being conjoined, the middle Note was the end of one, and the beginning of the other.

599 Meibomius seems to mistake the meaning of καταληφθέντα, and therefore put a point after λεγομένη.†

600 Theon of Smyrna, *Mathematica*, Chap.

601 Censorinus, *De Die Natale*, Chap. 2.

602 Boethius, *De Institutione Musica*, Liber I, Chap. 11.

603 Macrobius, *Ciceronis Somnium Scipionis*, Liber II.

604 Nicomachus, *Harmonices Manualis*, Chap. 6, repeated by Iamblichus, *De Vita Pythagorica*, Chap. 26.

605 πρὸς ἑαυτὸν ἀπηλλάγη, Meibomius otherwise.†

606 ἰσοστρόφους, which Meibomius, contrary to all MSS, would change unnecessarily into ισορρόπους , and renders *aeque graves*.†

607 Laertius, *De Vitis Philosophorum*, Liber VIII, Chap. 11

608 Aristides Quintilianus, *De Musica*, Liber 3.

609 Porphyry, *De Vita Pythagorae*, Chap. 3

610 Theon of Smyrna, *Mathematica*.

611 [While this sentence is incomplete as it appears in Stanley, the number 27 represents the last number of the "second quaternary." This "second tetractys" is formed by adding to the the number 1, the even number multiples 2, 4, and 8; then the odd number multiples of 3, 9, and 27. It is denominated by the number 27 because that is the sum of the other numbers: 1+2+3+4+8+9=27. For more on this, see *The Pythagorean Sourcebook*, pp. 317–19—Ed.]

612 Nicomachus, *Harmonices Manualis*, Chap. 1.

613 Euclid, *Sectio Canonis*.

614 Aristides Quintilianus, *De Musica*, Liber 3.

615 Iamblichus, *De Vita Pythagorica*, Chap. 15.

616 Iamblichus, *De Vita Pythagorica*, Chap. 25.

617 Reading ἀπὸ τῶν ἔργων.† This example of Pythagoras seems to relate to Hesiod; the other of Empedocles to Homer.

618 Seneca, *De Ira*, Liber III, Chap. 9. [The instrument was actually the lyre, not the lute. "*Pythagoras perturbationes animi lyra conponebat.*"—Ed.]

619 Cicero, *Tuscularum Disputationum* , Liber IV, Chap. 2.

620 Aelian, *Varia Historia*, Liber XIV, Chap. 23.

621 Porphyry, *De Vita Pythagorae*, Chap.32.

622 Aristides Quintilianus, *De Musica*, Liber II.

623 Porphyry, *De Vita Pythagorae*, Chap. 32.

624 Not the Philosopher, but the Cretan. See the life of Thales. [In Stanley's *History of Philosophy*—Ed.]

625 Ammonius, *Commentaria in quinque voces Porphyrii*.

626 Cited by Boethius, *De institutione musica*, Liber I, Chap. 1.

627 St. Basil of Caesarea, *Homilia XIV*.

628 Quintilian, Liber IX, Chap. 4.

629 Plutarch, *De Iside et Osiride*, Chap. 81.

630 Censorinus, *De Die Natale*, Chap.12.

631 Aristides Quintilianus, *De Musica*, Liber II.

632 Iamblichus, *De Vita Pythagorica*, Chap. 29.

633 Ibid.

634 Proclus, *In Primum Euclidis Elementorum*, Liber II.

635 Laertius, *De Vitis Philosophorum*, Liber VIII, Chap. 11.

636 Laertius, *De Vitis Philosophorum*, Liber VIII, Chap. 13.

637 Proclus, *In Primum Euclidis Elementorum*, Liber II, Def. 2.

638 Proclus, *In Primum Euclidis Elementorum*, Liber II, Def. 1.

639 Proclus, *In Primum Euclidis Elementorum*, Liber II, Def. 2.

640 Proclus, *In Primum Euclidis Elementorum*, Liber II, Def. 5.

641 Proclus, *In Primum Euclidis Elementorum*, Liber II, Def. 24.

642 Proclus, *In Primum Euclidis Elementorum*, Liber II, Def. 34.

643 Proclus, *In Primum Euclidis Elementorum*, Liber III, Com. 20.

644 Proclus, *In Primum Euclidis Elementorum*, Liber IV, Prop. 32, Com. 6.

645 Proclus, *In Primum Euclidis Elementorum*, Liber I, Prop. 47.

646 Vitruvius, *De Architectura*, Liber IX, Praefatio 5 & 6.

647 Laertius, *De Vitis Philosophorum*, Liber I, Chap. 3.

648 Vitruvius, Loco Citato.

649 Plutarch, *Non posse suaviter vivi secundum Epicurum*, Chap. 11.

650 Cicero, *De Natura Deorum*, Chap. 36.

651 Gregory Nazianzen, *Epistole 198*.

652 Plutarch, *Non Posse Suaviter Vivi Secundum Epicurum*, Chap. 11.

653 Proclus, *In Primum Euclidis Elementorum*, Liber IV, Prop. 44.

654 Reading ὅταν γὰρ εὐθείας ἐκκειμένης τὸ δοθὲν χωρίον πάσῃ τῇ εὐθείᾳ συμπαρατείνῃς, τότε παραβάλλειν ἐκεῖνο τὸ χωρίον φασίν, ὅταν δὲ μεῖζον, etc.†

655 Aulus Gellius, *Noctes Atticae*, Liber I, Chap. 1. [A. Gellius quotes a lost work by Plutarch, thus the indirect quotation by Stanley.—Ed.]

656 Iamblichus, *De Vita Pythagorica*, Chap. 29.

657 Anonymous, *De Vita Pythagorae apud Photius*, Chap. 19.

658 Ibid, Chap. 11.

659 Plutarch, *De Placitis Philosophorum*, Liber II, Chap. 29.

660 Aristotle, *Metaphysica*, Liber I, Chap 5.

661 Aristotle, *De Caelo*, Liber II, Chap. 13.

662 Stobaeus, *Eclogarum Physicarum et Ethicarum*, Liber I, Chap. 25.

663 Plutarch, *Numa*, Chap.11.

664 Clement of Alexandria, *Stromateis*, Liber V, Chap. 4.

665 Plutarch, *Numa*, Chap.11.

666 Aristotle, *De Caelo*, Liber II, Chap. 13.

667 Aristotle, Ibid.

668 Aristotle, Ibid.

669 Plutarch, *De Placitis Philosophorum*, Liber II, Chap. 29.

670 Laertius, *De Vitis Philosophorum*, Liber VIII, in *Philolaus*, Chap. 3.

671 Archimedes, *Arenarius et Dimensio Circuli*, Chap. 1 & Plutarch, *De Placitis Philosophorum*, Liber II, Chap. 29.

672 Plutarch, *Quaestiones Platonicae*, Ques. 7 & Plutarch, *Numa*, Chap. 11.

673 Anonymous, *De Vita Pythagorae* apud Photius, Chap. 14.

674 Loc. Cit.

675 Laertius, *De Vitis Philosophorum*, Liber VIII, in *Eudoxus*, Chap. 3.

676 Censorinus, *De Die Natale*, Chap. 13.†

677 Pliny, *Naturalis Historiae*, Liber II, Chap. 21, 22.

678 Pliny, *Naturalis Historiae*, Liber II, Chap. 8.

679 Aulus Gellius, *Noctes Atticae*, Liber I, Chap. 9.

680 Iamblichus, *De Vita Pythagorica*, Chap. 29.

681 Rufinus, *Apologiae In Sanctum Hieronimum*, Liber III, Chap. 40.

682 Stobaeus, *Eclogarum Physicarum et Ethicarum*, Liber II, Chap. 7.

683 Porphyry, *De Vita Pythagorae*, Chap. 46.

684 Hierocles of Alexandria, *Commentarius in Aurea Carmina*, Praefatio.

685 Anonymous, *De Vita Pythagorae* apud Photius, Chap. 5.

686 Laertius, *De Vitis Philosophorum*, Liber VIII, Chap. 19.

687 Ibid, citing Alexander.

688 Clement of Alexandria, *Stromateis*, Liber I, Chap. 19, citing Heraclides.

689 Iamblichus, *Protrepticus*, Chap. 9.

690 Laertius, *De Vitis Philosophorum*, Liber VIII, Chap. 19.

691 Stobaeus, *Eclogarum Physicarum et Ethicarum*, Liber II, Chap. 7.

692 Porphyry, *De Vita Pythagorae*, Chap.41.

693 Strabo, *Rerum Geographicarum*, Liber X, Chap. 3.

694 Porphyry, *De Vita Pythagorae*, Chap.41. See also Stobaeus, *Florilegium*, 11.

695 Pythagoras, *Aurea Carmina* , 70-71.

696 Stobaeus, *Florilegium*, 80.

697 Laertius, *De Vitis Philosophorum*, Liber VIII, Chap. 5.

698 Stobaeus, *Florilegium*, 1. Mentioned also by Plutarch, *De Exilio*, Chap. 8.

699 Stobaeus, *Florilegium*, 9.

700 Ibid.

701 Ibid.

702 Stobaeus, *Florilegium*, 13.

703 Stobaeus, *Florilegium*, 14.

704 Stobaeus, *Florilegium*, 24.

705 Stobaeus, *Florilegium*, 34.

706 Stobaeus, *Florilegium*, 35.

707 Porphyry, *De Vita Pythagorae*, Chap. 39.

708 Iamblichus, *De Vita Pythagorica*, Chap. 31.

709 Iamblichus, *De Vita Pythagorica*, Chap. 32.

710 Stobaeus, *Florilegium*, 44.

711 Cicero, *De Senectute*, Chap. 20.

712 Porphyry, *De Vita Pythagorae*, Chap. 22 & Iamblichus, *De Vita Pythagorica*, Chap. 31.

713 Stobaeus, *Florilegium*, 4.

714 Stobaeus, *Florilegium*, 5.

715 Ibid.

716 Ibid.

717 Stobaeus, *Florilegium*, 5.

718 Stobaeus, *Florilegium*, 14.

719 Stobaeus, *Florilegium*, 17.

720 Ibid.

721 Stobaeus, *Florilegium*, 18.

722 Stobaeus, *Florilegium*, 99.

723 Porphyry, *De Vita Pythagorae*, Chap.32.

724 Laertius, *De Vitis Philosophorum*, Liber VIII, Chap. 6.

725 Porphyry, *De Vita Pythagorae*, Chap. 39.

726 Clement of Alexandria, *Stromateis*, Liber I, Chap. 10.

727 Perhaps οὗτος (ἔφη) οὐ παύσῃ χαλεπώτερον σέαυτῶ κατασκευάζων τὸ δεσμωτήριον. See St. Basil of Caesarea, *Homilia ad Psalm. XIX.*†

728 Iamblichus

729 Reading αὐτὸν according to Stobaeis, *Florilegium* 99, who cites this fragment out of Aristoxenus; perhaps it belonged to his Book, *De Vitae Pythagorae.*†

730 Diodorus, *Excerpta Valesiana*, p. 247.

731 Stobaeus, *Florilegium*, 3.

732 Stobaeus, *Florilegium*, 4.

733 Stobaeus, *Florilegium*, 92.

734 Cicero, *Tusculanum Disputationum* , Liber V, Chap. 25. [i.e. He considered the 'defnition' of things to be a vital component of the scientific method required to secure wisdom. – Ed.]

735 Iamblichus, *De Vita Pythagorica*, Chap. 6.

736 Stobaeus, *Florilegium*, 9.

737 Stobaeus, *Florilegium*, 19.

738 Stobaeus, *Florilegium*, 44.

739 Iamblichus, *De Vita Pythagorica*, Chap. 30.

740 Iamblichus, *De Vita Pythagorica*, Chap. 16.

741 Cicero, *De Officis*, Liber I, Chap. 17.

742 Clement of Alexandria, *Stromateis*, Liber IV, Chap. 23.

743 Laertius, *De Vitis Philosophorum*, Liber VIII, Chap. 10.

744 Iamblichus, *De Vita Pythagorica*, Chap.18.

745 Cicero, *De Legibus*, Liber II, Chap. 11.

746 Laertius, *De Vitis Philosophorum*, Liber VIII, Chap. 19.

747 Diodorus, *Excerpta Valesiana*, p. 247.

748 Laertius, *De Vitis Philosophorum*, Liber VIII, Chap. 6.

749 Laertius, *De Vitis Philosophorum*, Liber VIII, Chap 33.

750 Diodorus, *Bibliotheca Historica*, Liber VI, Fragment 40.

751 Cicero, *De Amicitia*, Chap. 4.

752 Iamblichus, *De Vita Pythagorica*, Chap. 28.

753 Pliny, *Naturalis Historiae*, Liber XXXV, Chap. 46.

754 Iamblichus, *De Vita Pythagorica*, Chap. 28.

755 Iamblichus, *De Vita Pythagorica*, Chap. 27.

756 Laertius, *De Vitis Philosophorum*, Liber VIII, Chap. 8.

757 Iamblichus, *De Vita Pythagorica*, Chap. 30.

758 Porphyry, *De Vita Pythagorae*, Chap. 38.

759 Iamblichus, *De Vita Pythagorica*, Chap. 30.

760 Iamblichus, Ibid. Also mentioned by Laertius, *De Vitis Philosophorum*, Liber VIII, Chap. 19.

761 Stobaeus, *Florilegium*, 1.

762 Stobaeus, *Florilegium*, 25.

763 Varro, *De Lingua Latina*, Liber VI.

764 Stobaeus, *Florilegium*, 44.

765 Iamblichus, *De Vita Pythagorica*, Chap. 6.

766 Lactantius, *Divinarum Institutionum*, Liber I, Chap. 5.

767 Justin Martyr, *Dialogus cum Tryphone Judaeo*, Chap. 11.

768 Porphyry, *De Vita Pythagorae*, Chap. 41.

769 Clement of Alexandria, *Stromateis*,Liber IV, Chap. 3.

770 Plutarch, *Numa*, Chap. 8.

771 Laertius, *De Vitis Philosophorum*, Liber VIII, Chap. 19.

772 Iamblichus, *De Vita Pythagorica*, Chap. 6.

773 Pythagoras, *Aurea Carmina*, 1-4.

774 Laertius, *De Vitis Philosophorum*, Liber VIII, Chap. 19.

775 Anonymous, *De Vita Pythagorae* apud Photius, Chap. 11.

776 Laertius, *De Vitis Philosophorum*, Liber VIII, Chap. 19.

777 Iamblichus, *De Vita Pythagorica*, Chap. 28 and 29.

778 Plutarch *De Placitis Philosophorum*, Liber V, Chap. 1.

779 Porphyry, *De Vita Pythagorae*, Chap. 11.

780 Laertius, *De Vitis Philosophorum*, Liber VIII, Chap. 18.

781 Ibid.

782 Cicero, *De Divinatione*, Liber I, Chap. 3.

783 Cicero, *De Divinatione*, Liber I, Chap. 3.

784 Laertius, *De Vitis Philosophorum*, Liber I, Life of Pittacus, Chap. 8.†

785 Iamblichus, *De Vita Pythagorica*, Chap. 28.

786 Apuleius, *Florida*, Chap. 15.

787 St. Augustine, *De Civitate Dei*, Liber VII, Chap. 35. [quoting Marcus Tarentius Varro —Ed.]

788 Eustathius, *Ad Homeri Iliadem*.

789 Porphyry, *De Vita Pythagorae*, Chap. 41.

790 Iamblichus, *De Vita Pythagorica*, Chap. 6.

791 Sextus Empericus, *Adversus Mathematicos*, Liber IX.

792 Sextus Expiricus, *Adversus Logicos*, Liber I.

793 Laertius, *De Vitis Philosophorum*, Liber VIII, Chap. 19.

794 Plutarch, *De Placitis Philosophorum*, Liber II, Chap.1 & Stobaeus, *Eclogarum Physicarum et Ethicarum*, Liber I.

795 Plutarch, *De Placitis Philosophorum*, Liber II, Chap. 4.

796 Stobaeus, *Eclogarum Physicarum et Ethicarum*, Liber I, Chap.1.

797 Plutarch, *De Placitis Philosophorum*, Liber II, Chap. 6.

798 Plutarch, *De Placitis Philosophorum*, Liber II, Chap. 4.

799 Laertius, *De Vitis Philosophorum*, Liber VIII, Chap. 19.

800 Plutarch, *De Placitis Philosophorum*, Liber II, Chap 25.

801 Laertius, *De Vitis Philosophorum*, Liber VIII, Chap. 19.

802 Aristotle, *Physica*, Liber III, Chap. 4.

803 Plutarch, *De Placitis Philosophorum*, Liber II, Chap. 9.

804 Plutarch, *De Placitis Philosophorum*, Liber. II, Chap. 10.

805 Anonymous, *De Vita Pythagorae* apud Photius, Chap. 14.

806 Anonymous, *De Vita Pythagorae* apud Photius, Chap. 11.

807 Laertius, *De Vitis Philosophorum*, Liber VIII, Chap. 19.

808 Hierocles of Alexandria, *Commentarius in Aurea Carmina*, 70-71.

809 Plutarch, *De Placitis Philosophorum*, Liber. II, Chap.13.

810 Plutarch, *De Placitis Philosophorum*, Liber. II, Chap. 24.

811 Plutarch, *De Placitis Philosophorum*, Liber. II, Chap. 25.

812 Plutarch, *De Placitis Philosophorum*, Liber. II, Chap. 30.

813 Aristotle, *Meteorologica*, Liber I, Chap. 6.

814 Plutarch, *De Placitis Philosophorum*, Liber III, Chap.2.

815 Aelian, *Varia Historia*, Liber IV, Chap. 17.

816 Anonymous, *De Vita Pythagorae* apud Photius, Chap. 11.

817 Plutarch, *De Placitis Philosophorum*, Liber I, Chap. 14.

818 Anonymous, *De Vita Pythagorae* apud Photius, Chap. 11.

819 Laertius, *De Vitis Philosophorum*, Liber VIII, Chap. 19.

820 Plutarch, *De Placitis Philosophorum*, Liber I, Chap. 23.

821 Laertius, *De Vitis Philosophorum*, Liber VIII, Chap. 19.

822 Laertius, *De Vitis Philosophorum*, Liber VIII, Chap. 19.

823 Laertius, *De Vitis Philosophorum*, Liber VIII, Chap. 19.

824 Censorinus, *De Die Natale*, Chap. 11.

825 Varro, *De Re Rustica*, Liber II, Chap. 1 & Censorinus, *De Die Natale*, Chap. 4.

826 Nemesius, *De Natura Hominis*, Chap. 2.

827 Plutarch, *De Placitis Philosophorum*, Liber IV, Chap. 2.

828 Aristotle, *De Anima*, Liber I, Chap. 2.

829 Plutarch, *De Placitis Philosophorum*, Liber IV, Chap 4.

830 Laertius, *De Vitis Philosophorum*, Liber VIII, Chap.19.†

831 Plutarch, *De Placitis Philosophorum*, Liber IV, Chap. 20.†

832 Stobaeus, *Eclogarum Physicarum et Ethicarum*, Liber I, Chap. 1.

833 Anonymous, *De Vita Pythagorae* apud Photius, Chap. 10.

834 Plutarch, *De Placitis Philosophorum*, Liber I, Chap. 15

835 Anonymous, *De Vita Pythagorae* apud Photius, Chap. 10. For δώδεκα ["Twelve"], perhaps δέκα ["ten"].†

836 Plutarch, *De Placitis Philosophorum*, Liber IV, Chap. 14.

837 Of which the Ancients made their Mirrors, see Callimachus, *Hymn 5*.†

838 Anonymous, *De Vita Pythagorae* apud Photius, Chap. 10.

839 Plutarch, *De Placitis Philosophorum*, Liber IV, Chap. 20.

840 Anonymous, *De Vita Pythagorae* apud Photius, Chap. 10.

841 Plutarch, *De Placitis Philosophorum*, Liber IV, Chap. 2.

842 Clement of Alexandria, *Stromateis*, Liber V, Chap. 13.

843 Cicero, *De Senectute*, Chap. 21.

844 Cicero, *De Natura Deorum*, Liber I, Chap. 11.

845 Laertius, *De Vitis Philosophorum*, Liber VIII, Chap. 19.

846 Cicero, *Tuscularum Disputationum* , Liber I, Chap. 26.

847 Anonymous, *De Vita Pythagorae* apud Photius, Chap. 17.

848 Anonymous, *De Vita Pythagorae* apud Photius, Chap.17.

849 Porphyry, *De Vita Pythagorae*, Chap. 19.

850 Laertius, *De Vitis Philosophorum*, Liber VIII, Chap.12.

851 Cited by Eusebius, *Praeparatio Evangelica*, Liber X, Chapter 8.

852 *Herodotus*, Liber II, Chap. 123.

853 Anonymous, *De Vita Pythagorae* apud Photius, Chap. 6.

854 Laertius, *De Vitis Philosophorum*, Liber VIII, Chap. 12.

855 Iamblichus, *De Vita Pythagorica*, Chap. 24.

856 Porphyry, *De Vita Pythagorae*, Chap. 44.

857 Laertius, *De Vitis Philosophorum*, Liber VIII, Chap.4.

858 Tzetzes, *Chiliades*, II, 48.

859 Aulus Gellius, *Noctes Atticae*, Liber IV, Chap. 11.

860 Porphyry, *De Vita Pythagorae*, Chap. 45.

861 Ovid, *Metamorphoses*, Liber XV.

862 Rendered into English by my Uncle, Mr. Sandys. [George Sandys, *Ovid's Metamorphosis Englished Mythologized and Represented in Figures* (Oxford, 1632.) —Ed.]

863 Porphyry, *De Vita Pythagorae*, Chap. 26 & Iamblichus, *De Vita Pythagorica*, Chap. 14.

864 Porphyry, *De Vita Pythagorae*, Chap. 26.

865 Iamblichus, *De Vita Pythagorica*, Chap. 28. See also Aelian, *Varia Historia*, Liber IV, Chap. 17.

866 Stobaeus, *Eclogarum Physicarum et Ethicarum*.

867 Plutarch, *De Placitis Philosophorum*, Liber IV, Chap.7.

868 Laertius, *De Vitis Philosophorum*, Liber VIII, Chap. 19.

869 Plutarch, *Quaestiones Graecae*, Ques. 39.

870 Aelian, *Varia Historia*, Liber IV, Chap. 17.

871 Apuleius, *Florida*, Chap. 15

872 Laertius, *De Vitis Philosophorum*, Liber VIII, Chap. 11.

873 Aelian, *Varia Historia*, Liber IX, Chap. 22.

874 Iamblichus, *De Vita Pythagorica*, Chap. 29.

875 Laertius, *De Vitis Philosophorum*, Liber VIII, Chap. 33.

876 Laertius, *De Vitis Philosophorum*, Liber VIII, Chap. 19.

877 Iamblichus, *De Vita Pythagorica*, Chap. 29.

878 Iamblichus, *De Vita Pythagorica*, Chap 24.

879 The Pythagoreans.

880 Iamblichus, *De Vita Pythagorica*, Chap. 24.

881 The Pythagorists.

882 Iamblichus, *De Vita Pythagorica*, Chap. 21 & Athenaeus, *Deipnosophistarum*, Liber X, Chap. 13.

883 Porphyry, *De Vita Pythagorae*, Chap. 34 & Laertius, *De Vitis Philosophorum*, Liber VIII, Chap. 18.

884 Laertius, *De Vitis Philosophorum*, Liber VIII, Chap. 18.

885 Porphyry, *De Vita Pythagorae*, Chap. 34.

886 Porphyry, *De Vita Pythagorae*, Chap. 35.

887 Pliny, *Naturalis Historiae*, Liber XXIV, Chap. 17.

888 Pliny, Ibid.

889 Pliny, Ibid.

890 Pliny, *Naturalis Historiae*, Liber XXIV, Chap. 17.

891 Pliny, *Naturalis Historiae*, Liber XIX, Chap. 5.

892 Pliny, *Naturalis Historiae*, Liber XX, Chap. 9.

893 Pliny, *Naturalis Historiae*, Liber XXII, Chap. 8.

894 In ἐπαοιδή. [The "Greek etymologist" is Hesychius of Alexandria.—Ed.]

895 Homer, *Odyssea*, 19, 455.

896 Porphyry, *De Vita Pythagorae*, Chap. 30.

897 Pliny, *Naturalis Historiae*, Liber XXVIII, Chap. 3.

898 Porphyry, *De Vita Pythagorae*, Chap. 37.

899 Iamblichus, *De Vita Pythagorica*, Chap. 29.

900 Porphyry, *De Vita Pythagorae*, Chap. 41.

901 For τὴν θάλατταν ἐκάλει εἶνα δάκρυον, read ἐκάλει Κρόνου δάκρουν, for so Clement of Alexandria, *Stromateis*, Liber V, Chap. 8.†

902 Porphyry, Loc. cit.

903 Laertius, *De Vitis Philosophorum*, Liber VIII, Chap. 19.

904 Porphyry, *De Vita Pythagorae*, Chap. 42.

905 Iamblichus, *Protrepticus*, Chap. 21.

906 Iamblichus, *De Vita Pythagorica*, Chap. 23.

907 Perhaps ἀπιστήσομεν ["disbelieve"].†
908 Olympiodorus, *Platonis Phaedonem*, Chap. 1.
909 Plutarch, *Numa*, Chap. 8.
910 Iamblichus, *De Vita Pythagorica*, Chap.28
911 Plutarch, *De Liberis Educandis*, Chap. 17.
912 Porphyry, *De Vita Pythagorae*, Chap. 42.
913 Plutarch, *De Liberis Educandis*, Chap. 17.
914 Laertius, *De Vitis Philosophorum*, Liber VIII, Chap.17.
915 Athenaeus, *Deipnosophistarum*, Liber X, Chap. 77.
916 Plutarch, *De Liberis Educandis*, Chap.17.
917 Laertius, *De Vitis Philosophorum*, Liber VIII, Chap.17.
918 Clement of Alexandria, *Stromateis*, Liber V, Chap.5.
919 Porphyry, *De Vita Pythagorae*, Chap. 42.
920 Laertius, *De Vitis Philosophorum*, Liber VIII, Chap. 17.
921 Plutarch, *Symposiac*, Liber VIII, Ques. 7.
922 Clement of Alexandria, *Stromateis*, Liber V, Chap. 5.
923 Plutarch, *De Liberis Educandis*, Chap. 17.
924 Porphyry, *De Vita Pythagorae*, Chap. 42.
925 Iamblichus, *De Vita Pythagorica*, Chap. 18.
926 Clement of Alexandria, *Stromateis*, Liber V, Chap. 5.
927 Clement of Alexandria, Ibid.
928 Iamblichus, *De Vita Pythagorica*, Chap. 24.
929 Laertius, *De Vitis Philosophorum*, Liber VIII, Chap. 18-19.
930 Plutarch, *De Liberis Educandis*, Chap. 17.
931 Porphyry, *De Vita Pythagorae*, Chap. 44.
932 Origen, *Philosophumena*, Liber I, *Pythagoras*.
933 Aulus Gellius, *Noctes Atticae*, Liber IV, Chap. 11.
934 Clement of Alexandria, *Stromateis*, Liber III, Chap. 3.
935 Laertius, *De Vitis Philosophorum*, Liber VIII, Chap. 19.
936 Ibid.
937 Ibid.
938 Porphyry, *De Vita Pythagorae*, Chap. 42.
939 Porphyry, *De Vita Pythagorae*, Chap. 42.
940 Iamblichus, *De Vita Pythagorica*, Chap.18.
941 Porphyry, *De Vita Pythagorae*, Chap. 43.
942 Laertius, *De Vitis Philosophorum*, Liber VIII, Chap. 19.
943 Athenaeus, *Deipnosophistarum*, Liber VII, Chap. 80.

944 Plutarch, *De Liberis Educandis*

945 Olympiodorus, *Platonis Phaedonem*

946 Cicero, in *Cato* and *De Republica*

947 Iamblichus, *De Vita Pythagorica*, Chap. 28.

948 Laertius, *De Vitis Philosophorum*, Liber VIII, Chap. 8.

949 Iamblichus, *De Vita Pythagorica*, Chap. 28.

950 Plutarch, *De Iside et Osiride*, Chap. 10.

951 Iamblichus, *Protrepticus*, Chap. 21.

952 Laertius, *De Vitis Philosophorum*, Liber VIII, Chap. 19 & Porphyry, *De Vita Pythagorae*, Chap. 39.

953 Clement of Alexandria, *Stromateis*, Liber IV, Chap. 26.

954 Clement of Alexandria, *Stromateis*, Liber V, Chap. 5.

955 Iamblichus, *De Vita Pythagorica*, Chap. 18.

956 Iamblichus, Ibid.

957 Iamblichus, Ibid.

958 Iamblichus, Ibid.

959 Plutarch, *De Iside et Osiride*, Chap. 10.

960 Lactantius, *De Vero Cultu*, Liber VI, Chap. 3.

961 The Parts of the World

962 Animals.

963 πόθακόντων perhaps is for προσηκόντων. (Doric.)†

964 Reuchlin, *De Arte Cabalistica*, Liber II.

965 Reuchlin, *De Arte Cabalistica*, Liber II, out of which Paul Schalich collects his first Canon, *De Mysterius Pythagoricis* in *Theses Mysticae Philosophiae*, Chap. 7 [in *Encyclopaediae, seu Orbis disciplinarum.* —Ed.]

966 Apuleius, *Florida*, Chap. 15.

967 Reuchlin, *De Arte Cabalistica*, Liber II.

968 Laertius, *De Vitis Philosophorum*, Liber VIII, Chap. 16.

969 Reuchlin, *De Arte Cabalistica*, Liber II & Scalich, *De Mysterius Pythagoricis* in *Theses Mysticae Philosophiae*, Canon 4.

970 Pythagoras, *Aurea Carmina*, I.

971 Pythagoras, *Aurea Carmina*, 47–48.

972 Reuchlin, *De Arte Cabalistica*, Liber II.

973 Plutarch, *De Placitis Philosophorum*, Liber IV, Chap. 2.

974 Scalich, *De Mysterius Pythagoricis* in *Theses Mysticae Philosophiae*, Canon 2.

975 Laertius, *De Vitis Philosophorum*, Liber VIII, Chap. 27.

976 Reuchlin, *De Arte Cabalistica*, Liber II.

977 Scalich, *De Mysterius Pythagoricis* in Theses Mysticae Philosophiae, Canon 9.

978 Scalich, *De Mysterius Pythagoricis* in Theses Mysticae Philosophiae, Canon 10.

979 Scalich, *De Mysterius Pythagoricis* in *Theses Mysticae Philosophiae*, Canon 11.

980 Homer, *Iliadem*, 14.

981 Reuchlin, *De Arte Cabalistica*, Liber II.

982 Timaeus of Locri, *De Natura Mundi Et Animae*, Chap. 5.

983 Pythagoras, *Aurea Carmina*, 50-51.

984 Plotinus, *Ennead III*, 5-6.

985 Pythagoras, *Aurea Carmina*,70-71.

986 Reuchlin, *De Arte Cabalistica*, Liber II.

987 Timaeus of Locri, *De Natura Mundi Et Animae*, Chap. 5.

988 Scalich, *De Mysterius Pythagoricis* in *Theses Mysticae Philosophiae*, Canon 3.

989 Alcinous, *De Doctrina Platonis*, Chap. 13. [Translated by Thomas Stanley & included in the account of *Plato* in his *History of Philosophy*.—Ed.]

990 Timaeus of Locri, *De Natura Mundi Et Animae*, Chap. 2.

991 Reuchlin, *De Arte Cabalistica*, Liber II.

992 Pythagoras, *Aurea Carmina*, 63-64.

993 *Herodotus*, Liber I, Chap. 32.

994 Reuchlin, *De Arte Cabalistica*, Liber II.

995 Pythagoras, *Aurea Carmina*,65-66.

996 Virgil, *Aeneid*, Liber VI.

997 Scalich, *De Mysterius Pythagoricis* in *Theses Mysticae Philosophiae*, Canon 6.

998 Scalich, *De Mysterius Pythagoricis* in *Theses Mysticae Philosophiae*, Canon 5.

999 Scalich, *De Mysterius Pythagoricis* in *Theses Mysticae Philosophiae*, Canon 8.

1000 Reuchlin, *De Arte Cabalistica*, Liber II.

1001 Aristotle, *De Generatione et Corruptione*, Liber I, Chap. 1.

1002 Philostratus, *Vita Apollonii*, Chap.19.

ADDITIONAL NOTES TO THE TEXT
BY J. DANIEL GUNTHER

(marked with †)

p. 79 γνησίους, "Genuine."
From Iamblicus', *Life of Pythagoras*, Cap. 18 (Kiessling, *Iamblichi Chalcidensis Ex Coele-Suria De Vita Pythagorica*, Vol. 1, p.172)

p. 88 Γέντα, a Magician.
The word γέντα is not the normal word for "magician." It refers to one who examines animal entrails for the purpose of divination. Cf. Schmidt, *Hesychii Alexandrini Lexicon, Editionem Minorem* p.342, Liddell Scott, *A Greek-English Lexicon* p. 344b, γέντα and p.1628b, σπλαγχνο-σκοπία. The accusation of Timon that Pythagoras was a γέντα is contradicted by the account in Chapter 15, 'Divination by Numbers' (see page 169) where we find an account of divination where Pythagoras rejects the use of animal entrails: "The student of Pythagoras, Abaris, performed those kinds of sacrifices to which he was accustomed, and diligently practiced divination after the ways of the Barbarians by victims (principally of cocks,whose entrals they conceived to be most exact for inspection). Pythagoras, not willing to take him away from his study of truth; yet, in order to direct him by a safer way, without blood and slaughter (moreover esteeming the cock sacred to the Sun), taught Abaris to find out all truth by the science of arithmetic."

p. 96 And that he chiefly praised Homer, for saving, Ποιμένα λάων, the shepherd of the people.
The phrase is used by Homer multiple times as an epithet of a ruler.
For one example, see *The Odyssey*, III, line 156 and IV, line 541 where the phrase is applied to Agamemnon. (Palmer, *The Odyssey of Homer, Books I-XII. The Text, And An English Version In Rhythmic Prose*, pp. 74 & 132.)

p. 99 σωμασκητής ["One that practices bodily exercises".] ἀλειπτης, ("Exercitator"...)
For σωμασκητής , "One that practices bodily exercises," Cf. Liddell Scott, *A Greek-English Lexicon* p. 1749B, and Dindorf, *Clementis Alexandrini Opera*, p. 421 par. 266, 10. For ἀλειπτης, read literally "one who annoints," i.e. one who applied ointments in a gymnasium. Cf. Liddell

Scott, A Greek-English Lexicon p. 62a. The reference is to the Natural History of Pliny Secundi, Liber XXIII, Chap. 7 which extols the virtues of the fig: Pythagoras exercitator primus ad carnes eos transtulit. "Pythagoras, the gymnist (exercitator), being the first who introduced them to a flesh diet." (Perhaps meaning that he used figs to assist in putting on weight. Cf. Mayhoff, C. Plini Secundi Naturalis Historiae, Vol. 4 p. 38, and Bostock & Riley, The Natural History of Pliny, Vol. 4 , p. 503)

p. 99 αὐτὸς ἔφη, ["He said it"]
    The phrase αὐτὸς ἔφη implies "The Master said it"; Latin Ipse dixit.
    It was associated with Pythagoras whose students in a debate would argue ipse dixit, ("He said it himself"), meaning Pythagoras, and considered it sufficent proof of an argument even without evidence. Cf. Cicero, De Natura Deorum (Liber I, Cap.V,10. Latin text is given in Mayor, M. Tulli Ciceronis De Natura Deorum Libri Tres, Vol. 1, p. 4) Cicero was in turn quoted to this effect by Valerius Maximus, Memorable Doings And Sayings, Book VIII. 15. Ext. 1. According to Joseph Mayor, Socrates was also called αὐτὸς by his disciples. Both the Latin and Greek pronouns were used colloquially by slaves of their masters. (M. Tulli Ciceronis De Natura Deorum Libri Tres, Vol. 1, p. 77) It is interesting to note that Jeremy Bentham (1748-1832) would eventually utilize the Latin phrase to form the word ipse-dixitism, which is used to signify an unsupported or dogmatic argument.

p. 99 σκίλλη, "squill" or "sea-onion," Urginea maritima.
    The plant was used in the Mediterranean area medicinally and as rat poison. Pliny, in Liber XIX, Chapter 30 of his Natural History, wrote that, "the philosopher Pythagoras has written a whole volume on the merits of this plant, setting forth its various medicinal properties.," and further, in Liber XX, Chapter 39, "Pythagoras says that a squill suspended at the threshold of a door, effectively shuts all access to evil spells and incantations.." (See Bostock & Riley, The Natural History of Pliny, Vol. IV, pp. 168-169 and 243. The Latin text is in Mayhoff, C. Plini Secundi Naturalis Historiae, Vol. 3, pp. 273-274 and 372.)

p. 100 ποια
    An interrogative particle meaning in this case, "what?" i.e., "what clothes?"
    The passage in full reads as follows:
    τῇ δὲ πρὸς τὸν ἴδιον ἄνδρα μελλούσῃ πορεύεσθαι παρήνει ἅμα τοῖς ἐνδύμασι καὶ τὴν αἰσχύνην ἀποτίθεσθαι, ἀνισταμένην τε πάλιν ἅμ᾽ αὐτοῖσιν ἀναλαμβάνειν. ἐρωτηθεῖσα, "ποῖα"; ἔφη, "ταῦτα δι᾽ ἃ γυνὴ κέκλημαι."

"And she recommended a woman, who was going to her husband, to put off her modesty with her clothes, and when she left him, to resume it again with her clothes; and when she was asked, "What clothes?" she said, "Those which cause you to be called a woman."

(Yonge, *Diogenes Laërtius, The Lives And Opinions of Eminent Philosophers* p. 356. Cf. Hicks, *Diogenes Laertius, Lives of Eminent Philosophers*, Vol. 2, pp. 357-359)

p. 118 αὐτὸς ἔφα. "He said it."
See above, note to page 99.

p. 122 πενταετὴς σιωπή, a quinquennial silence.
From Iamblicus, *Life of Pythagoras*, Cap. 17 (Kiessling, *Iamblichi Chalcidensis Ex Coele-Suria De Vita Pythagorica*, Vol. 1, p. 154)

p. 122 ἐχερημοσύνη ["keeping silent"], ὑπὸ τοῦ ἐχων εν εαυτῷ τὸν λόγον, from keeping our speech within ourselves. Read ἐχερρημοσύνη ["keeping silent"], ὑπὸ τοῦ ἔχοντος ἑαυτῷ τὸν λόγον. The word ἐχερρημοσύνη is a synonym of ἐχεμυθία.

See Schmidt, M., *Hesychii Alexandrini Lexicon* under ἐχέμυθος, and Liddell-Scott, *A Greek-English Lexicon*, p. 747b under ἐχε-κήλης, (-μῡθία, *silence, reserve.*)

p. 134. Quinquennial silence, πενταετὴς ἐχεμυθία.
"Quinquennial silence" is the translation of πενταετὴς σιωπη, (Iamblicus, *Life of Pythagoras*, Cap. 17) which Stanley mentioned specifically earlier on page 122 (see note above.) The quinquennial silence was also called ἐχεμυθία.

p. 142 προκεντημα. ["a thing pricked," i.e. "traced out beforehand"].
A design for a finished work, perhaps etched into the raw material. Cf. Liddell Scott *A Greek-English Lexicon*, p. 1486a προκεντ-έω.

p. 149 μεμονῶσθαι. "separation" (from multitude).
The etymological signification of the word μονάς, "Monad," according to Theon Smyrnaeus, was based on the fact that it remained unaltered if multiplied by itself, or that is separated and isolated (μεμονῶσθαι) from the remaining multitude of numbers. (Heath, *The Thirteen Books of Euclid's Elements*, Vol. 2 , p. 279)

p. 152 διάκρεσις, judgment.
Derived from διακρίνω, "separate one from another," in the sense of "a discerning, distinguishing." Cf. Liddell Scott, A *Greek-English Lexicon*, p. 399a. "Meursius" refers to the classical scholar Johannes Meursius (1579–1639)

p. 153 ἀργυροπεζα, "silver-footed," or "silver-sandalled."
The word is used as an epithet of Thetis in Homer's *Iliad*, I, 538. Cf. Monro, *Iliad, Books I–XII*, p. 18. Cf. also Liddell Scott, A *Greek-English Lexicon*, p. 236b under ἀργυρό-Βιος.

p. 161 οὐλομέλεια.
The literal meaning is "whole of limb, not dismembered." Cf. Liddell Scott, A *Greek-English Lexicon* p. 1218a.

p. 162 Ζυγίτης ["central oarsman"].
This refers to the central oarsmen of the style of Greek warship called the "Trireme" (τριήρης.) The ship had three rows of oarsmen. The rowers with the longest oars who sat in the mid-most point of the boat. Used in the same sense as μεσόνεος. (Cf. Liddell Scott, A *Greek-English Lexicon*, pp. 1106b, 1107a.)

p. 162 Βολήσασαν, ["hurled forth"].
The notion is that the Triad (Hecate) is hurled forth and joined with another Triad to form the Hexad. Cf. Thomas Taylor, *Theoretic Arithmetic* p. 198.

p. 163 Ἀτρυτόνη "The Unwearied."
An epithet of Pallas Athena. Cf. Liddell Scott, A *Greek-English Lexicon*, p. 273b, Ἀτρυτώνη.

p. 164 Ὀβριμοπάτρα, Tritogenia
Literally, "daughter of a mighty father," an epithet of Athena. Thus also "Tritogenia" (Greek Τριτο-γένεια), "Trito-born," explained in antiquity as either the lake Tritonis (Τριτωνίς) in Libya from which Athena was said to have been born. Another explanation is from Triton, a spring in Arcadia. Yet another is from the word τριτώ, an Aeolic word for κεφαλή, "head," thus "head-born." Cf. Liddell Scott, A *Greek-English Lexicon*, p. 1823b.

p. 164 Γλαυκῶπις, ["Blue-eyed"].
Another epithet of Athena. From Pausanias' *Description of Greece* (1.14.6), "I was not surprised that an image of Athena stood beside Hep-

haestus; but observing that Athena's image had blue eyes, I recognized the Libyan version of the myth. For the Libyans say that she is a daughter of Poseidon and the Tritonian lake, and that she, like Poseidon, has blue eyes." (Frazer, *Pausanias's Description of Greece*, Vol. 1, p. 21). The belief that the Greeks understood the epithet Γλαυκῶπις to mean "blue-eyed" is strengthened by this passage in Pausanias. Cf. Frazer, *Pausanias's Description of Greece*, Vol. 2, p. 128 for his commentary on Pausanias' 1.14.6.

p. 164 Ἀλαλκομένεια. ["Protectress"].

An epithet of Athena mentioned by Homer in The Iliad, IV,8 (Ἀλαλκομένηις Ἀθήνη). Also mentioned by Pausanias, Book 9, Chapter 33, who says it was a villiage of no great size, which got its name from Alalkomenes, a native (αὐτοχθόνος), who is said to have reared Athena, or alternately, Alalkomenia was one of the daughters of Ogyges. (Cf. Sibelis, *Pausaniae Graeciae Descripto*, Vol. 4 pp. 222–223) In his commentary on *The Iliad*, Leaf writes, "It is hard to say whether the local or attributive sense prevails in this title. Pausanias testifies to a cultus of Athene at Alalkomenai, near the Tritonian lake Boiotia, down to the time of Sulla; but the word is evidently also significant, 'the guardian'. (We hear also of Ζεὺς Ἀλαλκομένευς in the Et. Mag. (i.e. Etymologia Magnum)) Probably the name of the town was taken was either taken from the title of the goddess or adapted to it from an older form, or was itself the cause of the adoption of the cultus; a local adjective being then formed with a distinct consciousness of its original significance." (Leaf, *The Iliad*, Vol. 1, p. 116)

p. 164 Ἐργάνη ["worker"].

An epithet of Athena mentioned in Pausanias' Book I, Cap. 24. Cf. Shilleto, *Pausanias' Description of Greece*, Vol. 1, p. 45)

p. 164 Οὐλομέλεια ["sound of limbs"].

Or, "wholeness of limbs," implying the general nature of a thing.

p. 164 Τελέσφορος, "leading to the end".

In simpler terms, to "be brought to completion."

p. 165 Θηλύποιος ["making weak"].

From Nicomachus' as quoted by Photius, *Bibliotheca* p.144B. In the sense of "feminine." Cf. Liddell Scott, *A Greek-English Lexicon*, p. 798a under θηλύ-παθεω. Thomas Taylor translated this as "the producing cause of females." (Cf. Taylor, *Theoretic Arithmetic*, p. 204)

p. 165 Πολιοῦχος ["guardian of the city"].
An epithet of the guardian diety of a city. Cf. Πολιοῦχη παλλάς in Aristophanes, *Equites*, 581 (Leeuwen, *Aristophanes Equites cum prolegomenis et commentariis*, p. 110).

p. 165 Ηλιτόμηνα ["untimely born"].
That is, born at the wrong time of the month, or "immature." Cf. Liddell Scott, *A Greek-English Lexicon* p. 769b under ἠλῖτο-εργός.

p. 165 Ἀσφάλεια ["stability"].
Literally, "security against stumbling or falling." Used as an epithet of Poseidon as "The Securer," who was also associated with the ogdoad. Cf. Plutarch, *Theseus*, 36: "they pay honors to Poseidon on the eighth day of every month. The number eight, as the first cube of an even number and the double of the first square, fitly represents the steadfast and immovable power of this god, to whom we give the epithets of Securer (ἀσφάλειον) and Earth-stayer." (Perrin, *Plutarch's Lives*, Vol. 1 pp. 84-86)

p. 165 Ἔδρασμα ["placing in position"].
Used with the sense of 'establishing' and 'making stable', being in the proper place.

p. 166 Ἀνεικεία ["reconciliation"].
Note that this same term is used for the Pentad. (cf. page 159, " Ἀνεικία, Reconciliation, because the fifth element, Aether, is free from the disturbances of the other four."

p. 166 Ἑκάεργος ["far-darting"], because there is no shooting beyond it.
The meaning intended is that it prevents the further progression of number (ἀπὸ τοῦ εἴργειν τὴν ἑκὰς πρόβασιν τοῦ ἀριθμοῦ, *Theol. Ar.* 58-59.) Cf. Ast, *Theologumena Arithmeticae*, p. 58)

p. 166 Τελέσφορος ["bringing to the end"].
Note that this term is also used of the Heptad. See page 164.

p. 182 ἐξαρτύσεις, ["preparations"] and ἐπαφὰς, ["contact, touch"].
'Preparations' in the sense of "musical arrangement." (Cf. Liddell Scott, *A Greek-English Lexicon*, p. 587b) Likewise, ἐπαφὰς in this case indicates the touch of a hand upon a musical instrument. (Cf. Guthrie, The Pythagorean Sourcebook and Library, p. 85. Guthrie translated ἐξαρτύσεις as "readiness.")

p. 184 ἔργα "work".
Hesiod's poem is fully titled Ἐργα καὶ Ἡμέραι, "Works and Days."

p. 185 ἐξάρτησις, "preparedness," and συναρμογὴ "musical combination,"
and ἐπαφὴ "contact".
Note that ἐξάρτησις is the same word that was discussed in note 182
above. Hence, "preparedness" in the sense of musical preparation. So also
συναρμογη, "musical combination." (Cf. Liddell Scott, A Greek-English
Lexicon, p.1699a). Ἐπαφη is also discussed in note 201 above, here rendered "contact.
This entire section is a quotation taken from Chapter 25 of Iamblicus'
Life of Pythagoras: "The Pythagoreans distinguished three states of mind,
called exartysis, or readiness: synarmoge, or fitness, and epaphe, or contact
…" (Guthrie, The Pythagorean Sourcebook and Library, p. 85)
Thomas Taylor's translation, with the exception of his reading of the
word ἐπαφη is not only florid, but curiously obtuse: "The whole Pythago-
rean school produced appropriate songs, which they called exartysis or adap-
tions, synarmoge or elegance of manners, and apaphe or contact…" (Taylor,
Iamblicus' Life of Pythagoras, p. 61)
For the Greek text, see Kiessling, Iamblichi Chalcidensis Ex Coele-Suria
De Vita Pythagorica, Vol. 1, p. 242.

p. 185 ἐπᾴδοντες, by charming them.
See Liddell Scott, A Greek-English Lexicon p. 603a, ἐπαείδω.

p. 193 ἐλλείπειν.
The original text erroneously had εκλείπειν "eclipse" instead of ἐλλεί-
πειν, "fall short" (in application of areas). Cf. Heath, The Thirteen Books of
Euclid's Elements, Vol. 2, p. 262 and 427.

p. 197 Διὸς φυλακὴν, the custody of Jupiter.
Διὸς φυλακὴν was a Pythagorean term for the center of the Universe.
(Cf. Liddell Scott, A Greek-English Lexicon, p. 1960a, φυλᾰκ-άρχης, 3.)
See Aristotle's "On the heavens" (ΠΕΡΙ ΟΥΡΑΝΟΥ, or De Cælo)
Book 2:
"They think (i.e. the Pythagoreans) that the most honourable place
belongs to the most honourable body, and that Fire is more honourable than
Earth; that the two extremes, centre and circumference, are more honour-
able than the parts intermediate between them. Upon these grounds, they
consider that Fire, and not Earth, is at the centre of the Universal Sphere;
and they have another reason, peculier to themselves, for this conclusion:
they hold that the centre is the most important place in the universe, and

that it ought as such to be the most carefully guarded; wherefore they call it the watch of Jupiter (Διὸς φυλακὴν), and regard it as occupied by Fire." (George Grote, Aristotle, Vol 2, De Cælo II, Cap. 13, p. 423) For the Greek text of Aristotle, see Bekker, Aristotelis Graece, Vol. 1, p. 293b, 3.

p. 200 " ἐπιπροσθήσεών τε καὶ ὑπολείψεων καὶ ἀνωμαλιῶν ἐκκεντρότη-τών τε καὶ ἐπικύκλων. ["their oppositions, their eclipses, inequalities, eccentricities and epicycles."] Ἐπιπρόσθησις is the anticipation of any planet, either in respect to some other planet, or to the fixed Stars."

This is a difficult passage to translate, as Ἐπιπρόσθεσις and ὑπολειψις may both be used in the sense of "eclipse" or "occultation." Thomas Taylor translated Ἐπιπρόσθεσις as "oppositions" which was likewise followed by Guthrie. (See Liddell Scott, A Greek-English Lexicon, p. 633a) The text is from Iamblicus' Life of Pythagoras, Chapter 6. Cf. Kiessling, Iamblichi Chalcidensis Ex Coele-Suria De Vita Vol. 1, p. 70. See also Thomas Taylor, Iamblicus' Life of Pythagoras, p. 15 and Guthrie, The Pythagorean Sourcebook and Library, p. 64.

p. 200 Ἀνωμαλία, Inequality.

Astronomically, the word signifies "irregular motion," hence the etymology of the English word "anomaly." Cf. Liddell Scott, A Greek-English Lexicon, p. 170a.

p. 215 προφερὲς, precocious.

From Stobaeus' Florilegium, 99. Καθόλου μὲν φυλάττεσθαι τὸ καλου-μενον προφερές.

Stanley read, "principally observe that which is called precocious." It probably should be understood as "guard against that which is called precocious." (Cf.Liddell Scott, A Greek-English Lexicon, p. 1961a, φῦλασσω). Cf. also Iamblicus' Life of Pythagoras, Cap. 31, where this same account also occurs. Thomas Taylor read, "In the first place, they thought it necessary to guard against what is called untimely [offspring]." (Taylor, Iamblicus' Life of Pythagoras, p. 108) Guthrie (The Pythagorean Sourcebook and Library, p.107), renders the translation, "First, they prevented untimely birth."

p. 222 παιδαρτάσεις ["admonitions"]

This is a Pythagorean word for νουθετέω. (See Liddell Scott, A Greek-English Lexicon, p. 1351b πεδαρτάω.) From Iamblicus' Life of Pythagoras, Cap. 22. (Cf. Kiessling, Iamblichi Chalcidensis Ex Coele-Suria De Vita Pythagorica, Vol. 1, p. 218, and Guthrie, The Pythagorean Sourcebook and Library, p.82)

p. 223 κοινὰ φέλων ["friends share in common"]
Read κοινὰ τά φέλων. From *Diogenes Laertius, Lives of Eminent Philosophers*, VIII, 10.

Hicks translated it "friends have all things in common," while Guthrie read "the property of friends is common" (Cf. Hicks, *Diogenes Laertius, Lives of Eminent Philosophers*, Vol. 2, p. pp. 328–329, and Guthrie, *The Pythagorean Sourcebook and Library*, p. 144.)

p. 223 φιλιαν ισότητα ["friendship is equality"]
From *Diogenes Laertius, Lives of Eminent Philosophers*, VIII, 10. (Cf. Hicks, *Diogenes Laertius, Lives of Eminent Philosophers*, Vol. 2, p. pp. 328–329, and Guthrie, *The Pythagorean Sourcebook and Library*, p. 144.)

p. 225 τελεταὶ, ["Rites of Fulfillment"]
The exact meaning of τελεται as understood by the ancient Greeks remains something of a mystery. We might also read, "rituals of Perfection." See Kevin Clinton's essay, *Stages of Initiation in the Eleusinian and Samothracian Mysteries* (pp. 50–78 in *Greek Mysteries, The Archaeology and Ritual of Ancient Greek Secret Cults* (London, 2003)

p. 226 Ὅρκος ["of oaths"].
Cf. Hicks, *Diogenes Laertius, Lives of Eminent Philosophers*, Vol. 2, pp. 348-349:
Ὅρκιόν τ᾽ εἶναι τὸ δίκαιον καὶ διὰ τοῦτο Δια ὄρκιον λέγεσθαι.
"Right has the force of an oath, and that is why Zeus (i.e. Jupiter) is called the God of Oaths."

p. 234 εἱμαρμένη, the Decree of God.
Read "εἱμαρμένην τοῦ θεοῦ, the Decree of God." The word εἱμαρμένη means "decree." Stanley translated the entire phrase, but the last two Greek words were omitted from the original book. From an Anonymous *Life of Pythagoras* which Photius preserved in his Codex CCXLIX of his *Bibliotheca*. (Cf. Migne, *Patrologiæ Cursus Completus, Series Græca*. Vol. 103, p. 1581, and Guthrie, *The Pythagorean Sourcebook and Library*, p. 138)

p. 234 εἱμαρμένη, a Fate of all things in general and in particular, the cause of their administration.
Cf. Hicks, *Diogenes Laertius, Lives of Eminent Philosophers*, Vol. 2, pp. 342–343.

p. 236 reading (perhaps) ἐναπειλημμένην

Stanley means to read the phrase ἐναπειλημμένην τῷ χαλκῷ, "enclosed in the brass." Thus also all the authorities. For the Greek, see Kiessling, *Iamblichi Chalcidensis Ex Coele-Suria De Vita Pythagorica*, Vol. 2, p. 72 and for the Greek with Latin translation, see Nauck, *Porphryii Philosophi Platonici Opuscula Tria*, p. 30. The latter renders the Greek by the Latin *includo*, which is more in keeping with the sense of the word, implying that the voice of the daimon was "confined" or "imprisoned" in the brass. For an English translation, see Guthrie, *The Pythagorean Sourcebook and Library*, p. 131.

p. 246 Κόσμον ["order"].

See *Anonymous: Life of Pythagoras Preserved by Photius* in Guthrie, *The Pythagorean Sourcebook and Library*, p. 139, "It was Pythagoras who first called heaven kosmos because it is perfect, and "adorned" with infinite beauty and living beings. In addition to "order," Κόσμος may also have the meaning "ornament" or "decoration," hence the last portion of the sentence in the quotation.

p. 254 by divine participation, θεία μείρα

Read θεία μοίρα . The quote is from Clement of Alexandria, Stromata V. It is found in Chapter 13. The Greek text reads:

Ἐντεῦθεν οἱ ἀμφὶ τὸν Πυθαγόραν θεία μοίρα τον νοῦν εἰς ἀνθρώπους ἥκειν φασὶ, καθάπερ Πλάτων καὶ Ἀριστοτέλης ὁμολογουσσιν.

"Thus, the Pythagoreans say that the mind (νοῦς) comes to man by divine providence, as Plato and Aristotle affirm." The common and accepted translation of θεία μοίρα is "divine providence." Thus also Xenophon, *Memorabilia* Book 2, Chapter 3, line 18. (Dindorf, *Clementis Alexandrini Opera*, Vol. 3, p. 68., Liddell Scott, *A Greek-English Lexicon*, p. 1141a, III., Schneider, *Xenophontes Quae Extant*, Vol. 4, p. 95)

p. 266 and Pindar, speaking of Aesculapius, ἀμφέπων, ["tending them"] with soft charms.

Aesculapius (Latin) is better known to the modern reader by his Greek name Asclepius, the god of medicine and healing, described in Pindar's Pythian Ode III:

"Them therefore, whoso came unto him,
having self-caused sores
or marred in limbs by the polished steel,
or far-hurled stone;
or wasted in body by summer's fire or winter's cold,

he cured, freeing various from various pains;
some he fixed healthful,
tending them with gentle spells..."

(Fennell, *Pindar: The Olypian and Pythian Odes*, p. 179, Laurent, *The Odes of Pindar in English Prose*, Vol. 1, p. 155)

p. 267 στώη καίετων

Unfortunately, it is unclear what Stanley understood this phrase to mean, since all the authorities declare it to be a corruption. The Greek text given by Kiessling is as follows:

ἢ ἐν τῷ κόσμος ὀνόματι, ἢ νὴ Δία ἐν τῷ φιλοσοφία, ἢ καὶ ἐν τῷ στώη καΐετων, ἤτὸ διαβόωμενον ἐν τῷ τετρακτύς.

Kiessling notes that στώη καίετων is *monstra verborum* (an "ill-formed word"), and would restore the passage to: ἐν τῷ εὐεστὼ καὶ ἀειεστώ, translated as "in *euesto* aut et *aeiesto*, id est, tranquillo et constanti animo." (in *euesto* (happiness) and *aeiesto* (everlastingness,) which is, peace and continual life")

The critical edition of Ludwig Deubner marks the passage but omits the two words.

The popular editions of Thomas Taylor and Kenneth Guthrie likewise ignore them.

(Kiessling, *Iamblichi Chalcidensis Ex Coele-Suria De Vita Pythagorica*, pp. 342-344, Taylor, *Iamblicus' Life of Pythagoras*, p. xxx, Guthrie, *The Pythagorean Sourcebook and Library*, p.97)

pp. 278, who named the more honorable hand δεξιὰν, the right, not only ἀπὸ τοῦ δέχεσθαι, from receiving; but likewise, ἀλλὰ καὶ ἀπὸ τοῦ δεκτὴν ὑπάρχειν ἐν τῷ μεταδιδόναι, from being ready to receive in communicating.

From the *Protrepticus* of Iamblicus, Chapter 21. Johnson translated this, "who called the right hand more excellent than the left, not only because it receives, but also because it is able to impart." (Cf. Pistelli, *Iamblichi Protrepticus Ad Fidem Codicis Florentini*, p. 117, Johnson, *Iamblicus: The Exhortation to Philosophy*, p. 104.)

p. 288. In the Twenty eighth, Lay not hold on every one readily with your right hand. Plutarch omits ῥαδίως , Suidus παντί.

From the *Protrepticus* of Iamblicus, Cap. XXI. The Greek reads, Δεξιὰν μὴ παντὶ ῥᾳδίως ἔμβαλλε, which Stanley translates as, "Lay not hold on everyone readily with your right hand." (i.e. "Do not hasten to offer everyone your right hand.")

In Suidas' *Lexicon*, the entry describing this Symbol omits the word
παντί, and reads:

μὴ ῥᾳδίως δεξιὰν εμβάλλειν, "Do not hasten to offer the right hand."
In Plutarch's Morals, "On Education," Chapter 17, it is written as: μὴ παντὶ
ἐμβάλλειν δεξιάν, "Do not offer everyone your right hand," omitting the
word ῥᾳδίως from the account of Pythagoras' Symbol. This Symbol is
recounted in full by Diogenes Laertius in his *Lives of Eminent Philosophers*,
Chapter VIII, 17, which Hicks translated liberally, "don't shake hands too
eagerly," but which effectively sums up the actual meaning of the sentence.
(Cf. Pistelli, *Iamblichi Protrepticus Ad Fidem Codicis Florentini*, p. 108, Bekker, *Suidae Lexicon*, p. 910a., Vernardakis, *Plutarchi Chaeronensis Moralia*,
Vol. 1, p. 28, Shilleto, *Plutarch's Morals, Ethical Essays*, p. 18., and Hicks,
Diogenes Laertius, Lives of Eminent Philosophers, Vol. 2, p. 337.)

p. 289 This last reason is confirmed by Plutarch, who explains this Symbol:
Abstain from Suffrages; which of old were given by Beans.

In *Liberis Educandis* (On the training of children), Plutarch wrote,
"Abstain from beans"; means that a man should keep out of politics, for
beans were used in earlier times for voting upon the removal of magistrates
from office." (Babbitt, *Plutarch, Moralia*, Vol. 1., Chap. 17) This process is
described by Robert Bateman Paul as follows:

"when [the assembly] deprived the magistrates of their power for mal-
administration, they gave their votes in private. The manner of voting privately was by casting pebbles (ψήφους) into vessels, (κάδους,) which the
prytanes [i.e. officers in the Senate] were obliged to place in the assembly
for this purpose. Before the use of pebbles, they voted with beans (κύαμοι.)
As soon as the people had done voting, the proëdri [i.e. other officers of the
Senate], having carefully examined the number of suffrages, pronounced
the decree ratified or thrown out, according as the majority part approved
or rejected it." (R.B. Paul, *The Antiquities of Greece*, p.228.) Beans were also
used in this manner for casting judgments against defendants on trial, as
well as voting for Senators.

"The Senators were elected by lots in the following manner: on a certain day, before the beginning of the month Hecatombæon, the president
of every tribe gave in the names of all the persons within his district who
were capable of this dignity, and chose to be candidates for it. These were
engraven on tables of brass, called πινάκια, and cast into a vessel set there
for that purpose. Into another vessel were cast the same number of beans,
fifty of which were white, and all the rest black. Then the names of the
candidates and the beans were drawn out one by one; and those whose
names were drawn out together with the white beans were elected for that
tribe." (Ibid, p. 229)

p. 291. διδύμων αἰδοίων, ["testicles (and) genitals"]

Read, διδύμων, καὶ αἰδοίων. From Porphyry's *Life of Pythagoras*, Chapter 43. (Cf. Kiessling, *Iamblichi Chalcidensis Ex Coele-Suria De Vita Pythagorica*, Vol. 2, p. 76, and Guthrie, *The Pythagorean Sourcebook and Library*, p. 132.)

p. 291 διδύμυς καὶ αἰδοῖα , Generation

Stanley translates διδύμυς καὶ αἰδοῖα as "Generation," instead of the literal "testicles and genitals".

p. 312. αὐτὸς ἔφα, He said.

See page 373 above, note to page 99.

p. 312. Thus the Cabalists answer אמרו הכמים The wise said; and Christians, πίστευσον, Believe.

The phrase, אמרו הכמים (*ameru hakamim*) "the sages say," was translated by Reuchlin in Latin as *dixerunt sapientes*, read by Stanley as "the wise said." The phrase is found, for example, in some of the Midrashim, such as the *Midrash 'Aseret Ha-Dibrot*, and the *Midrash Vayosha* where the authors introduced subject matter without feeling the necessity to quote their sources, intitiating significant sections with, *ameru hakamim*, "*the sages say...*"

In speaking of the corresponding Christian admonition "Believe," Reuchlin was in turn quoting Gregory of Nazienzus' *First Invective Against Julian*, Chapter 102, where Gregory says of Julian:

"Ours," says he, "are the words and speaking of Greek, whose right it is to worship the gods; yours are the want of words, and clownishness, and nothing beyond the faith in your own doctrine." At this, those I fancy will not laugh, who follow the sect of Pythagoras amongst you, with whom the "αὐτὸς ἔφα " is the first and greatest of articles of faith; and preferable to the "Golden (perhaps Leaden) Words." For after that preliminary and much celebrated training of *Silence* of such as were initiated into his doctrine (in order that they might be trained in bridling speech by dint of holding their tongues), it was the rule, 'tis said, that when questioned about any one of his tenets, they replied in explanation, when the reason was asked, that it had been so decreed by Pythagoras himself: and that the reason of the doctrine was what had come into that sage's head, without proof, and unquestioned. Thus your "He said so" comes to the same thing with our "Believe," but in other syllables and terms, although you never give over ridiculing and abusing the latter. For our saying means that it is not allowable to disbelieve things said by divinely-inspired persons, but that the proof of the Word is their *trustworthiness*, a thing more convincing than any logical argument or defense."

(Goodman, *Johann Reuchlin On the Art of the Kabbalah*, pp. 144–147, King, C.W. *Julian the Emperor containing Gregory Nazianzen's Two Invectives and Libanius' Monody*, pp. 68-69)

p. 317. That is the IDEA (from ἔιδω γινώσκω), ["seeing, *meaning* understanding"]

Stanley is paraphrasing Reuchlin's De Arte Cabalistica here, but the Greek as he gives it is problematical. The Reuchlin text has ἐκ τοῦ ἴδω, τὸ γνώσκω, " from seeing (ἔιδω), meaning understanding (γινώσκω)." Stanley has structured his parenthetical note in such a way that γινώσκω appears only as a gloss on ἔιδω , apparently intending to emphasize that IDEA is derived from ἔιδω , adding γινώσκω as an explanation or definition of ἔιδω. It is unclear why Stanley did not simply quote Reuchlin verbatim. (Cf. Goodman, *Johann Reuchlin, On the Art of the Kabbalah. De Arte Cabalistica*, p. 152-153.)

p. 318 Empedocles Ἔρις "strife"

Stanley is closely paraphrasing Reuchlin here, but he supplies the Greek term where Reuchlin remains in Latin. The doctrine of Empedocles asserted that creation and destruction were impossible, but that which appeared to be either of these arises from the union or separation of the four eternal elements of Air, Earth, Fire and Water. The unifying principle was signifed by φιλότης, "love," while the separative principle was its opposite νεῖκος, "strife" or "contention," the latter being a synonym of ἔρις .

ὦ ποποι, ὦ δειλὸν θνητῶν, ὦ δυσάνολβον, ποίων ἔκ τ᾽ ἐρίδων ἔκ τε στόαχῶν ἐγένεσθε. "O mortal kind! O ye poor sons of grief! From such contentions and such sighings sprung!" —Empedocles, 124.2.

(Leonard, *The Fragments of Empedocles*, p. 57)

p. 322 Having overcome these things (says Pythagoras) thou shalt know σύστασιν, the cohabitation of the immortal gods, and mortal men.

This quote is a short paraphrase of Reuchlin, whose longer version closely follows the Golden Verses: "from Pythagoras, who wrote in the the Golden Verses: 'When you cast aside the body you come to the free aether, you will be a god and immortal. When the things of this life are overcome, you will know the dwelling together (which he elegantly termed σύστασιν, because they 'stand together') of immortal gods and mortal men."

Reuchlin was quoting from two different places within the Golden Verses. The first portion of the quote is the last two lines of the Golden Verses: "Then should you be separated from the body, and soar in the aethyr. You will be imperishable, a divinity, a mortal no more." (Guthrie, *The Pythagorean Sourcebook*, p. 165). The second portion of the quote is lines 49-51: "If this you hold fast, soon will you recognize of Gods and mortal men." (Ibid, p. 164.) For the Greek text, see Gaisford, *Poetæ Minories Gracæ* Vol. 3, pp.282–283. Cf. Goodman, *Johann Reuchlin, On the Art of the Kabbalah. De Arte Cabalistica*, pp. 196-197.

p. 322 styled by Homer ἄσβεστος γέλως, inextinguishable laughter.

From the *Iliad*, I:595–600: "the white-armed goddess Hera smiled, and smiling took the cup at her son's hand. Then he poured wine to all the other gods from right to left, ladling the sweet nectar from the bowl. And **laughter unquenchable** arose amid the blessed gods to see Hephaistos bustling through the palace." (Lang, Leaf & Meyers. *Homer's Iliad done into English Prose*, p. 20) For the Greek text, see Monro, *Homer, Iliad, Books I–XII*, p. 20. Cf. Goodman, *Johann Reuchlin, On the Art of the Kabbalah. De Arte Cabalistica*, pp. 198-199.

p. 327 For men often straying from the rule of right reason precipitate themselves into misery, ἀυθαίρετα πήματ᾽ ἔχοντας, in Pythagoras's word, *incurring ills voluntary*.

From the Golden Verses, "Men shall you find whose sorrows they themselves have created." (Guthrie, The Pythagorean Sourcebook, p. 164. Greek text in Gainsford, *Poetæ Minories Gracæ*. Vol. 3, p. 283.)

p. 327 Thus is man placed between Virtue and Vice, like the stalk between the two branches in the Pythagorical Y.

"In this way, man seems poised between virtue and vice. This brings to mind the Pythagorean letter "Y," with its upright split into two branches." (Goodman, *Johann Reuchlin, On the Art of the Kabbalah. De Arte Cabalistica*, p. 167)

p. 327 Tartarus, by those who endure infinite torments, ὅθεν οὔποτε ἐκβαίνουσιν, (as Plato, imitating Pythagoras, says) whence they never come out.

From Plato's *Phaedra*: "But those who appear to be incurable, on account of the greatness of their wrong-doings, because they have committed many great deeds of sacrilege, or wicked and abominable murders, or any other such crimes, are cast by their fitting destiny into Tartarus, *whence they never emerge* (ὅθεν οὔποτε ἐκβαίνουσιν)*.

(Fowler, *Plato*, Vol. 1, *Phaedo*,62, p. 388–389) Reuchlin believed this passage from *Phaedo* was a direct quote from Pythagoras. (Goodman, *Johann Reuchlin, On the Art of the Kabbalah. De Arte Cabalistica*, p. 168–169.) Eduard Zeller discussed the influence of Pythagorean ideas of the soul on later writers such as Plato in his *History of Greek Philosophy from the earliest period to the time of Socrates* (See pp. 481–496.)

p. 330 Look on him as my Progenitor, or πρόγονον σῶμα, progeniting body;
From Philostratus' *The Life of Apollonius of Tyana*, Cap. XIX. Conybeare translated πρόγονον σῶμα as "ancestral body." (Conybeare, *Philostratus, The Life of Apollonius of Tyana*, Vol. 1, pp. 270–271)

p. 337 note 15. ἀντὶ Σάμης, ["instead of Same"].
According to Iamblicus, Ancaeus of Cephallenia was informed of his task by the Pythian Oracle in the words:
Ἀγκαῖ, εἰαλίαν νησον Σάμον ἀντί Σάμης σδ
οἰκίζειν κέλομαι · Φυλλὰς δ ὀνομάζεται αὔτη.
"I order you Ancaeus, to colonize the marine island Samos instead of Same, and to call it Phyllas." (Kiessling, *Iamblichi Chalcidensis Ex Coele-Suria De Vita Pythagorica*, Vol. 1, p.18 & Guthrie, *The Pythagorean Sourcebook and Library*, p. 58)

p. 337 note 20. Adding καὶ κυούσης αὐτὴν ἐκ μὴ οὔτως ἐχούσης καταστῆσαί.
"and got her with child" [i.e. "caused her to become pregnant"]
The text is added from Iamblicus, *De Vita Pythagorica*, Cap. 2. (Kiessling, *Iamblichi Chalcidensis Ex Coele-Suria De Vita Pythagorica*, Vol. 1, p.24)

p. 337 note 25. The manuscript of Porphyry's *Life of Pythagoras* gives the name Cleanthes (Κλεάνθες) as the source of these accounts, and Stanley is quoting it correctly. However, scholars now affirm that the word is a misspelling for Neanthes (Νεάνθης). Edouard Zeller, in *A History of Greek Philosophy from the earliest period to the time of Socrates*, Vol. 1, p. 329: "The Cleanthes of Porphyry is certainly not the Stoic but most likely a misspelling for Neanthes (of Cyzicus)." Guthrie likewise modifies Cleanthes to Neanthes (*The Pythagorean Sourcebook and Library*, p. 123). For the Greek text, see Nauck, *Porphryii Philosophi Platonici Opuscula Tria*, p. 14. Cf. Pearson, *The Fragments of Zeno and Cleanthes*, p. 294)

p. 338 note 44. Reading ἐξαιρέτως, ["principal"].
From Iamblicus, *De Vita Pythagorica*, Cap. 3 (Kiessling, *Iamblichi Chalcidensis Ex Coele-Suria De Vita Pythagorica*, Vol. 1, p.38)

p. 338 note 46. For μόνον τε ἐπιφθεγξάμενος, reading ἐπιφθεγξάμενος τε μῶν εἰς ᾽Αιγυπτον ὁ αποπλους, etc.

Stanley offered an emendation to Iamblicus' *Life of Pythagoras*, Cap. 3 which reads: μόνον τε ἐπιφθεγξάμενος εἰς Αιγυπτον ὁ ἀπόπλους. Thomas Taylor translated the original text, "he said nothing more than, 'Are you bound for Egypt?'" (Kiessling, *Iamblichi Chalcidensis Ex Coele-Suria De Vita Pythagorica*, Vol. 1, p.44. Taylor, *Iamblicus' Life of Pythagoras*, p. 8. Cf. Guthrie, *The Pythagorean Sourcebook and Library*, p. 60)

p. 340 note 98. δ᾽ ἐν τῷ καλουμένῳ Τρίοπι. Hesych. Τρίοψ, ὁ ὑπὸ τῶν Πυθάγορικῶν ἐν Δελφοῖς τρίπους.

The earliest edition of Porphyry's *Life of Pythagoras* that was available to consult, the 1630 edition by Cardinal Barberinus, does not concur with Stanley, but gives the reading δ᾽ ἐν τῷ καλουμένῳ Τρίποδι. Likewise, the 1731 Latin edition of Stanley's *History of Philosophy* notes that Stanley wrote Τρίοπι instead of Τρίποδι which is in the published text of Porphyry. "The later editions of Kiessling and Nauck likewise read δ᾽ ἐν τῷ καλουμέ-νῳ Τρίποδι, "in the place called Tripod." Guthrie follows Kiessling and Nauck, translating the entire passage quoted by Stanley:

"At Delphi he inscribed an elegy on the tomb of Apollo, declaring that Apollo was the son of Silenus, but was slain by Pytho, and buried in the place called "Tripod," so named from the local mourning for Apollo by the three daughters of Triopas."

Stanley's reference "Hesychius', Τρίοψ, ὁ ὑπὸ τῶν Πυθάγορικῶν ἐν Δελφοῖς τρίπους." refers to the Lexicon of Hesychius of Alexandria, where it is said that Triops for the Pythagoreans signified the Tripod of Delphi.

(Barberinus, *Porphyrii Philosophi Liber De Vita Pythagoræ*, pp. 10-11, Kiessling, *Iamblichi Chalcidensis Ex Coele-Suria De Vita Pythagorica*, Vol. 2, p. 30, Nauck, *Porphryii Philosophi Platonici Opuscula Tria*, p. 20, Guthrie, *The Pythagorean Sourcebook and Library*, p. 126. Cf. Schmidt, *Hesychii Alexandrini Lexicon, Editionem Minorem*, p. 1472)

p. 340 note 122. Cicero's reference to this event in his *Tusculan Disputations*, Book I, Chapter 4, is quite brief: "Pythagoras… came into Italy in the reign of Tarquin the proud."

Cicero referred to Pythagoras' arrival in Italy with more detail in his treatise, *On the Commonwealth*, Book 2, Chapter 15: "For it was not till the fourth year of the reign of Tarquinius Superbus that Pythagoras is ascertained to have come to Sybaris, Crotona, and this part of Italy." (Yonge, *Cicero's Tusculan Disputations; also treatises on the nature of the gods and on the Commonwealth*, pp. 25 & 406.)

p. 340 note 127. Eusebius, *Chronicon*

Stanley's footnote to the English edition does not identify the specific source, but merely indicates that it is from a work by Eusebius. The Latin edition of *The History of Philosophy* clearly identifies the source as the *Chronicon* or "Chronicle" of Eusebius. The original Greek for the Eusebius' *Chronicon* is lost and it is known only through an early Latin translation by Justin. However, in the year 1616 the scholar Joseph Justus Scaliger published an edition of the *Chronicon* under the title *Thesaurus Temporum: Eusebii Pamphili Caesareae Palaestinae Episcopi, Chronicorum Canonum Omnimodae Historiae*, in which he attempted to restore the Greek of Eusebius, relying heavily upon the Latin translation of Justin. In Stanley's time, this work was acknowledged as a very important work, and was widely read. It is probable that this was the work untilized by Thomas Stanley for referencing the Greek Olympiads.

p. 341 note 146. Μοῦσαι quasi μοῦσαι, ['Muse', practically the same as 'Music'] Synessius in *Dion*, Chap. 5 & Cassiodorus, *Variarum*, Liber II, 40.

Synessius, the Neo-Platonic philosopher who became the Bishop of Kyrenaica, in his work *Dion*, writes about Dio Cocceianus of Prusa, also known as *Chrysostom*, "goldvoice." Dio was a Greek philosopher and politician, considered by many to be one of the first representatives of the Second Sophistic movement of Greece. Synessius argues that Dio converted from sophism to philosophy. In Chapter 5 of *Dion*, Synessius extols the usefulness of the arts of the Muses, suggesting that while the Muses inspire a variety of arts, the philosopher harmonizes them into one. The passage in full reads:

"Now this speech would define as an artist and an expert the man who cuts off for himself any one branch of knowledge, one such man belonging to one divinity (daimon), another to another; but it would call philosopher that one who has been fitted together from the harmony of all, and has made the multitude of arts into one. Or rather he has not attained this yet, for this must be added to him also, namely, that he have a task of his own superior to that of his company. Thus the story goes that Apollo sings at one time with the Muses, leading off himself, and giving the time to the band, and at another sings by himself; but the first would be the sacred and ineffable melody. So our philosopher will commune, now with himself, and now with the god through philosophy, but he will commune with men by the subordinate powers of speech. He will possess knowledge indeed as a lover of literature, whereas he will pass judgment upon each and everything as a philosopher. But these immovable men who despise rhetoric and poetry do not seem to me to be what they are of their own free will, and owing to the poverty of their natural gifts they are incapable of even small achievements. You may more easily see such men than see anything in their minds, and their tongues are unable to interpret any thought."

(Migne, *Patrologiæ Cursus Completus, Series Græca. Vol. 66.* ΣΥΝΕΣΙΟΥ, p. 1125–1128, and Fitzgerald, *The Letters of Synesius of Cyrene: Translated into English with introduction and notes*)

Cassiodorus in Liber II, Letter 40 of his *Variarum* wrote concerning music:

"Reflections on the nature of music. She is the Queen of the senses; when she comes forth from her secret abiding place all other thoughts are cast out. Her curatiave influence on the soul. The five tones: the Dorian, influencing to modesty and purity; the Phrygian to fierce combat; the Aeolian to tranquility and slumber; the Ionian (Jastius), which sharpens the intellect of the dull and kindles the desire of heavenly things; the Lydian, which soothes the soul oppressed with too many cares. We distinguish the highest, middle and lowest in each tone, obtaining thus in all fifteen tones of artificial music. The diapason is collected from all, and unites all their virtues.

Classical instances of music: Orpheus. Amphion. Musaeus.

The human voice was an instrument of music. Oratory and Poesy as branches of the art.

The power of song: Ulysses and the Sirens. David, the author of the Psalter, who by his melody three times drove away the evil spirit from Saul. The lyre is called 'Chorda' because it so easily moves the hearts (corda) of men. As the diadem dazzles by the variegated luster of its gems, so the lyre with its diverse sounds. The lyre, the loom of the Muses. Mercury, the inventor of the lyre, is said to have derived the idea of it from the harmony of the spheres. This astral music, apprehended by reason alone, is said to form one of the delights of heaven."

(Cf. Migne, Jaques Paul. *Patrologiæ Cursus Completus, Series Latinae,* Vol. 69, Cassiodori, and Hodgkin, *The Letters of Cassiodorus being a condensed translation of the Variae Epistolae of Magnus Aurelius Cassiodorus Senator*, pp.193–194).

p. 341 note 147. Aristotle, *Analytica Priora et Posteriora*, Posterior Analytics Chap. 11. Ἐπικοινωνοῦσι δὲ πᾶσαι αἱ ἐπιστῆμαι ἀλλήλαις κατὰ τὰ κοινά. Cicero, *Oratio Pro Licinio Archia*, Oratio IX, "Quasi cognatione quadam" etc.

The translation of Ἐπικοινωνοῦσι δὲ πᾶσαι αἱ ἐπιστῆμαι ἀλλήλαις κατὰ τὰ κοινά is, "All sciences communicate with each other according to common (principles)" "Quasi cognatione quadam" etc." refers to a quote from Cicero's *Oratio Pro Licinio Archia*: "Etenim omnes artes, quae ad humanitatem pertinent, habent quoddam commune vinculum, et **quasi cognatione quadam** inter se continentur".

"all the liberal arts are nearly allied to each other, and have, as it were, one common bond of union."

(Cf. Bekker, *Aristoteles Opera*, Vol. 1, p. 198, and Owen, *The Organon, or Logical Treatises of Aristotle*, p. 270 & Duncan, *Cicero's Select Orations Translated Into English*, p. 287)

p. 341 note 152. The missing text from Laertius is as follows:

Τίμαιός τέ φηειν ἐν δεκάτῃ ἱστοριῶν λέγειν αὐτὸν τὰς συνοικου-´σας ἀδράσι Θεῶν ἔχειν ὀνόματα, Κορας, Νύμφας, εἶτα Μητέρας καλου-μενας.

"Timaeus, in the tenth book of his Histories, tells us, that he used to say that women who were married to men had the names of the Gods, being successively called Virgins, then Nymphs, and subsequently Mothers." (Hicks, *Diogenes Laertius, Lives of Eminent Philosophers*, Vol. 2, p. 330 and Yonge, *Diogenes Laërtius, The Lives And Opinions of Eminent Philosophers* p. 342.)

p. 341 note 157. Iamblichus, *De Vita Pythagorica*, Chap 6.

'Acousmatics' from ἀκουσματικοὺς, "eager to hear." (Liddell-Scott, *A Greek-English Lexicon*, p. 53b.)

p. 341 note 159. Clement of Alexandria, *Stromateis*, Liber I, Chap. 15.

Homacoeion from ὁμακοεῖον, "school," in turn derived from ὁμα-´κοοι, "fellow hearers," or "fellow students" in the school of Pythagoras. (Liddell-Scott, *A Greek-English Lexicon*, p. 1220a. Cf. Taylor, *Iamblicus' Life of Pythagoras*, pp. 38-41.)

page 342 note 190. So read, [Pyrrhus], not Pythius.

The Scholiast of Sophocles incorrectly rendered the name Πύθιος, thus Stanley's note.

(Cf. Mobeim, Marcus. *Diogenes Laertii De Vitis, Dogmatibus et Apophthegmatibus Clarorum Philosophorum*, p. 491)

p. 343 note 194. σπάνει τῶν ἀναγκαίων, ill rendered, *amicorum inopia* ["lack of friends".]

Stanley's note means that the Greek text of Porphyry's *Life of Pythagoras*, σπάνει τῶν ἀναγκαίων, should be rendered as "want of necessities" rather than the Latin translation *amicorum inopia, "lack of friends."* The 1630 edition of Cardinal Barberinus', *Porphyrii Philosophi Liber De Vita Pythagoræ* p. 39 translates the Greek by the Latin *amicorum inopia*, the phrase Stanley finds faulty. Likewise, the Eighteenth century translation of Kiessling, *Iamblichi Chalcidensis Ex Coele-Suria De Vita Pythagorica*, Vol. 2, p. 93, retains the reading *amicorum inopia*. The Greek text reads:

Ἐν δὲ τῇ περὶ μεταπόντιον καὶ Πυθαγόραν αὐτὸν λέγουσι τελευτῆσαι, καταφυγόντα ἐπὶ το μουσῶν ἱερὸν, σπάνει τῶν ἀναγκαίων τεσσαράκοντα ἡμέρας διαμείναντα.

Guthrie's version has, "Pythagoras fled to the temple of the Muses, in Metapontum. There he abode forty days, and starving, died." (Guthrie, *The Pythagorean Sourcebook and Library*, p. 134)

p. 343 note 198. Ibid, Chap. 2

"fair-haired Samian," τὸν ἐν Σάμῳ κομήτην, was correctly translated "long-haired Samian" by Taylor and Guthrie. (Cf. Taylor, *Iamblicus' Life of Pythagoras or Pythagoric Life*, p. 5, Guthrie, *The Pythagorean Sourcebook and Library*, p.59. Cf. Liddell-Scott, *A Greek-English Lexicon*, p. 975a., Kiessling, *Iamblichi Chalcidensis Ex Coele-Suria De Vita Pythagorica*, p. 30.)

p. 343 note 225. Perhaps τήλαυγες κλυτὲ κοῦρε, etc.

Stanley's original marginal note reads verbatum with the text of Laertius.

Cf. Huebner, *Diogenis Laertii De Vitis, Dogmatis Et Apophthegmatis Clarorum Philosophorum Libri Decem*, Vol. 2, p. 276 and Yonge, *Diogenes Laërtius, The Lives And Opinions of Eminent Philosophers* p. 355 : "Telauges, noble youth, whom in due time, Theano bore to wise Pythagoras."

p.344 note 235. κακοτεχνίην "poor workmanship," κακοτεχνως "mischevious art.

From Laertius Chapter 5." Ἐνιοι μὲν οὖβ Πυθαγόραν μεδὲ ἕν καταλιπεῖν σύγγραμμά φασιν παίζοντες. Ἡράκλειτος γοῦν ὁ φυσσικὸς μονονουχὶ κέκραγε καί φησι. "Πυθαγόρης Μνησάρχου ἱστορίην ἤσκησεν ἀνθρώπων μάλιστα πάντων καὶ ἐκλεξάμενος ταύτας τὰς συγγραφὰς ἐποιήσατο ἑαυτοῦ σοφίην, πολυμαθείην, κακοτεχνίην." Yonge translated it, "Now, some people say that Pythagoras did not leave behind him a single book; but they talk foolishly; for Heraclitus, the natural philosopher, speaks plainly enough of him saying, 'Pythagoras, the son of Mnesarchus, was the most learned of all men in history; and having selected from these writings, he thus formed his own wisdom, and extensive learning, and ***mischevious art***" (Yonge, *Diogenes Laërtius, The Lives And Opinions of Eminent Philosophers*, p. 340) Compare the version of Hicks: "There are some who insist, absurdly

enough, that Pythagoras left no writings whatever. At all events, Heraclitus, the physicist, almost shouts in our ear, "Pythagoras, son of Mnesarchus,
practised inquiry beyond all other men, and in this selection of his writings
made himself a wisdom of his own, showing much learning, but *poor workmanship.*" (Hicks, *Diogenes Laertius Lives of Eminent Philosophers,*Vol. 2 pp.
324–325). Cf. Huebner *Diogenis Laertii De Vitis, Dogmatis Et Apophthegmatis
Clarorum Philosophorum Libri Decem,* Vol. 2, p. 242.

"sometimes taken in a good sense; Gregory Nazianzus, *Adversus Julianus,*
Oratio 4. ἐπεὶ καὶ οὗτοι μιμεῖσθαι μεν λέγονται τῶν ανθρωπίων τινὰ
δελεασμάτων μεν τοι κακοτέχνως προστιθεμένων τούτοις καὶ ἁλίσκονται, the text being so to be restored."

(Cf. Migne, *Patrologiae Cursus Completus, Gregorius Nazianzenus* Vol.
XXXV, *Contra Julianum imperatorem,* Cap.112, 87-88. p. 649. Note that the
Greek is significantly different from that given by Stanley: ἐπεὶ καὶ οὗ
τοι μιμεῖσθαι μὲν λέγονται τῶν ἀνθρωπίων τινὰ δελεασμάτων, κακοτε-
ʹχνως προστιθεμένων · τούτοις μέντοι καὶ ἁλίσκονται.) Cf. King, *Julian
the Emperor containing Gregory Nazianzen's Two Invectives and Libanius'
Monody,* p. 75 where κακοτέχνως was rendered "treacherous intention."
Stanley's suggestion that the word is sometimes taken in a "good sense"
would appear to be dependent on his own restoration and interpretation of
the text of Nazianzus, not followed by other authorities.

p. 344 note 238. κοτ' οἴσω "bear ill-will." The original Ms. of Diogenes
Laertius' *Lives of Eminent Philosophers* has κατοίσω, which was copied by
Stanley. Hicks rendered the phrase "suffer censure" Yonge translated it, "be
blamed."

(For οἴσω see Liddel Scott, *A Greek-English Lexicon* under φέρω. Cf.
Hicks, *Diogenes Laertius Lives of Eminent Philosophers,*Vol 2 p. 325. Yonge,
Diogenes Laërtius, The Lives And Opinions of Eminent Philosophers, p. 340)

p. 345 note 259. For τέχνη perhaps read εχνη. The Greek text of Iamblicus' *Life of Pythagoras* Cap. 19, 77 reads: καὶ ἄλλα τοιαῦτα τέχνη ιετορεῖ
ται τῆς τοῦ Ἀβαριδος δυνάμεως. Kiessling also noted that τέχνη, "art,
craft," is corrupt in this context. (Cf. *Iamblichi Chalcidensis Ex Coele-Suria
De Vita Pythagorica,* Vol. 1, p. 200-201) The sentence requires the meaning
of "mark" or "sign," hence Kiessling's Latin translation *Etiam alia similia
potentiae Abaradis* **vestigia** *memorantur.* "Many other such signs of the power
of Abaris were reported."

p. 346 note 297. For σωθῆνας reading, ὡς φῆναι κατὰ τὸν Πλάτωνα, "Thus,
as said by Plato …"

From Iamblicus' Life of Pythagoras, Chapter 16, the passage in full reads:

ἀπὸ δὴ τούτων ἀπάντων δαιμονίως ἰᾶτο καὶ ἀπεκάθαιρε τὴν ψυχὴν, καὶ ἀνεζωπύρει τὸ θεῖον ἐν αὐτῇ καὶ ἀπέσωζε, καὶ περιῆγεν ἐπὶ τὸ ΄νοητὸν τὸ θεῖον ὄμμα, κρεῖττον ὂν σωθῆναι κατὰ τὸν Πλάτωνα μυρίων σαρχίνων ομμάτων.

"By all these inventions, therefore, he divinely healed and purified the soul, resuscitated and saved its divine part, and conducted to the intelligible its divine eye, which, as Plato says, is better worth saving than ten thousand corporeal eyes."

The reference to Plato is from his *Republic, Book VII, Chapter X*, where in the dialogue, the argument is made that the study of science and mathematics, while difficult, enlightens the soul: "that by these branches of study some organ of the soul in each individual is purified and rekindled like fire, after having been destroyed and blinded by other kinds of study – an organ, indeed, better worth saving than ten-thousand eyes, since by that alone truth can be seen."

This same passage from Plato is also quoted by Nicomachus in his Introduction To Arithmetic (Chapter 3) as a defense of the four sciences of Arithmetic, Geometry, Music and Astronomy.

(Kiessling, *Iamblichi Chalcidensis Ex Coele-Suria De Vita Pythagorica*, Vol. 1, p. 148. Taylor, *Iamblicus' Life of Pythagoras*, p. 37. Burges, *Works of Plato*, Vol. 2, p. 217. D'Ooge, *Introduction to Arithmetic, by Nicomachus of Gerasa* (pp. 181-190))

p. 346 note 308. For ἄγριος Αἰνεὺς, "savage Aenean" perhaps read Ἀγριανεύς "Agrinean."

Kiessling (*Iamblichi Chalcidensis Ex Coele-Suria De Vita Pythagorica*, Vol. 1 p. 188) mentions the option ἄγριος Αἰνεὺς (*rusticus Aeneus*) but suggested Αἰγεῖος "Aegean" and rendered the Latin, *Hippomedon Aegeus*, "Hippomedon the Aegean." Thomas Taylor rendered it "Hippomedon, an Aegean." (Taylor, *Iamblicus' Life of Pythagoras*, p.46) Cf. Guthrie, *The Pythagorean Sourcebook and Library*, p. 79. Stanley himself lists Hippomedon as one of the Aegeans. (See page 113.)

p. 346 note 310. For ἱματιλινά, perhaps read καὶ ἱμάτια λινᾶ. Yet Laertius expressly saith, that linen was not as yet used in those parts.

The reference to the linen garment is from Iamblicus, *Life of Pythagoras*, Cap. 21. Kiessling also corrected the reading to ἱμάτια λινᾶ, "linen garment," Diogenes Laertius however wrote: στολὴ δ᾽ αὐτῷ λευκή, καθαρά, καὶ στρώματα λευκὰ ἐξ ἐρίων· τὰ γὰρ λινᾶ οὔπω εἰς ἐκείνους ἀφῖκτο τοὺς τόπους. "His robe was white and spotless, his quilts of white wool, for linen had not yet reached those parts."

(Kiessling, Iamblichi Chalcidensis Ex Coele-Suria De Vita Pythagorica, Vol. 1, p. 216. Hicks, Diogenes Laertius, Lives of Eminent Philosophers, Vol. 2, pp. 336-337.)

p. 346 note 312. From Iamblichus restore Diodorus in Excerpta Valesiana page 245. reading οὐδὲν γὰρ μεῖζον πρὸς επιστήμην καὶ φρόνησιν, ἔπι δὲ τῶν πάντων ἐμπειρειαν, τοῦ δυνασθαι πολλὰ μνημονευειν.

The fragment from Excerpta Valesiana refers to a fragment of Diodorus Siculus' Bibliotheca Historica, originally published by Henricus Valesius in 1636. The text may be found in Dindorf, ΔΙΟΔΩΡΟΥ ΒΙΒΛΙΟΘΗΚΗ ΙΣΤΟΡΙΚΗ Diodori Bibliotheca Historica, Vol. 2, p. 166, where the actual fragment from Liber X, Chapter 5, Section 1 reads:

... πρὸς ἐπιστήμην καὶ φρονεσιν, ἔτι δὲ τῶν πάντων ἐμπειριαν τε τοῦ δύνασθαι πολλὰ μνημονεύειν...

Stanley's restoration comes from Iamblicus' Life of Pythagoras, Chapter 29. Cf. Kiessling, Iamblichi Chalcidensis Ex Coele-Suria De Vita Pythagorica, Vol. I, page 350 line 166: οὐδὲν γὰρ μεῖζον πρὸς επιστήμην καὶ ἐμπειρειαν και φρόνησιν τοῦ δυνασθαι μνημονευειν. "the ability of remembering was most important for experience, science and wisdom." See also Booth, The Historical Library of Diodorus The Sicilian in Fifteen Books to which are added The Fragments of Diodorus and Those published by H. Valesius, I. Rhodomannus, and F. Ursinus, Vol. 2 page 576 (No. 38). Where the entire passage of the fragment from Diodorus translated reads, "The Pythagoreans had a great art in improving their memories, and to that end employed their utmost care and diligence. For the first thing they did constantly after they rose from their beds in a morning, was to recollect and call to mind every thing they had done the day before, from the morning to the evening; if if they had time and leisure, they would go back to examine the actions of the second, third, and fourth days, and sometimes farther, conceiving it very helpful and advantageous for improving the memory, and increasing knowledge." From this, one can see that Stanley drew heavily on Diodorus for the text immediately preceding the note, and adding from Iamblicus.

p. 347 note 323. Τὸ καθ᾽ ἑκάτερον ὡρισμένον.

Also rendered the same by Friedlein, Procli Diadochi In Primum Euclidis Elementorum Librum Commentarii, p. 36. 'Barocius' refers to Franciscus Barocius (the Latin name of Francesco Barozzi) who published a translation of Euclid's Elements in Venice in the year 1560.

p. 347 note 324. ὡς οὐ τὴν καθ᾽ ἑκάτερον ἀπειρίαν γνώσει λαβεῖν κενόν.

Freidlein read this passage ὡς οὐχ ἐνὸν τὴν καθ᾽ ἑκάτερον ἀπειρίαν γνώσει περιλαβεῖν. (Friedlein, *Procli Diadochi In Primum Euclidis Elementorum Librum Commentarii*, p. 36)

p. 347 note 326. Ἀριθμετικῆς εἰσαγωγῆς "Introduction to Arithmetic" The subsequent text, "so supply the Title, as a page. 30. 35. 44. 62. 76) cap. 4. refers to the Greek Ἀριθμετικῆς εἰσαγωγῆς which is the title of the book by Nicomachus by that name, known by its Latin name *Introductionis Arithmeticae*. In Chapter 3, Nicomachus quotes Plato's *Republic*, Book VII, Chapter X, wherein the four *mathemata* of the *quadrivium* (the "higher subjects" — Arithmetic, Geometry, Music and "Spheric," i.e. Astronomy) are described and defended: "arithmetic for reckoning, distributions, contributions, exchanges and partnerships, geometry for sieges, the founding of cities and sanctuaries, and the partition of land, music for festivals, entertainment, and the worship of the gods, and the doctrine of the spheres, or astronomy, for farming, navigation and other undertaking, revealing beforehand the proper procedure and suitable season."

Chapter 4 of Nicomachus' "Introduction to Arithmetic" clarifies the reasoning to select Arithmetic as the first of the four methods (Music, Mathematics, Geometry or Spheric) should be studied first. The Chapter is given in full below:

"Which then of these four methods must we first learn? Evidently, the one which naturally exists before them all, is superior and takes the place of origin and root and, as it were, of mother to the others. And this is arithmetic, not solely because we said that it existed before all the others in the mind of the creating God like some universal and exemplary plan, relying upon which as a design and archetypal example the creator of the universe sets in order his material creations and makes them attain to their proper ends; but also because it is naturally prior in birth inasmuch as it abolishes other sciences with itself, but is not abolished together with them. For example, 'animal' is naturally antecedent to 'man,' for abolish 'animal' and 'man' is abolished; but if 'man' be abolished, it no longer follows that 'animal' is abolished at the same time. And again, 'man' is antecedent to 'schoolteacher,' but if 'schoolteacher' is nonexistent, it is still possible for 'man' to be. Thus since it has the property of abolishing the other ideas with itself, it is likewise the older. Conversely, that is called younger and posterior which implies the other thing with itself, but is not implied by it, like 'musician,' for this always implies 'man.' Again, take 'horse'; 'animal' is always implied along with 'horse,' but not the reverse; for if 'animal' exists, it is not necessary that 'horse' should exist, nor if 'man' exists, must 'musician' also be implied.   So it is with the foregoing sciences; if geometry exists, arithmetic must also needs be implied, for it is with the help of this latter that we can speak of triangle, quadrilateral, octahedron, icosahedron, double, eightfold, or one and one-half times, or anything else of the sort which is used as a term by geometry, and such things cannot be conceived of without the numbers that are implied with each one. For how can 'triple' exist, or be spoken of, unless the number 3 exists beforehand, or 'eightfold' without 8? But on the contrary, 3, 4, and the rest might be without the figures existing to which they give names. Hence arithmetic abolishes geometry along with itself, but is not abolished by it, and while it is implied by geometry, it does not itself imply geometry."

(Hoche, ΝΙΚΟΜΑΧΟΥ ΓΕΡΑΣΗΝΟΥ ΠΥΘΑΓΟΡΙΚΟΥ ΑΡΙΘΜΗ-ΤΙΚΗ ΕΙΣΑΓΩΓΗ, *Nicomachi Geraseni Pythagorei Introductionis Arithmeticae*, pp. 9–10, D'Ooge, *Introduction to Arithmetic*, by Nicomachus of Gerasa (pp. 181–190)

p. 347 note 342. Eustratius, *Ethica Nicomachea*.1 & Servius, *Incipit Expositio Primae Eclogae*, VIII.

Cf. Virgil, *Ecologue* VIII:

"Threefold first I twine about thee these diverse triple-hued threads, and thrice round these altars I draw thine image: an odd number is god's delight." (McKail, *The Eclogues and Georgics of Virgil*, p. 29)

p. 354 note 599. Meibomius seems to mistake the meaning of καταλη-φθέντα, and therefore puts a point after λεγομένη.

The quote is from Nicomachus' 'Manual of Harmonics' (ΑΡΜΟΝΙΚΟΝ ΕΓΧΕΙΡΙΔΙΟΝ).

Marcus Meibom, in the Greek text of his *Nicomachi Harmonices* p. 10 in *Antiquae Musicae*, Vol. 1, erroneously places a period after λεγομένη. The correct Greek text is supplied by Jan, *Musici Scriptoris Graeci* p. 245, given below with a translation by Mike Estell:

Τὴν δὲ κατ᾽ ἀριθμὸν ποσότητα ταύτην ἤτε διὰ τεσσάρων χορδῶν ἀπόστασις, ἤτε διὰ πέντε, καὶ ἡ κατ᾽ ἀμφοτέρων σύνοδον, διὰ πασῶν λεγομένη, καὶ ὁ προσκείμενος μεταξὺ τῶν δύο τετραχόρδων τόνος, τρόπῳ τινὶ τοιούτῳ ὑπὸ τοῦ Πυθαγόρου καταληφθέντι ἔχειν ἐβεβαιώθη.

"After the interval of four chords, that of five chords, and that by the joining of both, call diapason, and the tone added between the two four-chord intervals, were confirmed to have this numerical quantity, in some such manner seized upon by Pythagoras."

Whereas Meibom has καταληφθέντα, Jan's text from *Musici Scriptoris Graeci* correctly gives καταληφθέντι, which is the masculine dative with the final letter being iota, not alpha. The word is the aorist passive participle of καταλαμβάνω, "seize, catch" or "constrain." In the sentence above, καταληφθέντι modifies the phrase τρόπῳ τινὶ τοιούτῳ, "in some such manner." It refers to the manner in which Pythagoras came to establish the numerical quantity of intervals with the musical chords, which he "seized upon." The phrase, "in some such manner," refers to the following sentence which describes Pythagoras' trip to the Blacksmith shop. As Stanley observes, Meibom mistakes the meaning, or function in the sentence, of καταληφθέντι, not understanding it to modify τρόπῳ τινὶ τοιούτῳ, but apparently relating back to the phrase "the tone added between the two four-chord intervals," with a meaning something akin to "comprehended." καταλαμβάνω can mean "to seize with the mind, comprehend, understand," and this may have been the basis of his error. The period following λεγομένη may not be related to this error at all, and may just be a simple misprint in the Greek text printed by Meibom. He does not insert a period in the middle of the Latin text as he does in the Greek.

(For the Greek translation and scholarly commentary on this difficult passage above, we are indebted to Mike Estell.)

P. 355 note 605. πρὸς ἑαυτὸν ἀπηλλάγη, Meibomius otherwise.

The quotation is from Nicomachus' *Harmonicum Enchiridium*, which is verbatum with Iamblicus' *Life of Pythagoras*, Chapter 26:

σηκώματα ἀκριβῶς ἐκλαβὼν καὶ ῥοπὰς ἰσαιτάτας τῶν ῥαιστήρων πρὸς ἑαυτὸν ἀπηλλάγη. "After carefully examining the weights of the hammers and their impacts, which were identical, he went home." Marcus Meibom had the correct Greek πρὸς ἑαυτὸν ἀπηλλάγη but his Latin translation, *intra se est conversus*, "he returned by himself," is faulty, hence Stanley's note. Kiessling rendered it *domum rediit*, "he returned home." (Meibom, *Nicomachi Harmonices* p. 11 in *Antiquae Musicae* Vol. 1, Jan, *Musici Scriptoris Graeci*, p. 246., Levin, *The Manual of Harmonics of Nicomachus the Pythagorean*, p.83, Kiessling, *Iamblichi Chalcidensis Ex Coele-Suria De Vita Pythagorica*, Vol. 1, p. 248.)

p. 355 note 606. ἰσοστρόφους, which Meibomius, contrary to all MSS. Would change unnecessarily into ἰσορρόπους and renders *aeque graves*.

In the main body of the text Meibom printed ἰσοστρόφους which is correct. In his notes to the text on p. 48 however, he discussed ἰσορρόπων "in balance" and ἰσοστάθμων "equal in weight" in support of his Latin translation *aeque graves* (equal weight). The word ἰσοστρόφους means literally "equally twisted," and refers to the ropes. (See Meibom, *Nicomachi Harmonices* pp. 11 and 48 in *Antiquae Musicae* Vol. 1, and Liddell Scott, *A Greek-English Lexicon*, p. 839b under ἰσο-στάδην.)

p. 355 note 617. Reading ἀπὸ τῶν ἔργων.
Kiessling read it as ἐπὶ τῶν ἔργων. (*Iamblichi Chalcidensis Ex Coele-Suria De Vita Pythagorica*, Vol. 1 p. 238)

p. 356 note 654. "Reading ὅταν γὰρ εὐθείας ἐκκειμένης τὸ δοθὲν χωρίον πάσῃ τῇ εὐθείᾳ συμπαρατείνῃς, τότε παραβάλλειν ἐκεῖνο τὸ χωρίον φασίν, ὅταν δὲ μεῖζον, etc." (Cf. Freidlein, *Procli Diadochi In Primum Euclidis Elementorum Librum Commentarii*, p. 419-420.)

p. 357 note 676. For an English translation of Censorinus' *De Die Natale* ("The Natal Day"), and specifically Chapter XIII, on the "Music of the Spheres" quoted by Stanley, see Maude, *Die Die Natale by Censorinus*, pp. 10–11. For the Latin text, Cf. Hultsch, *CENSORINI, DE DIE NATALI LIBER* pp. 22–24."

p. 358 note 727. "Perhaps οὗτος (ἔφη) οὐ παύσῃ χαλεπώτερον σέαυτῷ κατασκευάζων τὸ δεσμωτήριον. See St. Basil of Caesarea, *Homilia ad Psalm. XIX.*"

The quotation is from from Basil's ΠΡΟΣ ΤΟΥΣ ΝΕΟΥΣ ΟΡΩΣ ΕΛΛΗ-ΝΙΚΩΝ ᾿ΩΦΕΛΟΙΝΤΟ ΛΟΓΩΝ, *To young men on how they might profit from Greek Literature*. ("Greek Literature" is alternately translated, "Pagan Literature" or "Profane Works") In Migne's *Patrologiæ Cursus Completus, Series Græca. Vol. 31* this work is listed as one of the Sermons, and falls between Homily 21 and 23. The 24th Homily is *Contra Sabellianos, et Arium, et Anomœos*. The entire quote, with a better restoration, reads:

καὶ τοῦ Πυθαγόρου μεμνῆσθαι ὃς τῶν συνόντων τινὰ καταμαθὼν γυμνασίοις τε καὶ σιτίοις ἑαυτὸν εὖ μάλα κατασαρχοῦντα, οὗτος ἔφη. οὐ παύσῃ χαλεπώτερον σεαυτῷ κατασκευάζων τὸ δεσμωτήριον.

"And it will be remembered of Pythagoras, that calling one of his familiars from the gymnastics and eating, which were fattening him very much, he said, 'Will you not cease making your imprisonment harder for yourself?' (Jacks, *St. Basil and Greek Literature*, p. 45) These words of Pythagoras were assigned by Stobaeus to Plato (Serm. 77)

For the Greek text see Migne, *Patrologiæ Cursus Completus, Series Græca. Vol. 31*, pp. 583-584, or for Greek text with another translation, Cf. Defarrari, *Saint Basil: The Letters & Address To Young Men On Reading Greek Literature*, Vol. 4, pp. 422-423.

The final portion of the note refers to St. Basil of Caesarea's, *Homilia ad Psalm. XXIX*, which contains the following condemnation of gluttony:

"On the other hand, what is uglier or more disgusting than a soul given over to base passions? Look at the hot-headed person: he is like a wild beast.

Consider the slave of lust or gluttony: who can bear the sight of him?" (PG 29, 316)

p. 358 note 727. "Reading αὐτὸν according to Stobaeus, *Florilegium* 99, who cites this fragment but of Aristoxenus; perhaps it belonged to his Book, *De Vitae Pythagorae*."

See above, page 373, note to page 99. By αὐτὸν, Stanley means αὐτὸς ἔφη, "He said it," referring to Pythagoras, since Stobaeus credits the source as Aristoxenus, but relates it as a quotation from Pythagoras himself.

p. 360 note 787. Laertius, *De Vitis Philosophorum*, Liber I, Life of Pittacus, Chap. 8.

The "Epigram of Callimachus upon Pittacus" is in full, as follows:

'Hyrradius' prudent son, old Pittacus
The pride of Mitylene, once was asked
By an Atarnean stranger; "Tell me, sage,
I have two marriages proposed to me;
One maid my equal is in birth and riches;
The other's far above me; which is best?
Advise me now which shall I take to wife?"
Thus spoke the stranger; but the aged prince,
Raising his old man's staff before his face,
Said, "These will tell you all you want to know;"
And pointed to some boys, who with quick lashes
Were driving whipping tops along the street.
"Follow their steps," said he; so he went near them
And heard them say, "Let each now mind his own."—
So when the stranger heard the boys speak thus,
He pondered on their words, and laid aside
Ambitious thoughts of an unequal marriage.
As then he took to shame the poorer bride,
So too do you, O reader, mind thy own.'

(Yonge, *Diogenes Laertius, Lives of Eminent Philosophers*, p. 37)

p. 361 note 830. These are termed νοῦς ["intelligence"], φρὴν ["reason"], θυμὸς ["passion"]. Νοῦς ["intelligence"] and θυμὸς ["passion"] are in other living creatures, φρὴν ["reason"], only in man.

τὴν δ᾽ ἀνθρώπου ψυχὴν διαρεῖσθαι τριχῇ, εἴς τε νοῦν καὶ φρένας καὶ θυμόν. νοῦν μὲν οὖν καί θυμὸν εἶναι καὶ ἐν τοῖς ἄλλοις ζώοις, φρένας δὲ μόνον ἐν ἀνθρώπῳ.

"The soul of man, he says, is divided into three parts: intelligence, reason, and passion. Intelligence and passion are possessed by other animals as well, but reason by man alone." (Hicks, *Diogenes Laertius, Lives of Eminent Philosophers*, Vol. 2, p. 347)

p. 361 note 831. λαλοῦσι μὲν γὰρ οὗτοι, οὐ φράζουσι δε, They talk, but cannot speak.

For the Greek text, see Wyttenbach, ΠΛΟΥΤΑΡΧΟΥ ΤΟΥ ΧΑΙΡΩΝΕΩΣ ΤΑ ΗΘΙΚΑ *PLUTARCHI CHÆRONENSIS MORALIA*, Vol. 4, part 2, p. 668. λαλοῦσι means "inarticulate speech" or "chatter." (Cf. the reading by Vernardakis, *Plutarchi Chaeronensis Moralia*, Vol. 5, p. 364.)

p. 361 note 835. Anonymous, *De Vita Pythagorae* apud Photius, Chap. 10. For δώδεκα ["Twelve"], perhaps δέκα ["ten"].

The Greek text in the Anonymous *De Vita Pythagorae* preserved by Photius, Chapter 10 reads:

῞Οτι ἡ ὄψις, κατὰ Πυθαγόραν, καὶ Πλάτωνα, καὶ ᾿Αριστοτέλην, τῶν δώδεκα χρωμάτων ἐστὶ κριτική. λευκοῦ καὶ μέλανος, καὶ τῶν μεταξὺ ξανθοῦ, φαιοῦ, ὠχροῦ, ἐρυθροῦ, κυανοῦ, ἀλουργοῦ, λαμποῦ, ὀρφνίνου.

"According to Pythagoras, Plato and Aristotle, sight is the judge of the twelve colors, white and black being the extremes of those in between: yellow, tawny, pale, red, blue, green, light blue, and gray".

One would expect a list of twelve colors to follow, however only ten colors are given. Thus Stanley corrects the text from "twelve" (δώδεκα) to "ten" (δέκα.)

(Kiessling, *Iamblichi Chalcidensis Ex Coele-Suria De Vita Pythagorica*, Vol. 2, pp. 106–108.)

p. 362 note 837. Of which the Ancients made their Mirrors, see Callimachus, *Hymn 5*.

The fifth Hymn of Callimachus gives the name given by the Greeks to the material from which mirrors were made: "bring not, ye companions of the Bath, for Pallas perfumes nor alabasters (for Athena loves not mixed unguents), neither bring ye a mirror. Always her face is fair, and, even when the Phrygian judged the strife on Ida, the great goddess looked not into orichak."

(A.W. Mair, *Callimachus and Lycophron*, p. 113) Orichak (ὀρείχαλκος) "mountain copper" was a mixture of copper and zinc, frequently given as "Aurichalcum," or Brass.

(Cf. Liddell Scott, *A Greek-English Lexicon*, p. 1247b)

p. 363 note 901. For τὴν θαλατταν ἐκάλει εἶνα δάκρυον, read ἐκάλει Κρόνου δάκρουν, for so Clement of Alexandria, *Stromateis*, Liber V, Chap. 8.

Stanley intended us to read, τὴν θαλατταν ἐκάλει Κρόνου δάκρουν, "the Sea, a tear of Saturn," supplying the wording from Clement of Alexander's *Stromata*, Liber V, Chapter 8: τοιαῦτα καὶ οἱ Πυθαγόρειοι ἠνισσοντο, Φερσεφόνης μὲν κύρας τοὺς πλανήτας, Κρόνου δε δάκρυον τὴν θάλασσαν ἀλληγοροῦτες. "In the same way too, the Pythagoreans figuratively called the planets the "dogs of Persephone," and to the sea they applied the metaphorical appellation of "the tears of Kronos."

The name of Saturn was omitted by Porphyry, and read only "the Sea, a tear." The full epithet was restored by Kenneth Guthrie, but who preferred translating Κρόνος using the Greek "Kronos" rather than the Roman equivalent "Saturn." (Dindorf, *Clementis Alexandrini Opera*, Vol. 3, p. 40; Kiessling, *Iamblichi Chalcidensis Ex Coele-Suria De Vita Pythagorica*, Vol. 2, p. 72., and Guthrie, *The Pythagorean Sourcebook and Library*, p.131.)

p. 364 note 907. Perhaps ἀπιστήσομεν, ["disbelieve".]

For "disbelieve." Cf. Liddell Scott, *A Greek-English Lexicon*, p.189b, ἀπιστ-εύω. In the listing of the Pythagorean Symbols in the *Protrepticus* of Iamblicus, the 25th Symbol is, περὶ θεῶν μηθὲν θαυμαστὸν ἀπίστει, μηδὲ περὶ θείων δογμάτων, "Concerning the gods, disbelieve nothing wonderful, nor concerning Divine Doctrines." When explained, it is switched to the position of Symbol #4. In this book, it is both listed and explained as Symbol #4. In the *Protrepticus* the explanation reads:

τὸ δὲ περὶ θεῶν μεδὲν θαυμαστὸν ἀπίστει μηδὲ περὶ θείων δογμάτων προτρέπει μετιέναι καὶ κτᾶσθαι ἐκεῖνα τὰ μαθήματα, δι᾽ ἅ οὐκ ἀπιστήσεις οὐκέτι περὶ θεῶν καὶ περὶ θείων δογμάτων ἔχων τὰ μαθήματα καὶ τὰς ἐπιστημονικὰς ἀποδείξεις.

Stanley's correction to ἀπίστειν appears to be unique, not followed by either Piscelli or Edouard Des Places. Thomas Moore Johnson approached the text a bit differently and translated, "For it urges us to acquire a science of that kind through which we shall be in no respect deficient in things asserted about the gods." (Cf. Pistelli, *Iamblichi Protrepticus Ad Fidem Codicis Florentini*, pp. 107 & 121, Des Places, *Jamblique Protreptique*, pp. 134 & 146, and Johnson, *Iamblicus: The Exhortation to Philosophy*, p. 98)

p. 365 note 963. πόθακόντων perhaps is for προσηκόντων. Doric.

The Doric word πόθακόντων the equivalent of the Attic πρροσηκόντων, "proper," or as Stanley has it, "good." From *Timaei Locri, De Anima Mundi*:

Καὶ ταῦτα μεν αἰτία ἐκ τῶν γενετόρων καὶ στοιχείων ἐπάγεται μᾶλλον ἢ ἐξ ἅμεων. ᾧ τι μὴ ἀργία ἔστίν, ἀφισταμένων ἡμων τῶν ποθακόντων ἔργων.

Thomas Tobin, following the restoration of William Marg to the first line and reads, Κατά ταῦτα κακίας μεν etc...

"Accordingly, the cause of vice comes rather from our parents and from our own basic elements than from ourselves, granted that there is no laziness and that we do not shrink from our **proper** duties."

(Cf. Tobin, *Timaios of Locri, On the Nature of the World and the Soul*, pp. 66–67, Marg, *Timaeus Locrus. De Natura Mundi et Animae*, p. 146, Burges, *Works of Plato*, Vol. 6, p. 166, and Stallbaum, *Platonis Opera Omnia*, Vol. 7, p. 439)

BIBLIOGRAPHY

Ahrens, Heinrich. *Bucolicorum Graecorum Theocriti Bionis, Moschi reliquae: accedentibus incertorum idylliis*. 2 Vols. Leipzig (1855)

Ammonius, Hermae. *Ammonii Hermiae in Quinque Voces Porphyrii Commentarius*, Venice (1546)

Anderson, Walter. *The Philosophy of Ancient Greece investigated, in its Origin and Progress to the Æras of its Greatest Celebrity, in the Ionian, Italic and Athenian Schools*. London (1791)

Anthon, Charles. *Select Orations of Cicero. With English Notes, Critical and Explanatory, and Historical, Geographical, and Legal Indexes*. New York (1841)

Arndts, Ludwig. *Iulii Paulli Receptarum Sententiarum ad Filium Libri Quinque*. Bologna (1833)

Arnold, T.K. and Browne, H. *A Copious Phraseological English-Greek Lexicon*. London (1875)

Ashmand, J. M. *Ptolemy's Tetrabiblios or Quadripartite being four books of the influence of the stars*. London (1822)

Ast, Frederich. *Theologumena Arithmeticae ad Rarissimum Exemplum Parisiense Emendatius Descripta*. Leipzig (1817) Contains Nicomachus' *Arithmetica Introductio*.

Aucher, J.B. ΕΥΣΕΒΙΟΥ ΤΟΥ ΠΑΜΦΙΛΟΥ ΧΡΟΝΙΚΑ *Eusebii Pamphilii Caesariensis Episcopi Chronicon Bipartitum*. Venice (1818)

Babbitt, Frank Cole. *Plutarch, Moralia, Vol. 1*. London (1928)

Bailey, D. R. Shackleton. *Valerius Maximus, Memorable Doings And Sayings*. London (2000)

Baker, George. *The History of Rome by Titus Livius*. 6 vols. New York (1823)

Bandini, Angelo Maria. ΘΕΟΓΝΙΔΟΣ ΜΕΓΑΡΕΟΣ ΓΝΟΜΑΙ ΦΩΚΥΔΙΔΟΥ ΠΟΙΗΜΑ ΝΟΥΘΕΤΙΚΟΝ ΠΥΘΑΓΟΡΟΥ ΧΡΥΣΑ *Theognidis Megarensis Sententiae: Phocylidis Poema Admonitorium. Pythagorae Aurae Carmina*. Florintine (1766). Contains the Greek text of The Golden Verses

Barberinus, Cardinal Franciscus. *Porphyrii Philosophi Liber De Vita Pythagoræ*. Porphyry's Life of Pythagoras, Greek & Latin. Rome, (1630)

Barocius, Fancesco. *Amirandum illud, geometricum problema, XIII modis demonstratum*. Ghent (1587)

Bekker, Immanuel. *Aristotelis Graece, Vol. 1*. Berlin (1831). Contains Aristotle's *Analytica priora et posteriora* & *De Coela*

_____. *Aristotelis Opera*. Vols. 1-3 Oxford (1837)

_____. *Diodori Siculi, Bibliotheca Historica*. 4 Vols. Liepzig (1853)

_____. *Flavii Iosephi opera omnia*. 5 Vols. Leipzig (1856)

_____. *Homeri Odyssea*. Berlin (1843)

_____. *Suidae Lexicon*. Berlin (1854)

_____. *Thucydidis De Bello Peloponnesiaco Libri Octo*. Berlin (1846)

Beloe, William. *The Attic Nights of Aulus Gellius*. 3 Vols. London (1795)

Benn, Alfred William. *The Greek Philosophers*. 2 Vols. London (1882)

Bergk, Theodore. *Zeitschrift für die Alterthumswissenschaft*. Marburg (1847)

Bettenham, J. *Hierocles Alexandrinus in aurea carmina commentarus: Graece et latine*. London (1742) Hierocles' commentary on the Golden Verses of Pythagoras, Greek & Latin.

Blatchford, Samuel. *Elements of the Greek Language*, New York (1807)

Boissonade, Jean François. *Michael Psellus, De Operatione Daemonum*. Nuremberg 1838.

Booth, George. *The Historical Library of Diodorus The Sicilian in Fifteen Books to which are added The Fragments of Diodorus and Those published by H. Valesius, I. Rhodomannus, and F. Ursinus..* 2 Vols. London (1814)

Bostock, John & Riley, H.T. *The Natural History of Pliny*. 6 Vols. London (1890)

Boulliau, Ismael. ΘΕΩΝΟΣ ΣΜΥΡΝΑΙΟΥ ΠΛΑΤΟΝΙΚΟΥ, *Theonis Smyrnaei Platonici*. Paris (1644)

Bridgman, William. *Translations From The Greek, viz. Aristotle's Synopsis of The Virtues and Vices, The Similitudes of Demophilus. The Golden Sentences of Democrates, and The Pythagoric Symbols, With The Explanations of Iamblicus, To Which Are Added , The Pythagoric Sentences of Demophilus by Mr. Thomas Taylor*. London (1804)

Browne, R.W. *The Nicomachian Ethics of Aristotle*. Oxford (1850)

Bullions, Peter. *Principles of Latin Grammar; comprising the substance of the most approved grammars extant, with an appendix for the use of schools and colleges*. New York (1854)

Bünemann, J. L. *Lactantii Firmiani opera omnia quae exstant*. Leipzig (1739)

Burges, George. *Works of Plato*, 6 Vols. London (1838) <Vol. 6 has a translation of *Timaeus of Locri*.

Butler, H. E. *The Apologia and Florida of Apuleius of Madaura*. Oxford (1909) Contains an English translation of Apuleius' *Florida* and *The Apology*.

Capella, Martianus. *De Nuptiis Philologiae et Mercurii et de septem Artibus liberalibus libri novem*. Erfurt (1500)

_____. (Ed. Franz Eyssenhardt) *Martianus Capella*. Leipzig (1866). Includes *De Nuptiis Philologiae et Mercurii et de septem Artibus liberalibus libri novem*.

_____. (Ed. Hugo Grotius) *Satyricon: in quo de nuptiis Philologiae & Mercurij libri duo, & de septem artibus liberalibus libri singulares*. Leiden (1599)

Cobet, C.G. *Diogenes Laertii de Clarorum Philosophorum*. Paris (1878)

Codrington, Robert. *The History of Justin, Taken Out of the Four and Forty Books of Trogus Pompeius: Containing the Affairs of All Aages and Countries, Both in Peace and War, from the Beginning of the World Until the Time of the Roman Emperors*. London (1688)

Conybeare, F. C. *Philostratus, The Life of Apollonius of Tyana. The Epistles of Apollonius and the Treatise of Eusebius*. 2 Vols. London (1912)

Cosmopoulos, Michael B. *Greek Mysteries, The Archaeology and Ritual of Ancient Greek Secret Cults*. London (2003)

Crucius, G. *A Complete Greek and English Lexicon of the Poems of Homer and the Homeridæ*. Trans. Henry Smith. Hartford (1844)

Cruse, C.F. *The Ecclesiastical History of Eusebius of Pamphilus, Bishop of Cæsarea, in Palestine.* London (1851)

Curterio, J. ἹΕΡΟΚΛΕΟΥΣ ΦΙΛΟΣΟΦΟΥ ὙΠΟΜΝΗΜΑ ἘΙΣ ΤΑ ΤΩΝ ΠΥΘΑΓ-ΟΡΕΙΩΝ ἔπη τὰ χρυσᾶ *Hieroclis Philosophi Commentarius in Aurea Pythagoreorum Carmina.* London (1673). Hieracles' commentary on The Golden Verses of Pythagoras, Greek & Latin.

Dacier, M. *The Life of Pythagoras With His Symbols and Golden Verses.* London (1707)

Dakyns, H. G. *The Works of Xenophon.* 4 Vols. London (1897)

Davis, J. M. *Tulli Ciceronis De Finibis Bonorum Et Malorum Libri Quinque.* Oxford (1809)

Dechair, Edward. *Sancti Athenagorae Atheniensis Philosophi Legatio Pro Christianis.* Oxford (1706)

Defarrari, Joseph R. & McGuire, Martin R.P. *Saint Basil: The Letters & Address To Young Men On Reading Greek Literature.* 4 Vols. London (1970)

Des Places, Edouard. *Jamblique Protreptique.* Paris (1989)

Deubner, Ludwig August. *Iamblichi De Vita Pythagorica Liber.* Leipzig (1899)

De Gelder, J. J. *Theon Smyrnaeus.* ΘΕΩΝΟΣ ΣΜΥΡΝΑΙΟΥ ΠΛΑΤΟΝΙΚΟΥ, ΤΩΝ ΚΑΤΑ ΑΡΙΘΜΕΤΙΚΗΝ ΧΡΗΣΙΜΩΝ ΕΙΣ ΤΗΝ ΤΟΥ ΠΛΑΤΩΝΟΣ ΑΝΑΓ-ΝΩΣΙΝ. *Theonis Smyrnaei Platonici, Expositio Eorum, Quæ in Arithmeticis Ad Platonis Lectionem Utilia Sunt.* Lyons (1827)

Diehl, Ernst. *Procli Diadoche In Platonis Timaeum Commentaria.* 3 Vols. Leipzig (1903)

Dindorf, Ludwig August. ΔΙΟΔΩΡΟΥ ΒΙΒΛΙΟΘΗΚΗ ΙΣΤΟΡΙΚΗ *Diodori Bibliotheca Historica.* 5 Vols. Leipzig (1866)

Dindorf, Wilhelm. *Aristides.* 2 Vols. Leipzig (1829)

_____. *Clementis Alexandrini Opera.* 4 Vols. Oxford (1869)

Deubner, Ludwig. *Iamblichi, De Vita Pythagorica Liber.* Stuttgart (1975)

Dods, Marcus. *The Works of Aurelius Augustine Bishop of Hippo. Vol. XIII, The Letters of Augustine,* Vol. 2. Edinburgh (1875)

D'Ooge, Martin Luther. Introduction to Arithmetic, by Nicomachus of Gerasa (ca. 100 AD), Macmillan, New York (1926)

Donnegan, James. *A New Greek and English Lexicon; principally on the plan of the Greek and German Lexicon of Schneider.* New York (1838)

Duncan, William. *Cicero's Select Orations Translated Into English; with the original Latin, from the best editions, in the opposite page; and notes historical, critical, and explanatory. Designed for the use of schools, as well as private gentlemen.* London (1792)

Emmenessius, Jacob. *P. Virgilii Maronis Opera in tres tomos divisa: cum integris notis Servii, Philargyrii, nec non J. Pierii variis lectionibus, & selectissimis plerisque commentariis Donati, Probi, Nannii, Sabini, Germani, Cerdæ, Taubmanni, & aliorum.* 3 Vols. Leiden (1676)

Enfield, William. *The History Of Philosophy,* 2 vols. London (1791)

Evelyn-White, Hugh G. *Hesiod, The Homeric Hymns and Homerica*. London (1920)

Everitt, Edward. *Greek Grammar*, Boston (1822)

Fairbanks, Arthur. *The First Philosophers of Greece, An edition and translation of the remaining fragments of the Pre-Sokratic philosophers, together with a translation of the most important accounts of their opinions contained in the early epitomes of their works*. New York (1898)

Fenelon, M. *Lives of the Ancient Philosophers*. London (1825)

Fennell, C. *Pindar: The Olympian and Pythian Odes*. Cambridge (1893)

Fitzgerald, Augustine. *The Letters of Synesius of Cyrene: Translated into English with introduction and notes*. Oxford (1926)

Flach, Johannes. *Hesiodi quæ feruntur Carmina ad optimorum codicum fidem*. Leipzig (1899)

Fletcher, James. *Epicteti stoici philosophi Enchiridion: unà cum Cebetis Thebani Tabula. Quibus adjiciuntur hac editione Simplicii Commentarius in Enchiridion Epicteti. Item Arriani Commentariorum de Epicteti disputationibus, Lib. IV.* London (1670)

Fletcher, William. *The Works of Lactantius*. 2 Vols. Edinburgh (1871)

Forman, Lewis Leaming. *Aristophanes Clouds*. New York (1915)

Fowler, H. N. *Plato*, Vol. 1. London (1913)

Fowler, H. W. and F.G. *The Works of Lucian of Samosata, complete with exceptions specified in the Preface*. 4 Vols. Oxford (1905)

Frazer, J.G. *Pausanias's Description of Greece*. 6 Vols. London (1898)

Friedlein, G. *Anicii Manlii Torquati Severini Boetii De institutione arithmetica Libri duo*. Leipzig. (1867)

_____. *Procli Diadochi In Primum Euclidis Elementorum Librum Commentarii*. Liepzig (1873)

Gaisford, Thomas. ΙΩΑΝΝΟΥ ΣΤΟΒΑΙΟΥ ΑΝΘΟΛΟΓΙΟΝ *Joannis Stobæi Florilegium*, 4 Vols. Oxford (1822)

_____. *Poetæ Minories Gracæ*. Vol. 3. Leipzig (1823) Contains The Golden Verse of Pythagoras, Greek & Latin.

_____. ΘΕΟΔΩΡΕΤΟΥ ΕΠΙΣΚΟΠΟΥ ΚΥΡΟΥ ΕΛΛΗΝΙΚΩΝ ΠΑΘΗ-ΜΑΤΩΝ ΘΕΡΑΠΕΥΤΙΚΗ *Theodoreti Episcopi Cyrensis Græcarum Affectionum Curatio*. Oxford (1839)

Gellius, Aulus. *Noctes Atticae* (Editio Stereotypa) Leipzig. 1835

Gifford, E.H., *Eusebii Pamphili, Evangelicae Praeparationis Libri XV*, 5 Vols. Oxford (1903) <Greek with English translation of Eusebius' "Preparation For The Gospel"

Giraldi, L. & Casaubon, M. *Hierocles De Providentia & Fatu*. London (1673)

Godley, Alfred Denis. *Herodotus*. 4 Vols. London (1920)

Gow, James. *A Short History Of Greek Mathematics*. Cambridge (1884)

Goodman, Martin and Sarah. *Johann Reuchlin, On the Art of the Kabbalah. De Arte Cabalistica*. New York (1983, facsimile of the 1517 edition of *De Arte Cabalistica* with English translation.)

Goodwin, William W. *Plutarch's Morals. Translated from the Greek by Several Hands. Corrected and Revised by William W. Goodwin.* 5 Vols. Boston (1878)

Grote, George. *Aristotle.* 2 Vols. London (1872)

Groves, John. *A Greek and English Dictionary, comprising all the words in the writing of the most popular Greek Authors; with the difficult inflections in them and in the Septuagint and New Testament.* Boston (1842)

Guthrie, Kenneth Sylvan. *The Pythagorean Sourcebook and Library,* Grand Rapids (1987)

——————. *The Complete Works of Plotinus.* 4 Vols. Alpine, NJ (1918)

Guthrie, W.K.C. *Aristotle: On the Heavens.* Cambridge (1939)

Hagan, Hermann and Georg Christian Thilo. *Servii Grammatici qvi fervntvr in Vergilii carmina commentarii.* 3 Vols. Leipzig. (1881-1902) Contains Servius' commentary on Virgil.

Hamilton, H.C. and Falconer, W. *The Geography of Strabo.* 3 Vols. London (1856)

Harwood, Edward. *A View of the Various Editions of the Greek and Roman Classics.* London (1790)

Hearne, Thomas. *T. Livii Patavini Historiarum Ab Urbe Condita.* 6 Vols. Oxford (1708)

Heath, T. L. *The Thirteen Books of Euclid's Elements.* 3 Vols. Cambridge (1908)

Henry, John and James Parker. *M. Tulli Ciceronis Tuscularum Disputationum Libri Quinque.* Oxford (1856)

Hercheri, Rudolph. *Claudii Aeliani Varia Historia.* Leipzig (1870)

Hermann, Johann Gottfried. *M. Tulli Ciceronis de republica.* Leipzig (1823)

Heylbut, Gustav. *Eustratii Et Michaelis Et Anonyma In Ethica Nicomachea Commentaria.* Vol. 20 of *Commentaria in Aristotelem Graeca.* Berlin (1892) Eustratius' *Ethica Nicomachea.*

Hicks, R. D. *Diogenes Laertius, Lives of Eminent Philosophers,* 2 Vols. London (1925)

Hiller, E. *Theonis Smyrnaei, Philosophi Platonici, Expositio Rerum Mathematicarum ad Legendum Platonem Utilium.* Leipzig (1878)

Hitzig, Hermann & Blümner, Hugo. *Pausaniae Graeciae Descriptio.* 5 Vols. Berlin/ Leipzig. (1896-1907)

Hoche, Richard Gottfried. ΝΙΚΟΜΑΧΟΥ ΓΕΡΑΣΗΝΟΥ ΠΥΘΑΓΟΡΙΚΟΥ ΑΡΙΘΜΗΤΙΚΗ ΕΙΣΑΓΩΓΗ, *Nicomachi Geraseni Pythagorei Introductionis Arithmeticae Libri II.* Liepzig (1866)

Hodgkin, Thomas. *The Letters of Cassiodorus being a condensed translation of the Variae Epistolae of Magnus Aurelius Cassiodorus Senator.* London (1886)

Holden, Hubert Ashton. *Aristophanis Nubes.* London (1873-1874)

Hort, John Anthony & Mayor, Joseph B. *Clement of Alexandria Miscellanies Book VII.* London (1902)

Hultsch, Frederick. *Censorini, De Die Natali Liber.* Leipzig (1867)

Humphries, David. *The Apologeticks Of The Learned Athenian Philosopher Athenagoras I. For the Christian Religion II. For the Truth of the Resurrection.* London (1714)

Huebner, H. G. *Diogenis Laertii De Vitis, Dogmatis Et Apophthegmatis Clarorum Philosophorum Libri Decem*. 4 Vols. Leipzig (1828-1831)

Jacks, Leo V. *St. Basil and Greek Literature*. (in *The Catholic University of America Patristic Studies*, Vol. 1)Washington, DC. (1922)

Jacobitz, Karl. *Luciani Samosatensis Opera*. 3 Vols. Leipzig (1864-1866)

Jan, Karl. *Musici Scriptoris Graeci*. Liepzig (1895). Contains Nicomacus' *Harmonicum Enchiridium*.

Johnson, George. *The Arithmetical Philosophy of Nicomachus of Gerasa*. Lancaster, PA. (1916)

Johnson, Thomas Moore. *Iamblicus: The Exhortation to Philosophy*. Grand Rapids (1988)

Jones, John. *The Tyro's Greek and English Lexicon*. London (1825)

Jonsius, J. *De scriptoribus historiae philosophiae libri IV, cura Jo. Christophori Dornii, cum prefatione Burc. Gotthelfii Struvii De scriptoribus historiae philosophiae libri IV, cura Jo. Christophori Dornii, cum prefatione Burc. Gotthelfii Struvii*, Jena (1716)

Kappio, Joanne. *Valerii Maximi Factorumque dictorumque moemorabilium libri novem*. Leipzig (1782)

Keble, John. *Five Books of S. Irenaeus Bishop of Lyons Against Heresies*. London (1872)

Kempf, Karl Freidreich. *Valeri Maximi Factorum et dictorum memorabilium libri novem*. Berlin (1854)

Kiessling, M. Theophilus. *Iamblichi Chalcidensis Ex Coele-Suria De Vita Pythagorica*. 2 Vols. Leipzig (1815-1816) Contains Iamblicus' *Life of Pythagoras*, Porphyry's *Life of Pythagoras*, & *Life of Pythagoras* by Anonymous, preserved by Photius.

_____. ΙΟΝΝΟΥ ΤΟΥ ΤΖΕΤΖΟΥ ΒΙΒΛΙΟΝ ΙΣΤΟΡΙΚΗΣ ΤΗΣ ΔΙΑ ΣΤΙΧΩΝ ΠΟΛΙΤΙΚΩΝ ΑΛΦΑ ΔΕ ΚΑΛΟΥΜΕΝΗΣ, *IONNIS TZETZAE Historiarum Viarum Chiliades*. Leipzig (1826)

King, C.W. *Julian the Emperor containing Gregory Nazianzen's Two Invectives and Libanius' Monody* London (1888)

Laertius, Diogenes. ΒΙΩΝ ΚΑΙ ΓΝΩΜΩΝ ΤΩΝ ΕΝ ΦΙΛΟΣΟΦΙΑ ΕΥΔΟΚΙΜΗΣΑΝΤΩΝ, ΤΩΝ ΕΙΣ ΔΕΚΑ ΤΟ ΓΡΩΤΟΝ (Greek Text is Editio Princeps) Basil (1533)

Laertius, Diogenes. *De Vitis Philosophorum Libri X*. 2 Vols. Leipzig (1833)

Lang, Leaf & Meyers. *Homer's Iliad done into English Prose*. London (1921)

Laurent, Peter Edmund. *The Odes of Pindar in English Prose*. 2 Vols. Oxford (1824)

Leaf, Walter. *The Iliad*, 2 Vols. London (1886)

Leeuwen, J. Van. *Aristophanes Equites cum prolegomenis et commentariis*. Lyons (1800)

Leonard, William E. *The Fragments of Empedocles*. Chicago (1908)

Leveritt, F. P. *A New and Copious Lexicon of the Latin Language. Compiled chiefly from the Magnum Totius Latinitatis Lexicon of Faccialoti and Forcellini and the German Works of Scheller and Luenemann*. Boston (1839)

Lewis, Charlton T. *An Elementary Latin Dictionary*. New York (1894)

Liddell, George H. & Scott, Robert. A Greek-English Lexicon. Oxford (1968)

Lindsay, Wallace Martin. Isidori Hispalensis episcopi Etymologiarvm sive Originvm. 3 Vols. Oxford (1921)

Lion, Henreich. Commentarii in Virgilium Serviani. 2 Vols. Göttingen (1826)

Long, George. M. Tulli Ciceronis Orationes, Vol. 3. London (1856) <Contains Oratio Pro Licinio Archia

MacKail, John William. The Eclogues and Georgics of Virgil. London (1915)

Macran, Henry S. ΑΡΙΣΤΟΞΕΝΟΥ ΑΡΜΟΝΙΚΑ ΣΤΟΙΧΕΙΑ The Harmonics of Aristoxenus. Oxford (1902)

Maloney, Edward R. St. Basil The Great To Students On Greek Literature. New York (1900)

Marg, Walter. Timaeus Locrus De Natura Mundi Et Animae. Leiden, E.J. Brill (1972)

Martyn, John. Publii Virgilii Maronis Bucolicorum eclogae decem: The Bucolicks of Virgil, with an English translation and notes. London (1749)

Maude, William. De Die Natale by Censorinus. New York (1900)

Mayhoff, Karl Frederich Theodor. C. Plini Secundi Naturalis Historiae, 6 Vols, Liepzig (1806-1865)

Mayor, Joseph. B. Guide To The Choice Of Classical Books. London (1874)

_____. M. Tulli Ciceronis De Natura Deorum Libri Tres, 3 Vols. Cambridge (1883-1885)

_____. Notes on Diogenis Laertius. Journal of Philology, xxix. pp. 1-23. London (1904),

McBean, Aleander. A Dictionary of Ancient Geography. London (1773)

Meibom, Marcus. Antiquæ Mvsicæ Avctores Septem. 2 Vols. Facsimile of the Amsterdam, 1652 Edition. New York (1977)

_____. Diogenes Laertii De Vitis, Dogmatibus et Apophthegmatibus Clarorum Philosophorum. Amsterdam (1692)

Meineke, August. ΙΩΝΝΟΥ ΣΤΟΒΑΙΟΥ ΑΝΘΟΛΟΓΙΟΝ - Ioannis Stobaei Florilegium. 3 Vols. Leipzig. (1855)

Migne, Jaques Paul. Patrologiæ Cursus Completus, Series Græca. Vols 8-9, ΚΛΗΜΕΝΤΙΣ ΤΟΥ ΑΛΕΞΑΝΔΡΕΩΣ ΤΑ ΕΥΡΙΣΚΟΜΕΝΑ ΠΑΝΤΑ. Clementis Alexandrini, Opera Quæ Exstant Omnia. Paris (1857)

_____. Patrologiæ Cursus Completus, Series Græca. Vols. 29-32 ΒΑΣΙΛΕΙΟΥ ΑΡΧΙΕΠΙΣΚΟΠΟΥ ΚΑΙΣΑΡΕΙΑΣ ΚΑΠΠΑΔΟΚΙΑΣ, ΤΑ ΕΥΡΙΣΚΟΜΕΝΑ ΠΑΝΤΑ. S.P.N. Basilii, Cæsare Cappadociæ Archiepiscopi, Opera Omnia Quæ Exstant. Paris (1857)

_____. Patrologiæ Cursus Completus, Series Græca. Vols. 35-38 S. ΓΡΗΓΟΡΙΟΥ ΤΟΥ ΘΕΟΛΟΓΟΥ, ΑΡΧΙΕΠΙΣΚΟΠΟΥ ΚΩΝΣΤΑΝΤΙΝΟΥΠΟΛΕΩΣ ΤΑ ΕΥΠΙΣΚΟΜΕΝΑ ΠΑΝΤΑ. Sancti Patris Nostri Gregorii Theologi Vulgo Nazianzeni, Archiepiscopi Constantinopolitani, Opera Queæ Exstant Omnia. Paris (1886)

_____. Patrologiæ Cursus Completus, Series Græca. Vol. 66 Saeculum v. ΣΥΝΕΣΙΟΥ ΕΠΙΣΚΟΠΟΥ ΚΥΡΗΝΗΣ ΤΑ ΕΥΡΙΣΚΟΜΕΝΑ ΠΑΝΤΑ Synesii Episcopi Cyrenes, Opera Quæ Exstant Omnia. Paris (1859)

_____. *Patrologiæ Cursus Completus, Series Græca. Vols. 101-104. ΦΩΤΙΟΥ, ΠΑΤΡΙΑΡΧΟΥ ΚΩΝΣΤΑΝΤΙΝΟΥΠΟΛΕΩΣ ΤΑ ΕΥΠΙΣΚΟΜΕΝΑ ΠΑΤΑ. Photii Constantinopolitani, Opera Omnia.* Paris (1900)

_____. *Patrologiæ Cursus Completus, Series Latina, Vol. 21 Tyranni RUFINI, Aquileiensis Presbyteri.* Paris (1849) Contains Rufinus' Apologiae In Sanctum Hieronimum p.543

_____. *Patrologiæ Cursus Completus, Series Latina, Vol. 69 Magni Aurelii CASSIODORI Senatoris, viri Patriarch, Consularis, et Vivariensis Arbatis Opera Omnia.* Paris (1865)

Monro, D.B. *Homer, Iliad, Books I-XII.* Oxford (1884)

Monro, D.B. *Homer, Iliad, Books XIII-XXIV.* Oxford (1888)

Mokot, Robert. *The Penquin Historical Atlas of Ancient Greece.* London (1996)

Morwood, John. *The Pocket Oxford Latin Dictionary.* Oxford (2005)

Moss, Joseph William. *A Manual of Classical Bibliography comprising a copious detail of the various editions of the Greek and Latin Classics.* 2 vols. London (1837)

Nauck, Augustus. *Porphryii Philosophi Platonici Opuscula Tria,* Leipzig (1860)

Needham, P. *Hieroclis Philosophi Alexandrini Commentarius in Aurea Carmina.* London (1709) contains the Greek text of *The Golden Verses*

New Shorter Oxford English Dictionary. 2 vols. Ed. Leslie Brown.Oxford: Clarendon Press (1993)

Orrey, John. *The Letters of Pliny the Younger: With Observations on Each Letter ; and an Essay on Pliny's Life.* 2 Vols. London (1752)

Orry, Marc. *Magni Aurelli Cassiodori Senatoris.* Paris (1588)

_____. *Synesii Cyrenæi Episcopi Epistolæ.* Paris (1605)

Owen, Octavius Freire. *The Organon, or Logical Treatises of Aristotle, with the introduction of Porphyry.* 2 Vols. London (1853)

Padelford, Frederick Morgan. *Essays On The Study And Use Of Poetry By Plutarch And Basil The Great.* New York (1902)

Palmer, George Herbert. *The Odyssey of Homer, Books I-XII. The Text, And An English Version In Rhythmic Prose.* Boston (1895)

Parker, S. *Ciceros's Five Books De Finibus; or Concerning The Last Object Of Desire And Aversion.* Oxford (1812)

Paul, Robert Bateman. *The Antiquities of Greece.* Oxford (1835)

Pearce, Peter and Susan *Polyhedra Primer.* New York (1978)

Pearson, A.C. *The Fragments of Zeno and Cleanthes.* London (1891)

Perier, Charles. *Ioannis Stobaei Sententiae, Ex Thesauris Graecorum collectae, quarum authores circiter ducentos & quinquaginta, & in Sermones etc.* Paris (1552)

Perizonius, Jacob. ΚΛ. ΑΙΛΙΟΝΟΥ ΣΟΦΙΣΤΟΥ ΠΟΙΚΙΛΗΙΣΤΟΡΙΑ, *Cl. Aeliani Sophistae Varia Historia.* 2 Vols. Leiden (1701)

Perrin, Bernadotte. *Plutarch's Lives.* 10 Vols. London (1914)

Peyron, Amadeo. *Empedoclis et Parmenidis Fragmenta.* Leipzig (1810)

Pistelli, Ermenegildo. *Iamblichi In Nicomachi Arithmeticam Introductionem Liber Ad Fidem Codicis Florentini.* Leipzig (1894)

_____. *Iamblichi Protrepticus Ad Fidem Codicis Florentini*. Leipzig (1888)

Plunket, Emmeline M. *The Judgment of Paris and some other legends astronomically considered*. London (1908)

Pontanus, Johann. *Aur. Theodosii Macrobii V. Cl. & inlustris Opera*. Leipzig (1670) Includes Macrobius' *Saturnalia*.

Pope, Alexander. *The Iliad of Homer*. 6 Vols. London (1796)

Prantl, Carl. *Aristotelis, De Coelo et De Generatione et Corruptione*. Leipzig. (1881)

_____. *Aristotelis, Physica*. Leipzig. (1879)

Ptolemy. *Almagestum: opus ingens ac nobile omnes celorum motus continens. Felicibus Astris eat in lucem*. Venice (1515)

_____. *The Almagest*. Trans. by R. Catesby Taliaferro. Vol. 16 of Brittanica Great Books Series. Chicago (1978)

Raeder, Johann. *Theodoreti Graecarum Affectionum Curatio*. Leipzig (1904)

Reiske, Johann Jacob. *Animadversionvm Ad Graecos Avcotores: Vol 1 Diodorvs Sicvlvs* Leipzig (1757)

Reiz, Frederich Wolfgang. *Poetæ Minores Græcae*. Leipzig (1823)

Rühl, Franz. M. *Iuniani Iustini Epitoma historiarum Philippicarum Pompei Trogi*. Leipzig (1886)

Sandys, George. *Ovid's Metamorphosis Englished, Mythologized and Represented in Figures*. Oxford (1632)

Savage, John. *A Select Collection of Letters of the Antients*. London (1703)

Schäfer, G.H. ΑΘΗΝΑΙΟΥ ΔΕΙΠΝΟΣΟΦΙΣΤΩΝ ΒΙΒΛΙΑ ΠΕΝΤΕΚΑΙΔΕΚΑ *Athenaei Deipnosophistarum Libri Quindecim*. 3 Vols. Leipzig (1838)

Schaff, Philip. *Nicene and Post-Nicene Fathers. Vol. II, Augustine's City of God and Christian Doctrine*. New York (1887)

Schmidt, M., *Hesychii Alexandrini Lexicon, Editionem Minorem*. Leipzig (1867)

Schneider, Jo Gottlob. *Xenophontes Quae Extant*. 6 Vols. Leipzig (1816)

Schrevel, Cornelis. ΗΣΙΟΔΟΥ ΑΣΚΡΑΙΟΥ ΤΑ ΕΥΡΙΣΚΟΜΕΝΑ. *Hesiodi Ascræi Quæ Exant*. Leipzig (1684)

Schulze, Johann Ludwig. ΤΟΥ ΜΑΚΑΡΙΟΥ ΘΕΟΔΩΡΗΤΟΥ ΕΠΙΣΚΟΠΟΥ ΚΥΡΟΥ ΑΠΑΝΤΑ Β. *Theodoreti Episcopi Cyri Opera Omnia*. 5 Vols. Hall, Germany (1769)

Schwegler, Albert. *Handbook of the History of Philosophy*. Trans. by James Hutchinson Sterling. New York (1875)

Selden, John. *De Diis Syris Syntagmata II*, Leipzig (1672)

Shilleto, Richard. *Pausanias' Description of Greece*. 2 Vols. London (1886)

_____. *Plutarch's Morals, Ethical Essays*. London (1888)

Sibelis, C.G. ΠΑΥΣΑΝΙΟΥ ΤΗΣ ΕΛΛΑΔΟΣ ΠΕΡΙΗΓΗΣΙΣ – *Pausaniae Graeciae Descripto*. 5 Vols. Liepzig (1822-1828)

Siebenkees, Johann Philipp *Strabonis Rerum Geographicarum Libri XVII*, 5 Vols. Leipzig (1796-1808)

Sigoni, Carlo. *T. Livii Patavini Historiarum Quod Extant*. 6 Vols. Basil (1740)

Sillig, Julius. C. *Plini Secundi Naturalis Historae Librii* XXXVII. Vol. 6 Gothae (1855)

Smith, Charles Foster. *Thucydides, The History of the Peloponnesian War.* 4 Vols. London (1920)

Smith, William. *A Dictionary of Greek and Roman Biography and Mythology.* 3 Vols. London (1880)

Smith, William. *A Latin-English Dictionary based upon the work of Forcelleni and Freund.* London (1855)

Spengel, Leonhard. *Themistii Paraphrases Aristotelis.* 2 Vols. Leipzig (1866) Themistius' Paraphrase of Aristotle – includes Physic.

Stallbaum, Gottfried. *Platonis Opera Omnia.* 7 Vols. London (1838)

Stallbaum, J. G. *Eustathii Archiepiscopi Thessalonicensis Comentarii ad Homeri Iliadem.* 3 Vols. Leipzig (1829) <Eustathius

Stanley, Thomas. *A History of Philosophy.* 3 Vols. London (1687) Fascimile edition by Garland Publishing (1978)

——————. *A History of Philosophy.* London (1701) Fascimile edition by The Apocryphile Press, Berkeley (2006)

Stanley, Thomas; Le Clerc, Jean; Olearius, Johann Gottfried. *Historia philosophiae, vitas, opiniones, resque gestas, et dicta philosophorum sectae cujusvis complexa, avtore Thema Stanlejo ex anglico sermone in latinum translata.* 3 Vols. (1731). <The first edition of Stanley's History of Philosophy, translated into Latin.

Stephani, Henri. *Auli Gellii Noctes Atticæ.* Paris (1585)

Stirling, James H. *Handbook of the History of Philosophy.* New York (1875)

Sylburg, Frederick. ΕΤΥΜΟΛΟΓΙΚΟΝ ΤΟ ΜΕΓΑ ΗΓΟΥΝ Ή ΜΕΓΑΛΗ ΓΡΑΜΜΑΤΙΚΗ *Etymologicon Magnvm Editio Nova Correctior.* Liepzig. (1816)

Taylor, Thomas. *Political Fragments of Archytas, Charondas, Zaleucus and other Ancient Pythagoreans, preserved by Stobaeus; and also the Ethical Fragments of Hierocles.* Chiswick (1822)

——————. *The Description of Greece, by Pausanias.* 3 Vols. London (1824)

——————. *Iamblicus' Life of Pythagoras or Pythagoric Life.* Rochester, VT (1986, reprinted from the edition of 1818)

——————. *Metamorphosis or Golden Ass and Philosophical Works of Apuleius.* London (1822)

——————. *The Philosophical and Mathematical Commentaries of Proclus surnamed, Plato's Successor, on the First Book of Euclid's Elements.* 2 Vols. London (1788)

——————. *Theoretic Arithmetic, In Three Books; containing the substance of all that has been written on this subject by Theo of Smyrna, Nicomachus, Iamblichus, and Boeius.* London (1816)

Thilo, George. *Servii Grammatici Qvi Fervuntvr in Vergilii Carmina Commentarii.* 4 Vols. Leipzig (1881-1902)

Thirlbius, S. ΙΟΥΣΤΙΝΟΥ Φιλοσόφου καὶ Μάρτυρος *Justini Philosophi & Martyris, Apologæ Duæ et Dialogus cum Tryphone Judæo.* London (1722) Contains Justin Martyr's Dialogue with Trypho the Jew.

Tighe, Mary Blachford. *The Works of Apuleius*. London (1902) Contains an English translation of Apuleius' Florida.

Tobin, Thomas. *Timaios of Locri: On the Nature of the World and the Soul*. Chico, CA. (1986)

Tornaesium, J. *Hieroclis Philosophi Stoici In Aureos Pithagorae Versus Commentarii*. Leiden (1551) Golden Verses

Ussher, James, Archbishop of Armagh. *Annales Veteris Testamenti, a prima mundi origine dedvcti: una cum rerum Asiaticarum et Aegyptiacarum chronico, a temporis historici principio usque ad Maccabaicorum initia producto*. London (1650) Latin Edition used by Thomas Stanley.

――――――――――. *The Annals Of The World*. Ed. Larry and Marion Pierce. Green Forest, AR. (2003)

Valpy, A.J. *Apuleii Opera Omnia*, 6 Vols. London (1825) Contains "Apuleius Florida"

Vernardakis, Gregory. *Plutarchi Chaeronensis Moralia*. 7 Vols. Leipzig (1893) Plutarch. Vol 2 has Fortuna Alexander.

Vossius, Gerard Johann. *De Philosophorum Sectis*. 2 Vols. Amsterdam (1657)

Waltz, Theodor. *Aristotelis Organon Graece*. Leipzig (1824)

Wyttenbach, Daniel. *Index Graecitatis In Plutarchi Opera*. 2 Vols. Leipzig (1829)

Wyttenbach, Daniel. ΠΛΟΥΤΑΡΧΟΥ ΤΟΥ ΧΑΙΡΩΝΕΩΣ ΤΑ ΗΘΙΚΑ *Plutarchi Chæronensis Moralia*. 8 Vols. Oxford (1797)

Wharton, Edward Ross. *Etymological Lexicon of Classical Greek*. Chicago: Ares Publishers Inc. (1974)

Whibley, Leonard. *A Companion To Greek Studies*. 3rd Edition. Cambridge (1916)

Whiston, William. *The Works of Flavius Josephus*. Halifax (1864)

Yonge, C. D. *An English-Greek Lexicon*. London (1849)

――――――――――. *The Academic Questions, Treatise de Finibis, and Tusculan Disputations of M.T. Cicero*. London (1853)

――――――――――. *Cicero's Tusculan Disputations; also treatises on the nature of the gods and on the Commonwealth*. New York (1899)

――――――――――. *The Deipnosophists, or Banquet Of The Learned of Athenæus*. London (1854)

――――――――――. *Diogenes Laërtius, The Lives And Opinions of Eminent Philosophers*. London (1853)

――――――――――. *The treatises of M. T. Cicero on the nature of the gods; on divination; on fate; on the republic; and on standing for the consulship*. London (1853)

Zeller, Edouard trans. S.F.Alleyne, *A History of Greek Philosophy from the earliest period to the time of Socrates*. 2 Vols. London (1881)

The Compact Edition of the Oxford English Dictionary, Complete Text Reproduced Micrographically in two volumes, New York, Oxford University Press, 1971. An invaluable resource throughout this project; it references Stanley's *History of Philosophy* repeatedly when providing examples of the first usage of obsolete words.

IBIS PRESS
Titles of Related Interest

~

Secret Societies
Illuminati, Freemasons,
and the French Revolution
Una Birch and James Wasserman

The greatest success of the Bavarian Illuminati conspiracy was the French Revolution of 1789. The profound impact of that Revolution is felt to this day in the political destinies of millions of people worldwide. The Illuminati had declared war against Church and State and worked feverishly to spread their gospel of Liberty and Reason. Although the Order was officially suppressed on the eve of the Revolution, its efforts do not appear to have been in vain.

The recruiting program of Illuminati founder Adam Weishaupt was focused on attracting powerful and influential members— government ministers, educators, the press, authors, philosophers, booksellers, publishers, even religious leaders open to agnostic or atheist views. Many such men belonged to the Masonic lodges of Germany, Austria and France. The European Masonic network offered Weishaupt a respectable vehicle by which he was able to propagate his clandestine doctrines.

The great philosophical/political battle of the Enlightenment was fought between the ideologies of individualism as exemplified in the American Revolution, and statism in the French.

Historian Una Birch provides a compelling account of the activities of these secret societies and the conditions of political oppression against which they rebelled. Secret society scholar James Wasserman provides an account of the Revolution itself along with biographical sketches of some 300 individuals referenced by Birch.

ISBN: 978-0-89254-132-4
288 Pages, 6" x 9". • Paperback. $18.95

Initiation in the Aeon of the Child
The Inward Journey
J. Daniel Gunther

In 1904, *The Book of the Law (Liber AL vel Legis)* declared the advent of a new period in the course of human history—the Aeon of Horus or Aeon of the Child. The doctrine codified in the *Book of the Law*, and numerous other Holy Books, is known as *Thelema* (a Greek word meaning "Will"). Aleister Crowley was revealed as the Prophet of the New Aeon.

In this ground-breaking book, author J. Daniel Gunther provides a penetrating and cohesive analysis of the spiritual doctrine underlying and informing the Aeon of the Child, and the sublime formulas of Initiation encountered by those who would probe its Mysteries. Drawing on more than thirty years of direct experience as a student and teacher within the Order of the A∴A∴, the author examines the doctrinal thread of Thelema in its historical, religious and practical context. He also provides detailed discussions and expositions of many of the cryptic passages within the Holy Books of Thelema.

Much of Thelemic doctrine is presented here for the first time in clear, precise language that will aid those students who seek to navigate the difficult terrain of the Spiritual quest. More advanced students will find tantalizing clues to serve as guideposts and eventual confirmation of direct experience.

With numerous diagrams and detailed references encompassing ancient Egyptian hieroglyphic texts, the Apocrypha, the Old and New Testaments, Alchemy, Hermetic Qabalah, and Tarot, as well as Carl Jung and Aleister Crowley.

ISBN: 978-0-89254-145-4
224 pages, 6" x 9". • Hardcover • $40.00

The Clavis or Key to the Magic of Solomon
From an Original Talismanic Grimoire in Full Color
by Ebenezer Sibley and Frederick Hockley
With Extensive Commentary by Joseph Peterson

The Clavis or Key to the Magic of Solomon is a notebook from the estate of Ebenezer Sibley, transcribed under the direction of Frederic Hockley (1808-1885). Sibley was a prominent physician and influential author, who complemented his scientific studies with writings on the "deeper truths." Both Sibley and Hockley were major inspirations in the occult revival of the past two centuries, influencing A.E. Waite, S.L. Mathers, Aleister Crowley, as well as the Golden Dawn, Rosicrucian, and Masonic movements.

This collection reflects Sibley's teachings on the practical use of celestial influences and harmonies. It contains clear and systematic instructions for constructing magical tools and pentacles. *The Mysterious Ring* gives directions for preparing magic rings. *Experiments of the Spirits Birto, Vassago, Agares,* and *Bealpharos,* show how to call upon angels and spirits, and perform crystal scrying. *The Wheel of Wisdom* gives concise directions for using celestial harmonies. The final text, the *Complete Book of Magic Science,* is closely akin to the *Secret Grimoire of Turiel,* but more complete.

The manuscript reproduced here is the most accurate and complete known, very beautifully and carefully written. With extraordinary hand-colored seals and colored handwritten text. (Blank pages have been eliminated so that the 384 page original has been reproduced here as 288 pages.)

ISBN: 978-089254-159-1
456 Pages, 7.5" x 9". Hardcover $95.00.

Arbatel
Concerning the Magic of the Ancients
Newly translated, edited and annotated
by Joseph H. Peterson

Arbatel is one of the most influential magical texts. Its many aphorisms are designed to guide us through a transition from an ordinary life to a magical life. It teaches that God created angels to help people, but that we need to learn how to attract and call upon them for help, both spiritual and material. The angels not only can help, protect, and heal, but the higher sciences can only be learned directly from them.

Arbatel also insists on the need to avoid superstition, and being constantly tricked and manipulated by evil forces which are always working against us.

This new edition includes the first English translation published since Turner's in 1655, and a fresh analysis utilizing important new research by Carlos Gilly, Antoine Faivre, and others. It illuminates many obscure points in the text, and explains the magical techniques employed, and its influence on esoteric literature, including the grimoires and the Theosophical movement. Includes illustrations, bibliography, index, and original Latin text.

ISBN: 978-0-89254-152-2
128 Pages, 6" x 9". Hardcover $35.00.

Necronomicon
Edited and Introduced by Simon
31st Anniversary Edition

• Gods that were ancient when Moses was a child.

• Temples that were gateways to the gods when Abraham came out of the desert.

• Rites that summoned forces Solomon never knew.

In the past thirty-one years, there has been a lot of ink—actual and virtual—spilled on the subject of the *Necronomicon*. As the decades have passed, more information has come to light both on the book's origins and discovery, and on the information contained within its pages. It has been found to contain formulae for spiritual transformation consistent with some of the most ancient mystical processes in the world, processes that involve communion with the stars.

This year, the original designer of the 1977 edition and the original editor have joined forces to present a new, deluxe hardcover edition of the most feared, most reviled, and most desired book on the planet. With a new preface by Simon, this edition will be strictly limited. It is intended for both the collector and the serious operator.

Two editions are available. The first is a quality hardcover bound in high quality cloth • 288 pages • printed on acid-free paper • 7-1/4 x 10-1/4 • ribbon marker • ISBN: 978-0-89254-146-1 • $125.00

The second is a deluxe, **leatherbound** edition • strictly limited to 220 **numbered** copies • **signed** by Simon • with three sided silver-gilding • ribbon-marker • deluxe end-papers • special binding boards • Copies are available for purchase exclusively from *www.studio31.com.* • ISBN: 978-0-89254-147-8. • Cost $275.00.